Metropolis

Center and Symbol of Our Times

Edited by

Philip Kasinitz
Associate Professor of Sociology
Hunter College, and the Graduate
Center of the City University of New York

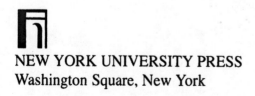

NEW YORK UNIVERSITY PRESS
Washington Square, New York

First published in the U.S.A. in 1995 by
NEW YORK UNIVERSITY PRESS
Washington Square
New York, N.Y. 10003
www.nyupress.nyu.edu

ISBN 0-8147-4640-3

This book is printed on paper suitable for recycling and
made from fully managed and sustained forest sources.

Library of Congress Cataloging-in-Publication Data
Metropolis: center and symbol of our times / edited by Philip Kasinitz.
    p. cm. — (Main trends of the modern world)
Includes bibliographical references and index.
ISBN 0-8147-4639-X. —ISBN 0-8147-4640-3 (pbk.)
1. Metropolitan areas. 2. Urbanization. 3. Urban sociology.
I. Kasinitz, Philip, 1957- . II. Title. III. Series.
HT330.M454 1995
307. 76—dc20   94-11576
                                                                    CIP

Contents

Contents

Series Preface

Main Trends of the Modern World is a series of books analyzing the main trends and the social psychology of our times. Each volume in the series brings together readings from social analysts who first identified a decisive institutional trend and from writers who explore its social and psychological effects in contemporary society.

The series works in the classical tradition of social theory. In this view, theory is the historically informed framing of intellectual problems about concrete social issues and the resolution of those problems through the analysis of empirical data. Theory is not, therefore, the study of the history of ideas about society, nor the abstract, ahistorical modeling of social realities, nor, as in some quarters, pure speculation often of an ideological sort unchecked by empirical reality. Theory is meaningful only when it illuminates the specific features, origins, and animating impetus of particular institutions, showing how these institutions shape experience and are linked to the social order as a whole.

Social analysts such as Karl Marx, Max Weber, Émile Durkheim, Sigmund Freud, Georg Simmel, Thorstein Veblen, and George Herbert Mead, whose works we now consider classics, never consciously set out to construct paradigms, models, or abstract theories of society. Instead they investigated concrete social phenomena such as the decline of feudal society and the emergence of industrial capitalism, the growth of bureaucracy, the consequences of the accelerating specialization of labor, the significance of religion in a scientific and secular age, the formation of self and the moral foundations of modern society, and the on-going rationalization of modern life. The continuing resonance of their ideas suggests the firmness of their grasp of deep-rooted structural trends in Western industrial society.

Later European and American social thinkers, deeply indebted though they were to the intellectual frameworks produced by the remarkable men who preceded them, faced a social order marked by increasing disarray, one that required fresh intellectual approaches. The social, cultural, and intellectual watershed was, of course, the Great War and its aftermath. The world's first total war ravaged a whole generation of youth. In Europe, it sowed the seeds of revolution, militarism, totalitarianism, fascism, and state socialism; in both Europe and America it signaled the age of mass propaganda. On both continents the aftermath of the war brought economic and political turmoil, cultural frenzies, widespread disenchantment and disillusionment, and social movements of every hue and description that led eventually to the convulsions of the Second World War. These later social thinkers grappled with issues such as:

- The deepening bureaucratization of all social spheres and the ascendance of the new middle classes.
- The collapse of old religious theodicies that once gave meaning to life and the emergence of complex social psychologies of individuals and masses in a rationalized world.
- The riddles posed by modern art and culture.
- The emergence of mass communications and propaganda as well as the manufacture of cultural dreamworlds of various sorts.
- War, militarism, and the advent of totalitarianism, fascism, and state socialism.
- The deepening irrational consequences and moral implications of the thoroughgoing rationalization of all life spheres.

Emil Lederer, Hans Speier, Joseph Schumpeter, Kenneth Burke, Robert MacIver, Harold Lasswell, Walter Lippmann, Robert Park, W. I. Thomas, Florian Znaniecki, Goerge Orwell, Hannah Arendt, Herbert Blumer, and Hans H. Gerth are only a few of the men and women who carried forward the theoretical attitude of the great classical thinkers in the course of working on the pressing issues of their own day. In this tradition, social theory means confronting head-on the social realities of one's own times, trying to explain both the main structural drift of institutions as well as the social psychologies of individuals, groups and classes.

What then are the major structural trends and individual experiences of our own epoch? Four major trends come immediately to mind, each with profound ramifications for individuals. We pose these as groups of research problems.

BUREAUCRACY AS THE ORGANIZATIONAL FORM OF MODERNITY

• What are the social and psychological consequences of living and working in a society dominated by mass bureaucratic structures? How do these structures affect the private lives of the men and women exposed to their influences?
• What is the structure and meaning of work in a bureaucratic society? In particular, how does bureaucracy shape moral consciousness? What are the organizational roots of the collapse of traditional notions of accountability in our society?
• What is the relationship between leaders and followers in a society dominated by a bureaucratic ethos? What are the changing roles of intellectuals, whether in the academy or in public life, in defining, legitimating, challenging, or serving the social order?

THE TECHNOLOGIES OF MASS COMMUNICATION AND THE MANAGEMENT OF MASS SOCIETY

• What role do public relations, advertising, and bureaucratized social research play in shaping the public opinions and private attitudes of the masses?
• What is the relationship between individuals' direct life experiences (with, for example, family, friends, occupations, sex, and marriage) and the definitions that the mass media suggest for these individual experiences? What illusions and myths now sustain the social order? What are the ascendant forms of this-worldly salvation in our time?
• What are the different origins, dynamics, and consequences of modern political, social, and cultural mass movements with their alternative visions of justice and morality?
• What social, economic, and cultural trends have made many great metropolises, once the epitomes of civilization and still the centers and symbols of modern life, into new wildernesses?

THE ON-GOING SOCIAL TRANSFORMATIONS OF CAPITALISM

- What are the prospects for a transformed capitalism in a post-Marxist, post-Keynesian era?
- How has the emergence of large bureaucratic organizations in every sector of the social order transformed the middle classes? What is the social and political psychology of these new middle classes?
- What transformations of the class and status structure have been precipitated by America's changing industrial order?
- What are the social, cultural, and historical roots of the pervasive criminal violence in contemporary American society? What social factors have fostered the breakdown of traditional mechanisms of social control and the emergence of violence as a primary means for effecting individual or group goals?

THE CLASH BETWEEN WORLD-VIEWS AND VALUES, OLD AND NEW

- How has science, particularly in its bureaucratized form, transformed the liberal doctrines of natural rights, individual rights, and concomitant conceptions of the human person, including notions of life and death?
- How have the old middle classes come to terms with mass bureaucratic institutions and the subsequent emergence of new classes and status groups? What social forces continue to prompt the framing of complicated social issues in terms of primal antagonisms of kith, kin, blood, color, soil, gender, and sexual orientation?
- What are the roots of the pervasive irrationalities evident at virtually every level of our society, despite our Enlightenment legacy of reason and rationality and our embrace of at least functional rationality in our organizational apparatus? To what extent is individual and mass irrationality generated precisely by formally rational bureaucratic structures?

In short, the modern epoch is undergoing social transformations every bit as dramatic as the transition from feudalism to industrial capitalism. The very complexity of the contemporary world impedes fixed social scientific understanding. Moreover we may lack the language and concepts necessary to provide coherent analyses of some emerging features of our social order. Nonetheless this series tries to identify and analyze the major trends of modern times. With an historical awareness of the great intellectual work of the past and with a dispassionate attitude toward contemporary social realities, the series fashions grounded, specific images of our world in the hope that future thinkers will find these more useful than speculation or prophecy.

Each volume in this series addresses one major trend. The book in hand analyzes the rise of the modern city and the social and spatial processes that have shaped contemporary urban life.

ROBERT JACKALL
ARTHUR J. VIDICH

Introduction
Philip Kasinitz

I'm crazy about this city. Daylight slants like a razor
cutting the buildings in half. In the top half I see faces
and it's not easy to tell which are people, which are the
work of stone masons. Below is shadow where any blasé
thing takes place: clarinets and lovemaking, fists and the
voices of sorrowful women. A city like this one makes me
dream tall and feel in on things. Hep. It's the bright
steel rocking above the shade below that does it. When I
look over the strips of green grass lining the river, at
church steeples and into cream-and-copper halls of apartment buildings, I'm strong. Alone, yes, but top notch and
indestructible.

Toni Morrison, Jazz, 1992.[1]

This is a book of readings about the modern city. It takes
as its starting point the assumption that modernity – the
way of life that emerged with the coming of the industrial
revolution – represents a fundamental break with the way
human communities were organized in the past. Some of
the characteristics of this new mode of social organization
are obvious: new technologies, the dominance of industry
and mass production, the emergence of a global economy
and the spread of wage labor, the rationalization and
commodification of space and time. Beyond all of these new
organizational forms, however, the overriding characteristic of modernity is its dynamism. The modern world is a
world of change, change unprecedented in its speed, scope
and the breath of its social impact.[2]

Modernity created new types of cities. This is sometimes
obscured by the fact that many modern cities contain the
physical remnants of their premodern origins. Yet, as Anthony
Giddens notes,

> Modern urban settlements often incorporate the sites of
> traditional cities, and may look as though they have merely
> grown out of them. In fact, modern urbanism is ordered

1

according to quite different principles from those which set off the pre-modern city from the countryside in prior periods.[3]

In different ways the essays in this book all make a contribution towards delineating these principles. The articles are written in various styles. They include works of sociological theory, polemics, critical essays, ethnography and historical accounts. What they all have in common, however, is an attempt to look beyond the pragmatic "social-problems" orientation that now dominates "urban sociology" and "urban studies." While many of the essay are concerned with some of the practical problems facing cities, they root these concerns in a broader inquiry into the nature of social life in the metropolis.

Given the historical specificity of the modern city, one might wonder if it really makes sense to speak of "the city" as a distinct social form. Indeed a few years ago it was fashionable among practitioners of the then "new" (that is, neo-Marxist) urban sociology to say there really was no such thing as "urban" social life. Nothing, they argued, was essentially "urban." The ways people lived in cities merely reflected the social organization of a particular economic order: capitalist urbanism was as fundamentally different from socialist urbanism as it was from feudal urbanism. To think otherwise was to lapse into "spatial determinism."[4]

Most of the authors in this volume would disagree. To be sure, the "new" urban sociology made a tremendously important contribution in pointing to the contingent nature of contemporary urbanism. In the wake of the riots of the 1960s and fiscal crises of the 1970s, it refocused much of scholarly writing about cities on the vital questions of how particular social orders produce particular urban outcomes and how "social divisions are reflected spatially."[5] Yet, for most of the authors represented here, there are aspects of modern urban culture that are distinct from both premodern urbanism and from the social life associated with nonurban, modern spatial forms. For some the differences are primarily matters of intensity and degree. But intensity and degree both count for a great deal in the lives of individuals.

If to live in the modern world is to cope with the fragmentation of social roles caused by a complex division of labor, then to live in the modern city means that one is acutely and constantly aware of this fragmentation. As the city is an inherently heterogeneous environment, to live in the modern city means to live in the presence of difference. For better or for worse, it requires frequent interaction with those who probably do not share one's beliefs and values. In the well-known paradox explored by the authors in Part I, the modern city brings together masses of people on a scale never before possible and yet produces a particular kind of individualism. The urbanite, as Morrison notes, is "alone" but "hep" and sometimes even "indestructible."

Finally, to live in the city means that one is acutely aware of the historical, man-made nature of one's environment.[6] As Witold Rybczynski reminds us: "whatever else they are, cities are also physical artifacts" made by people.[7] Those who distrust cities have long pointed to this artifice as evidence of thier morally dubious nature: "God made the Country, Man made the Town."[8] But while puritans, transcendentalists and a host of "back-to-nature" romantics have condemned the city for this reason, modernists have often celebrated it. For if God is dethroned and man is ascendent, then the great city – the largest and most complex of man's creations – is the embodiment of human genius. The exhilaration we feel when we view a great city from one of those rare vantage points where one can "take it all in" – Paris from the Eiffel Tower, Lower Manhattan from the Brooklyn Bridge – is the thrill of seeing in one moment the enormity of this human work.

Of course from the beginning of the modern era many people have been unhappy with the city. Some of their grievances are with aspects of social life particular to the metropolis. Others mask a deeper dissatisfaction with the nature of modernity itself. Seldom have these antiurban sentiments been as widely held as they are today, and looking at the shape contemporary cities are in, it is not hard to see why. Many of the authors in this volume share this dissatisfaction. Yet taken as a whole, these essays show us both the frightening, destructive force of the modern city and the enormous potential for human creativity that the metropolis has helped to unleash.

4 *Introduction*

Notes

1. Toni Morrison, *Jazz* (New York: Alfred A. Knopf, 1992), p. 7.
2. Anthony Giddens, *The Consequences of Modernity* (Stanford University Press, 1990); See also Marshall Berman, *All That is Solid Melts into Air* (New York: Simon and Schuster, 1982); Scott Lash and Jonathan Friedman (eds) *Modernity and Identity* (Cambridge: Basil Blackwell, 1992).
3. Giddens, *op. cit.*, p. 6.
4. See particularly the early work of Manuel Castells, much of which is collected in his *The Urban Question* (Cambridge: MIT Press, 1977). For other examples of the "new" urban sociology of the 1970s see David Harvey, *Social Justice and the City* (London: Arnold: 1973); C. G. Pickvance, *Urban Sociology: Critical Essays* (London: Tavistock: 1976); Sharon Zukin, "A Decade of the New Urban Sociology," *Theory and Society*, vol. 9 (1980), pp. 575–602.
5. William Tabb and Larry Sawers, *Marxism and the Metropolis* (New York: Oxford University Press, 1978), p. 16.
6. Of course most rural environments are also very much shaped by human habitation. But this fact is generally well hidden. Thus the tendency in modern culture is to imagine the rural landscape as "natural," "unspoiled" and "pristine."
7. Witold Rybczynski, "The Mystery of Cities", *The New York Review of Books*, vol. XL, no. 13 (15 July 1993), p. 13.
8. William Cowper, 1783. For a fascinating discussion of both the origins of this well-known couplet and the ways similar sentiments have been expressed since, see Eugene Weber, ". . . And Man Made the Town," *The American Scholar*, vol. 58 (1989), pp. 79–96.

Part I

Modernity and the Urban Ethos

1 Introduction
Philip Kasinitz

The rags of the squalid ballad-singer fluttered in the rich light that showed the goldsmith's treasures, pale and pinched up faces hovered about the windows where was tempting food, hungry eyes wandered over the profusion guarded by one thin sheet of glass – an iron wall to them; half naked shivering figures stopped to gaze at Chinese shawls and golden stuffs of India. There was a Christening party at the coffin-maker's, and a funeral hatchment had stopped some great improvements in the bravest mansion. Life and death went hand in hand, wealth and poverty stood side by side; repletion and starvation laid them down together. But it was London.

Charles Dickens, *Nicholas Nickelby*, 1839.[1]

All fixed, fast-frozen relations, with their train of ancient and venerable prejudices and opinions are swept away, all new formed ones become antiquated before they can ossify. All that is solid melts into air, all that is holy is profaned.

Karl Marx and Frederick Engels, *The Communist Manifesto*, 1848.[2]

In the nineteenth century the world changed. For most of recorded history, inded for aeons before history could be recorded, the overwhelming majority of human beings made their living scratching in the soil. Whatever the glorious achievements of the civilizations of antiquity – whatever art, science and philosophy they produced – these things were known only to the few. Most people lived and died on the land or in small villages, lashed to the cycle of the seasons, working as their parents had and as their children would after them. History, for most people, was a story of endless repetition, interrupted by occasional catastrophe.

Romantics like to think that such people were happier than we are today, living at one with nature and connected to their neighbors by the bonds of community. Cynics counter that they were probably miserable, struggling for existence

7

in a world of limited horizons. Who can say? What is certain is that their world was irretrievably different from the one we know.

In the nineteenth century there came into existence societies in which a considerable portion of the population lived by means other than agriculture. Capitalism, industry and revolutions in science and technology created a world in which people around the globe were connected to each other by the money economy, mass markets, mass media and bureaucratic institutions. Yet they frequently felt disconnected, isolated and alone. It was a world in which change was the only constant, in which "all things solid melt into air." Some saw in these changes the possibility for human liberation while others saw only the despair of rootless, normless, alienated individuals, locked ever more tightly into the "iron cage" of modern rationality. But, for bettter or for worse, it is clear that the world has changed.

The city changed most of all. As Peter Jukes notes (with only slight exaggeration) "the modern world began in London and Paris in the early nineteenth century when these two cities underwent a phenomenal burst of growth: it spread outward, through Europe to Russia, across the Atlantic to America, until it reached the cities of the south which are today creating their unique versions of metropolitan life."[3]

Of course there is nothing uniquely modern about cities. They are as old as civilization itself, as the common root of the "city" and "civilization" in the Latin *civitas* implies. Most of the people of the ancient or medieval worlds whose names we remember were city dwellers. Yet we sometimes forget that in their own times they belonged to a small and conspicuous minority. Until the modern age urban life was experienced by only a tiny part of the world's population.

As late as 1850 there was no predominantly urban society on the planet. In 1900 there was only one, Great Britain. By the middle of the twentieth century, however, most industrial societies were predominantly urban and urbanization was increasing rapidly throughout the rest of the world.[4] The speed with which this transition took place was truly remarkable. For example in 1800 there were only 15 cities and towns with populations of over 20 000 in all of England. By 1890 there were 185.[5] In the United States, in 1860 there were eight cities with populations over 100 000; by 1910 there were 50.[6] Throughout Europe and North America this urban growth brought with it gut-wrenching changes in people's daily lives: constant innovations in the labor process, a profusion of new goods and services, mass communication, industrial strife and a widening of the cultural and political gulf between the classes.

Like many of their generation, Marx and Dickens observed the early stages of these changes with profound ambivalence. Each had come to London as young men – Marx as a political refugee; Dickens driven there by economic upheavals. They found themselves in the midst of the largest and fastest-growing city in the world, a city at the center of a vast empire. Marx, who arrived in London shortly after the *Manifesto* was written, attributed these changes to capitalism. He was morally revolted by the exploitation and immiseration of industrial workers, which his collaborator Frederick Engels had already documented in Manchester. Yet in the *Manifesto* Marx is almost poetic in his awe at the transformative power of the new economic order. It had unified the nations of the world. It had created a vast profusion of new goods, and with them a host of "new wants" requiring ever more new products to be satisfied: "the cheap prices of its commodities" had knocked down "all Chinese walls." And it had created cities of unprecedented size and had "rescued a considerable part of the population from the idiocy of rural life."[7]

For Dickens, the central image of the new metropolis was that of stark contrasts and extraordinary juxtapositions. The new world was one of unprecedented complexity. The fact that starving London beggars might gaze at the luxury goods of China and India in the shop windows spoke of a global system of commerce. Yet the overall image the average man or woman in the London crowd perceived was not one of rational efficiency, but rather one of hurly-burly chaos. Further, for Dickens, it seemed that the creation of this new wealth was connected to the misery of the beggars. His London was both a place of evil and exploitation and a place of beauty and opportunity.

It was also a place of mystery. In Western European literature of the mid-nineteenth century the city, once the familiar center of civilization for the literate minority, was increasingly portrayed as an opaque and dangerous terrain. The urban poor started to appear as exotics whose strange ways and dialects had to be interpreted by authors writing for middle-class audiences living only a few miles away. In a popular genre of Victorian nonfiction, British social reformers and journalists borrowed the language of travel writers and early anthropologists to describe journeys into the urban slums. Salvation Army founder William Booth, for example, called his book on urban poverty *In Darkest England*. In Henry Mayhew's influential 1861 work, *London Labor and the London Poor*, the "denizens" of East London are presented as virtually a foreign race, "less a class in the Marxian sense than a species in the Darwinian sense" as Gertrude Himmelfarb notes.[8] Raymond Williams points out that it is during this period that the urban detective, "the man who can find his way through the fog, who can penetrate the intricacies of the streets," becomes a staple of popular fiction. In the city it takes a Sherlock Holmes to find order beneath the "complexity of modern life."[9]

The new discipline of sociology was in large part born out of late nineteenth- and early twentieth-century efforts to understand how order was possible in the modern world. Or, as Dennis Wrong puts it:

> One could even say that the discipline of sociology begins with a concern over the decline of such traditional forms of association as small towns, neighborhoods, religious congregations and social classes in the wake of that great wave of "creative destruction" (Schumpeter) we call the industrial revolution.[10]

Thus from the beginning, not surprisingly, the city has been one of sociology's central topics of research and analysis. Today much of what is called "urban sociology" is the study of "social problems" that happen to take place in cities. Beyond this, however, lies the broader question of how physical environments shape and are shaped by social life. Yet ultimately most good urban sociology – and most of the writers in this volume – comes back to the problems of social order and community life in industrial and (arguably) postindustrial societies.

The earliest of these efforts were generally attempts to conceptualize the differences between traditional and modern communities, often in the form of a continuum between two polar ideal types. Among the most influential of these formulations is that of Ferdinand Tönnies, whose 1887 work, *Gemeinschaft und Gesellschaft*, is an exploration of contrasting modes of social organization. For Tönnies, *Gemeinschaft* (community)[11] is a type social solidarity based on intimate bonds of sentiment, a common sense of place (social as well as physical) and a common sense of purpose. *Gemeinschafts*, he argues, are characterized by a high degree of face-to-face interaction in a common locality among people who have generally had common experiences. The sense of social norms is strong and individual deviation is relatively rare. There is a high degree of social consensus and behavior is governed by strong but usually informal institutions such as the family and peer group. In a *Gesellschaft*, in contrast, relationships between people tend to be impersonal, superficial and calculating, and self-interest is the prevailing motive for human action. Social solidarity is maintained by formal authority, contracts and laws. Yet for Tönnies, who like many early sociologists was deeply pessimistic about the modern age, such a reliance on calculable rules is a weak substitute for common sentiments: the *Gesellschaft* type of social solidarity was very close to no social solidarity at all.

Gemeinschaft is characteristic of the premodern world, *Gesellschaft* of modernity, and in German *Gemeinschaft* refers to a social relationship and does not imply a location, in the way that "community" often does in English. Nevertheless the conditions under which a *Gemeinschaft* is likely to form are clearly more associated with spatially separated, technologically simple settlements, whereas *Gesellschafts* are more typical of the bureaucratized mass societies we associate with large cities. Yet it remains unclear in this formulation whether the size of settlement (small town versus large city), the mode of production (agricultural versus industrial) or historical period is really central in creating these different bases for social order. In more recent times sociologists have pointed out that contemporary rural towns are far from simple *Gemeinschafts*[12] and that many

Gemeinschaft characteristics can be found in the midst of the modern metropolis,[13] a point taken up by the authors in Part III.

Emile Durkheim's continuum between "mechanical" and "organic" social solidarity in many ways parallels Tönnies, as Durkheim himself notes in his 1889 review of *Gemeinschaft und Gesellschaft*.[14] Yet Durkheim rejected Tönnies' description of modern social life as utterly utilitarian. If in a traditional "mechanical" society social solidarity is built on common world-views based on common experiences, Durkheim argued, in the modern, "organic" society social solidarity arises despite a complex division of labor and the rise of individualism. The collective consciousness of modern, and particularly urban, social life rest in shared abstract principals including, paradoxically, a common belief in the value of the individual. Yet the control exerted by these abstract principals is considerably looser than that afforded by the clear social norms of a mechanical society. The results in the modern city are often deviance, "anomie" (normlessness) and unhappiness.

Georg Simmel shared many common themes with his contemporaries Durkheim and Tönnies. Yet in "The Metropolis and Mental life," the third essay in Part I of this volume, he goes beyond them in detailing the psychological life of the modern urban person. Unlike Tönnies, and to an extent Durkheim, Simmel seems untouched by nostalgia for the world that preceded the advent of industrialization. He writes as an unapologetic urbanite, and while he lays out many of the negative aspects of the modern city it is clear that he speaks as its creature.

Simmel, as it is often noted, seems to have been destined for the role of explicating modern urbanism. He was born in Berlin and grew up in a house at the corner of Freidrichstrasse and Leizpzigerstrasse at the very center of metropolis (the nearest underground stop is called *Stadtmitte* – "midtown").[15] He was a Jew, albeit a nonobservant one, living in a period in which Jews were increasingly associated with the "rootless cosmopolitanism" of modernity.[16] Perhaps more importantly he was a public intellectual, a man equally capable of producing mammoth works of scholarship and short incisive essays for a broad audience.[17]

In "The Metropolis and Mental Life" Simmel explores the impact of urban living on the mental state of thinking people. He sees in the excessive psychic stimulation of the modern city the origins of the cold, intellectual, "blasé" attitude of urbanites. This attitude in part derives from the standardization of value, the calculation of time and the growth of the money economy; Simmel is not surprised that many are repulsed by it. And yet with this coldness comes a higher level of intellectual engagement with the environment and a greater sense of individuality. What is more, the highly specialized division of labor of the city forces people to play a number of different roles in a way that they do not in smaller communities. The result is a sort of self-hood that transcends the various roles one must play. As Richard Sennett notes, "Simmel believed that a man could, in a complex city, come to free his spirit from his acts, that is, come to understand that 'who I am' is not simply 'what I do ordinarily.' "[18] In the city, freedom and loneliness go hand in hand.

Like Simmel, the American historian, urban planner and cultural critic Lewis Mumford was a public intellectual on the margins of academe. Perhaps this is why his discussion of the city is so original. The excerpt included here as Chapter 2, from the introduction to his 1938 classic, *The Culture of Cities*, celebrates the role that cities play in human development. With their diversity of time structures cities make history and culture visible for their residents and thus "the mind takes form in the city." Yet while Simmel ambivalently embraces the modern city, Mumford is horrified by much of modern urbanism and has little sympathy for the direction of technological progress. Yet his nostalgia, unlike that of Tonnies and many early sociologists, is not for a mythical *Gemeinschaft* but rather for the medieval city, in which, he claims, the balance of dense neighborhoods, identities and broader civic unity created a world in which "both *Gemeinschaft* and *Gesellschaft* took on the same urban pattern."[19]

Using as its text the cultural ferment of nineteenth-century Paris, Walter Benjamin's essay gives a more impressionistic account of the early modern metropolis. Examining such diverse sources as the utopian politics of Saint Simon,

the poetry of Baudelaire, the commercial cornucopia of the
new retailing arcades and the fusion of commerce and mass
entertainment represented by the world exhibitions, Benjamin
finds in nineteenth-century Paris the roots of a new type of
public culture. Although Paris was one of the world's great
industrial centers during the nineteenth century, the culture that we most associate with Parisians of that day is
not that of industrial workers, but rather of consumers
and spectators. The world the impressionists painted was,
to a great extent, a world of white-collar workers; clerks,
bureaucrats, shop "girls" and entertainers; new people
in new positions that were neither proletarian nor bourgeois in the strict Marxian sense.

Describing this world of the new middle classes, Meyer
Shapiro writes that as the locus of urban sociability had

> shifted from community, family and church to commer-
> cialized or privately improvised forms – the streets, the
> cafes, the resorts – the resulting consciousness of indi-
> vidual freedom involved more and more estrangement from
> older ties; and those imaginative members of the middle
> class who accepted the norms of freedom but lacked the
> economic means to attain them were spiritually torn by
> a sense of helpless isolation in an anonymous, indifferent
> mass.[20]

In the background of this world looms Baron Georges-Eugene
Haussmann, who served as the prefect of the Seine between
1853 and 1870 and who supervised Napoleon III's rebuilding of Paris, the largest renovation of an existing city the
world had ever seen. Paris had already undergone substantial state-sponsored renewal efforts under both the direct-
orate and the republic, but nothing compared with what
Haussmann would accomplish. As Julia Trilling notes,
"Haussmann's plan was not just a choice of building style,
but a great civic redesign."[21] The result was "a spaciousness and scale which no other city possessed but which
city after city did its best to emulate."[22]

Like Le Corbusier and Robert Moses, who would follow
him, Haussmann saw controlling an exploding metropolis
and its diverse population as a technical problem, one that
lent itself to rational solutions. Long, straight boulevards

were drawn through the heart of the ancient city, mercilessly cutting through the cluttered maze of medieval streets and communities; in some cases the demolition crews used cannon fire to take down residential blocks. Traffic flow for horse-drawn vehicles became the paramount concern, and indeed Haussmann's system of boulevards served the city well into the automobile era. Ancient neighborhoods and monuments were swept aside as the modern city took shape. Yet the beautiful Paris we know was not universally beloved, at least not at first. As Norma Evenson notes:

In the view of many, the long straight vistas and uniform facades characterizing Haussmann's work reflected an insensitive and mechanical conception of urban design. New streets had been plotted across the map of Paris regardless of topography and existing buildings, and the resulting destruction inevitably generated protest. During the course of Haussmann's demolitions, the Ile de la Cite, the site of the oldest settlement of the city, was completely razed and its closely knit urban fabric replaced by new, coarsely scaled government offices. Two medieval monuments, the Notre Dame Cathedral and the church of Sainte Chapelle remained, but in totally altered surroundings.[23]

Haussmann and his successors built a city that was orderly, efficient and largely discontinuous with the past, except where that past could be taken out of context and reframed as a symbol or monument. For Baudelaire and his contemporaries these changes were frightening. Parisians increasingly did not recognize their new city as it took shape around them. But they were thrilled by it too. The city of lights was awash with change, and with change came new possibilities. Rootless and emancipated, Parisians invented a new sort of urban life in the cafe, in the department store, in the nightclub, and strolling on Sunday on the island of La Grande-Jatte. The city had become a spectacle and the painters who captured it taught the world a new way to see.[24]

Yet the painters told only half the story. Paris in the nineteenth century was also a world of real and deadly class conflicts, which always simmered just below the surface and occasionally exploded into the streets. The poor and the working classes fared badly under Haussmann's renovation. The ancient districts in which they had once lived in close proximity to more affluent Parisians were often destroyed, transformed into bourgeois neighborhoods or isolated by the new boulevards. For the most part the poor were banished to the outer edge of the city, where the Red Belt of suburbs, so named because of their propensity to vote communist, would grow up in the twentieth century. Where once a wall had protected Paris from external enemies, the new boulevards facilitated military movement *within* the city, for now the urban working class was perceived as at least as much of a threat to public order as any foreign army. The uprising of the Paris Commune of 1871 exposed the underside of the new Paris that Napoleon III and Haussmann had created, and, as Benjamin wryly notes, the boulevards, which were supposed to be too wide for the mob to block, simply forced them to build barricades that were stronger and higher.

For Benjamin, a Frankfurt-School Marxist and an aesthete, this contradiction between the free-floating world of the artist and the hard realities of inequality in the modern city was deeply troubling. Clearly he could no longer accept, as many nineteenth-century Parisians had, the Saint Simonian dream of industrial technology without class conflict. Yet he seemed unwilling to embrace either the bourgeois culture that produced the cafes and arcades, or the Stalinist uniformity that by the 1930s seemed the most obvious alternative. Benjamin, as Marshall Berman notes, was drawn

> irresistibly toward the city's brilliant lights, beautiful women, fashion, luxury, its play of dazzling surfaces and radiant scenes; meanwhile his Marxist conscience wrenches him insistently away from these temptations, instructs him that this whole glittering world is decadent, hollow, vicious, spiritually empty, oppressive to the proletariate, condemned by history. . . . [B]ut he cannot resist one last look down the boulevard or under the arcade; he wants to be saved, but not yet.[25]

The final essay in Part I, Louis Wirth's "Urbanism as a Way of Life" (Chapter 5), is perhaps the most systematic statement of the world-view and mission of the "Chicago School," the extraordinary tradition of urban sociological analysis that began at the University of Chicago in the early decades of the twentieth century. Chicago was an important beachhead for the discipline of sociology in the United States. If ever there was a place where people were motivated to understand what modern urban life was all about, it was Chicago. A village of a few dozen families in 1830, Chicago had grown to a city of 300 000 by 1870. By 1890 it was the nation's second-largest metropolis with a population of 1 200 000.[26] Immigrants and their children outnumbered natives, and the city combined modern anomie and class conflict with ethnic and racial divisions and patterns of residential segregation heretofore unknown in Europe.

For the sociologists of the Chicago School, this city of Louis Sullivan and Al Capone was the perfect laboratory for the study of modern life. Led by Robert Park, a progressive-era activist–journalist turned sociologist, the Chicago-School researchers drew on the German academic perspectives of Simmel and Max Weber, the American pragmatism of John Dewey and the social-reform tradition of Jane Adams. Park advocated using the ethnographic techniques of anthropology to study the metropolis and urged his students to

> Go and sit in the lounges of the luxury hotels and on the doorsteps of the flophouses; sit on the Gold Coast settees and on the slum shakedowns; sit in the Orchestra Hall and the Star and Garter Burlesque. In short, gentlemen, go get the seat of your pants dirty in real research.[27]

Generations of students did just that and turned out dozens of ethnographic studies of diverse urban communities, subcultures and occupational groups. If some of this work is occasionally frustrating in its localism, it remains one of the central traditions of American sociology and a vital link between grand theory and the way people actually live. Other Chicago students, working within the human-ecology perspective, used quantitative and qualitative data to develop models of the spatial development of cities, while still others conducted theoretical inquiries into the nature of urban

18   *Introduction*

life. All in all Chicago became, and remains, the most thoroughly sociologized location on the planet.[28]

Louis Wirth was among Park's most gifted students and collaborators, and in this essay he takes Simmel's insights as well as many of Durkheim's and Park's and systematically incorporates them into a coherent theoretical description of the modern city. Drawing on these earlier authors, he is particularly astute in working through the implications for urban life of the modern fragmentation of social roles and the complex division of labor. Writing in 1938, when the rise of fascism had made apparent the dark side of mass society, Wirth is also among the first to note the importance of electronic communication in modern politics and the particular vulnerability of "masses of men in the city" to "manipulation by symbols and stereotypes."

Notes

1. Charles Dickens, *Nicholas Nickleby* (New York: Penguin, 1981), p. 489.
2. Karl Marx, *The Communist Manifesto* (New York: International Publishers, 1948), p. 12.
3. Peter Jukes, *A Shout in the Street: An Excursion into the Modern City* (Berkeley: The University of California Press, 1991), p. xv.
4. Kingsley Davis, "The Urbanization of the Human Population", in Kingsley Davis (ed.), *Cities: A Scientific American Book* (New York: Alfred Knopf, 1973).
5. Janet L. Abu-Lughod, *Changing Cities* (New York: Harper Collins, 1991), p. 61.
6. Ibid., pp. 101-2.
7. Quotes from Karl Marx and Frederick Engels, *The Communist Manifesto* (New York: International Publisher, 1948), pp. 12-13.
8. Gertrude Himmelfarb, "the Culture of Poverty", in H. J. Dyos and Michael Wolff (eds), *The Victorian City* (Boston: Routledge and Kegan Paul, 1973), p. 719. See also Deborah Epstein Nord, "The Social Explorer as Anthropologist: Victorian Travellers Among the Urban Poor", in William Sharpe and Leonard Wallock (eds), *Visions of the Modern City* (Baltimore: Johns Hopkins University Press, 1987), pp. 122-34. Note that a similar form of proto-urban anthropology – with the same combination of horror and lurid fascination – emerges among social reformers in the United States a generation later. See in particular the work of Jacob Riis.
9. Raymond Williams, *The Country and the City* (Oxford and New York: Oxford University Press), pp. 226-7.

10. Dennis H. Wrong, "The Idea of Community: A Critique", *Dissent*, vol. 13 (May–June 1966), p. 290.

11. The terms *Gemeinschaft* and *Gesellschaft* are usually translated as "community" and "society," but as this does not adequately capture Tönnies' meaning, sociologists tend to use the original German.

12. See Arthur Vidich and Joseph Bensman, *Small Town in Mass Society* (Princeton University Press, 1958).

13. See Herbert Gans, *The Urban Villagers* (New York: Free Press, 1962).

14. Emile Durkheim, review of "Gemeinschaft und Gesellschaft," *Revue Philosophique*, vol. 27 (1889), pp. 421–422. Reprinted in *Selected Writings*, edited by Anthony Giddens (New York: Cambridge University Press, 1972), pp. 146–7.

15. Gianfranco Poggi, *Money and the Modern Mind: Georg Simmel's Philosophy of Money* (Berkeley: University of California Press, 1993), p. 39.

16. Simmel spent most of his career at Berlin University as a *privatdozent*: a lecturer at the margins of the University. Anti-Semitism and his own intellectual radicalism prevented him from attaining a regular university post until the last four years of his life. Simmel's biographers, inevitably college professors themselves, tend to see this as a tragic injustice. Yet it is hard to imagine Simmel in the small world of an exclusively academic community, apart from his urban milieux. In Berlin, not only were his lectures well attended and his writings influential, but he drew around him an extraordinary group of students, including Georg Lukacs, Ernst Bloch, Karl Mannheim and Robert Park. When he finally obtained a regular appointment at the University of Strasbourg at the age of 56, he accepted with the greatest reluctance. As he wrote to a friend, "if I accept it [the Strasbourg position] it will not be with a light heart. For the influence upon our philosophical culture, which I can exercise in Berlin, will not be achieved so easily elsewhere." See David Frisby, *Sociological Impressionism: A Reassessment of Georg Simmel's Social Theory* (London: Routledege, 1981), p. 29.

17. While Simmel's structural analysis had a profound influence on early American sociology, by the mid-twentieth century he came to be regarded as an important but ideosyncratic and ultimately secondary figure, particularly when compared with Durkheim and Max Weber. In recent years, however, there has been something of Simmel revival, particularly among contemporary sociologists of culture, who see in his impressionistic method and cultural criticism a sort of proto-postmodernism. This has led to an increased interest in Simmel's shorter and less academic works, many of which are only now being translated into English. See for example David Frisby, *Simmel and Since: Essays on Georg Simmel's Social Theory* (London: Routledge, 1992) and "Georg Simmel", a special issue of *Theory, Culture and Society* edited by Mike Featherstone, vol. 8, no. 3 (1991). For a critical response by a leading, traditional interpreter of Simmel see Lewis Coser, "The Many Faces of Georg Simmel," *Contemporary Sociology*, vol. 22, no. 3 (1993), pp. 452–4.

18. Richard Sennett, *Classic Essays on the Culture of Cities* (Englewood Cliffs, NJ: Prentice Hall, 1969), p. 10.
19. Lewis Mumford, "The Medieval City", in *The Lewis Mumford Reader*, edited by Donald Miller (New York: Pantheon, 1986), p. 122. This notion of balance and scale, influenced by the British social reformer Ebenezer Howard, characterizes not only Mumford's scholarly work, but also his activities as a member of the Regional Planning Association of America, and through those activities he became an important ideological touchstone for American regional planners.
20. Meyer Shapiro, in *Marxist Quarterly*, January 1937. Quoted in T. J. Clark, *The Painting of Modern Life: Paris in the Art of Manet and his Followers* (New York: Knopf, 1985), p. 3.
21. Julia Trilling, "A Future that looks like the Past", *The Atlantic Monthly*, July 1985, p. 31.
22. Mark Girouard, *Cities and People* (New Haven: Yale University Press, 1985), p. 283.
23. Norma Evenson, *Paris: A Century of Change* (New Haven: Yale University Press, 1982), p. 22.
24. See Clark, op. cit.
25. Marshall Berman, *All That is Solid Melts into Air* (New York: Simon and Schuster, 1982), p. 146.
26. Mark Girouard, *Cities and People* (New Haven: Yale University Press 1985), p. 304.
27. Robert E. Park, quoted in John C. McKinley, *Constructive Topology and Social Theory* (New York: Appleton-Century-Crofts, 1966), p. 71.
28. Which is wonderful in terms of the consistency of data that it provides but can at times create problems in knowing the difference between general social trends and the specifics of Chicago history.

2 The Culture of Cities*
Lewis Mumford

The city, as one finds it in history, is the point of maximum concentration for the power and culture of a community. It is the place where the diffused rays of many separate beams of life fall into focus, with gains in both social effectiveness and significance. The city is the form and symbol of an integrated social relationship: it is the seat of the temple, the market, the hall of justice, the academy of learning. Here in the city the goods of civilization are multiplied and manifolded; here is where human experience is transformed into viable signs, symbols, patterns of conduct, systems of order. Here is where the issues of civilization are focused; here, too, ritual passes on occasion into the active drama of a fully differentiated and self-conscious society.

Cities are a product of the earth. They reflect the peasant's cunning in dominating the earth; technically they but carry further his skill in turning the soil to productive uses, in enfolding his cattle for safety, in regulating the waters that moisten his fields, in providing storage bins and barns for his crops. Cities are emblems of that settled life which began with permanent agriculture: a life conducted with the aid of permanent shelters, permanent utilities like orchards, vineyards, and irrigation works, and permanent buildings for protection and storage.

Every phase of life in the countryside contributes to the existence of cities. What the shepherd, the woodman, and the miner know, becomes transformed and "etherealized" through the city into durable elements in the human heritage: the textiles and butter of one, the moats and dams and wooden pipes and lathes of another, the metals and jewels of the third, are finally converted into instruments of urban living: underpinning the city's economic existence,

* Reprinted from Lewis Mumford, *The Culture of Cities* (New York: Harcourt Brace and Company, 1938).

contributing art and wisdom to its daily routine. Within the city the essence of each type of soil and labor and economic goal is concentrated: thus arise greater possibilities for interchange and for new combinations not given in the isolation of their original habitats.

Cities are a product of time. They are the molds in which men's lifetimes have cooled and congealed, giving lasting shape, by way of art, to moments that would otherwise vanish with the living and leave no means of renewal or wider participation behind them. In the city, time becomes visible: buildings and monuments and public ways, more open than the written record, more subject to the gaze of many men than the scattered artifacts of the countryside, leave an imprint upon the minds even of the ignorant or the indifferent. Through the material fact of preservation, time challenges time, time clashes with time: habits and values carry over beyond the living group, streaking with different strata of time the character of any single generation. Layer upon layer, past times preserve themselves in the city until life itself is finally threatened with suffocation: then, in sheer defense, modern man invents the museum.

By the diversity of its time-structures, the city in part escapes the tyranny of a single present, and the monotony of a future that consists in repeating only a single beat heard in the past. Through its complex orchestration of time and space, no less than through the social division of labor, life in the city takes on the character of a symphony: specialized human aptitudes, specialized instruments, give rise to sonorous results which, neither in volume nor in quality, could be achieved by any single piece.

Cities arise out of man's social needs and multiply both their modes and their methods of expression. In the city remote forces and influences intermingle with the local: their conflicts are no less significant than their harmonies. And here, through the concentration of the means of intercourse in the market and the meeting place, alternative modes of living present themselves: the deeply rutted ways of the village cease to be coercive and the ancestral goals cease to be all-sufficient: strange men and women, strange interests, and stranger gods loosen the traditional ties of blood and neighborhood. A sailing ship, a caravan, stopping at the city, may bring a new dye for wool, a new glaze for the potter's dish, a new system of signs for long distance communication, or a new thought about human destiny. In the urban milieu, mechanical shocks produce social results; and social needs may take shape in contrivances and inventions which will lead industries and governments into new channels of experiment. Now the need for a common fortified spot for shelter against predatory attack draws the inhabitants of the indigenous village into a hillside fortification: through the compulsive mingling for defense, the possibilities for more regular intercourse and wider cooperation arise. That fact helps transform the nest of villages into a unified city, with its higher ceiling of achievement and its wider horizons. Now the collective sharing of experience, and the stimulus of rational criticism, turn the rites of the village festival into the more powerful imaginative forms of the tragic drama: experience is deepened, as well as more widely circulated, through this process. Or again, on another plane, the goldsmith's passive repository for valuables becomes, through the pressure of urban needs and the opportunities of the market, the dynamic agent of capitalism, the bank, lending money as well as keeping it, putting capital into circulation, finally dominating the processes of trade and production.

The city is a fact in nature, like a cave, a run of mackerel or an ant-heap. But it is also a conscious work of art, and it holds within its communal framework many simpler and more personal forms of art. Mind *takes form* in the city; and in turn, urban forms condition mind. For space, no less than time, is artfully reorganized in cities: in boundary lines and silhouettes, in the fixing of horizontal planes and vertical peaks, in utilizing or denying the natural site, the city records the attitude of a culture and an epoch to the fundamental facts of its existence. The dome and the spire, the open avenue and the closed court, tell the story, not merely of different physical accommodations, but of essentially different conceptions of man's destiny. The city is both a physical utility for collective living and a symbol of those collective purposes and unanimities that arise under such favoring circumstance. With language itself, it remains man's greatest work of art.

Through its concrete, visible command over space the city lends itself, not only to the practical offices of production, but to the daily communion of its citizens: this constant effect of the city, as a collective work of art, was expressed in a classic manner by Thomas Mann in his address to his fellow-townsmen of Lübeck on the celebration of the anniversary of Lübeck's foundation. When the city ceases to be a symbol of art and order, it acts in a negative fashion: it expresses and helps to make more universal the fact of disintegration. In the close quarters of the city, perversities and evils spread more quickly; and in the stones of the city, these antisocial facts become embedded: it is not the triumphs of urban living that awaken the prophetic wrath of a Jeremiah, a Savonarola, a Rousseau, or a Ruskin.

What transforms the passive agricultural regime of the village into the active institutions of the city? The difference is not merely one of magnitude, density of population, or economic resources. For the active agent is any factor that extends the area of local intercourse, that engenders the need for combination and co-operation, communication and communion; and that so creates a common underlying pattern of conduct, and a common set of physical structures, for the different family and occupational groups that constitute a city. These opportunities and activities superimpose upon primary groups, based upon traditional acceptances and daily face-to-face contact, the more active associations, the more specialized functions, and the more purposive interests of secondary groups: in the latter the purpose is not given, but chosen: the membership and the activities are selective: the group itself becomes specialized and differentiated.

Historically, the increase of population, through the change from hunting to agriculture, may have abetted this change; the widening of trade routes and the diversification of occupations likewise helped. But the nature of the city is not to be found simply in its economic base: the city is primarily a social emergent. The mark of the city is its purposive social complexity. It represents the maximum possibility of humanizing the natural environment and of naturalizing the human heritage: it gives a cultural shape to the first, and it externalizes, in permanent collective forms, the second.

"The central and significant fact about the city," as Geddes and Branford pointed out, "is that the city . . . functions as the specialized organ of social transmission. It accumulates and embodies the heritage of a region, and combines in some measure and kind with the cultural heritage of larger units, national, racial, religious, human. On one side is the individuality of the city – the sign manual of its regional life and record. On the other are the marks of the civilization, in which each particular city is a constituent element."

Today a great many things stand in the way of grasping the role of the city and of transforming this basic means of communal existence. During the last few centuries the strenuous mechanical organization of industry, and the setting up of tyrannous political states, have blinded most men to the importance of facts that do not easily fit into the general pattern of mechanical conquest, capitalistic forms of exploitation, and power politics. Habitually, people treat the realities of personality and association and city as abstractions, while they treat confused pragmatic abstractions such as money, credit, political sovereignty, as if they are concrete realities that had an existence independent of human conventions.

Looking back over the course of Western Civilization since the fifteenth century, it is fairly plain that mechanical integration and social disruption have gone on side by side. Our capacity for effective physical organization has enormously increased; but our ability to create an harmonious counterpoise to these external linkages by means of co-operative and civic associations on both a regional and a world-wide basis, like the Christian Church in the Middle Ages, has not kept pace with these mechanical triumphs. By one of those mischievous turns, from which history is rarely free, it was precisely during this period of flowing physical energies, social disintegration, and bewildered political experiment that the populations of the world as a whole began mightily to increase, and the cities of the Western World began to grow at an inordinate rate. Forms of social life that the wisest no longer understood, the more ignorant were prepared to build. Or rather, the ignorant were completely unprepared, but that did not prevent the building.

The result was not a temporary confusion and an occasional lapse in efficiency. What followed was a crystallization of chaos: disorder hardened uncouthly in metropolitan slum and industrial factory districts; and the exodus into the dormitory suburbs and factory spores that surrounded the growing cities merely widened the area of social derangement. The mechanized physical shell took precedence in every growing town over the civic nucleus: men became dissociated as citizens in the very process of coming together in imposing economic organizations. Even industry, which was supposedly served by this planless building and random physical organization, lost seriously in efficiency: it failed to produce a new urban form that served directly its complicated processes. As for the growing urban populations, they lacked the most elementary facilities for urban living, even sunlight and fresh air, to say nothing of the means to a more vivid social life. The new cities grew up without the benefit of coherent social knowledge or orderly social effort: they lacked the useful urban folkways of the Middle Ages or the confident esthetic command of the Baroque period: indeed, a seventeenth-century Dutch peasant, in his little village, knew more about the art of living in communities than a nineteenth century municipal councilor in London or Berlin. Statesmen who did not hesitate to weld together a diversity of regional interests into national states, or who wove together an empire that girdled the planet, failed to produce even a rough draft of a decent neighborhood.

In every department, form disintegrated: except in its heritage from the past, the city vanished as an embodiment of collective art and technics. And where, as in North America, the loss was not alleviated by the continued presence of great monuments from the past and persistent habits of social living, the result was a raw, dissolute environment, and a narrow, constricted, and baffled social life. Even in Germany and the Low Countries, where the traditions of urban life had lingered on from the Middle Ages, the most colossal blunders were committed in the most ordinary tasks of urban planning and building. As the pace of urbanization increased, the circle of devastation widened.

Today we face not only the original social disruption. We likewise face the accumulated physical and social results of the disruption: ravaged landscapes, disorderly urban districts, pockets of disease, patches of blight, mile upon mile of standardized slums, worming into the outlying areas of big cities, and fusing with their ineffectual suburbs. In short, a general miscarriage and defeat of civilized effort. So far have our achievements fallen short of our needs that even a hundred years of persistent reform in England, the first country to suffer heavily from disurbanization, have only in the last decade begun to leave an imprint. True, here and there patches of good building and coherent social form exist: new nodes of integration can be detected, and since 1920 these patches have been spreading. But the main results of more than a century of misbuilding and malformation, dissociation and disorganization still hold. Whether the observer focuses his gaze on the physical structure of communal living or upon the social processes that must be embodied and expressed, the report remains the same.

Today we begin to see that the improvement of cities is no matter for small one-sided reforms: the task of city design involves the vaster task of rebuilding our civilization. We must alter the parasitic and predatory modes of life that now play so large a part, and we must create region by region, continent by continent, an effective symbiosis, or co-operative living together. The problem is to coordinate, on the basis of more essential human values than the will-to-power and the will-to-profits, a host of social functions and processes that we have hitherto misused in the building of cities and polities, and of which we have never rationally taken advantage.

Unfortunately, the fashionable political philosophies of the past century are of but small help in defining this new task: they dealt with legal abstractions, like Individual and State, with cultural abstractions, like Humanity, the Nation, the Folk, or with bare economic abstractions like the Capitalist Class or the Proletariat – while life as it was lived in the concrete, in regions and cities and villages, in wheatland and cornland and vineland, in the mine, the quarry, the fishery, was conceived as but a shadow of the prevailing myths and arrogant fantasies of the ruling classes – or the often no less shadowy fantasies of those who challenged them.

Here and there one notes, of course, valiant exceptions both in theory and in action. Le Play and Reclus in France, W. H. Riehl in Germany, Kropotkin in Russia, Howard in England, Grundtvig in Denmark, Geddes in Scotland, began half a century ago to lay the ideological basis for a new order. The insights of these men may prove as important for the new biotechnic regime, based on the deliberate culture of life, as the formulations of Leonardo, Galileo, Newton, and Descartes were for the more limited mechanical order upon which the past triumphs of our machine civilization were founded. In the piecemeal improvement of cities, the work of sanitarians like Chadwick and Richardson, community designers like Olmsted, far-seeing architects, like Parker and Wright, laid the concrete basis for a collective environment in which the needs of reproduction and nurture and psychological development and the social processes themselves would be adequately served.

Now the dominant urban environment of the past century has been mainly a narrow by-product of the machine ideology. And the greater part of it has already been made obsolete by the rapid advance of the biological arts and sciences, and by the steady penetration of sociological thought into every department. We have now reached a point where these fresh accumulations of historical insight and scientific knowledge are ready to flow over into social life, to mold anew the forms of cities, to assist in the transformation of both the instruments and the goals of our civilization. Profound changes, which will affect the distribution and increase of population, the efficiency of industry, and the quality of Western culture, have already become visible. To form an accurate estimate of these new potentialities and to suggest their direction into channels of human welfare, is one of the major offices of the contemporary student of cities. Ultimately, such studies, forecasts, and imaginative projects must bear directly upon the life of every human being in our civilization.

Today [1938] our world faces a crisis: a crisis which, if its consequences are as grave as now seems, may not fully be resolved for another century. If the destructive forces in civilization gain ascendancy, our new urban culture will be stricken in every part. Our cities, blasted and deserted, will be cemeteries for the dead: cold lairs given over to less destructive beasts than man. But we may avert that fate: perhaps only in facing such a desperate challege can the necessary creative forces be effectually welded together. Instead of clinging to the sardonic funeral towers of metropolitan finance, ours to march out to newly plowed fields, to create fresh patterns of political action, to alter for human purposes the perverse mechanisms of our economic regime, to conceive and to germinate fresh forms of human culture.

Instead of accepting the stale cult of death that the fascists have erected, as the proper crown for the servility and the brutality that are the pillars of their states, we must erect a cult of life: life in action, as the farmer or the mechanic knows it: life in expression, as the artist knows it: life as the lover feels it and the parent practices it: life as it is known to men of good will who meditate in the cloister, experiment in the laboratory, or plan intelligently in the factory of the government office.

Nothing is permanent, certainly not the frozen images of barbarous power with which fascism now confronts us. Those images may easily be smashed by an external shock, cracked as ignominiously as fallen Dagon, the massive idol of the heathen: or they may be melted, eventually, by the internal warmth of normal men and women. Nothing endures except life: the capacity for birth, growth, and daily renewal. As life becomes insurgent once more in our civilization, conquering the reckless thrust of barbarism, the culture of cities will be both instrument and goal.

3 The Metropolis and Mental Life*
Georg Simmel

The deepest problems of modern life flow from the attempt of the individual to maintain the independence and individuality of his existence against the sovereign powers of society, against the weight of the historical heritage and the external culture and technique of life. This antagonism represents the most modern form of the conflict which primitive man must carry on with nature for his own bodily existence. The eighteenth century may have called for liberation from all the ties which grew up historically in politics, in religion, in morality and in economics in order to permit the original natural virtue of man, which is equal in everyone, to develop without inhibition; the nineteenth century may have sought to promote, in addition to man's freedom, his individuality (which is connected with the division of labor) and his achievements which make him unique and indispensable but which at the same time make him so much the more dependent on the complementary activity of others; Nietzsche may have seen the relentless struggle of the individual as the prerequisite for his full development, while Socialism found the same thing in the suppression of all competition – but in each of these the same fundamental motive was at work, namely the resistance of the individual to being levelled, swallowed up in the social-technological mechanism.

When one inquires about the products of the specifically modern aspects of contemporary life with reference to their inner meaning – when, so to speak, one examines the body of culture with reference to the soul, as I am to do con-

* Reprinted from Georg Simmel, *On Individuality and Social Forms* (Donald Levine, ed.) (Chicago: University of Chicago Press, 1971), translated by Edward Shills. Originally published as "Die Grossstadte und das Geistesleben" in T. Petermann (ed.), *Die Grossstadt* (Dresden, 1903).

cerning the metropolis today – the answer will require the investigation of the relationship which such a social structure promotes between the individual aspects of life and those which transcend the existence of single individuals. It will require the investigation of the adaptations made by the personality in its adjustment to the forces that lie outside of it.

The psychological foundation, upon which the metropolitan individuality is erected, is the intensification of emotional life due to the swift and continuous shift of external and internal stimuli. Man is a creature whose existence is dependent on differences, i.e., his mind is stimulated by the difference between present impressions and those which have preceded. Lasting impressions, the slightness in their differences, the habituated regularity of their course and contrasts between them, consume, so to speak, less mental energy than the rapid telescoping of changing images, pronounced differences within what is grasped at a single glance, and the unexpectedness of violent stimuli. To the extent that the metropolis creates these psychological conditions – with every crossing of the street, with the tempo and multiplicity of economic, occupational and social life – it creates in the sensory foundations of mental life, and in the degree of awareness necessitated by our organization as creatures dependent on differences, a deep contrast with the slower, more habitual, more smoothly flowing rhythm of the sensory–mental phase of small town and rural existence. Thereby the essentially intellectualistic character of the mental life of the metropolis becomes intelligible as over against that of the small town which rests more on feelings and emotional relationships. These latter are rooted in the unconscious levels of the mind and develop most readily in the steady equilibrium of unbroken customs. The locus of reason, on the other hand, is in the lucid, conscious upper strata of the mind and it is the most adaptable of our inner forces. In order to adjust itself to the shifts and contradictions in events, it does not require the disturbances and inner upheavals which are the only means whereby more conservative personalities are able to adapt themselves to the same rhythm of events. Thus the metropolitan type – which naturally takes on a thousand individual modifications – creates a protective organ for itself against the profound disruption with which the fluctuations and discontinuities of the external milieu threaten it. Instead of reacting emotionally, the metropolitan type reacts primarily in a rational manner, thus creating a mental predominance through the intensification of consciousness, which in turn is caused by it. Thus the reaction of the metropolitan person to those events is moved to a sphere of mental activity which is least sensitive and which is furthest removed from the depths of the personality.

This intellectualistic quality which is thus recognized as a protection of the inner life against the domination of the metropolis, becomes ramified into numerous specific phenomena. The metropolis has always been the seat of the money economy because the many-sidedness and concentration of commercial activity have given the medium of exchange an importance which it could not have acquired in the commercial aspects of rural life. But the money economy and the domination of the intellect stand in the closest relationship to one another. They have in common a purely matter-of-fact attitude in the treatment of persons and things in which a formal justice is often combined with an unrelenting hardness. The purely intellectualistic person is indifferent to all things personal because, out of them, relationship and reactions develop that are not to be completely understood by purely rational methods – just as the unique element in events never enters into the principle of money. Money is concerned only with what is common to all, i.e., with the exchange value which reduces all quality and individuality to a purely quantitative level. All emotional relationships between persons rest on their individuality, whereas intellectual relationships deal with persons as with numbers, that is, as with elements which, in themselves, are indifferent, but which are of interest only insofar as they offer something objectively perceivable. It is in this very manner that the inhabitant of the metropolis reckons with his merchant, his customer, and with his servant, and frequently with the persons with whom he is thrown into obligatory association.

These relationships stand in distinct contrast with the nature of the smaller circle in which the inevitable knowledge of individual characteristics produces, with an equal inevitability, an emotional tone in conduct, a sphere which is beyond the mere objective weighting of tasks performed and payments made. What is essential here as regards the economic–psychological aspect of the problem is that in less advanced cultures production was for the customer who ordered the product so that the producer and the purchaser knew one another. The modern city, however, is supplied almost exclusively by production for the market, that is, for entirely unknown purchasers who never appear in the actual field of vision of the producers themselves. Thereby, the interests of each party acquire a relentless matter-of-factness, and its rationally calculated economic egoism need not fear any divergence from its set path because of the imponderability of personal relationships. This is all the more the case in the money economy which dominates the metropolis in which the last remnants of domestic production and direct barter of goods have been eradicated and in which the amount of production on direct personal order is reduced daily. Furthermore, this psychological intellectualistic attitude and the money economy are in such close integration that no one is able to say whether it was the former that effected the latter or vice versa. What is certain is only that the form of life in the metropolis is the soil which nourishes this interaction most fruitfully, a point which I shall attempt to demonstrate only with the statement of the most outstanding English constitutional historian to the effect that through the entire course of English history London has never acted as the heart of England but often as its intellect and always as its money bag.

In certain apparently insignificant characters or traits of the most external aspects of life are to be found a number of characteristic mental tendencies. The modern mind has become more and more a calculating one. The calculating exactness of practical life which has resulted from a money economy corresponds to the ideal of natural science, namely that of transforming the world into an arithmetical problem and of fixing every one of its parts in a mathematical formula. It has been money economy which has thus filled the daily life of so many people with weighing, calculating, enumerating and the reduction of qualitative values to quantitative terms. Because of the character of calculability which money has there has come into the relationships of the elements of life a precision and a degree of certainty in the definition of the equalities and inequalities and an unambiguousness in agreements and arrangements, just as externally this precision has been brought about through the general diffusion of pocket watches.

It is, however, the conditions of the metropolis which are cause as well as effect for this essential characteristic. The relationships and concerns of the typical metropolitan resident are so manifold and complex that, especially as a result of the agglomeration of so many persons with such differentiated interests, their relationships and activities intertwine with one another into a many-membered organism. In view of this fact, the lack of the most exact punctuality in promises and performances would cause the whole to break down into an inextricable chaos. If all the watches in Berlin suddenly went wrong in different ways even only as much as an hour, its entire economic and commercial life would be derailed for some time. Even though this may seem more superficial in its significance, it transpires that the magnitude of distances results in making all waiting and the breaking of appointments an ill-afforded waste of time. For this reason the technique of metropolitan life in general is not conceivable without all of its activities and reciprocal relationships being organized and coordinated in the most punctual way into a firmly fixed framework of time which transcends all subjective elements.

But here too there emerge those conclusions which are in general the whole task of this discussion, namely, that every event, however restricted to this superficial level it may appear, comes immediately into contact with the depths of the soul, and that the most banal externalities are, in the last analysis, bound up with the final decisions concerning the meaning and the style of life. Punctuality, calculability, and exactness, which are required by the complications and extensiveness of metropolitan life are not only most intimately connected with its capitalistic and intellectualistic character but also color the content of life and are conducive to the exclusion of those irrational, instinctive, sovereign human traits and impulses which originally seek to determine the form of life from within instead of receiving it from the outside in a general, schematically precise form. Even though those lives which are autonomous and characterised by these vital impulses are not entirely impossible in the city, they are, none the less, opposed to it *in abstracto*. It is in the light of this that we can explain the passionate hatred of personalities like Ruskin and Nietzsche for the metropolis – personalities who found the value of life only in unschematized individual expressions which cannot be reduced to exact equivalents and in whom, on that account, there flowed from the same source as did that hatred, the hatred of the money economy and of the intellectualism of existence.

The same factors which, in the exactness and the minute precision of the form of life, have coalesced into a structure of the highest impersonality, have, on the other hand, an influence in a highly personal direction. There is perhaps no psychic phenomenon which is so unconditionally reserved to the city as the blasé outlook. It is at first the consequence of those rapidly shifting stimulations of the nerves which are thrown together in all their contrasts and from which it seems to use the intensification of metropolitan intellectuality seems to be derived. On that account it is not likely that stupid persons who have been hitherto intellectually dead will be blasé. Just as an immoderately sensuous life makes one blasé because it stimulates the nerves to their utmost reactivity until they finally can no longer produce any reaction at all, so, less harmful stimuli, through the rapidity and the contradictoriness of their shifts, force the nerves to make such violent responses, tear them about so brutally that they exhaust their last reserves of strength and, remaining in the same milieu, do not have time for new reserves to form. This incapacity to react to new stimulations with the required amount of energy constitutes in fact that blasé attitude which every child of a large city evinces when compared with the products of the more peaceful and more stable milieu.

Combined with this physiological source of the blasé metropolitan attitude there is another which derives from a money economy. The esssence of the blasé attitude is an indifference toward the distinctions between things. Not in the sense that they are not perceived, as is the case of mental dullness, but rather that the meaning and the value of the distinctions between things, and therewith of the things themselves, are experienced as meaningless. They appear to the blasé person in an homogeneous, flat and gray color with no one of them worthy of being preferred to another. This psychic mood is the correct subjective reflection of a complete money economy to the extent that money takes the place of all the manifoldness of things and expresses all qualitative distinctions between them in the distinction of "how much." To the extent that money, with its colorlessness and its indifferent quality, can become a common denominator of all values it becomes the frightful leveler – it hollows out the core of things, their peculiarities, their specific values and their uniqueness and incomparability in a way which is beyond repair. They all float with the same specific gravity in the constantly moving stream of money. They all rest on the same level and are distinguished only by their amounts. In individual cases this coloring, or rather this de-coloring of things, through their equation with money, may be imperceptibly small.

In the relationship, however, which the wealthy person has to objects which can be bought for money, perhaps indeed in the total character which, for this reason, public opinion now recognizes in these objects, it takes on very considerable proportions. This is why the metropolis is the seat of commerce and it is in it that the purchasability of things appears in quite a different aspect than in simpler economies. It is also the peculiar seat of the blasé attitude. In it is brought to a peak, in a certain way, that achievement in the concentration of purchasable things which stimulates the individual to the highest degree of nervous energy. Through the mere quantitative intensification of the same conditions this achievement is transformed into its opposite, into this peculiar adaptive phenomenon – the blasé attitude – in which the nerves reveal their final possibility of adjusting themselves to the content and the form of metropolitan life by renouncing the response to them. We see that the self-preservation of certain types of personalities is obtained at the cost of devaluing the entire objective world, ending inevitably in dragging the personality downward into a feeling of its own valuelessness.

Whereas the subject of this form of existence must come
to terms with it for himself, his self-preservation in the face
of the great city requires of him a no less negative type of
social conduct. The mental attitude of the people of the
metropolis to one another may be designated formally as
one of reserve. If the unceasing external contact of numbers of persons in the city should be met by the same number
of inner reactions as in the small town, in which one knows
almost every person he meets and to each of whom he has
a positive relationship, one would be completely atomized
internally and would fall into an unthinkable mental condition. Partly this psychological circumstance and partly the
privilege of suspicion which we have in the face of the
elements of metropolitan life (which are constantly touching one another in fleeting contact) necessitates in us that
reserve, in consequence of which we do not know by sight
neighbors of years standing and which permits us to appear to small-town folk so often as cold and uncongenial.
Indeed, if I am not mistaken, the inner side of this external reserve is not only indifference but more frequently than
we believe, it is a slight aversion, a mutual strangeness and
repulsion which, in a close contact which has arisen any
way whatever, can break out into hatred and conflict. The
entire inner organization of such a type of extended commercial life rests on an extremely varied structure of sym-
pathies, indifferences and aversions of the briefest as well
as of the most enduring sort. This sphere of indifference
is, for this reason, not as great as it seems superficially.
Our minds respond, with some definite feeling, to almost
every impression emanating from another person. The un-
consciousness, the transitoriness and the shift of these feelings seem to raise them only into indifference. Actually this
latter would be as unnatural to us as immersion into a chaos
of unwished-for suggestions would be unbearable.

From these two typical dangers of metropolitan life we
are saved by antipathy which is the latent adumbration of
actual antagonism since it brings about the sort of dis-
tanciation and deflection without which this type of life
could not be carried on at all. Its extent and its mixture,
the rhythm of its emergence and disappearance, the forms
in which it is adequate – these constitute, with the simplified

motives (in the narrower sense) an inseparable totality of
the form of metropolitan life. What appears here directly
as dissociation is in reality only one of the elementary forms
of socialization.

This reserve with its overtone of concealed aversion appears once more, however, as the form or the wrappings of
a much more general psychic trait of the metropolis. It
assures the individual of a type and degree of personal freedom to which there is no analogy in other circumstances.
It has its roots in one of the great developmental tendencies
of social life as a whole; in one of the few for which an
approximately exhaustive formula can be discovered. The
most elementary stage of social organization which is to be
found historically, as well as in the present, is this: a relatively small circle almost entirely closed against neighboring
foreign or otherwise antagonistic groups but which has
however within itself such a narrow cohesion that the individual member has only a very slight area for the development of his own qualities and for free activity for which
he himself is responsible. Political and familial groups began
in this way as do political and religious communities; the
self-preservation of very young associations requires a
rigorous setting of boundaries and a centripetal unity and
for that reason it cannot give room to freedom and the
peculiarities of inner and external development of the individual. From this stage social evolution proceeds simultaneously in two divergent but nonetheless corresponding
directions. In the measure that the group grows numerically, spatially, and in the meaningful content of life, its
immediate inner unity and the definiteness of its original
demarcation against others are weakened and rendered mild
by reciprocal interactions and interconnections. And at the
same time the individual gains a freedom of movement far
beyond the first jealous delimitation, and gains also a
peculiarity and individuality to which the division of labor
in groups, which have become larger, gives both occasion
and necessity. However much the particular conditions and
forces of the individual situation might modify the general
scheme, the state and Christianity, guilds and political parties
and innumerable other groups have developed in accord
with this formula.

This tendency seems, to me, however to be quite clearly recognizable also in the development of individuality within the framework of city life. Small town life in antiquity as well as in the Middle Ages imposed such limits upon the movements of the individual in his relationships with the outside world and on his inner independence and differentiation that the modern person could not even breathe under such conditions. Even today the city dweller who is placed in a small town feels a type of narrowness which is very similar. The smaller the circle which forms our environment and the more limited the relationships which have the possibility of transcending the boundaries, the more anxiously the narrow community watches over the deeds, the conduct of life and the attitudes of the individual and the more will a quantitative and qualitative individuality tend to pass beyond the boundaries of such a community. The ancient *polis* seems in this regard to have had a character of a small town. The incessant threat against its existence by enemies from near and far brought about that stern cohesion in political and military matters, that supervision of the citizen by other citizens, and that jealousy of the whole toward the individual whose own private life was repressed to such an extent that he could compensate himself only by acting as a despot in his own household. The tremendous agitation and excitement, and the unique colorfulness of Athenian life is perhaps explained by the fact that a people of incomparably individualized personalities were in constant struggle against the incessant inner and external oppression of a de-individualizing small town. This created an atmosphere of tension in which the weaker were held down and the stronger were impelled to the most passionate type of self-protection. And with this there blossomed in Athens, what, without being able to define it exactly, must be designated as "the general human character" in the intellectual development of our species. For the correlation, the factual as well as the historical validity of which we are here maintaining, is that the broadest and the most general contents and forms of life are intimately bound up with the most individual ones. Both have a common prehistory and also common enemies in the narrow formations and groupings, whose striving for self-preservation set

them in conflict with the broad and general on the outside, as well as the freely mobile and individual on the inside. Just as in feudal times the "free" man was he who
stood under the law of the land, that is, under the law of
the largest social unit, but he was unfree who derived his
legal rights only from the narrow circle of a feudal community – so today in an intellectualized and refined sense
the citizen of the metropolis is "free" in contrast with the
trivialities and prejudices which bind the small town person. The mutual reserve and indifference, and the intellectual conditions of life in large social units are never more
sharply appreciated in their significance for the independence of the individual than in the dense crowds of the
metropolis because the bodily closeness and lack of space
make intellectual distance really perceivable for the first
time. It is obviously only the obverse of this freedom that,
under certain circumstances, one never feels as lonely and
as deserted as in this metropolitan crush of persons. For
here, as elsewhere, it is by no means necessary that the
freedom of man reflects itself in his emotional life only as
a pleasant experience.

It is not only the immediate size of the area and population which, on the basis of world-historical correlation between the increase in the size of the social unit and the
degree of personal inner and outer freedom, makes the
metropolis the locus of this condition. It is rather in transcending this purely tangible extensiveness that the metropolis
also becomes the seat of cosmopolitanism. Comparable with
the form of the development of wealth – (beyond a certain
point property increases in ever more rapid progression as
out of its own inner being) – the individual's horizon is
enlarged. In the same way, economic, personal and intellectual relations in the city (which are its ideal reflection),
grow in a geometrical progression as soon as, for the first
time, a certain limit has been passed. Every dynamic extension becomes a preparation not only for a similar extension
but rather for a larger one and from every thread which is
spun out of it there continue, growing as out of themselves,
an endless number of others. This may be illustrated by
the fact that within the city the "unearned increment" of
ground rent, through a mere increase in traffic, brings to

the owner profits which are self-generating. At this point the quantitative aspects of life are transformed qualitatively. The sphere of life of the small town is, in the main, enclosed within itself. For the metropolis it is decisive that its inner life is extended in a wave-like motion over a broader national or international area. Weimar was no exception because its significance was dependent upon individual personalities and died with them, whereas the metropolis is characterised by its essential independence even of the most significant individual personalities; this is rather its antithesis and it is the price of independence which the individual living in it enjoys.

The most significant aspect of the metropolis lies in this functional magnitude beyond its actual physical boundaries and this effectiveness reacts upon the latter and gives to it life, weight, importance and responsibility. A person does not end with limits of his physical body or with the area to which his physical activity is immediately confined but embraces, rather, the totality of meaningful effects which emanates from him temporally and spatially. In the same way the city exists only in the totality of the effects which transcend their immediate sphere. These really are the actual extent in which their existence is expressed. This is already expressed in the fact that individual freedom, which is the logical historical complement of such extension, is not only to be understood in the negative sense as mere freedom of movement and emancipation from prejudices and philistinism. Its essential characteristic is rather to be found in the fact that the particularity and incomparability which ultimately every person possesses in some way is actually expressed, giving form to life. That we follow the laws of our inner nature – and this is what freedom is – becomes perceptible and convincing to us and to others only when the expressions of this nature distinguish themselves from others; it is our irreplaceability by others which shows that our mode of existence is not imposed upon us from the outside.

Cities are above all the seat of the most advanced economic division of labor. They produce such extreme phenomena as the lucrative vocation of the *quatorzieme* in Paris. These are persons who may be recognized by shields on

their houses and who hold themselves ready at the dinner
hour in appropriate costumes so they can be called upon
on short notice in case thirteen persons find themselves at
the table. Exactly in the measure of its extension the city
offers to an increasing degree the determining conditions
for the division of labor. It is a unit which, because of its
large size, is receptive to a highly diversified plurality of
achievements while at the same time the agglomeration of
individuals and their struggle for the customer forces the
individual to a type of specialized accomplishment in which
he cannot be so easily exterminated by the other. The decisive fact here is that in the life of a city, struggle with
nature for the means of life is transformed into a conflict
with human beings and the gain which is fought for is
granted, not by nature, but by man. For here we find not
only the previously mentioned source of specialization but
rather the deeper one in which the seller must seek to
produce in the person to whom he wishes to sell ever new
and unique needs. The necessity to specialize one's product in order to find a source of income which is not yet
exhausted and also to specialize a function which cannot
be easily supplanted is conducive to differentiation, refinement and enrichment of the needs of the public which
obviously must lead to increasing personal variation within
this public.

All this leads to the narrower type of intellectual
individuation of mental qualities to which the city gives
rise in proportion to its size. There is a whole series of
causes for this. First of all there is the difficulty of giving
one's own personality a certain status within the framework
of metropolitan life. Where quantitative increase of value
and energy has reached its limits, one seizes on qualitative
distinctions, so that, through taking advantage of the existing
sensitivity to differences, the attention of the social world
can, in some way, be won for oneself. This leads ultimately
to the strangest eccentricities, to specifically metropolitan
extravagances of self-distanciation, of caprice, of fastidious-
ness, the meaning of which is no longer to found in the
content of such activity itself but rather in its being a form
of "being different" – of making oneself noticeable. For many
types of persons these are still the only means of saving for

oneself, through the attention gained from others, some sort of self-esteem and the sense of filling a position. In the same sense there operates an apparently insignificant factor which in its effects however is perceptibly cumulative, namely, the brevity and rarity of meetings which are allotted to each individual as compared with social intercourse in a small city. For here we find the attempt to appear to-the-point, clear-cut and individual with extraordinarily greater frequency than where frequent and long association assures to each person an unambiguous conception of the other's personality.

This appears to me to be the most profound cause of the fact that the metropolis places emphasis on striving for the most individual forms of personal existence – regardless of whether it is always correct or always successful. The development of modern culture is characterised by the predominance of what one can call the objective spirit over the objective; that is, in language as well as in law, in the technique of production as well as in art, in science as well as in the objects of domestic environment, there is embodied a sort of spirit (*Geist*), the daily growth of which is followed only imperfectly and with an even greater lag by the intellectual development of the individual. If we survey for instance the vast culture which during the last century has been embodied in things and in knowledge, in institutions and comforts, and if we compare them with the cultural progress of the individual during the same period – at least in the upper classes – we would see a frightful difference in rate of growth between the two which represents, in many points, rather a regression of the culture of the individual with reference to spirituality, delicacy and idealism.

This discrepancy is in essence the result of the success of the growing division of labor. For it is this which requires from the individual an ever more one-sided type of achievement which, at its highest point, often permits his personality as a whole to fall into neglect. In any case this overgrowth of objective culture has been less and less satisfactory for the individual. Perhaps less conscious than in practical activity and in the obscure complex of feelings which flow from him, he is reduced to a negligible quantity.

He becomes a single cog as over against the vast overwhelming organization of things and forces which gradually take out of their hands everything connected with progress, spirituality and value. The operation of these forces results in the transformation of the latter from a subjective form into one of purely objective existence.

It need only be pointed out that the metropolis is the proper arena for this type of culture which has outgrown every personal element. Here in buildings and in educational institutions, in the wonders and comforts of space-conquering technique, in the formations of social life and in the concrete institutions of the State is to be found such a tremendous richness of crystallizing, depersonalized cultural accomplishments that the personality can, so to speak, scarcely maintain itself in the face of it. From one angle life is made infinitely more easy in the sense that stimulations, interests, and the taking up of time and attention, present themselves from all sides and carry it in a stream which scarcely requires any individual efforts for its ongoing. But from another angle, life is composed more and more of these impersonal cultural elements and existing goods and values which seek to suppress peculiar personal interests and incomparabilities. As a result, in order that this most personal element be saved, extremities and peculiarities and individualizations must be produced and they must be over-exaggerated merely to be brought into the awareness even of the individual himself. The atrophy of individual culture through the hypertrophy of objective culture lies at the root of the bitter hatred which the preachers of the most extreme individualism, in the footsteps of Nietzsche, directed against the metropolis. But it is also the explanation of why indeed they are so passionately loved in the metropolis and indeed appear to its residents as the saviors of their unsatisfied yearnings.

When both of these forms of individualism which are nourished by the quantitative relationships of the metropolis, i.e., individual independence and the elaboration of personal peculiarities, are examined with reference to their historical position, the metropolis attains an entirely new value and meaning in the world history of the spirit. The eighteenth century found the individual in the grip of powerful bonds which had become meaningless – bonds of a political, agrarian, guild and religious nature – delimitations which imposed upon the human being at the same time an unnatural form and for a long time an unjust inequality. In this situation arose the cry for freedom and equality – the belief in the full freedom of movement of the individual in all his social and intellectual relationships which would then permit the same noble essence to emerge equally from all individuals as Nature had placed it in them and as it had been distorted by social life and historical development.

Alongside of this liberalistic ideal there grew up in the nineteenth century from Goethe and the Romantics, on the one hand, and from the economic division of labor on the other, the further tendency, namely, that individuals who had been liberated from their historical bonds sought now to distinguish themselves from one another. No longer was it the "general human quality" in every individual but rather his qualitative uniqueness and irreplaceability that now became the criteria of his value. In the conflict and shifting interpretations of these two ways of defining the position of the individual within the totality is to be found the external as well as the internal history of our time. It is the function of the metropolis to make a place for the conflict and for the attempts at unification of both of these in the sense that its own peculiar conditions have been revealed to us as the occasion and the stimulus for the development of both. Thereby they attain a quite unique place, fruitful with an inexhaustible richness of meaning in the development of the mental life. They reveal themselves as one of those great historical structures in which conflicting life-embracing currents find themselves with equal legitimacy. Because of this, however, regardless of whether we are sympathetic or antipathetic with their individual expressions, they transcend the sphere in which a judge-like attitude on our part is appropriate. To the extent that such forces have been integrated, with the fleeting existence of a single cell, into the root as well as the crown of the totality of historical life to which we belong – it is our task not to complain or to condome but only to understand.

4 Paris: Capital of the Nineteenth Century*
Walter Benjamin[1]

> The waters are blue and the vegetation pink;
> The evening sweet to behold;
> People are out walking. Great ladies promenade;
> and behind them walk the small ladies.
> (Nguyen-Trong-Hiep. *Paris, Capital of France* (1897)

FOURIER, OR THE ARCADES

> De ces palais les colonnes magiques
> A l'amateur montrent de toutes parts
> Dans les objets qu'étalent leurs portiques
> Que l'industrie est rivale aux arts.
> (*Nouveaux tableaux de Paris*, 1828)[2]

Most of the Paris arcades are built in the decade and a half after 1822. The first condition for this new fashion is the boom in the textile trade. The *magasins de nouveauté*, the first establishments to keep large stocks of goods on their premises, begin to appear, precursors of the department stores. It is the time of which Balzac wrote, "The great poem of display chants its many-colored strophes from the Madeleine to the Porte-Saint-Denis." The arcades are a center of trade in luxury goods. In their fittings art is brought in to the service of commerce. Contemporaries never tire of admiring them. They long remain a center of attraction for foreigners. An *Illustrated Guide to Paris* said: "These arcades, a recent invention of industrial luxury, are glass-rooted, marble-walled passages cut through whole blocks of houses, whose owners have combined in this speculation. On either

* Reprinted from Walter Benjamin, *Reflections: Essays, Aphorisms, Autobiographical Writing* (New York: Harcourt Brace and Company, 1978).

side of the passages, which draw their light from above, run the most elegant shops, so that an arcade of this kind is a city, indeed, a world in miniature." The arcades are the scene of the first gas lighting. The second condition for the construction of the arcades is the advent of building in iron. The Empire saw in this technique an aid to a renewal of architecture in the ancient Greek manner. The architectural theorist Bötticher expresses a general conviction when he says, "with regard to the artistic form of the new system, the formal principle of the Hellenic style" should be introduced. *Empire* is the style of revolutionary heroism for which the state is an end in itself. Just as Napoleon failed to recognize the functional nature of the state as an instrument of domination by the bourgeois class, neither did the master builders of his time perceive the functional nature of iron, through which the constructive principle began its domination of architecture. These builders model their pillars on Pompeian columns, their factories on houses, as later the first railway stations are to resemble chalets. "Construction fills the role of the unconscious." Nevertheless the idea of the engineer, originating in the revolutionary wars, begins to assert itself, and battle is joined between constructor and decorator, Ecole Polytechnique and Ecole des Beaux-Arts.

In iron, an artificial building material makes its appearance for the first time in the history of architecture. It undergoes a development that accelerate in the course of the century. The decisive breakthrough comes when it emerges that the locomotive, with which experiments had been made since the end of the twenties, could only be used on iron rails. The rail becomes the first prefabricated iron component, the forerunner of the girder. Iron is avoided in residential buildings and used in arcades, exhibition halls, stations – buildings serving transitory purposes. Simultaneously, the architectonic scope for the application of glass expands. The social conditions for its intensified use as a building material do not arrive, however, until a hundred years later. Even in Scheerbart's "glass architecture" (1914) it appears in utopian contexts.

Chaque époque rêvê la suivante. (Michelet, *Avenir! Avenir!*)[3]

Corresponding in the collective consciousness to the forms of the new means of production, which at first were still dominated by the old (Marx), are images in which the new is intermingled with the old. These images are wishful fantasies, and in them the collective seeks both to preserve and to transfigure the inchoateness of the social product and the deficiencies in the social system of production. In addition, these wish-fulfilling images manifest an emphatic striving for dissociation with the outmoded – which means, however, with the most recent past. These tendencies direct the visual imagination, which has been activated by the new, back to the primeval past. In the dream in which, before the eyes of each epoch, that which is to follow appears in images, the latter appear wedded to elements from prehistory, that is, of a classless society. Intimations of this, deposited in the unconscious of the collective, mingle with the new to produce the utopia that has left its traces in thousands of configurations of life, from permanent buildings to fleeting fashions.

This state of affairs is discernible in Fourier's utopia. Its chief impetus comes from the advent of machines. But this is not directly expressed in his accounts of it; these have their origin in the morality of trade and the false morality propagated in its service. His phalanstery is supposed to lead men back to conditions in which virtue is superfluous. Its highly complicated organization is like a piece of machinery. The meshing of passions, the intricate interaction of the *passions mécanistes* with the *passion cabaliste*, are primitive analogies to machinery in the material of psychology. This human machinery produces the land of milk and honey, the primeval wish symbol that Fourier's utopia filled with new life.

In the arcades, Fourier saw the architectonic canon of the phalanstery. His reactionary modification of them is characteristic: whereas they originally serve commercial purposes, he makes them into dwelling places. The phalanstery becomes a city of arcades. Fourier installs in the austere, formal world of the Empire the colorful idyll of Biedermeier. Its radiance lasts, though paled, till Zola. He takes up Fourier's ideas in *Travail*, as he takes leave of the arcades in *Thérèse Raquin*. Marx defends Fourier to Carl Grün, emphasizing his "colossal vision of man." He also draws attention to Fourier's humor. And in fact Jean Paul in *Levana* is as closely related to Fourier the pedagogue as Scheerbart in his "glass architecture" is to Fourier the utopian.

GRANDVILLE, OR THE WORLD EXHIBITIONS

Oui, quand le monde entier, de Paris jusqu'en Chine,
O divin Saint-Simon, sera dans la doctrine,
L'âge d'or doit renaître avec tout son éclat,
Les fleuves rouleront du thé, du chocolat;
Les moutons tous rôtis bondiront dans la plaine,
Et les brochets au bleu nageront dans la Seine;
Les épinards viendront au monde fricassés,
Avec des croûtons frits tout au tour concassés.
Les arbres produiront des pommes en compotes
Et l'on moissonnera des cerricks et des bottes;
Il neigera du vin, it pleuvera des poulets,
Et du ciel les canards tomberont aux navets.
(Lauglé and Vanderbusch, *Louis et le Saint-Simonien*,1832)[4]

World exhibitions are the sites of pilgrimages to the commodity fetish. "Europe is on the move to look at merchandise," said Taine in 1835. The world exhibitions are preceded by national industrial exhibitions, the first of which takes place in 1798 on the Champ-de-Mars. It proceeds from the wish "to entertain the working classes, and becomes for them a festival of emancipation." The workers stand as customers in the foreground. The framework of the entertainment industry has not yet been formed. The popular festival supplies it. Chaptal's speech on industry opens this exhibition. The Saint-Simonists, who plan the industrialization of the earth, take up the idea of world exhibitions. Chevalier, the first authority in the new field, is a pupil of Enfantin and editor of the Saint-Simonist journal, *Globe*. The Saint-Simonists predicted the development of the world economy, but not of the class struggle. Beside their participation in industrial and commercial enterprises about the middle of the century stands their helplessness in questions concerning the proletariat.

The world exhibitions glorify the exchange value of commodities. They create a framework in which commodities'
intrinsic value is eclipsed. They open up a phantasmagoria
that people enter to be amused. The entertainment industry facilitates this by elevating people to the level of commodities. They submit to being manipulated while enjoying
their alienation from themselves and others. The enthronement of merchandise, with the aura of amusement surrounding it, is the secret theme of Grandville's art. This is reflected
in the discord between its utopian and its cynical elements.
Its subtleties in the presentation of inanimate objects correspond to what Marx called the "theological whims" of
goods. This is clearly distilled in the term *spécialité* – a
commodity description coming into use about this time in
the luxury industry; under Grandville's pencil the whole
of nature is transformed into *spécialités*. He presents them
in the same spirit in which advertising – a word that is
also coined at this time – begins to present its articles. He
ends in madness.

> Fashion: My dear Mr. Death! (Leopardi, *Dialogue Between
> Fashion and Death*).

The world exhibitions build up the universe of commodities. Grandville's fantasies extend the character of a commodity to the universe. They modernize it. Saturn's ring
becomes a cast-iron balcony on which the inhabitants of
the planet take the air in the evening. The literary counterpart of this graphic utopia is presented by the book of the
Fourierist natural scientist Toussenal. Fashion prescribes
the ritual according to which the commodity fetish wishes
to be worshipped; Grandville extends fashion's claims both
to the objects of everyday use and to the cosmos. By pursuing it to its extremes he discloses its nature. This resides
in its conflict with the organic. It couples the living body
to the inorganic world. Against the living it asserts the rights
of the corpse. Fetishism, which is subject to the sex appeal of the inorganic, is its vital nerve. The cult of commodities places it in its service.

On the occasion of the 1867 World Exhibition, Victor
Hugo issues a manifesto: *To the Peoples of Europe*. Earlier,
and more unambiguously, their interests had been represented

by the French workers' delegations, the first of which had been sent to the London World Exhibition of 1851, and the second, consisting of seven hundred and fifty representatives, to that of 1862. The latter was of indirect importance for the foundation of the International Workingmen's Association by Marx. The phantasmagoria of capitalist culture reaches its most brilliant display in the World Exhibition of 1867. The Empire is at the height of its power. Paris reaffirms itself as the capital of luxury and fashion: Offenbach sets the rhythm of Parisian life. The operetta is the ironic utopia of the capital's lasting rule.

LOUIS-PHILIPPE, OR THE INTERIOR

> Une tête, sur la table de nuit, repose
> Comme un renoncule.
> (Baudelaire, "Un martyre")[5]

Under Louis-Philippe the private citizen enters the stage of history. The extension of the democratic apparatus through a new franchise coincides with the parliamentary corruption organized by Guihot. Under its protection the ruling class makes history by pursuing its business interests. It promotes railway construction to improve its share holdings. It favors Louis-Philippe as a private citizen at the head of affairs. By the time of the July Revolution, the bourgeoisie has realized the aims of 1789 (Marx).

For the private person, living space becomes, for the first time, antithetical to the place of work. The former is constituted by the interior; the office is its complement. The private person who squares his accounts with reality in his office demands that the interior be maintained in his illusions. This need is all the more pressing since he has no intention of extending his commercial considerations into social ones. In shaping his private environment he represses both. From this spring the phantasmagorias of the interior. For the private individual the private environment represents the universe. In it he gathers remote places and the past. His drawing room is a box in the world theater.

BAUDELAIRE, OR THE STREETS OF PARIS

Tout pour moi devient Allégorie.
(Baudelaire, "Le cygne")[6]

Baudelaire's genius, which is fed on melancholy, is an allegorical genius. In Baudelaire Paris becomes for the first time a subject of lyric poetry. This poetry is not regional art; rather, the gaze of the allegorist that falls on the city is estranged. It is the gaze of the *flâneur,* whose mode of life still surrounds the approaching desolation of city life with a propitiatory luster. The *flâneur* is still on the threshold, of the city as of the bourgeois class. Neither has yet engulfed him; in neither is he at home. He seeks refuge in the crowd. Early contributions to a physiognomics of the crowd are to be found in Engels and Poe. The crowd is the veil through which the familiar city lures the *flâneur* like a phantasmagoria. In it the city is now a landscape, now a room. Both, then, constitute the department store that puts even *flânerie* to use for commodity circulation. The department store is the *flâneur's* last practical joke.

In the *flâneur* the intelligentsia pays a visit to the marketplace, ostensibly to look around, yet in reality to find a buyer. In this intermediate phase, in which it still has patrons but is already beginning to familiarize itself with the market, it appears as bohemianism. The uncertainty of its political function corresponds to the uncertainty of its economic position. This is most strikingly expressed in the professional conspirators, who are certainly a part of Bohemia. Their first field of activity is the army; later it becomes the petit bourgeoisie, occasionally the proletariat. Yet this stratum sees its opponents in the real leaders of the latter. The *Communist Manifesto* puts an end to their political existence. Baudelaire's poetry draws its strength from the rebellious emotionalism of this group. He throws his lot in with the asocial. His only sexual communion is realized with a whore.

Facilis descensus Averni
(Virgil, *Aeneid*)

What is unique in Baudelaire's poetry is that the images of women and death are permeated by a third, that of Paris. The Paris of his poems is a submerged city, more submarine than subterranean. The chthonic elements of the city – its topographical formation, the old deserted bed of the Seine – doubtless left their impression on his work. Yet what is decisive in Baudelaire's "deathly idyll" of the city is a social, modern substratum. Modernity is a main accent in his poetry. He shatters the ideal as spleen (*Spleen et Idéal*). But it is precisely modernity that is always quoting primeval history. This happens here through the ambiguity attending the social relationships and products of this epoch. Ambiguity is the pictorial image of dialectics, the law of dialectics seen at a standstill. This standstill is utopia and the dialectic image therefore a dream image. Such an image is presented by the pure commodity: as fetish. Such an image are the arcades, which are both house and stars.

HAUSSMANN, OR THE BARRICADES

J'ai le culte du Beau, du Bien, des grandes choses,
De la belle nature inspirant le grand art,
Qu'il enchante l'oreille ou charme le regard;
J'ai l'amour du printemps en fleurs: femmes et roses.
(Baron Haussmann, *Confession d'un lion devenu vieux*)[7]

The blossomy realm of decoration,
Landscape and architecture's charm
And all effects of scenery repose
Upon perspective's law alone.
(Franz Böhle, *Theatrical Catechism*)

Haussmann's urban ideal was of long perspectives of streets and thoroughfares. This corresponds to the inclination, noticeable again and again in the nineteenth century, to ennoble technical necessities by artistic aims. The institutions of the secular and clerical dominance of the bourgeoisie were to find their apotheosis in a framework of streets. Streets, before their completion, were draped in canvas and unveiled like monuments. Haussmann's efficiency is integrated with Napoleonic idealism. The latter favors finance capi-

tal. Paris experiences a flowering of speculation. Playing
the stock exchange displaces the game of chance in the forms
that had come down from feudal society. To the
phantasmagorias of space to which the *flâneur* abandons himself, correspond the phantasmagorias of time indulged in by
the gambler. Gambling converts time into a narcotic. Lafargue
declares gaming an imitation in miniature of the mysteries of
economic prosperity. The expropriations by Haussmann call
into being a fraudulent speculation. The arbitration of the
Court of Cassation, inspired by the bourgeois and Orleanist
opposition, increases the financial risk of Haussmannization.
Haussmann attempts to strengthen his dictatorship and to place
Paris under an emergency regime. In 1864 he gives expression
in a parliamentary speech to his hatred of the rootless population of big cities. The latter is constantly increased by his
enterprises. The rise in rents drives the proletariat into the
suburbs. The *quartiers* of Paris thus lose their individual physi-
ognomies. The red belt is formed. Haussmann gave himself
the name of "artist in demolition." He felt himself called to
his work and stresses this in his memoirs. Meanwhile, he es-
tranges Parisians from their city. They begin to be conscious
of its inhuman character. Maxime du Camp's monumental
work *Paris* has its origin in this consciousness. The *Jérémiades
d'un Haussmannisé* give it the form of a biblical lament.

The true purpose of Haussmann's work was to secure
the city against civil war. He wanted to make the erection
of barricades in Paris impossible for all time. With such
intent Louis-Philippe had already introduced wooden paving.
Yet the barricades played a part in the February Revolution. Engels studies the technique of barricade fighting.
Haussmann seeks to prevent barricades in two ways. The
breadth of the streets is intended to make their erection impossible, and new thoroughfares are to open the shortest route
between the barracks and the working-class districts. Contemporaries christen the enterprise "strategic embellishment."

> *Fais voir, en déjouant la ruse,*
> *O République, à ces pervers*
> *Ta grande face de Méduse*
> *Au milieu de rouges éclairs.*
> (Workers' song, about 1850)[8]

The barricade is resurrected in the Commune. It is stronger and better secured than ever. It stretches across the great boulevards, often reaching the height of the first floor, and covers the trenches behind it. Just as the *Communist Manifesto* ends the epoch of the professional conspirator, the Commune puts an end to the phantasmagoria that dominates the freedom of the proletariat. It dispels the illusion that the task of the proletarian revolution is to complete the work of 1789 hand in hand with the bourgeoisie. This illusion prevailed from 1831 to 1871, from the Lyons uprising to the Commune. The bourgeoisie never shared this error. The struggle of the bourgeoisie against the social rights of the proletariat has already begun in the Great Revolution and coincides with the philanthropic movement that conceals it, attaining its fullest development under Napoleon III. Under him is written the monumental work of this political tendency: Le Play's *European Workers*. Besides the covert position of philanthropy, the bourgeoisie was always ready to take up the overt position of class struggle. As early as 1831 it recognizes, in the *Journal des Débats*, "Every industrialist lives in his factory like the plantation owners among their slaves." If, on the one hand, the lack of a guiding theory of revolution was the undoing of the old workers' uprisings, it was also, on the other, the condition for the immediate energy and enthusiasm with which they set about establishing a new society. This enthusiasm, which reached its climax in the Commune, for a time won over to the workers the best elements of the bourgeoisie, but in the end led them to succumb to their worst. Rimbaud and Courbet declare their support for the Commune. The Paris fire is the fitting conclusion to Haussmann's work of destruction.

My good father had been in Paris. (Karl Gutzkow, *Letters from Paris*, 1842)

Balzac was the first to speak of the ruins of the bourgeoisie. But only Surrealism exposed them to view. The development of the forces of production reduced the wish symbols of the previous century to rubble even before the monuments representing them had crumbled. In the nineteenth century this development emancipated constructive forms from art, as the sciences freed themselves from philosophy in the sixteenth. Architecture makes a start as constructional engineering. The reproduction of nature in photography follows. Fantasy creation prepares itself to become practical as commercial art. Literature is subjected to montage in the *feuilleton*. All these products are on the point of going to market as wares. But they hesitate on the brink. From this epoch stem the arcades and interiors, the exhibitions and panoramas. They are residues of a dream world. The realization of dream elements in waking is the textbook example of dialectical thinking. For this reason dialectical thinking is the organ of historical awakening. Each epoch not only dreams the next, but also, in dreaming, strives toward the moment of waking. It bears its end in itself and unfolds it – as Hegel already saw – with ruse. In the convulsions of the commodity economy we begin to recognize the monuments of the bourgeoisie as ruins even before they have crumbled.

Notes

1. Translations of material in this chapter by Susan Dunn, prepared for this volume.
2. The magic columns of those palaces
   Show the lover of the art,
   Through the objects that their porticos reveal,
   That industry is the rival of the arts.
3. Each epoch already dreams of the following one (Michelet, *The Future! The Future!*)
4. Yes, when the whole world, form Paris to China,
   O divine Saint-Simon, will follow the doctrine,
   The golden age will be reborn in all its splendor,
   The rivers will flow with tea, with chocolate;
   Sheep nicely roasted will leap in the fields,
   Grilled pike will swim in the Seine;
   Spinach will enter the world already fricaseed,
   Garnished with fried croutons evenly crushed.
   Trees will yield stewed apples,
   And the harvest will include cerricks and bushels;
   It will snow wine, it will rain chickens,
   And out from the sky ducks will fall into turnips.
5. A head, on the night table, rests
   Like a buttercup.
   (Baudelaire, "A Martyr").

6. Everything, for me, becomes Allegory (Baudelaire "Le cygne").
7. I worship, Beauty, Goodness, wondrous things,
   Beautiful nature that inspires great art;
   Whether art enchants the ear or charms the eye;
   I love spring in bloom: women and roses.
   (Baron Hausman, *Confessions of a now old lion*)
8. Oh Republic, thwart their schemes
   And show these depraved minds
   Your great Medusa face
   Against red bolts of lightning.

5 Urbanism as a Way of Life*
Louis Wirth

THE CITY AND CONTEMPORARY CIVILIZATION

Just as the beginning of Western civilization is marked by the permanent settlement of formerly nomadic peoples in the Mediterranean basin, so the beginning of what is distinctively modern in our civilization is best signalized by the growth of great cities. Nowhere has mankind been farther removed from organic nature than under the conditions of life characteristic of great cities. The contemporary world no longer presents a picture of small isolated groups of human beings scattered over a vast territory, as Sumner described primitive society.[1] The distinctive feature of the mode of living of man in the modern age is his concentration into gigantic aggregations around which cluster lesser centers and from which radiate the ideas and practices that we call civilization.

The degree to which the contemporary world may be said to be "urban" is not fully or accurately measured by the proportion of the total population living in cities. The influences which cities exert upon the social life of man are greater than the ratio of the urban population would indicate, for the city is not only in ever larger degrees the dwelling-place and the workshop of modern man, but it is the initiating and controlling center of economic, political, and cultural life that has drawn the most remote parts of the world into its orbit and woven diverse areas, peoples, and activities into a cosmos.

The growth of cities and the urbanization of the world is one of the most impressive facts of modern times. Although it is impossible to state precisely what proportion of the estimated total world population of approximately

* Reprinted from the *American Journal of Sociology*, vol. 44, no. 1 (1938).

1 800 000 000 is urban, 69.2 per cent of the total population of those countries that do distinguish between urban
and rural areas is urban.[2] Considering the fact, moreover,
that the world's population is very unevenly distributed and
that the growth of cities is not very far advanced in some
of the countries that have only recently been touched by
industrialism, this average understates the extent to which
urban concentration has proceeded in those countries where
the impact of the industrial revolution has been more forceful
and of less recent date. This shift from a rural to a predominantly urban society, which has taken place within the
span of a single generation in such industrialized areas as
the United States and Japan, has been accompanied by
profound changes in virtually every phase of social life. It
is these changes and their ramifications that invite the attention of the sociologist to the study of the differences
between the rural and the urban mode of living. The pursuit of this interest is an indispensable prerequisite for the
comprehension and possible mastery of some of the most
crucial contemporary problems of social life since it is likely
to furnish one of the most revealing perspectives for the
understanding of the ongoing changes in human nature and
the social order.[3]

Since the city is the product of growth rather than of
instantaneous creation, it is to be expected that the influences
which it exerts upon the modes of life should not be able
to wipe out completely the previously dominant modes of
human association. To a greater or lesser degree, therefore, our social life bears the imprint of an earlier folk
society, the characteristic modes of settlement of which were
the farm, the manor, and the village. This historic influence
is reinforced by the circumstance that the population of
the city itself is in large measure recruited from the countryside, where a mode of life reminiscent of this earlier form
of existence persists. Hence we should not expect to find
abrupt and discontinuous variation between urban and rural types of personality. The city and the country may be
regarded as two poles in reference to one or the other of
which all human settlements tend to arrange themselves.
In viewing urban–industrial and rural–folk society as ideal
types of communities, we may obtain a perspective for the

analysis of the basic models of human association as they appear in contemporary civilization.

A SOCIOLOGICAL DEFINITION OF THE CITY

Despite the preponderant significance of the city in our civilization, however, our knowledge of the nature of urbanism and the process of urbanization is meager. Many attempts have indeed been made to isolate the distinguishing characteristics of urban life. Geographers, historians, economists, and political scientists have incorporated the points of view of their respective disciplines into diverse definitions of the city. While in no sense intended to supersede these, the formulation of a sociological approach to the city may incidentally serve to call attention to the interrelations between them by emphasizing the peculiar characteristics of the city as a particular form of human association. A sociologically significant definition of the city seeks to select those elements of urbanism which mark it as a distinctive mode of human group life.

The characterization of a community as urban on the basis of size alone is obviously arbitrary. It is difficult to defend the present census definition which designates a community of 2500 and above as urban and all others as rural. The situation would be the same if the criterion were 4000, 8000, 10 000, 25 000, or 100 000 population, for although in the latter case we might feel that we were more nearly dealing with an urban aggregate than would be the case in communities of lesser size, no definition of urbanism can hope to be completely satisfying as long as numbers are regarded as the sole criterion. Moreover, it is not difficult to demonstrate that communities of less than the arbitrarily set number of inhabitants lying within the range of influence of metropolitan centers have greater claim to recognition as urban communities than do larger ones leading a more isolated existence in a predominantly rural area. Finally, it should be recognized that census definitions are unduly influenced by the fact that the city, statistically speaking, is always an administrative concept in that the corporate limits play a decisive role in delineating the urban area. Nowhere is this more clearly apparent than in the concentrations of population on the peripheries of great metropolitan centers which cross arbitrary administrative boundaries of city, county, state, and nation.

As long as we identify urbanism with the physical entity of the city, viewing it merely as rigidly delimited in space, and proceed as if urban attributes abruptly ceased to be manifested beyond an arbitrary boundary line, we are not likely to arrive at any adequate conception of urbanism as a mode of life. The technological developments in transportation and communication which virtually mark a new epoch in human history have accentuated the role of cities as dominant elements in our civilization and have enormously extended the urban mode of living beyond the confines of the city itself. The dominance of the city, especially of the great city, may be regarded as a consequence of the concentration in cities of industrial and commercial, financial and administrative facilities and activities, transportation and communication lines, and cultural and recreational equipment such as the press, radio stations, theaters, libraries, museums, concert halls, operas, hospitals, higher educational institutions, research and publishing centers, professional organizations, and religious and welfare institutions. Were it not for the attraction and suggestions that the city exerts through these instrumentalities upon the rural population, the differences between the rural and the urban modes of life would be even greater than they are. Urbanization no longer denotes merely the process by which persons are attracted to a place called the city and incorporated into its system of life. It refers also to that cumulative accentuation of the characteristics distinctive of the mode of life which is associated with the growth of cities, and finally to the changes in the direction of modes of life recognized as urban, which are apparent among people, wherever they may be, who have come under the spell of the influences which the city exerts by virtue of the power of its institutions and personalities operating through the means of communication and transportation.

The shortcomings which attach to number of inhabitants as a criterion of urbanism apply for the most part to density of population as well. Whether we accept the density of 10 000 persons per square mile as Mark Jefferson[4] proposed, or 1000, which Willcox[5] preferred to regard as the criterion of urban settlements, it is clear that unless density is correlated with significant social characteristics it can furnish only an arbitrary basis for differentiating urban from rural communities. Since our census enumerates the night rather than the day population of an area, the locale of the most intensive urban life – the city center – generally has low population density, and the industrial and commercial areas of the city, which contain the most characteristic economic activities underlying urban society, would scarcely anywhere be truly urban if density were literally interpreted as a mark of urbanism. Nevertheless, the fact that the urban community is distinguished by a large aggregation and relatively dense concentration of population can scarcely be left out of account in a definition of the city. But these criteria must be seen as relative to the general cultural context in which cities arise and exist and are sociologically relevant only insofar as they operate as conditioning factors in social life.

The same criticisms apply to such criteria as the occupation of the inhabitants, the existence of certain physical facilities, institutions, and forms of political organization. The question is not whether cities in our civilization or in others do exhibit these distinctive traits, but how potent they are in molding the character of social life into its specifically urban form. Nor in formulating a fertile definition can we afford to overlook the great variations between cities. By means of a typology of cities based upon size, location, age, and function, such as we have undertaken to establish in our recent report to the National Resources Committee,[6] we have found it feasible to array and classify urban communities ranging from struggling small towns to thriving world-metropolitan centers; from isolated trading centers in the midst of agricultural regions to thriving world-ports and commercial and industrial conurbations. Such differences as these appear crucial because the social characteristics and influences of these different "cities" vary widely.

A serviceable definition of urbanism should not only denote the essential characteristics which all cities – at least those in our culture – have in common, but should lend itself to the discovery of their variations. An industrial city will differ significantly in social respects from a commercial, mining, fishing, resort, university, and capital city. A one-industry city will present different sets of social characteristics from a multi-industry city, as will an industrially balanced from an imbalanced city, a suburb from a satellite, a residential suburb from an industrial suburb, a city within a metropolitan region from one lying outside, an old city from a new one, a southern city from a New England city, a middle-western from a Pacific-Coast city, a growing from a stable and from a dying city.

A sociological definition must obviously be inclusive enough to comprise whatever essential characteristics these different types of cities have in common as social entities, but it obviously cannot be so detailed as to take account of all the variations implicit in the manifold classes sketched above. Presumably some of the characteristics of cities are more significant in conditioning the nature of urban life than others, and we may expect the outstanding features of the urban social scene to vary in accordance with size, density, and differences in the functional type of cities. Moreover, we may infer that rural life will bear the imprint of urbanism in the measure that through contact and communication it comes under the influence of cities. It may contribute to the clarity of the statements that follow to repeat that while the locus of urbanism as a mode of life is, of course, to be found characteristically in places which fulfil the requirements we shall set up as a definition of the city, urbanism is not confined to such localities but is manifest in varying degrees wherever the influences of the city reach.

While urbanism, or that complex of traits which makes up the characteristic mode of life in cities, and urbanization, which denotes the development and extensions of these factors, are thus not exclusively found in settlements which are cities in the physical and demographic sense, they do, nevertheless, find their most pronounced expression in such areas, especially in metropolitan cities. In formulating a definition of the city it is necessary to exercise caution in order to avoid identifying urbanism as a way of life with any specific locally or historically conditioned cultural influences which, while they may significantly affect the specific character of the community, are not the essential determinants of its character as a city.

It is particularly important to call attention to the danger of confusing urbanism with industrialism and modern capitalism. The rise of cities in the modern world is undoubtedly not independent of the emergence of modern power-driven machine technology, mass production, and capitalistic enterprise. But different as the cities of earlier epochs may have been by virtue of their development in a preindustrial and precapitalistic order from the great cities of today, they were, nevertheless, cities.

For sociological purposes a city may be defined as a relatively large, dense, and permanent settlement of socially heterogeneous individuals. On the basis of the postulates which this minimal definition suggests, a theory of urbanism may be formulated in the light of existing knowledge concerning social groups.

A THEORY OF URBANISM

In the rich literature on the city we look in vain for a theory of urbanism presenting in a systematic fashion the available knowledge concerning the city as a social entity. We do indeed have excellent formulations of theories on such special problems as the growth of the city viewed as a historical trend and as a recurrent process,[7] and we have a wealth of literature presenting insights of sociological relevance and empirical studies offering detailed information on a variety of particular aspects of urban life. But despite the multiplication of research and textbooks on the city, we do not as yet have a comprehensive body of compendent hypotheses which may be derived from a set of postulates implicitly contained in a sociological definition of the city, and from our general sociological knowledge which may be substantiated through empirical research. The closest approximations to a systematic theory of urbanism that we have are to be found in a penetrating essay, "Die Stadt," by Max Weber,[8] and a memorable paper by Robert E. Park on "The City: Suggestions for the Investigation of Human Behavior in the Urban Environment."[9] But even these excellent contributions are far from constituting an ordered and coherent framework of theory upon which research might profitably proceed.

In the pages that follow we shall seek to set forth a limited number of identifying characteristics of the city. Given these characteristics we shall then indicate what consequences or further characteristics follow from them in the light of general sociological theory and empirical research. We hope in this manner to arrive at the essential propositions comprising a theory of urbanism. Some of these propositions can be supported by a considerable body of already available research materials; others may be accepted as hypotheses for which a certain amount of presumptive evidence exists, but for which more ample and exact verification would be required. At least such a procedure will, it is hoped, show what in the way of systematic knowledge of the city we now have and what are the crucial and fruitful hypotheses for future research.

The central problem of the sociologist of the city is to discover the forms of social action and organization that typically emerge in relatively permanent, compact settlements of large numbers of heterogeneous individuals. We must also infer that urbanism will assume its most characteristic and extreme form in the measure in which the conditions with which it is congruent are present. Thus the larger, the more densely populated, and the more heterogeneous a community, the more accentuated the characteristics associated with urbanism will be. It should be recognized, however, that in the social world institutions and practices may be accepted and continued for reasons other than those that originally brought them into existence, and that accordingly the urban mode of life may be perpetuated under conditions quite foreign to those necessary for its origin.

Some justification may be in order for the choice of the principal terms comprising our definition of the city. The attempt has been made to make it as inclusive and at the same time as denotative as possible without loading it with unnecessary assumptions. To say that large numbers are necessary to constitute a city means, of course, large numbers in relation to a restricted area or high density of settlement. There are, nevertheless, good reasons for treating large numbers and density as separate factors, since each may be connected with significantly different social consequences. Similarly the need for adding heterogeneity to numbers of population as a necessary and distinct criterion of urbanism might be questioned, since we should expect the range of differences to increase with numbers. In defense, it may be said that the city shows a kind and degree of heterogeneity of population which cannot be wholly accounted for by the law of large numbers or adequately represented by means of a normal distribution curve. Since the population of the city does not reproduce itself, it must recruit its migrants from other cities, the countryside, and – in this country until recently – from other countries. The city has thus historically been the melting-pot of races, peoples, and cultures, and a most favorable breeding ground of new biological and cultural hybrids. It has not only tolerated but rewarded individual differences. It has brought together people from the ends of the earth *because* they are different and thus useful to one another, rather than because they are homogeneous and like-minded.[10]

There are a number of sociological propositions concerning the relationship between (1) numbers of population, (2) density of settlement and (3) heterogeneity of inhabitants and group life, which can be formulated on the basis of observation and research.

Size of the Population Aggregate

Ever since Aristotle's *Politics*,[11] it has been recognized that increasing the number of inhabitants in a settlement beyond a certain limit will affect the relationships between them and the character of the city. Large numbers involve, as has been pointed out, a greater range of individual variation. Furthermore, the greater the number of individuals participating in a process of interaction, the greater is the *potential* differentiation between them. The personal traits, the occupations, the cultural life, and the ideas of the members of an urban community may, therefore, be expected to range between more widely separated poles than those of rural inhabitants.

That such variations should give rise to the spatial segregation of individuals according to color, ethnic heritage, economic and social status, tastes and preferences, may readily be inferred. The bonds of kinship, of neighborliness, and the sentiments arising out of living together for generations under a common folk tradition are likely to be absent or, at best, relatively weak in an aggregate the members of which have such diverse origins and backgrounds. Under such circumstances competition and formal control mechanisms furnish the substitutes for the bonds of solidarity that are relied upon to hold a folk society together.

Increase in the number of inhabitants of a community beyond a few hundred is bound to limit the possibility of each member of the community knowing all the others personally. Max Weber, in recognizing the social significance of this fact, pointed out that from a sociological point of view large numbers of inhabitants and density of settlement mean that the personal mutual acquaintanceship between the inhabitants which ordinarily inheres in a neighborhood is lacking.[12] The increase in numbers thus involves a changed character of the social relationships. As Simmel points out:

> [If] the unceasing external contact of numbers of persons in the city should be met by the same number of inner reactions as in the small town, in which one knows almost every person he meets and to each of whom he has a positive relationship, one would be completely atomized internally and would fall into an unthinkable mental condition.[13]

The multiplication of persons in a state of interaction under conditions which make their contact as full personalities impossible produces that segmentalization of human relationships which has sometimes been seized upon by students of the mental life of the cities as an explanation for the "schizoid" character of urban personality. This is not to say that the urban inhabitants have fewer acquaintances than rural inhabitants, for the reverse may actually be true; it means rather that in relation to the number of people whom they see and with whom they rub elbows in the course of daily life, they know a smaller proportion, and of these they have less intensive knowledge.

Characteristically, urbanites meet one another in highly segmental roles. They are, to be sure, dependent upon more people for the satisfaction of their life-needs than are rural people and thus are associated with a greater number of organized groups, but they are less dependent upon particular persons, and their dependence upon others is confined to a highly fractionalized aspect of the other's round of activity. This is essentially what is meant by saying that the city is characterized by secondary rather than primary contacts. The contacts of the city may indeed be face to face, but they are nevertheless impersonal, superficial, transitory, and segmental. The reserve, the indifference, and the blasé outlook which urbanites manifest in their relationships may thus be regarded as devices for immunizing themselves against the personal claims and expectations of others.

The superficiality, the anonymity, and the transitory character of urban–social relations make intelligible, also, the sophistication and the rationality generally ascribed to city dwellers. Our acquaintances tend to stand in a relationship of utility to us in the sense that the role which each one plays in our life is overwhelmingly regarded as a means for the achievement of our own ends. Whereas, therefore, the individual gains, on the one hand, a certain degree of emancipation or freedom from the personal and emotional controls of intimate groups, he loses, on the other hand, the spontaneous self-expression, the morale, and the sense of participation that comes with living in an integrated society. This constitutes essentially the state of *anomie* or the social void to which Durkheim alludes in attempting to account for the various forms of social disorganization in technological society.

The segmental character and utilitarian accent of interpersonal relations in the city find their institutional expression in the proliferation of specialized tasks which we see in their most developed form in the professions. The operations of the pecuniary nexus leads to predatory relationships, which tend to obstruct the efficient functioning of the social order unless checked by professional codes and occupational etiquette. The premium put upon utility and efficiency suggests the adaptability of the corporate device for the organization of enterprises in which individuals can engage only in groups. The advantage that the corporation has over the individual entrepreneur and the partnership in the urban–industrial world derives not only from the possibility it affords of centralizing the resources of thousands of individuals or from the legal privilege of limited liability and perpetual succession, but from the fact that the corporation has no soul.

The specialization of individuals, particularly in their occupations, can proceed only, as Adam Smith pointed out, upon the basis of an enlarged market, which in turn accentuates the division of labor. This enlarged market is only in part supplied by the city's hinterland; in large measure it is found among the large numbers that the city itself contains. The dominance of the city over the surrounding hinterland becomes explicable in terms of the division of labor which urban life occasions and promotes. The extreme degree of interdependence and the unstable equilibrium of urban life are closely associated with the division of labor and the specialization of occupations. This interdependence and instability is increased by the tendency of each city to specialize in those functions in which it has the greatest advantage.

In a community composed of a larger number of individuals than can know one another intimately and can be assembled in one spot, it becomes necessary to communicate through indirect mediums and to articulate individual interests by a process of delegation. Typically in the city, interests are made effective through representation. The individual counts for little, but the voice of the representative is heard with a deference roughly proportional to the numbers for whom he speaks.

While this characterization of urbanism, insofar as it derives from large numbers, does not by any means exhaust the sociological inferences that might be drawn from our knowledge of the relationship of the size of a group to the characteristic behavior of the members, for the sake of brevity the assertions made may serve to exemplify the sort of propositions that might be developed.

Density

As in the case of numbers, so in the case of concentration in limited space, certain consequences of relevance in sociological analysis of the city emerge. Of these only a few can be indicated.

As Darwin pointed out for flora and fauna and as Durkheim[14] noted in the case of human societies, an increase in numbers when area is held constant (that is, an increase in density) tends to produce differentiation and specialization, since only in this way can the area support increased numbers. Density thus reinforces the effect of numbers in diversifying men and their activities and in increasing the complexity of the social structure.

On the subjective side, as Simmel has suggested, the close physical contact of numerous individuals necessarily produces a shift in the mediums through which we orient ourselves to the urban milieu, especially to our fellow-men. Typically, our physical contacts are close but our social contacts are distant. The urban world puts a premium on visual recognition. We see the uniform which denotes the role of the functionaries and are oblivious to the personal eccentricities that are hidden behind the uniform. We tend to acquire and develop a sensitivity to a world of artefacts and become progressively farther removed from the world of nature.

We are exposed to glaring contrasts between splendor and squalor, between riches and poverty, intelligence and ignorance, order and chaos. The competition for space is great, so that each area generally tends to be put to the use which yields the greatest economic return. Place of work tends to become dissociated from place of residence, for the proximity of industrial and commercial establishments makes an area both economically and socially undesirable for residential purposes.

Density, land values, rentals, accessibility, healthfulness, prestige, aesthetic consideration, absence of nuisances such as noise, smoke, and dirt determine the desirability of various areas of the city as places of settlement for different sections of the population. Place and nature of work, income, racial and ethnic characteristics, social status, custom, habit, taste, preference, and prejudice are among the significant factors in accordance with which the urban population is selected and distributed into more or less distinct settlements. Diverse population elements inhabiting a compact settlement thus tend to become segregated from one another in the degree in which their requirements and modes of life are incompatible with one another and in the measure in which they are antagonistic to one another. Similarly, persons of homogeneous status and needs unwittingly drift into, consciously select, or are forced by circumstances into, the same area. The different parts of the city thus acquire specialized functions. The city consequently tends to resemble a mosaic of social worlds in which the transition from one to the other is abrupt. The juxtaposition of divergent personalities and modes of life tends to produce a relativistic perspective and a sense of toleration of differences which may be regarded as prerequisites for rationality and which lead toward the secularization of life.[15]

The close living together and working together of individuals who have no sentimental and emotional ties foster a spirit of competition, aggrandizement, and mutual exploitation. To counteract irresponsibility and potential disorder, formal controls tend to be resorted to. Without rigid adherence to predictable routines a large compact society would scarcely be able to maintain itself. The clock and the traffic signal are symbolic of the basis of our social order in the urban world. Frequent close physical contact, coupled with great social distance, accentuates the reserve of unattached individuals toward one another and, unless compensated for by other opportunities for response, gives rise to loneliness. The necessary frequent movement of great numbers of individuals in a congested habitat gives occasion to friction and irritation. Nervous tensions which derive from such personal frustrations are accentuated by the rapid tempo and the complicated technology under which life in dense areas must be lived.

Heterogeneity

The social interaction among such a variety of personality types in the urban milieu tends to break down the rigidity of caste lines and to complicate the class structure, and thus induces a more ramified and differentiated framework of social stratification than is found in more integrated societies. The heightened mobility of the individual, which

brings him within the range of stimulation by a great number
of diverse individuals and subjects him to fluctuating status
in the differentiated social groups that compose the social
structure of the city, tends toward the acceptance of instability and insecurity in the world at large as a norm. This
fact helps to account too, for the sophistication and cosmopolitanism of the urbanite. No single group has the undiv-
ided allegiance of the individual. The groups with which
he is affiliated do not lend themselves readily to a simple
hierarchical arrangement. By virtue of his different interests
arising out of different aspects of social life, the individual
acquires membership in widely divergent groups, each of
which functions only with reference to a single segment of
his personality. Nor do these groups easily permit of a
concentric arrangement so that the narrower ones fall within
the circumference of the more inclusive ones, as is more
likely to be the case in the rural community or in primitive societies. Rather the groups with which the person
typically is affiliated are tangential to each other or intersect in highly variable fashion.

Partly as a result of the physical footlooseness of the
population and partly as a result of their social mobility,
the turnover in group membership generally is rapid. Place
of residence, place and character of employment, income
and interests fluctuate, and the task of holding organizations together and maintaining and promoting intimate and
lasting acquaintanceship between the members is difficult.
This applies strikingly to the local areas within the city
into which persons become segregated more by virtue of
differences in race, language, income, and social status, than
through choice or positive attraction to people like themselves. Overwhelmingly the city dweller is not a home-owner,
and since a transitory habitat does not generate binding
traditions and sentiments, only rarely is he truly a neighbor.
There is little opportunity for the individual to obtain a
conception of the city as a whole or to survey his place in
the total scheme. Consequently he finds it difficult to determine what is to his own "best interests" and to decide
between the issues and leaders presented to him by the
agencies of mass suggestion. Individuals who are thus detached from the organized bodies which integrate society

comprise the fluid masses that make collective behavior in the urban community so unpredictable and hence so problematical.

Although the city, through the recruitment of variant types to perform its diverse tasks and the accentuation of their uniqueness through competition and the premium upon eccentricity, novelty, efficient performance, and inventiveness, produces a highly differentiated population, it also exercises a leveling influence. Wherever large numbers of differently constituted individuals congregate, the process of depersonalization also enters. This leveling tendency inheres in part in the economic basis of the city. The development of large cities, at least in the modern age, was largely dependent upon the concentrative force of steam. The rise of the factory made possible mass production for an impersonal market. The fullest exploitation of the possibilities of the division of labor and mass production, however, is possible only with standardization of processes and products. A money economy goes hand in hand with such a system of production. Progressively as cities have developed upon a background of this system of production, the pecuniary nexus which implies the purchasability of services and things has displaced personal relations as the basis of association. Individuality under these circumstances must be replaced by categories. When large numbers have to make common use of facilities and institutions, an arrangement must be made to adjust the facilities and institutions to the needs of the average person rather than to those of particular individuals. The services of the public utilities, of the recreational, educational, and cultural institutions must be adjusted to mass requirements. Similarly, the cultural institutions, such as the schools, the movies, the radio, and the newspapers, by virtue of their mass clientele, must necessarily operate as leveling influences. The political process as it appears in urban life could not be understood without taking account of the mass appeals made through modern propaganda techniques. If the individual would participate at all in the social, political, and economic life of the city, he must subordinate some of his individuality to the demands of the larger community and in that measure immerse himself in mass movements.

THE RELATION BETWEEN A THEORY OF URBANISM AND SOCIOLOGICAL RESEARCH

By means of a body of theory such as that illustratively sketched above, the complicated and many-sided phenomena of urbanism may be analyzed in terms of a limited number of basic categories. The sociological approach to the city thus acquires an essential unity and coherence enabling the empirical investigator not merely to focus more distinctly upon the problems and processes that properly fall in his province but also to treat his subject matter in a more integrated and systematic fashion. A few typical findings of empirical research in the field of urbanism, with special reference to the United States, may be indicated to substantiate the theoretical propositions set forth in the preceding pages, and some of the crucial problems for further study may be outlined.

On the basis of the three variables – number, density of settlement, and degree of heterogeneity – of the urban population, it appears possible to explain the characteristics of urban life and to account for the differences between cities of various sizes and types.

Urbanism as a characteristic mode of life may be approached empirically from three interrelated perspectives: (1) as a physical structure comprising a population base, a technology, and an ecological order; (2) as a system of social organization involving a characteristic social structure, a series of social institutions, and a typical pattern of social relationships; and (3) as a set of attitudes and ideas, and a constellation of personalities engaging in typical forms of collective behavior and subject to characteristic mechanisms of social control.

Urbanism in Ecological Perspective

Since in the case of physical structure and ecological processes we are able to operate with fairly objective indices, it becomes possible to arrive at quite precise and generally quantitative results. The dominance of the city over its hinterland becomes explicable through the functional characteristics of the city which derive in large measure from the effect of numbers and density. Many of the technical facilities and the skills and organizations to which urban life gives rise can grow and prosper only in cities where the demand is sufficiently great. The nature and scope of the services rendered by these organizations and institutions and the advantage which they enjoy over the less developed facilities and smaller towns enhances the dominance of the city of the dependence of ever wider regions upon the central metropolis.

The urban-population composition shows the operation of selective and differentiating factors. Cities contain a large proportion of persons in the prime of life than rural areas which contain more old and very young people. In this, as in so many other respects, the larger the city the more this specific characteristic of urbanism is apparent. With the exception of the largest cities, which have attracted the bulk of the foreign-born males, and a few other special types of cities, women predominate numerically over men. The heterogeneity of the urban population is further indicated along racial and ethnic lines. The foreign born and their children constitute nearly two-thirds of all the inhabitants of cities of one million and over. Their proportion in the urban population declines as the size of the city decreases, until in the rural areas they comprise only about one-sixth of the total population. The larger cities similarly have attracted more Negroes and other racial groups than have the smaller communities. Considering that age, sex, race, and ethnic origin are associated with other factors such as occupation and interest, it becomes clear that one major characteristic of the urban dweller is his dissimilarity from his fellows. Never before have such large masses of people of diverse traits as we find in our cities been thrown together into such close physical contact as in the great cities of America. Cities generally, and American cities in particular, comprise a motley of peoples and cultures, of highly differentiated modes of life between which there often is only the faintest communication, the greatest indifference and the broadest tolerance, occasionally bitter strife, but always the sharpest contrast.

The failure of the urban population to reproduce itself appears to be a biological consequence of a combination of factors in the complex of urban life, and the decline in the birth-rate generally may be regarded as one of the most significant signs of the urbanization of the Western world. While the proportion of deaths in cities is slightly greater than in the country, the outstanding difference between the failure of present-day cities to maintain their population and that of cities of the past is that in former times it was due to the exceedingly high death-rates in cities, whereas today, since cities have become more livable from a health standpoint, it is due to low birth-rates. These biological characteristics of the urban population are significant sociologically, not merely because they reflect the urban mode of existence but also because they condition the growth and future dominance of cities and their basic social organization. Since cities are the consumers rather than the producers of men, the value of human life and the social estimation of the personality will not be unaffected by the balance between births and deaths. The pattern of land use, of land values, rentals, and ownership, the nature and functioning of the physical structures, of housing, of transportation and communication facilities, of public utilities – these and many other phases of the physical mechanism of the city are not isolated phenomena unrelated to the city as a social entity, but are affected by and affect the urban mode of life.

Urbanism as a Form of Social Organization

The distinctive features of the urban mode of life have often been described sociologically as consisting of the substitution of secondary for primary contacts, the weakening of bonds of kinship, and the declining social significance of the family, the disappearance of the neighborhood, and the undermining of the traditional basis of social solidarity. All these phenomena can be substantially verified through objective indices. Thus, for instance, the low and declining urban reproduction rates suggest that the city is not conducive to the traditional type of family life, including the rearing of children and the maintenance of the home as the locus of a whole round of vital activities. The transfer of industrial, educational, and recreational activities to specialized institutions outside the home has deprived the family of some of its most characteristic historical functions. In cities mothers are more likely to be employed, lodgers are more frequently part of the household, marriage tends to be postponed, and the proportion of single and unattached people is greater. Families are smaller and more frequently without children than in the country. The family as a unit of social life is emancipated from the larger kinship group characteristic of the country, and the individual members pursue their own diverging interests in their vocational, educational, religious, recreational, and political life.

Such functions as the maintenance of health, the methods of alleviating the hardships associated with personal and social insecurity, the provisions for education, recreation, and cultural advancement have given rise to highly specialized institutions on a community-wide, statewide, or even national basis. The same factors which have brought about greater personal insecurity also underlie the wider contrasts between individuals to be found in the urban world. While the city has broken down the rigid caste lines of preindustrial society, it has sharpened and differentiated income and status groups. Generally, a larger proportion of the adult urban population is gainfully employed than is the case with the adult rural population. The white-collar class, comprising those employed in trade, in clerical, and in professional work, are proportionately more numerous in large cities and in metropolitan centers and in smaller towns than in the country.

On the whole, the city discourages an economic life in which the individual in time of crisis has a basis of subsistence to fall back upon, and it discourages self-employment. While incomes of city people are on average higher than those of country people, the cost of living seems to be higher in the larger cities. Home ownership involves greater burdens and is rarer. Rents are higher and absorb a larger proportion of income. Although the urban dweller has the benefit of many communal services, he spends a large proportion of his income on such items as recreation and advancement and a smaller proportion on food. What the communal services do not furnish the urbanite must purchase, and there is virtually no human need which has

remained unexploited by commercialism. Catering to thrills
and furnishing means of escape from drudgery, monotony,
and routine thus become one of the major functions of urban
recreation, which at its best furnishes means for creative
self-expression and spontaneous group association, but which
more typically in the urban world results in passive spec-
tatorism on the one hand, or sensational record-smashing
feats on the other.

Being reduced to a state of virtual impotence as an individual, the urbanite is bound to exert himself by joining
with others of similar interest into organized groups to obtain
his ends. This results in the enormous multiplication of
voluntary organizations directed toward as great a variety
of objectives as there are human needs and interests. While
on the one hand the traditional ties of human association
are weakened, urban existence involves a much greater degree
of interdependence between man and man and a more complicated, fragile, and volatile form of mutual interrelations
over many phases of which the individual as such can exert
scarcely any control. Frequently there is only the most tenuous
relationship between the economic position or other basic
factors that determine the individual's existence in the urban
world and the voluntary groups with which he is affiliated.
While in a primitive and in a rural society it is generally
possible to predict on the basis of a few known factors who
will belong to what and who will associate with whom in
almost every relationship of life, in the city we can only
project the general pattern of group formation and affiliation,
and this pattern will display many incongruities and contradictions.

Urban Personality and Collective Behavior

It is largely through the activities of voluntary groups, be
their objectives economic, political, educational, religious,
recreational, or cultural, that the urbanite expresses and
develops his personality, acquires status, and is able to carry
on the round of activities that constitute his life-career. It
may easily be inferred, however, that the organizational
framework which these highly differentiated functions call
into being does not of itself ensure the consistency and

integrity of the personalities whose interests it enlists. Personal disorganization, mental breakdown, suicide, delinquency, crime, corruption, and disorder might be expected under these circumstances to be more prevalent in the urban than in the rural community. This has been confirmed insofar as comparable indices are available; but the mechanisms underlying these phenomena require further analysis.

Since for most group purposes it is impossible in the city to appeal individually to the large number of discrete and differentiated individuals, and since it is only through the organizations to which men belong that their interests and resources can be enlisted for a collective cause, it may be inferred that social control in the city should typically proceed through formally organized groups. It follows, too, that the masses of men in the city are subject to manipulation by symbols and stereotypes managed by individuals working from afar or operating invisibly behind the scenes through their control of the instruments of communications. Self-government either in the economic, the political, or the cultural realm is under these circumstances reduced to a mere figure of speech or, at best, is subject to the unstable equilibrium of pressure groups. In view of the ineffectiveness of actual kinship ties we create fictional kinship groups. In the face of the disappearance of the territorial unit as a basis of social solidarity we create interest units. Meanwhile the city as a community resolves itself into a series of tenuous segmental relationships superimposed upon a territorial base with a definite center but without a definite periphery and upon a division of labor which far transcends the immediate locality and is world-wide in scope. The larger the number of persons in a state of interaction with one another the lower the level of communication and the greater the tendency for communication to proceed on an elementary level, that is on the basis of those things which are assumed to be common or to be of interest to all.

It is obviously, therefore, to the emerging trends in the communication system and to the production and distribution technology that has come into existence with modern civilization that we must look for the symptoms which will indicate the probable future development of urbanism as a mode of social life. The direction of the ongoing changes in urbanism will for good or ill transform not only the city but the world. Some of the more basic of these factors and processes and the possibilities of their direction and control invite further detailed study.

It is only insofar as the sociologist has a clear conception of the city as a social entity and a workable theory of urbanism that he can hope to develop a unified body of reliable knowledge, which what passes as "urban sociology" is certainly not at the present time. By taking his point of departure from a theory of urbanism such as that sketched in the foregoing pages to be elaborated, tested, and revised in the light of further analysis and empirical research, it is to be hoped that the criteria of relevance and validity of factual data can be determined. The miscellaneous assortment of disconnected information which has hitherto found its way into sociological treatises on the city may thus be sifted and incorporated into a coherent body of knowledge. Incidentally, only by means of some such theory will the sociologist escape the futile practice of voicing in the name of sociological science a variety of often unsupportable judgments concerning such problems as poverty, housing, city planning, sanitation, municipal administration, policing, marketing, transportation, and other technical issues. While the sociologist cannot solve any of these practical problems – at least not by himself – he may, if he discovers his proper function, have an important contribution to make to their comprehension and solution. The prospects for doing this are brightest through a general, theoretical, rather than through an *ad hoc* approach.

Notes

1. William Graham Sumner, *Folkways* (Boston, 1906), p. 12.
2. S. V. Pearson, *The Growth and Distribution of Population* (New York, 1935), p. 211.
3. Whereas rural life in the United States has for a long time been a subject of considerable interest on the part of governmental bureaus, the most notable case of a comprehensive report being that submitted by the Country Life Commission to President Theodore Roosevelt in 1909, it is worthy of note that no equally comprehensive official inquiry into urban life was undertaken until the estab-

lishment of a Research Committee on Urbanism of the National Resources Committee. Cf. *Our Cities: Their Role in the National Economy* (Washington: Government Printing Office, 1937).

4. Mark Jefferson, "The Anthropogeography of Some Great Cities," *Bulletin of the American Geographical Society,* vol. XLI (1909), pp. 537–66.
5. Walter F. Willcox, "A Definition of 'City' in Terms of Density," in E. W. Burgess, *The Urban Community* (Chicago, 1916), p. 119.
6. Louis Wirth, *Our Cities, Their Role in the National Economy* (Washington, Government Printing Office, 1937) p. 8.
7. See Robert E. Park, Ernest W. Burgess, *et al., The City* (Chicago, 1925), esp. chaps. ii and iii; Werner Sombart, "Städtische Siedlung, Stadt," *Handwörterbuch der Soziologie,* ed. Alfred Vierkandt (Stuttgart, 1931).
8. Max Weber, *Wirtschaft und Gesellschaft* (Tübingen, 1925), Part II, chap. vii, pp. 514–601.
9. Robert E. Park, Burgess, *et al., op. cit.,* chap. i.
10. The justification for including the term "permanent" in the definition may appear necessary. Our failure to give an extensive justification for the qualifying mark of the urban rests on the obvious fact that unless human settlements take a fairly permanent root in a locality the characteristics of urban life cannot arise, and conversely the living together of large numbers of heterogeneous individuals under dense conditions is not possible without the development of a more or less technological structure.
11. See esp. vii 4. 4–14. Translated by B. Jowett, from which the following may be quoted:

To the size of states there is a limit, as there is to other things, plants, animals, implements; for none of these retain their natural power when they are too large or too small, but they either wholly lose their nature, or are spoiled. . . . [A] state when composed of too few is not as a state ought to be, self-sufficing; when of too many, though self-sufficing in all mere necessaries, it is a nation and not a state, being almost incapable of constitutional government. For who can be the general of such a vast multitude, or who the herald, unless he have the voice of a Stentor?

A State then only begins to exist when it has attained a population sufficient for a good life in the political community: it may indeed somewhat exceed this number. But, as I was saying, there must be a limit. What should be the limit will be easily ascertained by experience. For both governors and governed have duties to perform; the special functions of a governor are to command and to judge. But if the citizens of a state are to judge and to distribute offices according to merit, then they must know each other's characters; where they do not possess this knowledge, both the election to offices and the decision of lawsuits will go wrong. When the population is very large they are manifestly settled at haphazard, which clearly ought not to be. Besides, in an overpopulous state foreigners and metics will readily acquire the rights of citizens, for who will find them out? Clearly, then, the best limit of the population of a state is the largest number which suffices for the purposes of life, and can be taken in at a single view. Enough concerning the size of a city.

12. Max Weber, op. cit., p. 514.
13. Georg Simmel, "Die Grossstädte und das Geistesleben," *Die Grossstadt,* ed. Theodor Petermann (Dresden, 1903), pp. 187–206.
14. E. Durkheim, *De la division du travail social* (Paris, 1932), p. 248.
15. The extent to which the segregation of the population into distinct ecological and cultural areas and the resulting social attitude of tolerance, rationality, and secular mentality are functions of density as distinguished from heterogeneity is difficult to determine. Most likely we are dealing here with phenomena which are consequences of the simultaneous operation of both factors.

Part II

Rationality and its Discontents: The Making of the Metropolis in New York City

6 Introduction
Philip Kasinitz

Power seemed to have outgrown its servitude and to have asserted its freedom. The cylinder had exploded, and thrown great masses of steam against the sky. The city had the air and movement of hysteria, and the citizens were crying, in every accent of anger and alarm, that the new forces must at any cost be brought under control. Prosperity never before imagined, power never yet wielded by man, speed never reached by anything but a meteor, had made the world irritable, nervous, querulous, unreasonable and afraid. All New York was demanding new men and all the new forces, condensed into corporations, were demanding a new type of man – a man with ten times the endurance, energy, will and mind of the old type – for whom they were ready to pay millions at sight.

Henry Adams *The Education of Henry Adams*, on New York in 1905.[1]

Here I was in New York, city of prose and fantasy, of capitalist automatism, its streets a triumph of cubism, its moral philosophy that of the dollar. New York impressed me tremendously because, more than any other city in the world, it is the fullest expression of our modern age.

Leon Trotsky, *My Life*, on New York in 1917.[2]

While some have sought to understand the modern metropolis, others have sought to change it. The three essays in this part are all polemics on modern urban life. All seek to describe the creation of what is perhaps the premier metropolis of the twentieth century: New York City. At the same time each of the authors is making an argument about how urban life *should* be organized, what has gone right and what has gone wrong in the modern city. In each case the intended audience is not only those who study cities, but also those who build them.

New York may seem a strange setting for a discussion of urban planning. Conventional wisdom maintains that among

North American cities New York is singularly unplanned and unplannable. Today the technical discussions of professional urban planners rarely address this city because it is generally thought to be so exceptional. Yet during the first two thirds of the twentieth century, New York, more than any other location on the planet, epitomized the forces of modernity. The very names of its streets – Madison Avenue, Wall Street and Broadway – became synonymous with the structures of mass communication and persuasion, finance, capitalism and popular culture that have defined the modern way of life. New York dominates the conceptual and symbolic vocabulary with which we think of the modern city. Thus it is not really surprising that it should figure so prominently in the type of discussions represented in Part II of this volume.

New York presents a paradoxical image. For Adams, the aging conservative, and Trotsky, the exiled revolutionary, viewing the city at the beginning of this century, New York was a triumph of modern technology and capitalist accumulation. Yet at the same time automation seemed to have "outgrown its servitude", threatening to overwhelm its human masters. Beneath the orderly geometry of its street grid New York seemed (and still seems) to teeter on the verge of hysteria and chaos.[3] The contradiction of unprecedented technological progress and mastery over the environment, coupled with deeply felt alienation and the sense of society gone out of control, epitomizes and ambivalence of many observers of the modern metropolis.

With the merger of the five boroughs in 1898 New York became the largest city in the Americas and, after London, the second largest in the world. Throughout the century it has had more than twice the population and nearly twice the population density of America's "second city," Chicago. Although it reached its zenith during the industrial age, New York has never been an industrial town in the sense that Pittsburgh, Detroit or even Chicago have been. While it has long housed a large industrial working class,[4] New York, like London and Paris, has always been more a center of commerce, finance, mass communication and corporate administration than of industrial production. Yet whereas London and Paris are popularly viewed as quintessentially

"British" or "French," Americans often point to and exaggerate the ways in which New York is unlike the rest of the country – "an island off the coast of America" in the words of humorist Spalding Grey.

To some degree the denial of the Americanness of New York reflects a deeply entrenched suspicion of centralized authority: that New York City is not the capital of the United States nor even of New York State is not surprising. Beyond this there is the sense that the "real America" is in its small-town and rural areas, a sense that lingered long after the United States became the world's premier industrial power and most of its population lived in metropolitan areas. More than any other city, New York embodies the diversity, complexity and artifice of modern urban life, which many Americans find morally suspect. When explaining the reluctance of Congress to extend financial assistance to the city during the fiscal crisis of 1976, Senator Joseph Biden observed that "Cities are viewed as the seed of corruption and duplicity, and New York is the biggest City."[5]

Given the enormous role that New York plays in American economic and cultural life, it is striking that until recently it has received relatively little attention from social scientists.[6] In contrast historians, literary observers and cultural critics – particularly those concerned with the built environment – have often based their arguments on New York.[7] The three observers in Part II all use the city as the site for arguments about how cities ought to be built. Their discussions shift our attention from seeing the city as the site of networks of social relations to seeing the city as an artifact: a thing built and rebuilt by people, shaped by and in turn shaping the culture of those who live there.

Le Corbusier (born Charles-Edouard Jeanneret) the Swissborn French architect and planner, was probably the single most central figure in the history of twentieth-century urban landscapes. The degree of his influence is striking given the fact that his practice as an architect was generally unsuccessful. He built few buildings, much less the cities that he continually planned on paper, although he was partially responsible for Chandigrath, the new capital of the Punjab built in the late 1950s. Nor are his many books, with their breathless celebration of technology and their

pompous, capitalized pronouncements, widely read anymore.
Yet his tireless efforts as the apostle of the high-rise "radiant city," with its relentless geometry, its soaring glass towers
and wide open spaces connected by winding ribbons of highways, have left their mark on most of the large cities of
the industrialized world. Today Le Corbusier is blamed for
a great deal of what has gone wrong in the modern city,
from Brasilia, the new capital of Brazil completed by his
disciples in 1960, to Pruitt-Igoe, the St Louis housing project
so unlivable it had to be demolished in 1972. Yet if Corbusier's
dream of the rational city proved entirely too easy for both
state and corporate bureaucrats to replicate on a brutal
and dehumanizing scale, it must also be remembered that
he and many of his contemporaries had a vision, not only
of what cities should look like, but of how the technological achievements of the modern age could be used to change
people's lives for the better.

For today's planners or architects, beset by bureaucratic
regulations and often preoccupied by narrow, technical issues,
this notion that their work can profoundly shape the way
people live probably seems grandiose, if not absurd. Yet
this was not always the case. From the mid-nineteenth to
the mid-twentieth century, in the work of planners and architects as diverse as Frederick Law Olmstead, Patrick
Geddes, Ebenezer Howard, Frank Lloyd Wright, the early
Soviet planners, the Bauhaus designers and, most centrally,
Le Corbusier, social utopianism was linked inextricably with
the reform of the built environment.[8] For these men and
women, new ways of building cities meant new ways of living, and their diverse visions continue to affect the lives of
people throughout the world. Today their faith that a more
rational and efficient city might create a more humane social
order often seems hopelessly naïve. Their willingness to uproot
established social patterns to realize their utopias can be, in
retrospect, quite frightening. Yet the fact that people once
widely believed that the improvement of the physical structure of cities could make a better society, and the fact that,
by and large, we no longer do, both speak volumes about the
changes that have taken place during the twentieth century.

Of course people have tried to plan cities since time
immemorial. Yet entirely planned cities are actually quite

rare. In the ancient and medieval worlds, as Max Weber notes, most cities grew up around centers of trade, centers of worship or military garrisons. Governmental and religious authorities often shaped the physical pattern of the settlement by laying out streets, constructing important public buildings and maintaining the walls and other public works. Yet the cities that developed were usually the product of a multitude of individual decisions made by thousands of different actors rather than a response to any given plan.

With the growth of centralized states a more unitary urban vision became more common. Most often this involved rebuilding existing cities after a fire or other form of destruction or the deliberate attempt by the authorities to impose a new order on complex urban realities. Speaking of the cities of the early Renaissance, Mumford notes:

> If one uses the term precisely, there is no renascence city. But there are patches of renascence order, openings and clarifications, that beautifully modify the structure of the medieval city. If the new buildings, with their impersonal gravity and decorous regularity break up the harmony of the medieval pattern, they established a contrapuntal relationship which brings out, by contrast, otherwise unregarded, often invisible, aesthetic qualities of older streets and buildings. . . . The symbols of this new movement are the straight street, the unbroken horizontal roof line, the round arch, and the repetition of uniform elements.[9]

Yet as the power of state over daily life grew, planners found that they now had both the ability and desire to impose order on a scale Mumford disapproved of:

> As soon as the baroque order became widespread, uniform and absolute . . . its weaknesses lay revealed. Clarification gave place to regimentation, oneness to emptiness, greatness to grandiosity.[10]

With the dawn of the industrial age centralized states frequently undertook even more ambitious missions. Not content to remake ancient settlements in their own image, both Peter and Great and the American founding fathers thought it important to build entirely new, monumental capital cities in highly unlikely locales to express their different visions of governmental power.

Modern urban planning, however, with its mission of remaking urban society, truly begins in the Paris of Napoleon III and Baron Haussmann. Like the planners of Renaissance city states, Haussmann sought to impose regularity on what was seen as the disorder of the dense, ancient city. Unlike the Renaissance planners, the "artist of demolition" brought to bear on this task the full authority of the modern state and the destructive capacity of industrial technology.

Haussmann's vision was soon emulated, generally in less radical forms, throughout the world. When Daniel H. Burnham, founder of the "City Beautiful" movement, presented his plan for the rebuilding of Chicago in 1909 he noted "The task which Haussmann accomplished in Paris corresponds with the work which must be done for Chicago in order to overcome the intolerable conditions which invariably arise from a rapid growth in population."[11] From Frederick Law Olmstead's gracious parks and parkways to Vienna's Ringstrasse to the early advocates of workers' housing, late nineteenth- and early twentieth-century urbanists put forward many different ideas of what the good city should be. Yet throughout Europe and North America these visions shared a faith that the city, as a social entity, could be made *rational*. Mechanical efficiency could overcome, or at least push to the side, the conflicts of industrial society. Safe, sanitary, orderly living would improve the lives of the poor and affirm the standards of middle-class morality.

Before dismissing this naïve faith in technology we should remember the problems urban reformers were trying to solve. Not only had the industrial cities of Europe and North America grown at a completely unprecedented pace during the nineteenth century, they had grown in a largely unplanned and unregulated way. For example, in 1847 New York, which had started the year with a population of 375 000, received 129 000 immigrants in eight months – half of them starving refugees from the Irish potato famine. There was *one* public-health inspector for the entire city.[12] In much of the industrialized world the new working classes were being squeezed into shoddily built tenement housing. The result was unprecedented overcrowding: by the turn of the century New York, Paris and Berlin all had population densities higher than that of Calcutta today.[13] If the planners' obsessions with light, air and the "moral hygiene" of urban population reects a confusion of metaphor and reality, it should be remembered that the impoverished and disease-ridden slums were real enough.

While we should resist the nostalgic impulse to romanticize the premodern world, it is also true that in most preindustrial cities rich and poor lived in something like a common community, sharing, albeit unequally, in certain common institutions. Early industrial towns, at least smaller ones, continued to reflect much of this interclass unity: churches, political life and other social events brought workers and owners together on common ground if not on an equal footing.[14] But in the growing metropolis of the late nineteenth century, class, and in the United States ethnic segregation, had become pronounced and relations between classes and ethnic groups were increasingly hostile.[15]

It was against this background that Le Corbusier and the other utopian planners forwarded their arguments for a spatial and social reorganization of urban living.[16] For Le Corbusier, the profound contradiction of modern life was that industrial workers, whose labors created the fabulous wealth of the modern age, benefited little from it. They "each day make use of the brilliant and effective tools that the age has provided, but they are not permitted to use them for themselves."[17] While Le Corbusier's political affiliations varied across the spectrum from syndicalism to Vichy fascism in his search for allies and patrons, the core of his philosophy remained rooted in the simple Saint Simonian notion that technology and central planning was an alternative to class conflict.

In many ways his proposals draw on the highly influential "Garden-City" plans of the turn-of-the-century British social reformer Ebenezer Howard. In both cases the planners sought to reintegrate people with their natural environments. Both believed that new, carefully planned spatial forms could undo the concentrations of wealth and poverty of the modern city. Yet Howard's model is ultimately antimodernist. He proposed decentralizing the urban population into

manageable, class-integrated "Garden Cities" of approximately 30 000. While this notion requires modern transportation technology, it remains fundamentally nostalgic.
As Nathan Glazer describes it: "the image was the English
country town – with the manor house and its park replaced
by the community center and some factories hidden behind
a screen of trees, to supply work."[18] Le Corbusier, in contrast, embraced technology. By building higher and larger
than ever before possible, by making full use of innovations in transportation, by wiping out the old spatial forms
and "killing the street," the "city of tomorrow" would be a
"vertical community," full of light and air, without political conflicts.[19]

That this simple vision should have had the effect it did
is only understandable if one realizes that it came into fashion
at precisely the moment when it could do the most damage. The post-Second-World-War period needed a new way
to build cities. The bombed-out cities of Europe and the
Soviet Union, the urban-renewal and slum-clearance programs of the United States, the need for new capitals in
emerging Third-World countries and the task of reorganiz-
ing space for the automobile all necessitated massive building
at the very moment when faith in technology was at its zenith.
If Howard's gentle garden cities won the hearts of intellectuals, it was Le Corbusier's bold, automobile-friendly fu-
turism that caught the spirit of the age. Perhaps more
importantly, building high was cheap, a fact that instantly
won the hearts of bureaucrats the world over. By 1961 Jane
Jacobs would observe that, despite the difference in appearances, Le Corbusier's ideas were really not that different
from Howard's – the "radiant city" with its mass-produced
rows of repetitive "towers in the park" had made the garden-city ideals practical and attainable on a scale consistent with modern urban densities.

The excerpt from Le Corbusier in Chapter 7 is a reflection on his 1930 trip to New York, from his book *When the
Cathedrals Were White*. New York, for Le Corbusier, was the
epitome of the energy of the modern world. He approved
of the grid pattern of its streets, its tall buildings and, most
of all, its willingness to remake itself every few years. Yet
he did not like its chaos and found the city still too dependent

on historic spatial forms. The skyscrapers were not big enough and were jumbled too closely together: in the radiant city they would be more symmetrical, and would require streets and highways that matched their scale. Ultimately, however, Le Corbusier saw in Manhattan evidence that, if American energy could be tempered with a bit of Gallic sensibility and taste for centralized authority, his vision of the future, while not yet achieved, would be obtainable.

Between the skyscrapers of downtown and those of midtown, Le Corbusier noted in passing "an urban no man's land made up of miserable low building – poor streets of dirty red brick." It was from precisely these "poor" streets of dirty red brick." It was from precisely these "poor" streets that the great refutation of his model of urbanism would be launched. Jane Jacob's *The Death and Life of the Great American City,* first published in 1961, may be the single most influential book on American urban space of the last half century. It was hardly the first attack on modern architecture or urban renewal: Mumford and other followers of Howard had been doing battle with the disciples Le Corbusier for years. Sociologists,[20] muckraking journalists and grass-roots activists had already started to challenge the destruction of urban neighborhoods. But Jacobs, with her deceptively modest description of the rhythm of daily life on Hudson Street in New York's Greenwich Village, provided something more. She gave a growing movement of people throughout the industrialized world a vocabulary with which to oppose the seemingly irresistible force of "progress." In the face of generations of utopians and reformers she provided an intellectually coherent rationale for explaining why many people love the "miserable" low red brick streets of the dense urban neighborhoods *as they are.*

She accomplishes this in part through sociology. *The Death and Life of Great American Cities* is perhaps the first book about urban planning that takes as its starting point the way people actually live in cities, rather than a planner's image of how they should live. Jacobs unearths the complex web of social life of in the small-scale urban neighborhood. Yet this is not a nostalgic vision of an imagined *Gemeinschaft* (although it has at times been read this way). Her neighborhood includes dense networks of personal relationships, but also many strangers, some of whom are potentially dangerous. Her story of how a successful modern urban neighborhood balances openness to strangers, thus supporting the vitality of the city, with the unity of neighbors, moves beyond the *Gemeinschaft/Gesellschaft* dichotomy and provides valuable insight as to how urban communities function.[21] In addition, Jacobs makes a claim for the centrality of public spaces, particularly streets, in establishing urban communal life. In contrast with those who would rationalize the urban form, she makes the case for the social and economic functions of irrationality. If crowded multifunction streets impede traffic flow, they also promote the space for serendipitous encounters, the unplanned social interaction and intellectual exchange that are the essence of urbanity.

But there is far more to Jacobs' book than one woman's description of her neighborhood. The second half of the *Death and Life of Great American Cities* is a detailed account of the types of spatial forms that promote and that impede this sort of urban life. Finally the book is an attack on planning. Its almost anarchist embrace of the unplanned community, and its early celebration of small groups and organizations over large ones, made its author a hero to both the new left and some elements of the new right.[22] Yet herein lies what may be the book's major weakness. Ultimately many of Jacobs solutions seem insufficient to the problems of the modern city: "Mother Jacobs' home remedies for urban cancer" is how Mumford described the work.[23]

Marshall Berman juxtaposes Jacobs with Robert Moses, New York's master builder, as symbols of two divergent forms of urban modernism. Moses, the multiple-office-holding public-sector entrepreneur who for half a century ruled over the reorganization of New York, shared much of Le Corbusier's vision about the future of cities. Unlike Le Corbusier, he also possessed a unique gift for gathering and using political power. Thus he was able to remake the landscape of America's largest city and provide the model copied in many other American cities. Drawing on Robert Caro's Pulitzer-Prize-winning biography *The Power Broker*,[24] Berman notes how Moses made New York accessible to the airplane and the automobile, and, like a latterday Baron Haussmann, destroyed neighborhoods and displaced thousands from their homes in the process. For Berman, and generation of New Yorkers, Moses came to symbolize the force of progress. In Jacobs Berman sees the disillusionment with that version of progress, and with the "expressway world" it produced. Yet while he sympathizes with Jacobs' celebration of the human-scale community, he is left wondering about the limits of her vision. Can any defense of the world as it is, however necessary, be sufficient to address the deep social and political divisions in contemporary urban life? Ultimately Berman is relieved that urban utopianism is largely a thing of the past. Yet he misses the grandeur of its vision.

Notes

1. Henry Adams, *The Education of Henry Adams* (New York: Random House, 1931), p. 499.
2. Leon Trotsky, *My life* (New York: The Trotsky Estate, 1930), p. 185.
3. Although the grid pattern of street layout aids greatly in the rationalization and commodification of space, it is, of course, not a particularly modern innovation, nor is it particular to New York. Late Roman towns often used the pattern and it is a long-time favorite of urban utopians: William Penn's grid plan for Philadelphia is but one example. Still, for pure planning hubris and faith in rational development it is hard to match the New Yorkers who laid out the street grid for the whole of Manhattan in 1811, decades before most of the island was settled.
4. Indeed many would point to the post-1960 decline of that class as the most important factor in the decline of New York. See for example, Joseph Epstein, "The Tragedy of New York," *The New York Review of Books*, 9 April 1992.
5. *The new York Times*, 25 May 1976.
6. Although in recent years there has been something of an explosion of social scientific writing on New York. See for example Sharon Zukin, *Loft Living: Culture and Capital in Urban Change* (Baltimore: Johns Hopkins Press, 1982); Jonathan Rieder, *Canarsie: The Jews and Italians of Brooklyn Against Liberalism* (Cambridge: Harvard University Press, 1985; Roger Waldinger, *Through the Eye of the Needle: Immigrants and Enterprise in New York's Garment Trades* (New York: New York University Press, 1986); Mercer Sullivan, *Getting Paid: Youth Crime and Work in the Inner City* (Ithaca: Cornell University

Press, 1989); John Hull Mollenkopf (ed.), *Power, Culture and Place: Essays on New York City* (New York: Russell Sage, 1989); Philip Kasinitz, *Caribbean New York: Black Immigrants and the Politics of Race* (Ithaca: Cornell University Press, 1992).

7. The dearth of social science on New York may in part be simply a function of the location of leading graduate schools; no New-York based university has ever played a role comparable to that of the University of Chicago. There may be a deeper reasons as well. American sociologists have tended be primarily concerned with unearthing the patterns that are supposed to shape social behavior. Studies of specific people and places are usually seen as valid only to the extent that they are generalizable to some larger universe. Yet New York is impossible to render generic. Its people and places are too prominent in the national culture, yet at the same time too often seen as exceptional, to become the building blocks of social-scientific theory.

8. For one of the best treatments of architectural utopianism, see Robert Fishman, *Urban Utopias in the Twentieth Century* (Cambridge MA: MIT Press, 1982).

9. Lewis Mumford, "The Baroque City", in Donald Miller (ed.), *The Lewis Mumford Reader* (New York: Pantheon, 1986), p. 130.

10. Ibid, p. 132.

11. Daniel Burnham, *A Plan for Chicago* (Chicago: Commercial Club, 1909), p. 18.

12. Cecil Woodham-Smith, *The Great Hunger* (New York, Harper and Row, 1962), pp. 253, 263.

13. Mark Girouard, *Cities and People* (New Haven, Yale University Press, 1985), p. 312.

14. See, for example Herbert Gutman, *Work Culture and Society in Early Industrializing America* (New York: Alfred A. Knopf, 1973).

15. Of course, in many ways the work of planners only exacerbated these conflicts. After Haussmann Paris was a far more spatially segregated city. Similarly, in London and New York great building and rebuilding efforts often reinforced the tendency towards physical and social separation of classes and races already present in industrialism. In the twentieth century, council housing in Britain and public housing in the United States were built by planners with highly idealistic motives, and they often did improve the physical conditions in which the poor lived. Yet they also isolated the poor and paved the way for the current crises of the ghetto discussed by Wacquant in Part V.

16. My discussion of Le Corbusier, Howard and Wright draws heavily on Mark Fishman, *Urban Utopias of the Twentieth Century* (Cambridge MA: MIT Press, 1982).

17. Le Corbusier, *Towards a New Architecture* (New York: Holt, Rinehart and Winston, 1960), pp. 259. Quoted in Fishman, op. cit., p. 187.

18. Quoted in Jane Jacobs, *The Death and Life of the Great American Cities* (New York: Random House, 1961), p. 18.

19. Fishman, op. cit., p. 263.

20. Most notably Herbert Gans in the United States and Young and Wilmot in Britain.

21. Of course it might be argued that in this respect Jacobs's primary example, Greenwich Village, is an extremely atypical urban community, a fact somewhat obscured by Jacobs' folksy account.

22. Roger Scruton, for example, compares Jacobs' role in challenging spatial planning to F. A. Hayek's challenge to economic planning. See Roger Scruton, "Public Space and the Classical Vernacular", *The Public Interest*, winter 1984, pp. 5–16.

23. Lewis Mumford, "Mother Jacobs' Home Remedies", *New Yorker*, 1 December 1962, p. 148.

24. Robert Caro, *The Power Broker: Robert Moses and the Fall of New York* (New York: Random House, 1974).

7 New York is not a Completed City*
Le Corbusier

It is a city in the process of becoming. Today it belongs to the world. Without anyone expecting it, it has become the jewel in the crown of universal cities in which there are dead cities whose memories and foundations alone remain and whose evocation is exalting; in which there are living cities injured by the narrow mold of past civilizations. Here is nobility, grandeur of outlines. Here are expressive, animated, proud topographies, exciting landscapes. Here are the old wisdoms accumulated century after century, harmoniously joined together by the simple passage of years, although everything in its has been contrasts, contradictions, revolutionary progress in techniques and conceptions. Here is Paris, for example, jumbled, yet with a gracious harmony: vertical Gothic, pure rectilinear Renaissance, pure *Grand Siècle* horizontal, strong Louis XV, elegant and sober Louis XVI, square Napoleon, Eiffel filigree. Crown of noble cities, soft pearls, or glittering topazes, or radiant lapis, or melancholy amethysts! New York is a great diamond, hard and dry, sparkling, triumphant.

Suddenly New York has entered the family of the cities of the world, and not by the back door. The American is a Janus: one face absorbed by the anxieties of adolescence, looking toward the troubles of his consciousness; the other face as solid as an Olympic victor's, looking toward an old world which at certain moments he believes he can dominate. Reverse the situation: imagine in an urban drawing room a slightly awkward young man, sympathetic and hardworking, who has come a long way and who causes many well-established people to smile. One day his book, his speech, the battle he has won, explodes in the face of the

* Reprinted from Le Corbusier, *When the Cathedrals Were White* (New York: Harcourt Brace and Company, 1947), translated by Francis E. Hyslap, Jr.

world. He dominates. Look at his eyes: a hard flame of pride shines in them! Will he become an ass or a king?

New York is not a finished or completed city. It gushes up. On my next trip it will be different. Those of us who have visited it are asked this question: "When you were there in 1939, or in 1928, or in 1926, or in 1920, was such and such already there? Oh, really, you don't know then what an effect that makes!" Such is the rhythm of the city.

The architects rush in with their heads down; after having worked over the "styles" firmly and worthily, they are launched on the paths of the modern spirit. How are they getting along? Badly, very badly, and nevertheless there are successes. Detail, that is all trash! *Style* is developing without them, outside of them, by the result itself, by the formidable internal pressure which mobilizes their efforts. These debatable results, strange, amusing, or striking, are being worked out in the sky. A thousand feet of height is the rule in this frightening type of football. Well then! A thousand feet of height, in stone, steel and glass, standing up in the magnificently blue sky of New York, is a new event in human history which up to now had only a legend on that theme: that of the Tower of Babel.

A thousand feet of height looked at from the streets, or appearing as an ineffable spectacle from the plains of New Jersey, above the Palisades – the cliffs along the Hudson River – that is the scale of the new times.

At present, it is like a house-moving, all the furniture in confusion, scattered about, unkempt. But order will come.

And the express elevators take forty-five seconds to go from the bottom to the top, that is, for sixty-five stories, a time equal to that taken by our elevators, sanctimoniously installed in the Haussmann stair wells, to go to the sixth story.

IT IS A SAVAGE CITY!

Yes. But the men and women are clean and healthy.

Cleanliness is a national virtue in America. No filth, no dust. Sea breezes incessantly sweep through the limpid maritime sky. The offices are clean; the bath tubs, the shops, the glistening hotels; the dazzling restaurants and bars. The immaculate personnel, in shirt sleeves, is shining white. Food is wrapped up in bright cellophane. There is no more real dust than there is symbolic dust, everything is new and spotless, including the collegiate Gothic of the universities.

Paris bistro, you disappointed me on my return, with your faded charm. It's too old, too old, saddening! Not even a nice little old, something neat and clean!

In contrast, there is a style, a true style, in American cleanliness.

People who wash their shirts, paint their houses, clean the glass in their windows, have an ethic different from those who cultivate dust and filth. To prove that they possess an age-old culture, the latter preserve the cracks in the walls, the patina, and what is worse, they have even established the taste for patina, the love of the old, and because of that they hammer out modern "wrought iron" and soil the new wainscoting of their apartments with bistre.

A true culture manifests itself in fresh color, white linen, and clean art. Among the Cyclades of Greece, in the islands where a volcanic topography has prevented the introduction of the wheel – cart, bicycle, car – where transportation is possible only by mule-back; where consequently customs have remained millenary; where you still seem to recognize Agamemnon or Ulysses in the villages, the tradition of a living culture demands that, each Saturday, the joints of the stones forming the steps of the house and those of the flagstones in front of the house, be painted with bright whitewash – a radiant filigree. Thus in the Islands each Sunday begins in cleanliness and whiteness; life is magnified by this testimony: be clean. Go through beautiful France in a car and you will see that this fundamental feeling of life, always renewed or renewable, has died down; that cracked walls, dirt, and negligence are masters of our spirits ... except here and there, where there is still faith in the virtue of each hour.

THE STREETS ARE AT RIGHT ANGLES TO EACH OTHER AND THE MIND IS LIBERATED

Your mind is free instead of being given over every minute to the complicated game imposed on it by the puzzle of our European cities. Do you want to go from your home to the Opera, to Père-Lachaise, to the Luxembourg Museum, or to the Eiffel Tower? First get the city plan out of your drawer and look for the route. It is a task. Old gentlemen will pretend to discover in that the charm of Paris. I do not agree; nevertheless I accept the inconvenience imposed by the very history of the city; on my way I thank Louis XIV, Napoleon, and Haussmann for having cut through the city with some clear and intelligent axes.

Manhattan, in New York, is a granite rock more than twelve miles long and two miles wide, between the Hudson River and the East River. In length it is laid out in nine parallel avenues; across, in nearly two hundred streets parallel to each other and at right angles to the avenues. The avenue in the middle, Fifth Avenue, serves as a spinal column for this gigantic sole. On one side it is west, on the other east. The first street is at the south, on the ocean side, the last is at the north, on the land side. Everything is ordered accordingly. You have to go to 135 East 42nd Street? Everything is determined with a Euclidean clearness. 42nd Street? You are at your hotel on 55th Street; you go to Fifth Avenue, go down thirteen streets. East? You turn left. 135? You walk to number 135. Thus you know instantly whether to walk, whether to take a taxi, or whether to catch the bus on the avenue or use the subway. I say that it is an immense and beneficent freedom for the mind. It will be said that I am stopping over an anatomical detail of the city and that I attach a great deal of importance to it. This is not an anatomical detail, but the outstanding and essential biological structure of the city. It is a question of a fundamental principle. Do you wish the proof of our own vagaries? This grille of streets, this "American layout," is precisely the excuse for the attacks of academicians and romantics. It is our particular vanity to be plunged in disorder down to the very base. We make a virtue of it; we affirm that it is life, rich, subtle, agreeable, and what not! Now the Romans laid out their cities in "the American way"; and the Greeks before them. The Egyptians also. And the French, in the time of the white cathedrals, when new cities were being born – the towns of the South in particular – planned in "the American way."

Thus Saint Louis had Aigues Mortes executed, in one building campaign, in "the American way."

When the conquistadors left on caravels for the New World, they took along geometers with plans for cities conceived in advance, laid out in "the American way": the Spanish *cuadra* is one hundred ten square meters, the *cuadra* that you see everywhere from a plane, from Buenos Aires, going north, to Montevideo, to Ascension in Paraguay, in the immense pampas, as in the savanna of North America.

Are the Americans then the founders of civilization through the ages? Such is the conclusion to which you lead us, exiles of our own day, lost in the underbrush of romantic garden cities! One man sowed that foolish idea. He was an intelligent and sensitive Viennese, Camillo Sitte, who, quite simply, posed the problem badly. In travels of discovery through Italy, in medieval cities strategically placed on hills and tightly encircled by military walls, he was won over by the art which so exactly adjusted house to house and palace to church – each stone of each city, a living and subtle plastic character, a spectacle of quality. The existence of these exquisite things, and on the other hand, the vast vulgarities of the second half of the nineteenth century, dedicated to great railroad projects, which brought about the dreary, sinister, and soulless expanses of the great modern cities: Vienna, Berlin, Munich, Budapest, etc. . . . On the basis of the urban horrors of 1870 he concluded his reasoning and declared: Confusion is beautiful, and rectitude is base. And because on a small scale, in small Italian towns – Orvieto, Siena, Perugia, etc. – the walls hung on the sides of hills, the uneven levels of the ground, pocket-sized open spaces bowed the streets under their yoke to allow a greater number of houses to pile up like the scales of a pineapple, he concluded that the beautiful was curved and that large cities should be contorted. The fashion was launched: Berlin and Vienna and Munich, and cities throughout the world, developed curves, became entangled in a net like that which a cat makes out of a skein of wool. The garden cities near London, *idem*, etc. . . . Morocco was constructed in a crooked way, since straightness was considered an enemy of the heart! One day in a committee meeting, M. Louis Bonnier, head architect of the City of Paris, who

loves cathedrals and many excellent things, apostrophized
a bewildered young architect in connection with his city
plan project for Saint Raphael: "What is this, sir, this completely straight two-hundred-meter "artillery range"? We shall
not allow that to be executed!"
The ten main avenues of New York are nearly fifteen
kilometers long. Such are the minds of the same epoch:
one saying gee, another haw!
Fifteen kilometers long? It is imaginable, is it allowable!
Traditions, which have become academized, demand that
every straight avenue terminate in a blaze of glory, or if
you prefer, in a set piece: the Opera at the end of the avenue
of that name, the Saint-Augustin church at the end of the
Boulevard Malesherbes. A code established in the name of
true beauty. Here again, let us denounce the deformation
of accomplishments which had a harmonious origin: the
Place de la Concorde is a notable composition: Gabriel's
palaces, the rue Royale in the axis, and the Madeleine, one
hundred and fifty meters away. Opposite, the Palais-Bour-
bon. A "classic" composition with a comprehensible axis;
dimensions on a human scale. The spectacle is real, plastic. A royal composition. It is a place of glory, a porch of
honor. It is not a street, much less a traffic artery. Let's
not confuse things! Period of the carriage and pedestrian.
A city has a biological life. It is justly said of a man that
he is "a digestive tube with an entrance and an exit." At
the entrance or exit of the tube there is neither a church
nor a palace. There is a free passage! A fundamental condition of health of a city is being traversed, irrigated,
nourished from end to end, being free! Let's not graft plastic
forms on this need which has a biological character. The
occasion for that ought to be an appropriate one.
New York lives by its clear checkerboard. Millions of beings
act simply and easily within it. Freedom of mind. From the
first hour, the stranger is oriented, sure of his course.
We shall see that a plastic spectacle exists along the gigantic
avenue. Also, that it could have a different character.
We shall see, further, that the street-plan of Manhattan,
proud and strong, established in colonial times, a model of
wisdom and greatness of vision, is today in mortal danger
because of the motorcar.

And that remedies as vigorous as the first plan are necessary, if the city does not wish to decline.

Life never stops. The torment of men will be eternal, unless the function of creating and acting and changing, living intensely through each day, be considered an eternal joy.

THE SKYSCRAPERS OF NEW YORK ARE TOO SMALL!

The skyscraper is not a plume rising from the face of the city. It has been made that, and wrongly. The plume was a poison to the city. The skyscraper is an instrument. A magnificent instrument for the concentration of population, for getting rid of land congestion, for classification, for internal efficiency. A prodigious means of improving the conditions of work, a creator of economies and, through that,a dispenser of wealth. But the skyscraper as plume, multiplied over the area of Manhattan, has disregarded experience. The New York skyscrapers are out of line with the rational skyscraper which I have called: *the Cartesian skyscraper* ("Plans," *Revue internationale*, Paris, 1931).

Let me explain the Cartesian skyscraper:

(a) First of all, it is *realizable*, thanks to modern techniques: bold steel skeletons; lifting machinery; technique of sound-proofing. Extraordinary perfection of electric lighting, creation of precisely *conditioned air*, demonstrated efficiency of elevators, etc. . . .

(b) The skyscraper easily reaches a height of a thousand feet. Intuitively, I accept sixty stories, or seven hundred and twenty feet, a dimension that seems to me good.

(c) The skyscraper is normally vertical, plumb, from top to bottom, without setbacks or slopes – unlike the New York skyscrapers, handled nonsensically as the result of a deplorably romantic city ordinance.

(d) The skyscraper is a light radiator, which means that no office surface can be deprived of solar light. Consequently, it should have a form independent of that belonging to the ground plot, and developing from its three fundamental organs: elevators, corridors, offices planned with a depth directly proportioned to the height of the windows.

(e) The skyscraper should not have offices on the north side. Its layout will depend on the path of the sun in the sky – which should be diagrammed. Combined with the necessities of stability of resistance to the wind (the greatest adversary of the skyscraper), it will take, in plan, a characteristic form.

(f) The skyscraper is built of steel – a skeleton woven like a filigree in the sky, a spidery thing, marvelously clear and free. There are no *walls* in the skyscraper, since a wall is not easily put in place at six hundred and fifty feet; why have one anyway? Until the introduction of new methods of construction in reinforced concrete or steel, a wall served to *support floors*. Today they are carried by posts which do not take up a thousandth part of the surface of the ground, and not by walls. The exterior of the skyscraper, the facade – the facades – can be a film of glass, a skin of glass. Why repudiate richness itself: oods of light coming in.

(g) The skyscraper should be large. It can contain ten thousand, twenty thousand, thirty thousand, forty thousand occupants easily. It is worthwhile, then, to arrange its approaches and flawless means of transportation: subways, buses or trolleys, roads for cars.

(h) Now we are ready to state the fundamental principle: the skyscraper is a *function of capacity* (the offices) *and of the area of free ground at its base*. A skyscraper which does not fulfill this function harmoniously is a disease. That is the disease of New York.

The Cartesian skyscraper is a miracle in the urbanization of the cities of machine civilization. It makes possible extraordinary concentrations, from three to four thousand persons on each two and one-half acres. It does so while taking up only 8 to 12 per cent of the ground, 88–92 per cent being restored, usable, available for the circulation of pedestrians and cars! These immense free areas, this whole ward in the business section, will become a park. The glass skyscrapers will rise up like crystals, clean and transparent in the midst of the foliage of the trees. It is sufficient to discover the proper relation of parcels of ground, of skyscraper distribution, of their spacing, of their capacity. A new law appears among the rules of this new game: the technical conditions of automobile traffic. It requires a new dimensioning of the stages between the intersections of automobile highways; the right spacing of these highways.

This must be explained still further: if the skyscraper is large enough, the expenses of foundations are immediately divided up among admirably efficient installations: the common services of the skyscraper restaurants, bars, showrooms, barber shops, dry-goods stores, etc. ... Office life, made intensely productive through mechanical rationalization: post office, telephone, telegraph, radio, pneumatic tubes, etc. ... Thus the benefit of excellent psycho-physiological conditions: luxury, perfection, quality in the whole building – halls, elevators, the offices themselves (quiet and pure air). Here I call to mind the business offices of Paris. Ah! wretched, mediocre and miserable offices, an unsuspected degradation of the spirit of work – those entrances, those grotesque, ridiculous, idiotic elevators, those dark and bleak vestibules, and the series of dim rooms open on the hubbub of the street or on the dreariness of courts. Ah! no, let no one continue to defend the "good-natured" charm of these Homaisian installations where nothing, nothing, is efficient. I repeat: where the spirit is afflicted. Already in New York Rockefeller Center affirms to the world the dignity of the new times by its useful and noble halls, just as the skyscraper of Howe and Lescaze does in Philadelphia.

Here I wish to evoke the true splendor of the Cartesian skyscraper: the tonic spectacle, stimulating, cheering, radiant, which, from each office, appears through the transparent glass walls leading into space. Space! That response to the aspiration of the human being, that relaxation for breathing and for the beating heart, that outpouring of self in looking far, from a height, over a vast, infinite, unlimited expanse. Every bit of sun and fresh, pure air furnished mechanically. Do you try to maintain the fraud of hypocritical affirmations, to throw discredit on these radiant facts, to argue, to demand the "good old window," open on the stenches of the city and street, the noise, air currents, and the company of flies and mosquitoes? For thirty years I have known the offices of Paris: conversations cut to pieces by the uproar, suffocating atmosphere, the view broken thirty feet away by the walls of houses, dark corners, half-light, etc. ... Impostors should no longer deny the gains of our

period and by their fright prevent changing from one thing
to another, keeping the city or cities in general from going
their joyously destined way.

The skyscrapers of New York are too small and there are
too many of them. They are proof of the new dimensions
and the new tools; the proof also that henceforth everything can be carried out on a new general plan, a sym-
phonic plan – extent and height.

Their history is mixed up with questions of utility and
questions of vanity. They built tall buildings in Wall Street
because it was necessary to be grouped around the Stock
Exchange, in order to be able to act quickly. One sees canyons surging up, deep and violent fissures, streets such as
no one had ever seen before. Not ugly either! I will even
say: a very strong architectural sensation which is equal to
that experienced in the narrow streets of Rouen and Toulon,
with in this case the enthronement of a grandeur and intensity well calculated to inspire courage. Later, I shall speak
of one of the most remarkable architectural sights in the
world: the face of Washington seen against the Doric columns
of the Sub-Treasury, at the foot of the cliff formed by the
skyscrapers of Wall Street.

The skyscrapers born out of national conditions in Wall
Street multiplied thereafter, first on that site, establishing
the mystically alluring city seen far out at sea by the traveler,
which gives him a high idea of American destiny before
suddenly assaulting him, a half hour later, with its sav-
agery and brutality, when the boat comes into direct contact with it in the Hudson.

The skyscrapers then disappear in an area of several miles,
an urban no man's land made up of miserable low buildings – poor streets of dirty red brick. They spring up again
suddenly in mid-town (the center of the city) much higher,
fitted out with "architecture" and charged with a mission;
the proclamation of a proper name, that of a financial success, a fortune, a monetary power. Thus in the Middle Ages,
at San Gimignano in Tuscany, the struggles for control among
the families of the little city brought about the construction of fantastically high towers, one after another, each
one higher than the last; height indicated the triumph of

one family and the crushing of another. San Gimignano has the appearance of a pincushion, and the spectacle delights tourists while troubling common sense; hirsute beauty – yes, beauty, why not? The cataclysms of nature – jagged rocks, Niagara, Alps, or canyons, do they not compel our admiration by the effect of power, the feeling of catastrophe? In New York, it is by a thousand feet of height that the game is played – the game of skyscrapers, the sport of skyscrapers. Those mad Americans, how they have enjoyed themselves! Competition – football, boxing, the risky diversions of cowboys – there is a quality of spirit in all that. They celebrate the completion of each skyscraper. There are festivities, while building everyone laughs, is gay, fires rockets: a success is crowned. The troubadours of the new world sing of their loves. That was during the period of prosperity. Friends! it is all new, it is the burst of youth of a new world; there are in the world, in Manhattan, new white cathedrals.

They are sublime, naïve, touching idiotic. I admire the enthusiasm which projects them into the sky. In the Olympic Games their pole vaulters surpass previous world records. Theirs are record skyscrapers.

From that task, once accomplished, resulted the death of the city at the base. The ground was killed. The fields should have been preserved. The overwhelmed local authorities inconsiderately allowed a policy of laissez faire. Nevertheless, they intervened in order to encourage further these floral games. The lawmakers concerned themselves with preventing a nocturnal darkness in the streets, in full daylight. Is their intention supported by rational considerations? No legislation has ever been so contrary to common sense. The laws forbid skyscrapers rising vertically from their bases; thus the skyscraper will become a pyramid, will fade away from the street, will slide into oblique wall surfaces and will appear to be a stylus flanked by other styluses. The drawings supplied in support of the law show that the Cartesian spirit was brushed aside in conceiving this ravishing delirium: they wanted to do something "beautiful," "living," "triumphant." They wished to make the city a tiara of innumerable cathedrals. In the twentieth century, a period of the steel skeleton and big money, everything was sacrificed to a thought which was in some ways disinterested. The debate was not dragged out, as with us, through fifty years of disputes between architects' councils, supported by magazines and exhibitions of projects on paper. No. It is in this that the USA is the USA. The city was constructed at a tremendous rate; it sprang up vertically, a skyscraper every month or it may be every three months. Skyscrapers? The city is full of them, the sky is full of them; from below it is a prodigious flaming holocaust. Let no one say lightly that Americans act only in order to pile up dollars. Here they have given proof of the strength of their enthusiasm, of their youthful openness, of their nascent exuberance.

During this epic period, in Paris – Paris stimulated by these new cries – the magistrates responsible for the destiny of the city were also trying to legislate: the six-story houses heretofore allowed are too high; their height should be limited by law to four stories. In particular, the thirty-three kilometers of the zone fortified by Napoleon III, in process of destruction, was involved; money questions cut short so many "high" thoughts. In ten years – while New York moved as a unit to a position of leadership through its gigantic undertakings – were constructed the thirty kilometers of low cost housing of the City of Paris which will remain in history. Will it be a glaring proof of definitive abdication? "French" was opposed to "American." Without ever going to see what was there, they definitively ennobled "French" by a flattering characterization: measure, our beautiful measure. These flowers of perfumed rhetoric covered a little the disturbing musty odor which assailed our noses.

Everything finally bears fruit, a tangible result was attained: the socialist commune of Boulogne, independent of Paris though representing an eminent industrial and working-class district of Paris, animated by the purest intentions, saddled itself with a magistrate's law forbidding thenceforth buildings of more than four stories. At the edge of this commune, on the very border of the zone of Napoleon III, I succeeded in completing the last normal six-story building, and I personally live in the attic comprising the seventh and eighth stories. I live at an altitude of seventy-two feet while my friend Harrison works at a height of eight hundred and twenty feet in Rockefeller Center. And when we take the elevator at the same moment, we arrive at our doors at the same time, in forty-five seconds.

During these ten years New York raised itself into the sky; but the Soviets in Moscow denounced the skyscraper as "capitalist." A denaturing of the objects in question.

During this time, also, New York, having built too many skyscrapers too small, ossified its soil, disorganized the streets to such an extent that the city officials are still disturbed by it. They no longer know what to do with their city, their streets, their destroyed circulation. In the beautiful maritime sky of Manhattan they have made sparkling cathedrals for themselves.

I am not dismayed. Americans are strong enough to admit that this tremendous flowering of the "boom period" should be demolished and replaced by structures which are noble, but also efficient. The skyscraper as a useful instrument, a function of height and the area of available ground, that is the next task for New York. It will be the third metamorphosis of the city.

8 The Uses of Sidewalks*
Jane Jacobs

Streets in cities serve many purposes besides carrying vehicles, and city sidewalks – the pedestrian parts of the streets – serve many purposes besides carrying pedestrians. These uses are bound up with circulation but are not identical with it and in their own right they are at least as basic as circulation to the proper workings of cities.

A city sidewalk by itself it nothing. It is an abstraction. It means something only in conjunction with the buildings and other uses that border it, or border other sidewalks very near it. The same might be said of streets, in the sense that they serve other purposes besides carrying wheeled traffic in their middles. Streets and their sidewalks, the main public places of a city, are its most vital organs. Think of a city and what comes to mind? Its streets. If a city's streets look interesting, the city looks interesting; if they look dull, the city looks dull.

More than that, and here we get down to the first problem, if a city's streets are safe from barbarism and fear, the city is thereby tolerably safe from barbarism and fear. When people say that a city, or a part of it, is dangerous or is a jungle what they mean primarily is that they do not feel safe on the sidewalks.

But sidewalks and those who use them are not passive beneficiaries of safety or helpless victims of danger. Sidewalks, their bordering uses, and their users, are active participants in the drama of civilization versus barbarism in cities. To keep the city safe is a fundamental task of a city's streets and its sidewalks.

This task is totally unlike any service that sidewalks and streets in little towns or true suburbs are called upon to do. Great cities are not like towns, only larger. They are not like suburbs, only denser. They differ from towns and suburbs

* Reprinted from Jane Jacobs *The Death and Life of the Great American Cities* (New York: Random House, Inc., 1961).

in basic ways, and one of these is that cities are, by definition, full of strangers. To any one person, strangers are far more common in big cities than acquaintances. More common not just in places of public assembly, but more common at a man's own doorstep. Even residents who live near each other are strangers, and must be, because of the sheer number of people in small geographical compass.

The bedrock attribute of a successful city district is that a person must feel personally safe and secure on the street among all these strangers. He must not feel automatically menaced by them. A city district that fails in this respect also does badly in other ways and lays up for itself, and for its city at large, mountain on mountain of trouble.

Today barbarism has taken over many city streets, or people fear it has, which comes to much the same thing in the end. "I live in a lovely, quiet residential area," says a friend of mine who is hunting another place to live. "The only disturbing sound at night is the occasional scream of someone being mugged." It does not take many incidents of violence on a city street, or in a city district, to make people fear the streets. And as they fear them, they use them less, which makes the streets still more unsafe.

To be sure, there are people with hobgoblins in their heads, and such people will never feel safe no matter what the objective circumstances are. But this is a different matter from the fear that besets normally prudent, tolerant and cheerful people who show nothing more than common sense in refusing to venture after dark – or in a few places, by day – into streets where they may well be assaulted, unseen or unrescued until too late.

The barbarism and the real, not imagined, insecurity that gives rise to such fears cannot be tagged a problem of the slums. The problem is most serious, in fact, in genteel-looking "quiet residential areas" like that my friend was leaving.

It cannot be tagged as a problem of older parts of cities. The problem reaches its most baffling dimensions in some examples of rebuilt parts of cities, including supposedly the best examples of rebuilding, such as middle-income projects. The police precinct captain of a nationally admired project of this kind (admired by planners and lenders) has recently admonished residents not only about hanging around outdoors after dark but has urged them never to answer their doors without knowing the caller. Life here has much in common with life for the three little pigs or the seven little kids of the nursery thrillers. The problem of sidewalk and doorstep insecurity is as serious in cities which have made conscientious efforts at rebuilding as it is in those cities that have lagged. Not is it illuminating to tag minority groups, or the poor, or the outcast with responsibility for city danger. There are immense variations in the degree of civilization and safety found among such groups and among the city areas where they live. Some of the safest sidewalks in New York City, for example, at any time of day or night, are those along which poor people or minority groups live. And some of the most dangerous are in streets occupied by the same kinds of people. All this can also be said of other cities.

Deep and complicated social ills must lie behind delinquency and crime, in suburbs and towns as well as in great cities. This book will not go into speculation on the deeper reasons. It is sufficient, at this point, to say that if we are to maintain a city society that can diagnose and keep abreast of deeper social problems, the starting point must be, in any case, to strengthen whatever workable forces for maintaining safety and civilization do exist – in the cities we do have. To build city districts that are custom made for easy crime is idiotic. Yet that is what we do.

The first thing to understand is that the public peace – the sidewalk and street peace – of cities is not kept primarily by the police, necessary as police are. It is kept primarily by an intricate, almost unconscious, network of voluntary controls and standards among the people themselves, and enforced by the people themselves. In some city areas – older public housing projects and streets with very high population turnover are often conspicuous examples – the keeping of public sidewalk law and order is left almost entirely to the police and special guards. Such places are jungles. No amount of police can enforce civilization where the normal, casual enforcement of it has broken down.

The second thing to understand is that the problem of insecurity cannot be solved by spreading people out more thinly, trading the characteristics of cities for the characteristics of suburbs. If this could solve danger on the city streets, then Los Angeles should be a safe city because superficially Los Angeles is almost all suburban. It has virtually no districts compact enough to quality as dense city areas. Yet Los Angeles cannot, any more than any other great city, evade the truth that, being a city, it *is* composed of strangers not all of whom are nice. Los Angeles' crime figures are flabbergasting. Among the seventeen standard metropolitan areas with populations over a million, Los Angeles stands so pre-eminent in crime that it is in a category by itself. And this is markedly true of crimes associated with personal attack, the crimes that make people fear the streets.

Los Angeles, for example, has a forcible rape rate (1958 figures) of 31.9 per 100 000 population, more than twice as high as either of the next two cities, which happen to be St. Louis and Philadelphia; three times as high as the rate of 10.1 for Chicago, and more than four times as high as the rate of 7.4 for New York.

In aggravated assault, Los Angeles has a rate of 185, compared with 149.5 for Baltimore and 139.2 for St. Louis (the two next highest), and with 90.9 for New York and 79 for Chicago.

The overall Los Angeles rate for major crimes is 2507.6 per 100 000 people, far ahead of St. Louis and Houston, which come next with 1634.5 and 1541.1, and of New York and Chicago, which have rates of 1145.3 and 943.5.

The reasons for Los Angeles' high crime rates are undoubtedly complex, and at least in part obscure. But of this we can be sure: thinning out a city does not ensure safety from crime and fear of crime. This is one of the conclusions that can be drawn within individual cities too, where pseudosuburbs or superannuated suburbs are ideally suited to rape, muggings, beatings, holdups and the like.

Here we come up against an all-important question about any city street: How much easy opportunity does it offer to crime? It may be that there is some absolute amount of crime in a given city, which will find an outlet somehow (I do not believe this). Whether this is so or not, different kinds of city streets garner radically different shares of barbarism and fear of barbarism.

Some city streets afford no opportunity to street barbarism. The streets of the North End of Boston are outstanding examples. They are probably as safe as any place on earth in this respect. Although most of the North End's residents are Italian or of Italian descent, the district's streets are also heavily and constantly used by people of every race and background. Some of the strangers from outside work in or close to the district; some come to shop and stroll; many, including members of minority groups who have inherited dangerous districts previously abandoned by others, make a point of cashing their paychecks in North End stores and immediately making their big weekly purchases in streets where they know they will not be parted from their money between the getting and the spending.

Frank Havey, director of the North End Union, the local settlement house, says, "I have been here in the North End twenty-eight years, and in all that time I have never heard of a single case of rape, mugging, molestation of a child or other street crime of that sort in the district. And if there had been any, I would have heard of it even if it did not reach the papers." Half a dozen times or so in the past three decades, says Havey, would-be molesters have made an attempt at luring a child or, late at night, attacking a woman. In every such case the try was thwarted by passers-by, by kibitzers from windows, or shopkeepers.

Meantime, in the Elm Hill Avenue section of Roxbury, a part of inner Boston that is suburban in superficial character, street assaults and the ever present possibility of more street assaults with no kibitzers to protect the victims, induce prudent people to stay off the sidewalks at night. Not surprisingly, for this and other reasons that are related (dispiritedness and dullness), most of Roxbury has run down. It has become a place to leave.

I do not wish to single out Roxbury or its once fine Elm Hill Avenue section especially as a vulnerable area; its disabilities, and especially its Great Blight of Dullness, are all too common in other cities too. But differences like these in public safety within the same city are worth noting. The Elm Hill Avenue section's basic troubles are not owing to a criminal or a discriminated against or a poverty-stricken population. Its troubles stem from the fact that it is physically quite unable to function safely and with related vitality as a city district.

Even within supposedly similar parts of supposedly similar places, drastic differences in public safety exist. An incident at Washington Houses, a public housing project in New York, illustrates this point. A tenants' group at this project, struggling to establish itself, held some outdoor ceremonies in mid-December 1958, and put up three Christmas trees. The chief tree, so cumbersome it was a problem to transport, erect, and trim, went into the project's inner "street," a landscaped central mall and promenade. The other two trees, each less than six feet tall and easy to carry, went on two small fringe plots at the outer corners of the project where it abuts a busy avenue and lively cross streets of the old city. The first night, the large tree and all its trimmings were stolen. The two smaller trees remained intact, lights, ornaments and all, until they were taken down at New Year's. "The place where the tree was stolen, which is *theoretically* the most safe and sheltered place in the project, is the same place that is unsafe for people too, especially children," says a social worker who had been helping the tenants' group. "People are no safer in that mall than the Christmas tree. On the other hand, the place where the other trees were safe, where the project is just one corner out of four, happens to be safe for people."

This is something everyone already knows: A well-used city street is apt to be a safe street. A deserted city street is apt to be unsafe. But how does this work, really? And what makes a city street well used or shunned? Why is the sidewalk mall in Washington Houses, which is supposed to be an attraction, shunned? Why are the sidewalks of the old city just to its west not shunned? What about streets that are busy part of the time and then empty abruptly?

A city street equipped to handle strangers, and to make a safety asset, in itself, out of the presence of strangers, as the streets of successful city neighborhoods always do, must have three main qualities.

First, there must be a clear demarcation between what is public space and what is private space. Public and private spaces cannot ooze into each other as they do typically in suburban settings or in projects.

Second, there must be eyes upon the street, eyes belonging to those we might call the natural proprietors of the street. The buildings on a street equipped to handle strangers and to insure the safety of both residents and strangers, must be oriented to the street. They cannot turn their backs or blank sides on it and leave it blind.

And third, the sidewalk must have users on it fairly continuously, both to add to the number of effective eyes on the street and to induce the people in buildings along the street to watch the sidewalks in sufficient numbers. Nobody enjoys sitting on a stoop or looking out a widow at an empty street. Almost nobody does such a thing. Large numbers of people entertain themselves, off and on, by watching street activity.

In settlements that are smaller and simpler than big cities, controls on acceptable public behavior, if not on crime, seem to operate with greater or lesser success through a web of reputation, gossip, approval, disapproval and sanctions, all of which are powerful if people know each other and word travels. But a city's streets, which must control not only the behavior of the people of the city but also of visitors from suburbs and towns who want to have a big time away from the gossip and sanctions at home, have to operate by more direct, straightforward methods. It is a wonder cities have solved such an inherently difficult problem at all. And yet in many streets they do it magnificently.

It is futile to try to evade the issue of unsafe city streets by attempting to make some other features of a locality, say interior courtyards, or sheltered play spaces, safe instead. By definition again, the streets of a city must do most of the job of handling strangers for this is where strangers come and go. The streets must not only defend the city against predatory strangers, they must protect the many, many peaceable and well-meaning strangers who use them, ensuring their safety too as they pass through. Moreover, no normal person can spend his life in some artificial haven, and this includes children. Everyone must use the streets.

On the surface, we seem to have here some simple aims: To try to secure streets where the public space is unequivocally public, physically unmixed with private or with nothing-at-all space, so that the area needing surveillance has clear and practicable limits; and to see that these public street spaces have eyes on them as continuously as possible.

But it is not so simple to achieve these objects, especially the latter. You can't make people use streets they have no reason to use. You can't make people watch streets they do not want to watch. Safety on the streets by surveillance and mutual policing of one another sounds grim, but in real life it is not grim. The safety of the street works best, most casually, and with least frequent taint of hostility or suspicion precisely where people are using and most enjoying the city streets voluntarily and are least conscious, normally, that they are policing.

The basic requisite for such surveillance is a substantial quantity of stores and other public places sprinkled along the sidewalks of a district; enterprises and public places that are used by evening and night must be among them especially. Stores, bars and restaurants, as the chief examples, work in several different and complex ways to abet sidewalk safety.

First, they give people – both residents and strangers – concrete reasons for using the sidewalks on which these enterprises face.

Second, they draw people along the sidewalks past places which have no attractions to public use in themselves but which become traveled and peopled as routes to somewhere else; this influence does not carry very far geographically, so enterprises must be frequent in a city district if they are to populate with walkers those other stretches of street that lack public places along the sidewalk. Moreover, there should be many different kinds of enterprises, to give people reasons for crisscrossing paths.

Third, storekeepers and other small businessmen are typically strong proponents of peace and order themselves; they hate broken windows and holdups; they hate having customers made nervous about safety. They are great street watchers and sidewalk guardians if present in sufficient numbers.

Fourth, the activity generated by people on errands, or people aiming for food or drink, is itself an attraction to still other people.

This last point, that the sight of people attracts still other people, is something that city planners and city architectural designers seem to find incomprehensible. They operate on the premise that city people seek the sight of emptiness, obvious order and quiet. Nothing could be less true. People's love of watching activity and other people is constantly evident in cities everywhere. This trait reaches an almost ludicrous extreme on upper Broadway in New York, where the street is divided by a narrow central mall, right in the middle of traffic. At the cross-street intersections of this long north–south mall, benches have been placed behind big concrete buffers and on any day when the weather is even barely tolerable these benches are filled with people at block after block after block, watching the pedestrians who cross the mall in front of them, watching the traffic, watching the people on the busy sidewalks, watching each other. Eventually Broadway reaches Columbia University and Barnard College, one to the right, the other to the left. Here all is obvious order and quiet. No more stores, no more activity generated by the stores, almost no more pedestrians crossing – and no more watchers. The benches are there but they go empty in even the finest weather. I have tried them and can see why. No place could be more boring. Even the students of these institutions shun the solitude. They are doing their outdoor loitering, outdoor homework and general street watching on the steps overlooking the busiest campus crossing.

It is just so on city streets elsewhere. A lively street always has both its users and pure watchers. Last year I was on such a street in the Lower East Side of Manhattan, waiting for a bus. I had not been there longer than a minute, barely long enough to begin taking in the street's activity of errand goers, children playing, and loiterers on the stoops, when my attention was attracted by a woman who opened a window on the third floor of a tenement across the street and vigorously yoo-hooed at me. When I caught on that she wanted my attention and responded, she shouted down, "The bus doesn't run here on Saturdays!" Then by a combination of shouts and pantomime she directed me around the corner. This woman was one of thousands upon thousands of people in New York who casually take care of the streets.

They notice strangers. They observe everything going on. If they need to take action, whether to direct a stranger waiting in the wrong place or to call the police, they do so. Action usually requires, to be sure, a certain self-assurance about the actor's proprietorship of the street and the support he will get if necessary, matters which will be gone into later in this book. But even more fundamental than the action and necessary to the action, is the watching itself.

Not everyone in cities helps to take care of the streets, and many a city resident or city worker is unaware of why his neighborhood is safe. The other day an incident occurred on the street where I live, and it interested me because of this point.

My block of the street, I must explain, is a small one, but it contains a remarkable range of buildings, varying from several vintages of tenements to three- and four-story houses that have been converted into low-rent flats with stores on the ground floor, or returned to single-family use like ours. Across the street there used to be mostly four-story brick tenements with stores below. But twelve years ago several buildings, from the corner to the middle of the block, were converted into one building with elevator apartments of small size and high rents.

The incident that attracted my attention was a suppressed struggle going on between a man and a little girl of eight or nine years old. The man seemed to be trying to get the girl to go with him. By turns he was directing a cajoling attention to her, and then assuming an air of nonchalance. The girl was making herself rigid, as children do when they resist, against the wall of one of the tenements across the street.

As I watched from our second-floor window, making up my mind how to intervene if it seemed advisable, I saw it was not going to be necessary. From the butcher shop beneath the tenement had emerged the woman who, with her husband, runs the shop; she was standing within earshot of the man, her arms folded and a look of determination on her face. Joe Cornacchia, who with his sons-in-law keeps the delicatessen, emerged about the same moment and stood solidly to the other side. Several heads poked out of the tenement windows above, one was withdrawn quickly and its owner reappeared a moment later in the doorway behind the man. Two men from the bar next to the butcher shop came to the doorway and waited. On my side of the street, I saw that the locksmith, the fruit man and the laundry proprietor had all come out of their shops and that the scene was also being surveyed from a number of windows besides ours. That man did not know it, but he was surrounded. Nobody was going to allow a little girl to be dragged off, even if nobody knew who she was.

I am sorry – sorry purely for dramatic purposes – to have to report that the little girl turned out to be the man's daughter.

Throughout the duration of the little drama, perhaps five minutes in all, no eyes appeared in the windows of the high-rent, small-apartment building. It was the only building of which this was true. When we first moved to our block, I used to anticipate happily that perhaps soon all the buildings would be rehabilitated like that one. I know better now, and can only anticipate with gloom and foreboding the recent news that exactly this transformation is scheduled for the rest of the block frontage adjoining the high-rent building. The high-rent tenants, most of whom are so transient we cannot even keep track of their faces,[1] have not the remotest idea of who takes care of their street, or how. A city neighborhood can absorb and protect a substantial number of these birds of passage, as our neighborhood does. But if and when the neighborhood finally *becomes* them, they will gradually find the streets less secure, they will be vaguely mystified about it, and if things get bad enough they will drift away to another neighborhood which is mysteriously safer.

In some rich city neighborhoods, where there is little do-it-yourself surveillance, such as residential Park Avenue or upper Fifth Avenue in New York, street watchers are hired. The monotonous sidewalks of residential Park Avenue, for example, are surprisingly little used; their putative users are populating, instead, the interesting store-, bar- and restaurant-filled sidewalks of Lexington Avenue and Madison Avenue to east and west, and the cross streets leading to these. A network of doormen and superintendents, of delivery boys and nursemaids, a form of hired neighborhood, keeps residential Park Avenue supplied with eyes. At night, with the security of the doormen as a bulwark, dog walkers safely venture forth and supplement the doormen. But this street is so blank of built-in eyes, so devoid of concrete reasons for using or watching it instead of turning the first corner off of it, that if its rents were to slip below the point where they could support a plentiful hired neighborhood of doormen and elevator men, it would undoubtedly become a woefully dangerous street.

Once a street is well equipped to handle strangers, once it has both a good, effective demarcation between private and public spaces and has a basic supply of activity and eyes, the more strangers the merrier.

Strangers become an enormous asset on the street on which I live, and the spurs off it, particularly at night when safety assets are most needed. We are fortunate enough, on the street, to be gifted not only with a locally supported bar and another around the corner, but also with a famous bar that draws continuous troops of strangers from adjoining neighborhoods and even from out of town. It is famous because the poet Dylan Thomas used to go there, and mentioned it in his writing. This bar, indeed, works two distinct shifts. In the morning and early afternoon it is a social gathering place for the old community of Irish longshoremen and other craftsmen in the area, as it always was. But beginning in midafternoon it takes on a different life, more like a college bull session with beer, combined with a literary cocktail party, and this continues until the early hours of the morning. On a cold winter's night, as you pass the White Horse, and the doors open, a solid wave of conversation and animation surges out and hits you; very warming. The comings and goings from this bar do much to keep our street reasonably populated until three in the morning, and it is a street always safe to come home to. The only instance I know of a beating in our street occurred in the dead hours between the closing of the bar and dawn. The beating was halted by one of our neighbors who saw it from his window and, unconsciously certain that even at night he was part of a web of strong street law and order, intervened.

A friend of mine lives on a street uptown where a church youth and community center, with many night dances and other activities, performs the same service for his street that the White Horse bar does for ours. Orthodox planning is much imbued with puritanical and Utopian conceptions of how people should spend their free time, and in planning, these moralisms on people's private lives are deeply confused with concepts about the workings of cities. In maintaining city street civilization, the White Horse bar and the church-sponsored youth center, different as they undoubtedly are, perform much the same public street civilizing service. There is not only room in cities for such differences and many more in taste, purpose and interest of occupation; cities also have a need for people with all these differences in taste and proclivity. The preferences of Utopians, and of other compulsive managers of other people's leisure, for one kind of legal enterprise over others is worse than irrelevant for cities. It is harmful. The greater and more plentiful the range of all legitimate interests (in the strictly legal sense) that city streets and their enterprises can satisfy, the better for the streets and for the safety and civilization of the city.

Suppose we continue with building, and with deliberate rebuilding, of unsafe cities. How do we live with this insecurity? From the evidence thus far, there seem to be three modes of living with it; maybe in time others will be invented but I suspect these three will simply be further developed, if that is the word for it.

The first mode is to let danger hold sway, and let those unfortunate enough to be stuck with it take the consequences. This is the policy now followed with respect to low-income housing projects, and to many middle-income housing projects.

The second mode is to take refuge in vehicles. This is a technique practiced in the big wild-animal reservations of Africa, where tourists are warned to leave their cars under no circumstances until they reach a lodge. It is also the technique practiced in Los Angeles. Surprised visitors to that city are forever recounting how the police of Beverly Hills stopped them, made them prove their reasons for being afoot, and warned them of the danger. This technique of public safety does not seem to work too effectively yet in Los Angeles, as the crime rate shows, but in time it may. And think what the crime figures might be if more people without metal shells were helpless upon the vast, blind-eyed reservation of Los Angeles.

People in dangerous parts of other cities often use automobiles as protection too, of course, or try to. A letter to the editor in the *New York Post*, reads, "I live on a dark street off Utica Avenue in Brooklyn and therefore decided to take a cab home even though it was not late. The cab driver asked that I get off at the corner of Utica, saying he did not want to go down the dark street. If I had wanted to walk down the dark street, who needed him?"

The third mode was developed by hoodlum gangs and has been adopted widely by developers of the rebuilt city. This mode is to cultivate the institution of Turf.

Under the Turf system in its historical form, a gang appropriates as its territory certain streets or housing projects or parks – often a combination of the three. Members of other gangs cannot enter this Turf without permission from the Turf-owning gang, or if they do so it is at peril of being beaten or run off. In 1956, the New York City Youth Board, fairly desperate because of gang warfare, arranged through its gang youth workers a series of truces among fighting gangs. The truces were reported to stipulate, among other provisions, a mutual understanding of Turf boundaries among the gangs concerned and agreement not to trespass.

The city's police commissioner, Stephen P. Kennedy, thereupon expressed outrage at agreements respecting Turf. The police, he said, aimed to protect the right of every person to walk any part of the city in safety and with impunity as a basic right. Pacts about Turf, he indicated, were intolerably subversive both of public rights and public safety.

I think Commissioner Kennedy was profoundly right. However, we must reflect upon the problem facing the Youth Board workers. It was a real one, and they were trying as well as they could to meet it with whatever empirical means they could. The safety of the city, on which public right and freedom of movement ultimately depend, was missing from the unsuccessful streets, parks and projects dominated by these gangs. Freedom of the city, under these circumstances, was a rather academic ideal.

Now consider the redevelopment projects of cities: the middle- and upper-income housing occupying many acres of city, many former blocks, with their own grounds and their own streets to serve these "islands within the city," "cities within the city," and "new concepts in city living," as the advertisements for them say. The technique here is also to designate the Turf and fence the other gangs out. At first the fences were never visible. Patrolling guards were sufficient to enforce the line. But in the past few years the fences have become literal.

Under the seeming disorder of the old city, wherever the old city is working successfully, is a marvelous order for maintaining the safety of the streets and the freedom of the city. It is a complex order. Its essence is intricacy of sidewalk use, bringing with it a constant succession of eyes. This order is all composed of movement and change, and although it is life, not art, we may fancifully call it the art form of the city and liken it to the dance – not to a simple-minded precision dance with everyone kicking up at the same time, twirling in unison and bowing off en masse, but to an intricate ballet in which the individual dancers and ensembles all have distinctive parts which miraculously reinforce each other and compose an orderly whole. The ballet of the good city sidewalk never repeats itself from place to place, and in any one place is always replete with new improvisations.

The stretch of Hudson Street where I live is each day the scene of an intricate sidewalk ballet. I make my own first entrance into it a little after eight when I put out the garbage can, surely a prosaic occupation, but I enjoy my part, my little clang, as the droves of junior high school students walk by the center of the stage dropping candy wrappers. (How do they eat so much candy so early in the morning?)

While I sweep up the wrappers I watch the other rituals of morning: Mr. Halpert unlocking the laundry's handcart from its mooring to a cellar door, Joe Cornacchia's son-in-law stacking out the empty crates from the delicatessen, the barber bringing out his sidewalk folding chair, Mr Goldstein arranging the coils of wire which proclaim the hardware store is open, the wife of the tenement's superintendent depositing her chunky three-year-old with a toy mandolin on the stoop, the vantage point from which he is learning the English his mother cannot speak. Now the primary children, heading for St. Luke's, dribble through to the south; the children for St. Veronica's cross, heading to the west, and the children for P.S. 41, heading toward the east. Two new entrances are being made from the wings: well-dressed and even elegant women and men with briefcases emerge from doorways and side streets. Most of these are heading for the bus and subways, but some hover on the curbs, stopping taxis which have miraculously appeared at the right moment, for the taxis are part of a wider morning ritual: having dropped passengers from midtown in the downtown financial district, they are now bringing downtowners up to midtown. Simultaneously numbers of women in housedresses have emerged and as they crisscross with one another they pause for quick conversations that sound with either laughter or joint indignation, never, it seems, anything between. It is time for me to hurry to work too, and I exchange my ritual farewell with Mr Lofaro, the short, thick-bodied, white-aproned fruit man who stands outside his doorway a little up the street, his arms folded, his feet planted, looking solid as earth itself. We nod; we each glance quickly up and down the street, then look back to each other and smile. We have done this many a morning for more than ten years, and we both know what it means: all is well.

The heart-of-the-day ballet I seldom see, because part of the nature of it is that working people who live there, like me, are mostly gone, filling the roles of strangers on other sidewalks. But from days off, I know enough of it to know that it becomes more and more intricate. Longshoremen who are not working that day gather at the White Horse or the Ideal or the International for beer and conversation. The executives and business lunchers from the industries just to the west throng the Dorgene restaurant and the Lion's Head coffee house; meat-market workers and communications scientists fill the bakery lunchroom. Character dancers come on, a strange old man with strings of old shoes over his shoulders, motor-scooter riders with big beards and girl friends who bounce on the back of the scooters and wear their hair long in front of their faces as well as behind, drunks who follow the advice of the Hat Council and are always turned out in hats, but not hats the Council would approve. Mr Lacey, the locksmith, shuts up his shop for a while and goes to exchange the time of day with Mr Slube at the cigar store. Mr Koochagian, the tailor, waters the luxuriant jungle of plants in his window, gives them a critical look from the outside, accepts a compliment on them from two passers-by, fingers the leaves on the plane tree in front of our house with a thoughtful gardener's appraisal, and crosses the street for a bite at the Ideal where he can keep an eye on customers and wigwag across the message that he is coming. The baby carriages comes out, and clusters of everyone from toddlers with dolls to teen-agers with homework gather at the stoops.

When I get home after work the ballet is reaching its crescendo. This is the time of roller skates and stilts and tricycles, and games in the lee of the stoop with bottletops and plastic cowboys; this is the time of bundles and packages, zigzagging from the drug store to the fruit stand and back over to the butcher's; this is the time when teen-agers, all dressed up, are pausing to ask if their slips show or their collars look right; this is the time when beautiful girls get out of MG's; this is the time when the fire engines go through; this is the time when anybody you know around Hudson Street will go by.

As darkness thickens and Mr Halpert moors the laundry cart to the cellar door again, the ballet goes on under lights, eddying back and forth but intensifying at the bright spotlight pools of Joe's sidewalk pizza dispensary, the bars, the delicatessen, the restaurant and the drug store. The night workers stop now at the delicatessen, to pick up salami and a container of milk. Things have settled down for the evening but the street and its ballet have not come to a stop.

I know the deep night ballet and its seasons best from waking long after midnight to tend a baby and, sitting in the dark, seeing the shadows and hearing the sounds of the sidewalk. Mostly it is a sound like infinitely pattering snatches of party conversation and, about three in the morning, singing, very good singing. Sometimes there is sharp-

ness and anger or sad, sad weeping, or a flurry of search
for a string of beads broken. One night a young man came
roaring along, bellowing terrible language at two girls whom
he had apparently picked up and who were disappointing
him. Doors opened, a wary semicircle formed around him,
not too close, until the police came. Out came the heads,
too, along Hudson Street, offering opinion, "Drunk...
Crazy... A wild kid from the suburbs."[2]

Deep in the night, I am almost unaware how many people
are on the street unless something calls them together, like
the bagpipe. Who the piper was and why he favored our
street I have no idea. The bagpipe just skirled out in the
February night, and as if it were a signal the random,
dwindled movements of the sidewalk took on direction.
Swiftly, quietly, almost magically a little crowd was there,
a crowd that evolved into a circle with a Highland fling
inside it. The crowd could be seen on the shadowy sidewalk,
the dancers could be seen, but the bagpiper himself was
almost invisible because his bravura was all in his music.
He was a very little man in a plain brown overcoat. When
he finished and vanished, the dancers and watchers ap-
plauded, and applause came from the galleries too, half a
dozen of the hundred windows on Hudson Street. Then the
windows closed, and the little crowd dissolved into the random movements of the night street.

The strangers on Hudson Street, the allies whose eyes
help us natives keep the peace of the street, are so many
that they always seem to be different people from one day
to the next. That does not matter. Whether they are so
many always-different people as they seem to be, I do not
know. Likely they are. When Jimmy Rogan fell through a
plate-glass window (he was separating some scuffling friends)
and almost lost his arm, a stranger in an old T shirt emerged
from the Ideal bar, swiftly applied an expert touniquet
and, according to the hospital's emergency staff, saved
Jimmy's life. Nobody remembered seeing the man before
and no one has seen him since. The hospital was called in
this way: a woman sitting on the steps next to the accident
ran over to the bus stop, wordlessly snatched the dime from
the hand of a stranger who was waiting with his fifteen-
cent fare ready, and raced into the Ideal's phone booth.

The stranger raced after her to offer the nickel too. Nobody remembered seeing him before, and no one has seen him since. When you see the same stranger three or four times on Hudson Street, you begin to nod. This is almost getting to be an acquaintance, a public acquaintance, of course.

I have made the daily ballet of Hudson Street sound more frenetic that it is, because writing it telescopes it. In real life, it is not that way. In real life, to be sure, something is always going on, the ballet is never at a halt, but the general effect is peaceful and the general tenor even leisurely. People who know well such animated city streets will know how it is. I am afraid people who do not will always have it a little wrong in their heads – like the old prints of rhinoceroses made from travelers' descriptions of rhinoceroses.

On Hudson Street, the same as in the North End of Boston or in any other animated neighborhoods of great cities, we are not innately more competent at keeping the sidewalks safe than are the people who try to live off the hostile truce of Turf in a blind-eyed city. We are the lucky possessors of a city order that makes it relatively simple to keep the peace because there are plenty of eyes on the street. But there is nothing simple about that order itself, or the bewildering number of components that go into it. Most of those components are specialized in one way or another. They unite in their joint effect upon the sidewalk, which is not specialized in the least. That is its strength.

Notes

1. Some, according to the storekeepers, live on beans and bread and spend their sojourn looking for a place to live where all their money will not go for rent.
2. He turned out to be a wild kid from the suburbs. Sometimes, on Hudson Street, we are tempted to believe the suburbs must be a difficult place to bring up children.

9 In the Forest of Symbols: Some Notes on Modernism in New York*
Marshall Berman

ROBERT MOSES: THE EXPRESSWAY WORLD

When you operate in an overbuilt metropolis, you have to hack your way with a meat ax.

I'm just going to keep right on building. You do the best you can to stop it.

Maxims of Robert Moses

> . . . She it was put me straight
> about the city when I said, it
>
> makes me ill to see them run up
> a new bridge like that in a few months
>
> and I can't find time even to get
> a book written. They have the power,
>
> that's all, she replied. That's what you all
> want. If you can't get it, acknowledge
>
> at least what it is. And they're not
> going to give it to you.
> (William Carlos Williams, "The Flower")

What sphinx of cement and aluminum hacked open their skulls and ate up their brains and imagination? . . . Moloch whose buildings are judgment!

Allen Ginsberg, "Howl"

Among the many images and symbols that New York has contributed to modern culture, one of the most striking in

---

* Reprinted from Marshall Berman, *All that is Solid Melts into Air* (New York: Simon and Schuster, 1982).

recent years has been an image of modern ruin and devastation. The Bronx, where I grew up, has even become an international code word for our epoch's accumulated urban nightmares: drugs, gangs, arson, murder, terror, thousands of buildings abandoned, neighborhoods transformed into garbage- and brick-strewn wilderness.

The Bronx's dreadful fate is experienced, though probably not understood, by hundreds of thousands of motorists every day, as they negotiate the Cross-Bronx Expressway, which cuts through the borough's center. This road, although jammed with heavy traffic day and night, is fast, deadly fast; speed limits are routinely transgressed, even at the dangerously curved and graded entrance and exit ramps; constant convoys of huge trucks, with grimly aggressive drivers, dominate the sight lines; cars weave wildly in and out among the trucks: it is as if everyone on this road is seized with a desperate, uncontrollable urge to get out of the Bronx as fast as wheels can take him. A glance at the cityscape to the north and south – it is hard to get more than quick glances, because much of the road is below ground level and bounded by brick walls ten feet high – will suggest why: hundreds of boarded-up abandoned buildings and charred and burnt-out hulks of buildings; dozens of blocks covered with nothing at all but shattered bricks and waste.

Ten minutes on this road, an ordeal for anyone, is especially dreadful for people who remember the Bronx as it used to be: who remember these neighborhoods as they once lived and thrived, until this road itself cut through their heart and made the Bronx, above all, a place to get out of. For children of the Bronx like myself, this road bears a load of special irony: as we race through our childhood world, rushing to get out, relieved to see the end in sight, we are not merely spectators but active participants in the process of destruction that tears our hearts. We fight back the tears, and step on the gas.

Robert Moses is the man who made all this possible. When I heard Allen Ginsberg ask at the end of the 1950s, "Who was that sphinx of cement and aluminum," I felt sure at once that, even if the poet didn't know it, Moses was his man. Like Ginsberg's "Moloch, who entered my

soul early," Robert Moses and his public works had come
into my life just before my Bar Mitzvah, and helped bring
my childhood to an end. He had been present all along, in
a vague subliminal way. Everything big that got built in
or around New York seemed somehow to be his work: the
Triborough Bridge, the West Side Highway, dozens of
parkways in Westchester and Long Island, Jones and Orchard
beaches, innumerable parks, housing developments, Idlewild
(now Kennedy) Airport, a network of enormous dams and
power plants near Niagara Falls; the list seemed to go on
forever. He had generated an event that had special magic
for me: the 1939–40 World's Fair, which I had attended
in my mother's womb, and whose elegant logo, the trylon
and perisphere, adorned our apartment in many forms –
programs, banners, postcards, ashtrays – and symbolized
human adventure, progress, faith in the future, all the heroic
ideals of the age into which I was born.

But then, in the spring and fall of 1953, Moses began to
loom over my life in a new way: he proclaimed that he was
about to ram an immense expressway, unprecedented in
scale, expense and difficulty of construction, through our
neighborhood's heart. At first we couldn't believe it; it
seemed to come from another world. First of all, hardly
any of us owned cars: the neighborhood itself, and the
subways leading downtown, defined the flow of our lives.
Besides, even if the city needed the road – or was it the
state that needed the road? (in Moses' operations, the location of power and authority was never clear, except for
Moses himself – they surely couldn't mean what the stories
seemed to say: that the road would be blasted directly
through a dozen solid, settled, densely populated neighborhoods like our own; that something like 60 000 working-
and lower-middle-class people, mostly Jews, but with many
Italians, Irish and Blacks thrown in, would be thrown out
of their homes. The Jews of the Bronx were nonplussed:
could a fellow-Jew really want to do this to us? (We had
little idea of what kind of Jew he was, or of how much we
were all an obstruction in his path.) And even if he did
want to do it, we were sure it couldn't happen here, not in
America. We were still basking in the afterglow of the New
Deal: the government was *our* government, and it would

come through to protect us in the end. And yet, before we knew, it, stream shovels and bulldozers were there, and people were getting notice that they had better clear out fast. They looked numbly at the wreckers, at the disappearing streets, at each other, and they went. Moses was coming through, and no temporal or spiritual power could block his way.

For ten years, through the late 1950s and early 1960s, the center of the Bronx was pounded and blasted and smashed. My friends and I would stand on the parapet of the Grand Concourse, where 174th Street had been, and survey the work's progress – the immense steam shovels and bulldozers and timber and steel beams, the hundreds of workers in their variously colored hard hats, the giant cranes reaching far above the Bronx's tallest roofs, the dynamite blasts and tremors, the wild, jagged crags of rock newly torn, the vistas of devastation stretching for miles to the east and west as far as the eye could see – and marvel to see our ordinary nice neighborhood transformed into sublime, spectacular ruins.

In college, when I discovered Piranesi, I felt instantly at home. Or I would return from the Columbia library to the construction site and feel myself in the midst of the last act of Goethe's *Faust*. (You had to hand it to Moses: his works gave you ideas). Only there was no humanistic triumph here to offset the destruction. Indeed, when the construction was done, the real ruin of the Bronx had just begun. Miles of streets alongside the road were choked with dust and fumes and deafening noise – most strikingly, the roar of trucks of a size and power that the Bronx had never seen, hauling heavy cargoes through the city, bound for Long Island or New England, for New Jersey and all points south, all through the day and night. Apartment houses that had been settled and stable for twenty years emptied out, often virtually overnight; large and impoverished black and Hispanic families, fleeing even worse slums, were moved in wholesale, often under the auspices of the Welfare Department, which even paid inflated rents, spreading panic and accelerating flight. At the same time, the construction had destroyed many commercial blocks, cut others off from most of their customers and left the storekeepers not only close to bankruptcy but, in their enforced isolation, increasingly vulnerable to crime. The borough's great open market, along Bathgate Avenue, still flourishing in the late 1950s, was decimated; a year after the road came through, what was left went up in smoke. Thus depopulated, economically depleted, emotionally shattered – as bad as the physical damage had been the inner wounds were worse – the Bronx was ripe for all the dreaded spirals of urban blight.

Moses seemed to glory in the devastation. When he was asked, shortly after the Cross-Bronx road's completion, if urban expressways like this didn't pose special human problems, he replied impatiently that "there's very little hardship in the thing. There's a little discomfort and even that is exaggerated." Compared with his earlier, rural and suburban highways, the only difference here was that "There are more houses in the way . . . more people in the way – that's all." He boasted that "When you operate in an over built metropolis, you have to hack your way with a meat ax."[1] The subconscious equation here – animals' corpses to be chopped up and eaten, and "people in the way" – is enough to take one's breath away. Had Allen Ginsberg put such metaphors into his Moloch's mouth, he would have never been allowed to get away with it: it would have seemed, simply, too much. Moses' flair for extravagant cruelty, along with his visionary brilliance, obsessive energy and megalo-maniac ambition, enabled him to build, over the years, a quasi-mythological reputation. He appeared as the latest in a long line of titanic builders and destroyers, in history and in cultural mythology: Louis XIV, Peter the Great, Baron Haussmann, Joseph Stalin (although fanatically anti-com-munist, Moses loved to quote the Stalinist maxim "You can't make an omelette without breaking eggs"), Bugsy Siegel (master builder of the mob, creator of Las Vegas), "Kingfish" Huey Long; Marlowe's Tamburlaine, Goethe's Faust, Cap-tain Ahab, Mr Kurtz, Citizen Kane. Moses did his best to raise himself to gigantic stature, and even came to enjoy his increasing reputation as a monster, which he believed would intimidate the public and keep potential opponents out of the way.

In the end, however – after forty years – the legend he cultivated helped to do him in: it brought him thousands

of personal enemies, some eventually as resolute and resource-
ful as Moses himself, obsessed with him, passionately dedicated to bringing the man and his machines to a stop. In
the late 1960s they finally succeeded, and he was stopped
and deprived of his power to build. But his works still
surround us, and his spirit continues to haunt our public
and private lives.

It is easy to dwell endlessly on Moses' personal power
and style. But this emphasis tends to obscure one of the
primary sources of his vast authority: his ability to convince a mass public that he was the vehicle of impersonal
world-historical forces, the moving spirit of modernity. For
forty years, he was able to pre-empt the vision of the modern. To oppose his bridges, tunnels, expressways, housing
developments, power dams, stadia, cultural centers, was –
or so it seemed – to oppose history, progress, modernity
itself. And few people, especially in New York, were prepared to do that. "There are people who like things as
they are. I can't hold out any hope to them. They have to
keep moving further away. This is a great big state, and
there are other states. Let them go to the Rockies."[2] Moses
struck a chord that for more than a century has been vital
to the sensibility of New Yorkers: our identification with
progress, with renewal and reform, with the perpetual transformation of our world and ourselves – Harold Rosenberg
called it "the tradition of the New." How many of the Jews
of the Bronx, hotbed of every form of radicalism, were willing
to fight for the sanctity of "things as they are"? Moses was
destroying our world, yet he seemed to be working in the
name of values that we ourselves embraced.

I can remember standing above the construction site for
the Cross-Bronx Expressway, weeping for my neighborhood
(whose fate I foresaw with nightmarish precision), vowing
remembrance and revenge, but also wrestling with some of
the troubling ambiguities and contradictions that Moses'
work expressed. The Grand Concourse, from whose heights
I watched and thought, was our borough's closest thing to
a Parisian boulevard. Among its most striking features were
rows of large, splendid 1930s apartment houses: simple and
clear in their architectural forms, whether geometrically
sharp or biomorphically curved; brightly colored in con-

trasting brick, offset with chrome, beautifully interplayed with large areas of glass; open to light and air, as if to proclaim a good life that was open not just to the elite residents but to us all. The style of these buildings, known as Art Deco today, was called "modern" in their prime. For my parents, who proudly described our family as a "modern" family, the Concourse buildings represented a pinnacle of modernity. We couldn't afford to live in them – though we did live in a small, modest, but still proudly "modern" building, far down the hill – but they could be admired for free, like the rows of glamorous ocean liners in port downtown. (The buildings look like shell-shocked battleships in drydock today, while the ocean liners themselves are all but extinct.)

As I saw one of the loveliest of these buildings being wrecked for the road, I felt a grief that, I can see now, is endemic to modern life. So often the price of ongoing and expanding modernity is the destruction not merely of "traditional" and "pre-modern" institutions and environments but – and here is the real tragedy – of everything most vital and beautiful in the modern world itself. Here in the Bronx, thanks to Robert Moses, the modernity of the urban boulevard was being condemned as obsolete, and blown to pieces, by the modernity of the interstate highway. *Sic transit!* To be modern turned out to be far more problematical, and more perilous, than I had been taught.

Moses was perhaps the first person in America to grasp the immense possibilities of the Roosevelt administration's commitment to public works; he grasped, too, the extent to which the destiny of American cities was going to be worked out in Washington from this point on. Now holding a joint appointment as City and State Parks Commissioner, he established close and lasting ties with the most energetic and innovative planners of the New Deal bureaucracy. He learned how to free millions of dollars in federal funds in a remarkably short time. Then, hiring a staff of first-rate planners and engineers (mostly from off the unemployment lines), he mobilized a labor army of 80 000 men and went to work with a great crash program to regenerate the city's 1700 parks (even more rundown at the nadir of the Depression than they are today) and create hundreds of new ones, plus hundreds of playgrounds and several zoos. Moses got the job done by the end of 1934. Not only did he display a gift for brilliant administration and execution, he also understood the value of ongoing public work as public spectacle. He carried on the overhauling of Central Park, and the construction of its reservoir and zoo, twenty-four hours a day, seven days a week: floodlights shined and jackhammers reverberated all through the night, not only speeding up the work but creating a new showplace that kept the public enthralled.

The workers themselves seem to have been caught up in the enthusiasm: they not only kept up with the relentless pace that Moses and his straw bosses imposed but actually outpaced the bosses, and took initiative, and came up with new ideas, and worked ahead of plans, so that the engineers were repeatedly forced to run back to their desks and redesign the plans to take account of the progress the workers had made on their own.[3] This is the modern romance of construction at its best – the romance celebrated by Goethe's Faust, by Carlyle and Marx, by the constructivists of the 1920s, by the Soviet construction films of the Five-Year Plan period, and the TVA and FSA documentaries and WPA murals of the later 1930s. What gave the romance a special reality and authenticity here is the fact that it inspired the men who were actually doing the work. They seem to have been able to find meaning and excitement in work that was physically gruelling and ill-paying, because they had some vision of the work as a whole, and believed in its value to the community of which they were a part.

The tremendous public acclaim that Moses received for his work on the city's parks served him as a springboard for something that meant far more to him than parks. This was a system of highways, parkways and bridges that would weave the whole metropolitan area together: the elevated West Side Highway, extending the length of Manhattan, and across Moses' new Henry Hudson Bridge, into and through the Bronx, and into Westchester; the Belt Parkway, sweeping around the periphery of Brooklyn, from the East River to the Atlantic, connected to Manhattan through the Brooklyn-Battery Tunnel (Moses would have preferred a bridge), and to the Southern State; and – here was the heart of the system – the Triborough Project, an enormously complex network of bridges and approaches and parkways that would link Manhattan, the Bronx and Westchester with Queens and Long Island.

These projects were incredibly expensive, yet Moses managed to talk Washington into paying for most of them. They were technically brilliant: the Triborough engineering is still a classic text today. They helped, as Moses said, to "weave together the loose strands and frayed edges of the New York metropolitan arterial tapestry," and to give this enormously complex region a unity and coherence it had never had. They created a series of spectacular new visual approaches to the city, displaying the grandeur of Manhattan from many new angles – from the Belt Parkway, the Grand Central, the upper West Side – and nourishing a whole new generation of urban fantasies.[4] The uptown Hudson riverfront, one of Moses' finest urban landscapes, is especially striking when we realize that (as Caro shows, in pictures) it was a wasteland of hoboes' shacks and garbage dumps before he got there. You cross the George Washington Bridge and dip down and around and slide into the gentle curve of the West Side Highway, and the lights and towers of Manhattan flash and glow before you, rising above the lush greenness of Riverside Park, and even the most embittered enemy of Robert Moses – or, for that matter, of New York – will be touched: you know you have come home again, and the city is there for you, and you can thank Moses for that.

At the very end of the 1930s, when Moses was at the height of his creativity, he was canonized in the book that, more than any other, established the canon of the modern movement in architecture, planning and design: Siegfried Giedion's *Space, Time and Architecture*. Giedion's work, first delivered in lecture form at Harvard in 1938–9, unfolded the history of three centuries of modern design and planning – and presented Moses' work as its climax. Giedion presented large photos of the recently completed West Side Highway, the Randall's Island cloverleaf, and the "pretzel" interchange of the Grand Central Parkway. These works, he said, "proved that possibilities of a great scale are inherent in our period." Giedion compared Moses' parkways to cubist paintings, to abstract sculptures and mobiles, and to the movies. "As with many of the creations born out of the spirit of this age, the meaning and beauty of the parkway cannot be grasped from a single point of observation, as was possible from a window of the château at Versailles. It can be revealed only by movement, by going along in a steady flow, as the rules of traffic prescribe. The space–time feeling of our period can seldom be felt so keenly as when driving."[5]

Thus Moses' projects marked not only a new phase in the modernization of urban space but a new breakthrough in modernist vision and thought. For Giedion, and for the whole generation of the 1930s – Corbusierian or Bauhaus formalists and technocrats, Marxists, even agrarian neopopulists – these parkways opened up a magical realm, a kind of romantic bower in which modernism and pastoralism could intertwine. Moses seemed to be the one public figure in the world who understood "the space–time conception of our period"; in addition, he had "the energy and enthusiasm of a Haussmann." This made him "uniquely equal, as Haussmann himself had been equal, to the opportunities and needs of the period," and uniquely qualified to build "the city of the future" in our time. Hegel in 1806 had conceived of Napoleon as "the *Weltseele* on horse"; for Giedion in 1939, Moses looked like the *Weltgeist* on wheels.[6]

Moses received a further apotheosis at the 1939–40 New York World's Fair, an immense celebration of modern technology and industry: "Building the World of Tomorrow." Two of the fair's most popular exhibits – the commercially oriented General Motors Futurama and the utopian Democracity – both envisioned elevated urban expressways and arterial parkways connecting city and country, in precisely the forms that Moses had just built. Spectators on their way to and from the fair, as they flowed along Moses' roads and across his bridges, could directly experience something of this visionary future, and see that it seemed to work.

Moses, in his capacity as Parks Commissioner, had put together the parcel of land on which the fair was being held. With lightning speed, at minimal cost, with his typical fusion of menace and finesse, he had seized from hundreds of owners a piece of land the size of downtown Manhattan. His proudest accomplishment in this affair was to have destroyed the notorious Flushing ash heaps and mounds of garbage that Scott Fitzgerald had immortalized as one of the great modern symbols of industrial and human waste:

> a valley of ashes – a fantastic farm where ashes grow like wheat into ridges and hills and grotesque gardens; where ashes take the forms of houses and chimneys and rising smoke and, finally, with a transcendent effort, of men who move dimly and already crumbling through the powdery air. Occasionally a line of gray cars crawls along an invisible track, gives out a ghastly creak, and comes to rest, and immediately the ash-gray men swarm up with leaden spades and stir up an impenetrable cloud, which screens their obscure operations from your sight. (*The Great Gatsby*, Chapter 2).

Moses obliterated this dreadful scene and transformed the site into the nucleus of the fairgrounds, and later of Flushing Meadow Park. This action moved him to a rare effusion of Biblical lyricism: he invoked the beautiful passage from Isaiah (61:1–4) in which "the Lord has anointed me to bring good tidings to the afflicted; he has sent me to bind up the brokenhearted, to proclaim liberty to the captives, and the opening of the prison to those that are bound; . . . to give unto them beauty for ashes . . . [so that] they shall repair the ruined cities, the devastations of many generations." Forty years later, in his last interviews, he still pointed to this with special pride: I am the man who destroyed the Valley of Ashes and put beauty in its place. It is on this note – with the fervent faith that modern technology and social organization could create a world without ashes – that the modernism of the 1930s came to an end.

Where did it all go wrong? How did the modern visions of the 1930s turn sour in the process of their realization?

The dark side was always there in Moses himself. Here is the testimony of Frances Perkins – America's first Secretary of Labor under FDR – who worked closely with Moses for many years and admired him all her life. She recalls the people's heartfelt love for Moses in the early years of the New Deal, when he was building playgrounds in Harlem and on he Lower East Side; however, she was disturbed to discover, "he doesn't love the people" in return:

> It used to shock me because he was doing all these things for the welfare of the people. . . . To him, they were lousy, dirty people, throwing bottles all over Jones Beach. "I'll get them! I'll teach them!" He loves the public, but not as people. The public is . . . a great amorphous mass to him; it needs to be bathed, it needs to be aired, it needs recreation, but not for personal reasons – just to make it a better public.[7]

"He loves the public, but not as people": Dostoevsky warned us repeatedly that the combination of love for "humanity" with hatred for actual people was one of the fatal hazards of modern politics. During the New Deal period, Moses managed to maintain a precarious balance between the poles and to bring real happiness not only to "the public" he loved but also to the people he loathed. But no one could keep up this balancing act forever. "I'll get them! I'll teach them!" The voice here is unmistakably that of Mr Kurtz: "It was very simple," Conrad's narrator says, "and at the end of every idealistic sentiment it blazed at you, luminous and terrifying, like a flash of lightning in a serene sky: 'Exterminate all the brutes!'" We need to know what was Moses' equivalent for Mr Kurtz's African ivory trade, what historical chances and institutional forces opened up the floodgates of his most dangerous drives: What was the road that led him from the radiance of "give unto them beauty for ashes" to "you have to hack your way with a meat ax" and the darkness that cleft the Bronx?

Part of Moses' tragedy is that he was not only corrupted but in the end undermined by one of his greatest achievements. This was a triumph that, unlike Moses' public works, was for the most part invisible: it was only in the late 1950s that investigative reporters began to perceive it. It was the creation of a network of enormous, interlocking "public authorities," capable of raising virtually unlimited sums of money to build with, and accountable to no executive, legislative or judicial power.[8]

The English institution of a "public authority" had been grafted onto American public administration early in the twentieth century. It was empowered to sell bonds to construct particular public works – e.g., bridges, harbors, railroads. When its project was completed, it would charge tolls for use until its bonds were paid off; at that point it would ordinarily go out of existence and turn its public work over to the state. Moses, however, saw that there was no reason for an authority to limit itself in time or space: so long as money was coming in – say, from tolls on the Triborough Bridge – and so long as the bond market was encouraging, an authority could trade in its old bonds for new ones, to raise more money, to build more works; so long as money (all of it tax-exempt) kept coming in, the banks and institutional investors would be only too glad to underwrite new bond issues, and the authority could go on building forever. Once the initial bonds were paid off, there would be no need to go to the city, state or federal governments, or to the people, for money to build. Moses proved in court that no government had any legal right even to look into an authority's books. Between the late 1930s and the late 1950s, Moses created or took over a dozen of these authorities – for parks, bridges, highways, tunnels, electric power, urban renewal and more – and integrated them into an immensely powerful machine, a machine with innumerable wheels within wheels, transforming its cogs into millionaires, incorporating thousands of businessmen and politicians into its production line, drawing millions of New Yorkers inexorably into its widening gyre.

Kenneth Burke suggested in the 1930s that whatever we might think of the social value of Standard Oil and U.S. Steel, Rockefeller's and Carnegie's work in creating these giant complexes had to be rated as triumphs of modern art. Moses' network of public authorities clearly belongs in this company. It fulfills one of the earliest dreams of modern science, a dream renewed in many forms of twentieth-century art: to create a system in perpetual motion. But Moses' system, even as it constitutes a triumph of modern art, shares in some of that art's deepest authorities. It carries the contradiction between "the public" and the people so far that in the end not even the people at the system's center – not even Moses himself – had the authority to shape the system and control its ever-expanding moves.

If we go back to Giedion's "bible," we will see some of the deeper meanings of Moses' work which Moses himself never really grasped. Giedion saw the Triborough Bridge, the Grand Central Parkway, the West Side Highway, as expressions of "the new form of the city." This form de- manded "a different scale from that of the existing city, with its *rues corridors* and rigid divisions into small blocks." The new urban forms could not function freely within the framework of the nineteenth-century city: hence, "It is the actual structure of the city that must be changed." The first imperative was this: "There is no longer any place for the city street; it cannot be permitted to persist." Giedion took on an imperial voice here that was strongly reminiscent of Moses' own. But the destruction of the city streets was, for Giedion, only a beginning: Moses' highways "look ahead to the time when, after the necessary surgery has been performed, the artificially swollen city will be reduced to its natural size."[9]

Leaving aside the quirks in Giedion's own vision (what makes any urban size more "natural" than any other?), we see here how modernism makes a dramatic new departure: the development of modernity has made the modern city itself old-fashioned, obsolete. True, the people, visions and institutions of the city have created the highway – "To New York . . . must go the credit for the creation of the parkway."[10] Now, however, by a fateful dialectic, because the city and the highway don't go together, the city must go. Ebenezer Howard and his "Garden City" disciples had been suggesting something like this since the turn of the century. Moses' historical mission, from the standpoint of this vision, is to have created a new superurban reality that makes the city's obsolescence clear. To cross the Triborough Bridge, for Giedion, is to enter a new "space–time con- tinuum," one that leaves the modern metropolis forever behind. Moses has shown that it is unnecessary to wait for some distant future: we have the technology and the or- ganizational tools to bury the city here and now.

Moses never meant to do this: unlike the "Garden City" thinkers, he genuinely loved New York – in his blind way – and never meant it any harm. His public works, whatever we may think of them, were meant to add something to

city life, not to subtract the city itself. He would surely
have recoiled at the thought that his 1939 World's Fair,
one of the great moments in New York's history, would be
the vehicle of a vision which, taken at face value, would
spell the city's ruin. But when have world-historical figures ever understood the long-range meaning of their acts
and works? In fact, however, Moses' great construction in
and around New York in the 1920s and 30s served as a
rehearsal for the infinitely greater reconstruction of the whole
fabric of America after World War Two. The motive forces
in this reconstruction were the multibillion-dollar Federal
Highway Program and the vast suburban housing initiatives of the Federal Housing Administration. This new order integrated the whole nation into a unified flow whose
lifeblood was the automobile. It conceived of cities principally as obstructions to the flow of traffic, and as junk-
yards of substandard housing and decaying neighborhoods
from which Americans should be given every chance to
escape. Thousands of urban neighborhoods were obliterated by this new order; what happened to my Bronx was
only the largest and most dramatic instance of something
that was happening all over. Three decades of massively
capitalized highway construction and FHA suburbanization
would serve to draw millions of people and jobs, and billions of dollars in investment capital, out of America's cities,
and plunge these cities into the chronic crisis and chaos that
plague their inhabitants today. This wasn't what Moses meant
at all; but it was what he inadvertently helped to bring about.[11]

Moses' projects of the 1950s and 60s had virtually none
of the beauty of design and human sensitivity that had distinguished his early works. Drive twenty miles or so on the
Northern State Parkway (1920s), then turn around and cover
those same twenty miles on the parallel Long Island Expressway (1950s/60s), and wonder and weep. Nearly all he
built after the war was built in an indifferently brutal style,
made to overawe and overwhelm: monoliths of steel and
cement, devoid of vision or nuance or play, sealed off from
the surrounding city by great moats of stark empty space,
stamped on the landscape with a ferocious contempt for
all natural and human life. Now Moses seemed scornfully
indifferent to the human quality of what he did: sheer

quantity – of moving vehicles, tons of cement, dollars received and spent – seemed to be all that drove him now. There are sad ironies in this, Moses' last, worst phase.

The cruel works that cracked open the Bronx ("more people in the way – that's all") were part of a social process whose dimensions dwarfed even Moses' own megalomaniac will to power. By the 1950s he was no longer building in accord with his own visions; rather, he was fitting enormous blocks into a pre-existing pattern of national reconstruction and social integration that he had not made and could not have substantially changed. Moses at his best had been a true creator of new material and social possibilities. At his worst, he would become not so much a destroyer – though he destroyed plenty – as an executioner of directives and imperatives not his own. He had gained power and glory by opening up new forms and media in which modernity could be experienced as an adventure; he used that power and glory to institutionalize modernity into a system of grim, inexorable necessities and crushing routines. Ironically, he became a focus for mass personal obsession and hatred, including my own, just when he had lost personal vision and initiative and become an Organization Man; we came to know him as New York's Captain Ahab at a point when, although still at the wheel, he had lost control of the ship.

This old man possessed an undeniable tragic grandeur; but it is not so clear that he ever achieved the self-awareness that is supposed to go with that grandeur. Replying to *The Power Broker*, Moses appealed plaintively to us all: Am I not the man who blotted out the Valley of Ashes and gave mankind beauty in its place? It is true, and we owe him homage for it. And yet, he did not really wipe out the ashes, only moved them to another site. For the ashes are part of us, no matter how straight and smooth we make our beaches and freeways, no matter how fast we drive – or are driven no matter how far out on Long Island we go.

THE 1960s: A SHOUT IN THE STREET

  – History, Stephen said, is a nightmare from which I am trying to awake.

From the playfield the boys raised a shout. A whirring whistle: goal. What if that nightmare gave you a back kick?
– The ways of the Creator are not our ways, Mr. Deasy said. All history moves toward one goal, the manifestation of God.
Stephen jerked his thumb toward the window, saying:
– That is God.
Hooray! Ay! Whrrwhee!
– What? Mr. Deasy asked.
– A shout in the street, Stephen answered.

James Joyce, Ulysses

I am for an art that tells you the time of day, or where such and such a street is. I am for an art that helps old ladies across the street.

Claes Oldenburg

The expressway world, the modern environment that emerged after World War Two, would reach a pinnacle of power and self-confidence in the 1960s, in the America of the New Frontier, the Great Society, Apollo on the moon. I have been focusing on Robert Moses as the New York agent and incarnation of that world, but Secretary of Defense McNamara, Admiral Rickover, NASA Director Gilruth, and many others, were fighting similar battles with equal energy and ruthlessness, far beyond the Hudson, and indeed beyond the planet Earth. The developers and devotees of the expressway world presented it as the only possible modern world: to oppose them and their works was to oppose modernity itself, to fight history and progress, to be a Luddite, an escapist, afraid of life and adventure and change and growth. This strategy was effective because, in fact, the vast majority of modern men and women do not want to resist modernity: they feel its excitement and believe in its promise, even when they find themselves in its way.

Before the Molochs of the modern world could be effectively fought, it would be necessary to develop a modernist vocabulary of opposition. This is what Stendhal, Buechner, Marx and Engels, Kierkegaard, Baudelaire, Dostoevsky, Nietzsche, were doing a century ago; it is what Joyce and Eliot, the dadaists and surrealists, Kafka, Zamyatin,

Babel and Mandelstam, were doing earlier in our century. However, because the modern economy has an infinite capacity for redevelopment and self-transformation, the modernist imagination, too, must reorient and renew itself again and again. One of the crucial tasks for modernists in the 1960s was to confront of the expressway world; another was to show that this was not the only possible modern world, that there were other, better directions in which the modern spirit could move.

If there is one work that perfectly expresses the modernism of the street in the 1960s, it is Jane Jacobs' remarkable book *The Death and Life of Great American Cities.* Jacobs' work has often been appreciated for its role in changing the whole orientation of city and community planning. This is true, and admirable, but it suggests only a small part of what the book contains. By quoting Jacobs at length in the next few page, I want to convey the richness of her thought. I believe that her book played a crucial role in the development of modernism: its message was that much of the meaning for which modern men and women were desperately searching in fact lay surprisingly close to home, close to the surface and immediacy of their lives: it was all right there, if we could only learn to dig.[12]

Jacobs develops her vision with a deceptive modesty: all she is doing is talking about her everyday life. "The stretch of Hudson Street where I live is each day the scene of an intricate sidewalk ballet." She goes on to trace twenty-four hours in the life of her street and, of course, of her own life on that street. Her prose often sounds plain, almost artless. In fact, however, she is working within an important genre in modern art: the urban montage. As we go through her twenty-four-hour life cycle, we are likely to experience a sense of déjà vu. Haven't we been through this somewhere before? Yes, we have, if we have read or heard or seen Gogol's "Nevsky Prospect," Joyce's *Ulysses,* Walter Ruttmann's *Berlin, Symphony of a Great City,* Dziga Vertov's *Man with the Movie Camera,* Dylan Thomas' *Under Milk Wood.* Indeed, the better we know this tradition, the more we will appreciate what Jacobs does with it.

Jacobs begins her montage in the early morning: she enters the street to put out her garbage and to sweep up the candy wrappers that are being dropped by junior high school students on their way to school. She feels a ritual satisfaction from this, and, as she sweeps, "I watch the other rituals of morning: Mr Halpert unlocking the laundry's handcart from its mooring to a cellar door, Joe Cornacchia's son-in-law stacking out the empty crates from the delicatessen, the barber bringing out his sidewalk folding chair, Mr Goldstein arranging the coils of wire that proclaim that the hardware store is open, the wife of the tenement's superintendent depositing her chunky three-year-old with a toy mandolin on the stoop, the vantage point from which he is learning the English his mother cannot speak."

Interwoven with these known and friendly faces, there are hundreds of strangers passing through: housewives with baby carriages, teenagers gossiping and comparing their hair, young secretaries and elegant middle-aged couples on their way to work, workers coming off the night shift and stopping by the corner bar. Jacobs contemplates and enjoys them all: she experiences and evokes what Baudelaire called the "universal communion" available to the man or woman who knows how to "take a bath of multitude."

By and by, it is time for her to rush off to work, "and I exchange my ritual farewell with Mr. Lofaro, the short, thick-bodied, white-aproned fruit man who stands outside his door a little up the street, his arms folded, his feet planted, looking solid as earth itself. We nod; ew each glance quickly up the street, then look back to each other and smile. We have done this many a morning for more than ten years, and we both know what it means: All is well." So it goes as Jacobs takes us through the day and into the night, bringing the children home from school and the adults back from work, bringing forth an abundance of new characters – businessmen, longshoremen, young and old bohemians, scattered solitaries – as they come to and pass along the street in search of food or drink or play or sex or love.

Gradually the life of the street subdues, but it never stops. "I know the deep night ballet and its seasons best from waking long after midnight to tend a baby, and sitting in the dark, seeing the shadows and hearing the sounds of the sidewalk." She attunes herself to these sounds. "Sometimes there is sharpness and anger, or sad, sad weeping . . .

about three in the morning, singing, very good singing." Is
that a bagpipe out there? Were can the piper be coming
from, and where is he going? She'll never know; but this
very knowledge, that her street's life is inexhaustibly
rich, beyond her (or anyone's) power to grasp, helps her
sleep well.

This celebration of urban vitality, diversity and fullness
of life is in fact, as I have tried to show, one of the oldest
themes in modern culture. Throughout the age of
Haussmann and Baudelaire, and well into the twentieth
century, this urban romance crystallized around the street,
which emerged as a primary symbol of modern life. From
the small-town "Main Street" to the metropolitan "Great
White Way" and "Dream Street," the street was experienced
as the medium in which the totality of modern material
and spiritual forces could meet, clash, interfuse and work
out their ultimate meanings and fates. This was what Joyce's
Stephen Dedalus had in mind in his cryptic suggestion that
God was out there, in the "shout in the street."

However, the makers of the post-World War One "modern movement" in architecture and urbanism turned radically against this modern romance: they marched to Le
Corbusier's battle cry, "We must kill the street." It was
their modern vision that triumphed in the great wave of
reconstruction and redevelopment that began after World
War Two. For twenty years, streets everywhere were at best
passively abandoned and often (as in the Bronx) actively
destroyed. Money and energy were rechanneled to the new
highways and to the vast system of industrial parks, shopping centers and dormitory suburbs that the highways were
opening up. Ironically, then, within the space of a generation, the street, which had always served to express dynamic
and progressive modernity, now came to symbolize everything dingy, disorderly, sluggish, stagnant, worn-out, obsolete – everything that the dynamism and progress of
modernity were supposed to leave behind.[13]

In this context, the radicalism and originality of
Jacobs' work should be clear. "Under the seeming disorder of the old city," she says, and "old" here means nineteenth-century modern, the remains of the city of the
Haussmann age,

Under the seeming disorder of the old city is a marvelous order for maintaining the safety of the streets and the freedom of the city. It is a complex order. Its essence is intricacy of sidewalk use, bringing with it a constant succession of eyes. This order is all composed of movement and change, and although it is life, not art, we may fancifully call it the art form of the city, and liken it to the dance.

Thus we must strive to keep this "old" environment alive, because it is uniquely capable of nourishing modern experiences and values: the freedom of the city, an order that exists in a state of perpetual motion and change, the evanescent but intense and complex face-to-face communication and communion, of what Baudelaire called the family of eyes. Jacobs' point is that the so-called modern movement has inspired billions of dollars' worth of "urban renewal" whose paradoxical result has been to destroy the only kind of environment in which modern values can be realized. The practical corollary of all this – which sounds paradoxical at first, but in fact makes perfect sense – is that in our city life, for the sake of the modern we must preserve the old and resist the new. With this dialectic, modernism takes on a new complexity and depth.

There is another crucial prophetic theme in Jacobs' book that no one seems to have noticed at the time. *The Death and Life of Great American Cities* gives us the first fully articulated woman's view of the city since Jane Addams. In one sense Jacobs' perspective is even more fully feminine: she writes out of an intensely lived domesticity that Addams knew only at second hand. She knows her neighborhood in such precise twenty-four-hour detail because she has been around it all day, in ways that most women are normally around all day, especially when they become mothers, but hardly any men ever are, except when they become chronically unemployed. She knows all the shopkeepers, and the vast informal social networks they maintain, because it is her responsibility to take care of her household affairs. She portrays the ecology and phenomenology of the sidewalks with uncanny fidelity and sensitivity, because she has spent years piloting children (first in carriages and strollers, then on roller skates and bikes) through these troubled waters, while balancing heavy shopping bags, talking to neighbors and trying to keep hold of her life. Much of her intellectual authority springs from her perfect grasp of the structures and processes of everyday life. She makes her readers feel that women know what it is like to live in cities, street by street, day by day, far better than the men who plan and build them.[14]

Jacobs never uses expressions like "feminism" or "women's rights" – in 1960 there were few words that were remoter from current concerns. Nevertheless, in unfolding a woman's perspective on a central public issue, and in making that perspective rich and complex, trenchant and compelling, she opened the way for the great wave of feminist energy that burst at the end of the decade. The feminists of the 1970s would do much to rehabilitate the domestic worlds, "hidden from history," which women had created and sustained for themselves through the ages. They would argue, too, that many of women's traditional decorative patterns, textiles, quilts and rooms possessed not only aesthetic value in their own right but also the power to enrich and deepen modern art. For anyone who had encountered the Jacobs persona, the author of *The Death and Life*, at once lovingly domestic and dynamically modern, this possibility made instant sense. Thus she nourished not only a renewal of feminism but also an increasingly widespread male realization that, yes, women had something to tell us about the city and the life we shared, and that we had impoverished our own lives as well as theirs by not listening to them till now.

Jacobs' thought and action heralded a great new wave of community activism, and activists, in all dimensions of political life. These activists have very often been wives and mothers, like Jacobs, and they have assimilated the language – celebration of the family and neighborhood, and their defense against outside forces that would shatter their life – that she did so much to create. But some of their activities suggest that a shared language and emotional tone may conceal radically opposed visions of what modern life is and what it should be. Any careful reader of *The Death and Life of Great American Cities* will realize that Jacobs is celebrating the family and the block in distinctively modernist terms: her ideal street is full of strangers passing through, of people of many different classes, ethnic groups, ages, beliefs and life-styles; her ideal family is one in which women go out to work, men spend a great deal of time at home, both parents work in small and easily manageable units close to home, so that children can discover and grow into a world where there are two sexes and where work plays a central role in everyday life.

Jacobs' street and family are microcosms of all the diversity and fullness of the modern world as a whole. But for some people who seem at first to speak her language, family and locality turn out to be symbols of radical anti-modernism: for the sake of the neighborhood's integrity, all racial minorities, sexual and ideological deviants, controversial books and films, minority modes of music and dress, are to be kept out; in the name of the family, woman's economic, sexual and political freedom must be crushed – she must be kept in her place on the block literally twenty-four hours a day. This is the ideology of the New Right, an inwardly contradictory but enormously powerful movement as old as modernity itself, a movement that utilizes every modern technique of publicity and mass mobilization to turn people against the modern ideals of life, liberty and the pursuit of happiness for all.

What is relevant and disturbing here is that ideologues of the New Right have more than once cited Jacobs as one of their patron saints. Is this connection entirely fraudulent? Or is there something in Jacobs that leaves her open to this misuse? It seems to me that beneath her modernist text there is an anti-modernist subtext, a sort of undertow of nostalgia for a family and a neighborhood in which the self could be securely embedded, *ein 'feste Burg*, a solid refuge against all the dangerous currents of freedom and ambiguity in which all modern men and women are caught up. Jacobs, like so many modernists from Rousseau and Wordsworth to D. H. Lawrence and Simone Weil, moves in a twilight zone where the line between the richest and most complex modernism and the rankest bad faith of modernist anti-modernism is very thin and elusive, if indeed there is a line at all.

There is another order of difficulty in Jacobs' perspective. Sometimes her vision seems positively pastoral: she insists, for instance, that in a vibrant neighborhood with a mixture of shops and residences, with constant activity on the sidewalks, with easy surveillance of the streets from within houses and stores, there will be no crime. As we read this, we wonder what planet Jacobs can possibly have been thinking of. If we look back a little skeptically at her vision of her block, we may see the trouble. Her inventory of the people in her neighborhood has the aura of a WPA mural or a Hollywood version of a World War Two bomber crew: every race, creed and color working together to keep America free for you and me. We can hear the roll call: "Holmstrom ... O'Leary ... Scagliano... Levy ... Washington..." But wait – here is the problem: there is no "Washington" in Jacobs' bomber, i.e., no blacks on her block. This is what makes her neighborhood vision seem pastoral: it is the city before the blacks got there. Her world ranges from solid working-class whites at the bottom to professional middle-class whites at the top. There is nothing and no one above; what matters more here, however, is that there is nothing and no one below – there are no stepchildren in Jacobs' family of eyes.

In the course of the 1960s, however, millions of black and Hispanic people would converge on America's cities – at precisely the moment when the jobs they sought, and the opportunities that earlier poor immigrants had found, were departing or disappearing. (This was symbolized in New York by the closing of the Brooklyn Navy Yard, once the city's largest employer.) Many of them found themselves desperately poor, chronically unemployed, at once racial and economic outcasts, an enormous *lumpenproletariat* without prospects or hopes. In these conditions, it is no wonder that rage, despair and violence spread like plagues – and that hundreds of formerly stable urban neighborhoods all over America disintegrated completely. Many neighborhoods, including Jacobs' own West Village, remained relatively intact, and even incorporated some blacks and Hispanics into their families of eyes. But it was clear by the late 1960s that, amid the class disparities and racial polarities that skewered American city life, no urban neighborhood anywhere, not even the liveliest and healthiest, could be free from crime, random violence, pervasive rage and fear. Jacobs' faith in the benignness of the sounds she heard from the street in the middle of the night was bound to be, at best, a dream.

What light does Jacobs' vision shed on the life of the Bronx? Even if she misses some of the shadows of neighborhood life, she is marvelous at capturing its radiance, an inner as well as outer radiance that class and ethnic conflict might complicate but could not destroy. Any child of the Bronx who goes through Hudson Street with Jacobs will recognize, and mourn for, many streets of our own. We can remember attuning ourselves to their sights and sounds and smells, and feeling ourselves in harmony with them – even if we knew, perhaps better than Jacobs knew, that there was plenty of dissonance out there as well. But so much of this Bronx, our Bronx, is gone today, and we know we will never feel so much at home anywhere again. Why did it go? Did it have to go? Was there anything we could have done to keep it alive? Jacobs' few fragmentary references to the Bronx display a Greenwich Villager's snobbish ignorance: her theory, however, clearly implies that shabby but vibrant neighborhoods like those of the central Bronx should be able to find the inner resources to sustain and perpetuate themselves. Is the theory right?

Here is where Robert Moses and his Expressway come in: he turned potential long-range entropy into sudden inexorable catastrophe; destroying scores of neighborhoods from without, he left it forever unknown whether they would have collapsed or renewed themselves from within. But Robert Caro, working from a Jacobean perspective, makes a powerful case for the inner strength of the central Bronx, had it only been left to itself. In two chapters of *The Power Broker*, both entitled "One Mile," Caro describes the destruction of a neighborhood about a mile from my own. He begins by painting a lovely panorama of this neighborhood, a sentimental but recognizable blend of Jacobs' Hudson Street with *Fiddler on the Roof*. Caro's evocative power sets us up for shock and horror when we see Moses on the horizon moving inexorably ahead. It appears that the Cross-Bronx Expressway could have been slightly curved around this neighborhood. Even Moses' engineers found it feasible to reroute. But the great man would not have it: he deployed every form of force and fraud, intrigue and mystification, at his command, obsessively determined to grind this little world into dust. (When Caro asked him twenty years later how come a leader of the people's protest had suddenly caved in, Moses' reply was cryptic but gloating: "After he was hit over the head with an ax.")[15] Caro's prose becomes incandescent, and utterly devastating, as he shows the blight spreading outward from the Expressway, block by block, year by year, while Moses, like a reincarnated General Sherman run wild in the streets of the North, blazed a path of terror from Harlem to the Sound.

All Caro says here seems to be true. And yet, and yet, it is not the whole truth. There are more questions we need to ask ourselves. What if the Bronxites of the 1950s had possessed the conceptual tools, the vocabulary, the widespread public sympathy, the flair for publicity and mass mobilization, that residents of many American neighborhoods would acquire in the 1960s? What if, like Jacobs' lower Manhattan neighbors a few years later, we had managed to keep the dread road from being built? How many of us would still be in the Bronx today, caring for it and fighting for it as our own? Some of us, no doubt, but I suspect not so many, and in any case – it hurts to say it – not me. For the Bronx of my youth was possessed, inspired, by the great modern dream of mobility. To live well meant to move up socially, and this in turn meant to move out physically; to live one's life close to home was not to be alive at all. Our parents, who had moved up and out from the Lower East Side, believed this just as devoutly as we did – even though their hearts might break when we went. Not even the radicals of my youth disputed this dream – and the Bronx of my childhood was full of radicals – their only complaint was that the dream wasn't being fulfilled, that people weren't able to move fast or freely or equally enough. But when you see life this way, no neighborhood or environment can be anything more than a stage along life's way, a launching pad for higher flights and wider orbits than your own. Even Molly Goldberg, earth goddess of the Jewish Bronx, had to move. (After Philip Loeb, who played Molly's husband, had been moved – by the Blacklist – off the air and, soon after, off the earth.) Ours was, as Leonard Michaels put it, "the mentality of neighborhood types who, quick as possible, got the hell out of their neighborhoods." Thus we had no way to resist the wheels that drove the American dream, because it was driving us ourselves – even though we knew the wheels might break us. All through the decades of the postwar boom, the desperate energy of this vision, the frenzied economic and psychic pressure to move up and out, was breaking down hundreds of neighborhoods like the Bronx, even where there was no Moses to lead the exodus and no Expressway to make it fast.

Thus there was no way a Bronx boy or girl could avoid the drive to move on: it was planted within us as well as outside. Moses entered our souls early. But it was at least possible to think about what directions to move in, and at what speed, and with what human toll. One night in 1967, at an academic reception, I was introduced to an older child of the Bronx, Herman Khan, who had grown up to be a famous futurologist and creator of scenarios for nuclear war. He had just come back from Vietnam, and I was active in the anti-war movement, but I didn't want trouble just then, so I asked about his years in the Bronx instead. We talked pleasantly enough, till I told him that Moses' road was going to blow every trace of both our childhoods away. Fine, he said, the sooner the better; didn't I understand that the destruction of the Bronx would fulfill the Bronx's own basic moral imperative? What moral imperative? I asked. He laughed as he bellowed in my face: "You want to know the morality of the Bronx? 'Get out, schmuck, get out!'" For once in my life, I was stunned into silence. It was the brutal truth: I had left the Bronx, just as he had, and just as we were all brought up to, and now the Bronx was collapsing not just because of Robert Moses but also because of all of us. It was true, but did he have to laugh? I pulled back and went home as he began to explain Vietnam.

Why did the futurologist's laughter make me want to cry? He was laughing off what struck me as one of the starkest facts of modern life: that the split in the minds and the wound in the hearts of the men and women on the move – like him, like me – were just as real and just as deep as the drives and dreams that made us go. His laughter carried all the easy confidence of our official culture, the civic faith that America could overcome its inner contradictions simply by driving away from them.

As I thought this over, it made me see more clearly what my friends and I were up to when we blocked traffic throughout the decade. We were trying to open up our society's inner wounds, to show that they were still there, sealed but never healed, that they were spreading and festering, that unless they were faced fast they would get worse. We knew that the glittering lives of the people in the fast lane were just as deeply maimed as the battered and buried lives of the people in the way. We knew, because we ourselves were just learning to live in that lane, and to love the pace. But this meant that our project was shot through with paradox from the start. We were working to help other people, and other peoples – blacks, Hispanics, poor whites, Vietnamese – to fight for their homes, even as we fled our own. We, who knew so well how it felt to pull up roots, were throwing ourselves against a state and a social system that seemed to be pulling up, or blowing up, the roots of the whole world. In blocking the way, we were blocking our own way. So long as we grasped our self-divisions, they infused the New Left with a deep sense of irony, a tragic irony that haunted all our spectacular productions of political comedy and melodrama and surreal farce. Our political theater aimed to force the audience to see that they, too, were participants in a developing American tragedy: all of us, all Americans, all moderns, were plunging forward on a thrilling but disastrous course. Individually and collectively, we needed to ask who we were and what we wanted to be, and where we were racing to, and at what human cost. But there was no way to think any of this through under pressure of the traffic that was driving us all on: hence the traffic had to be brought to a halt.

So the 1960s passed, the expressway world gearing itself up for ever more gigantic expansion and growth, but finding itself attacked by a multitude of passionate shouts from the street, individual shouts that could become a collective call, erupting into the heart of the traffic, bringing the gigantic engines to a stop, or at least radically slowing them down.

Notes

1. These statements are quoted by Robert Caro in his monumental study. *The Power Broker: Robert Moses and the Fall of New York* (New York: Alfred A. Knopf, 1974), pp. 849, 876. The "meat ax" passage is from Moses' memoir, *Public Works: A Dangerous Trade* (New York: McGraw-Hill, 1970). Moses' appraisal of the Cross-Bronx Expressway occurs in an interview with Caro. *The Power Broker* is the main source for my narrative of Moses' career. See also my article on Caro and Moses, "Buildings Are Judgment: Robert Moses and the Romance of Construction," *Ramparts*, March 1975, and a further symposium in the June issue.
2. Speech to the Long Island Real Estate Board, 1972, quoted in Caro, op. cit., p. 275.
3. For details of this episode, Caro, op. cit., pp. 368–72.
4. On the other hand, these projects made a series of drastic and near-fatal incursions into Manhattan's grid. Koolhaas (*Delirious New York*, New York: Oxford University Press, 1978, p. 15) explains incisively the importance of this system to the New York environment: "The Grid's two-dimensional discipline creates undreamt-of freedom for three-dimensional anarchy. The Grid defines a new balance between control and decontrol. . . . With its imposition, Manhattan is forever immunized against any [further] totalitarian intervention. In the single block – the largest possible area that can fall under architectural control – it develops a maximum unit of urbanistic Ego." It is precisely these urban ego-boundaries that Moses' own ego sought to sweep away.
5. Siegfried Giedion, *Space, Time and Architecture* (Cambridge: Harvard University Press, 1941), pp. 823–32.
6. Giedion, Space, Time and Architecture.
7. Frances Perkins, "Oral History Reminiscences" (Columbia University Collection), quoted in Caro, op. cit., p. 318.
8. A definitive analysis of public authorities in America can be found in Ame-Marie Walsh, *The Public's Business: The Politics and Practices of Government Corporations* (Cambridge MA: MIT Press, 1978), especially chapters 1, 2, 8, 11 and 12. Walsh's book contains much fascinating material on Moses, but she places his work in a broad institutional and social context taht Caro tends to leave out. Robert Fitch, in a perceptve 1976 essay, "Planning New York," tries to deduce all Moses' activities from the fifty-year agenda that was established by the financiers and officials of the Regional Plan Association; it appears in Roger Alcaly and David Mermelstein (eds), *The Fiscal Crisis of American Cities* (New York: Random House, 1977), pp. 247–84.
9. Giedion, *Space, Time and Architecture*.
10. Ibid., pp. 831–2.
11. Moses at least was honest enought to call a meat ax by its real name, to recognize the violence and devastation at the heart of his works. Far more typical of postwar planning is a sensibility like

Giedion's, for whom, "after the necessary surgery has been performed, the artificially swollen city will be reduced to its natural size." This genial self-delusion, which assumes that cities can be hacked to pieces without blood or wounds or shrieks of pain, points the way forward to the "surgical precision" bombing of Germany, Japan, and, later, Vietnam.

12. Jane Jacobs, *The Death and Life of Great American Cities* (New York: Random House, 1961). The passages that follow are from pages 50–54. For interesting critical discussion of Jacobs' vision, see, for instance, Herbert Gans, "City Planning and Urban Realities," *Commentary*, February 1962; Lewis Mumford, "Mother Jacobs' Home Remedies for Urban Cancer," *The New Yorker*, 1 December 1962, reprinted in the *Urban Prospect* (New York: Harcourt, 1966); and Roger Starr, *The Living End: The City and Its Critics* (New York: Coward-McCann, 1966).

13. In New York, this irony had a special twist. Probably no American politician incarnated the romance and the hopes of the modern city as well as Al Smith, who used as the anthem for his 1928 presidential campaign the popular song "East Side, West Side, All around the town. . . . We'll trip the light fantastic on the sidewalks of New York." It was Smith, however, who appointed and ardently supported Robert Moses, the figure who did more than anyone else to destroy those sidewalks. The 1928 election returns showed that Americans were not ready or willing to accept the sidewalks of New York. On the other hand, as it turned out, America was only too glad to embrace "the highways of New York" and to pave itself over in their image.

14. Contemporaneous with Jacobs' work, and similar in texture and richness, is the urban fiction of Grace Paley (whose stories are set in the same neighborhood), and, an ocean away, Doris Lessing.

15. Quoted in Caro, op. cit., p. 876.

Part III

Community Rediscovered, Community Reassessed: Social Bonds in the Modern City

10 Introduction
Philip Kasinitz

The processes of segregation establish moral distances which make the city a mosaic of little worlds which touch but do not interpenetrate. This makes it possible for individuals to pass quickly and easily from one moral milieu to another and encourages the fascinating but dangerous experiment of living at the same time in several contiguous, but otherwise widely separate, worlds.

Robert Park, "The City", 1916.[1]

The city is literally a composite of tens of thousands of tiny neighborhood units. So complete is each neighborhood, and so strong the sense of neighborhood that many a New Yorker spends a lifetime within the confines of an area smaller than a country village. Let him walk two blocks from his corner and he is in a strange land and will feel uneasy till he gets back.

E.B. White, Here is New York, 1949.[2]

Virtually all of the major social theorists of the late nineteenth and early twentieth centuries assumed that the bonds that hold people together underwent a radical transformation with the coming of modernity. Whether they spoke of *Gmeinschaft* versus *Gesellschaft*, feudalism versus capitalism, mechanical versus organic solidarity, the ideal typed community of the old order was envisioned as the rural village as contrasted with the teeming modern metropolis: Paris, Berlin, London, New York, Chicago.[3] By the mid-twentieth century the "loss of community" had become a virtual sociological cliché. A wide variety of social problems were (and are) popularly attributed to this loss: when middle-class Americans left urban areas in the post-Second-World-War period they were said to be in search of lawns, open space and community. When some of their children abandoned suburbia for the dense neighborhoods of the cities their parents had left, that was attributed to the search for "authenticity" and community.

163

The *Gemeinschaft/Gesellschaft* distinction has never been a clear dichotomy. Robert Park, at the beginning of his Chicago-school research, recognizes in this a seeming contradiction. He saw the city, particularly in the United States with its history of racial conflict and immigration, as a mosaic of utterly different worlds. The "Little Italys", "Little Polands," "ghettos," "gold coasts" and "Chinatowns" did not interpenetrate and many of the people in them lived in a world apart from the larger city. Though the modern urbanite may be tempted to live in many worlds at once, if many people did this the tiles of mosaic would become less distinct and eventually indistinguishable. So was the modern urban American really as parochial as any rural villager, as E. B. White implies? Was the urban freedom Simmel wrote about actually limited to a few cosmopolitan intellectuals, floating above the social structures in which most people actually live?

For the most part the Chicago writers of Park's era thought these dense neighborhoods were destined to last only one or two generations. Except in those cases where racial segregation prevented the dissolution of ethnic enclaves,[4] it was expected that urban anonymity and individualism would eventually overwhelm them. The immigrants might hold on to some of their peasant ways. They might even adjust them to the conditions of the industrial city. But their children would inevitably be swept up into the urban maelstrom. The bonds of community might not disappear completely, but they were surely destined to lose most of their strength.

By the post-Second-World-War era this proposition looked far less certain. For the next generation of urban sociologists, one important task was to account for the persistence of community in the face of the supposedly individualizing effects of modernity, while at the same time trying to understand what community meant in the metropolis.

An important early effort along these lines was set out by Morris Janowitz in his book *The Community Press in an Urban Setting: The Social Elements of Urbanism.*[5] Janowitz' formulation, termed the "community of limited liability," is a vision of urbanism somewhere in between Simmel's notion of the metropolis and the idea that modern urban neighborhoods are actually the equivalent of small towns. In Janowitz' vision, "communities," by which he generally means residential neighborhoods, continue to be important in the shaping of daily lives of urbanites. Yet he argues that, in contrast with the rural village, participation in urban communities is by and large voluntary, intentional and highly contingent; not all people living in a neighborhood need be embedded deeply, or at all, in local social life. Further, in the community of limited liability, both physical and social boundaries are as much a creation of political structures, voluntary organizations and local institutions as a reflection of the patterns of face-to-face interaction of the residents.

This view was redefined and expanded by Chicago-School sociologists during the 1960s and 1970s. Of particular importance is the work of Gerald Suttles, who delineated with considerable subtlety the conditions under which residential solidarity does or does not develop among neighborhood residents. Suttles' work points to the importance of political conflicts, perceived threats from ethnic and racial "outsiders," the "defense" of turf by "vigilante" peer groups in collective determination of neighborhood boundaries and identity.[6] Another variation on the nature of contemporary urban communities may be found in the work of Claude Fischer, who suggests that the demographic critical mass and density of social interaction of the modern city actually creates and intensifies subcultures. Fischer argues that, far from being the destroyer of community bonds, the modern city creates the possibility for new types of social networks and subcultures based on a wide variety of identities and tastes, some of which would scarcely be possible in smaller and simpler human settlements.[7]

Yet while it is clear that Fischer's work of the mid-1970s anticipates the development of what would later come to be known as "identity politics," he actually pays relatively little attention to the importance of political conflicts in the creation and promotion of these new forms of solidarity. In contrast Bensman and Vidich, in the essay presented here (Chapter 12), clearly see the form of solidarity practiced by ethnic groups and other types of subcultural communities as being shaped to a considerable degree by the political climate in which they function. This insight became all the more crucial during the 1980s, as politics based on collective identity and collective grievance became common to the point of being the norm.

Herbert Gans, originally an urban planner and one of the most important figures in the rethinking of the role of community in American sociology, is known for skewering theoretical and political truisms with a combination of skepticism and common sense. In his first major ethnographic study, *The Urban Villagers*, Gans explored daily life in the West End of Boston, a dense, working-class community. As the title of the book suggests, Gans documents the web of face-to-face interaction and community life that prevailed in the city. Yet the "urban village" is not a rural village, as Gans clearly demonstrates. Although the actual level of neighborhood interaction is quite high, consciousness of the neighborhood as a collectivity is still based to a large degree on media presentations and politics, and that consciousness is likely to become more sharply focused when the neighborhood is under attack.[8]

Gans does not romanticize the West End and he documents the costs to the individual of this sort of community life. Yet he concludes that the West End is ultimately a community that its members both need and value. This was a politically crucial point. The West End was widely perceived as a slum by policy makers and was already scheduled for demolition when Gans' study began. In fact Gans' study was funded in part in order to document the problems of the slums and to support the benefits of urban renewal. The fact that he came to the opposite conclusion did not save the West End – the area was demolished shortly after his study ended. Yet Gans' work called attention to the great hardships and dubious benefits of many urban-renewal projects. This conclusion, along with similar studies by Young and Wilmot in Great Britain, gave new intellectual weight to the attack on urban-renewal policies that gained force during the 1960s.

Gans' 1968 essay, included in this volume as Chapter 11, draws on both *The Urban Villagers* and Gans' subsequent ethnography of the new suburbs, *The Levittowners*. In this essay, a direct challenge to Louis Wirth, Gans argues that urban residence in and of itself has far less sociological significance than the Chicago tradition implies. The degree of social embeddedness experienced by modern Americans varies with their economic status, their age and stage in their life course and even their cultural tastes, but not generally by the size of the community they live in. In modern America, Gans argues, the line between city and suburb is often a political artifact and suburanization was thus not likely to be the huge force for social change many in the 1960s assumed it would be. In retrospect one might argue that in many cases "mere" political artifacts count for a great deal: consider the urban versus suburban conflicts over public education in contemporary America. Still this essay stands as an important corrective to Wirth's spatial determinism.

Another factor of effecting the nature of urban communities is the perception of public safety. In recent years many Americans have become obsessed, not without cause, with the issue of crime and safety in their neighborhoods. In his contribution to Part III of this volume, Albert Hunter (Chapter 13) explores the roles that crime and urban incivility play in the formation of various sorts of public life and modes of urban fraternization.

Since the 1960s the concept of community has taken on new cultural baggage. As opposition spread to Robert Moses' style urban growth and large-scale urban-renewal efforts, a new localism came to characterize urban politics, illustrated by the profusion of "community planning boards," "community school boards" and "community advisory groups." Many of these "communities" were fairly transparent, synthetic creations, as the hyphen in the name of one of the most famous sites "Ocean Hill-Brownsville") of the "community-control" struggle in public education attests. It is also questionable how much real decentralization of power these innovations represented and ironic to note that while many of these arrangements began as concessions to racial minorities they are now most effectively used by middle-class white "communities." Nevertheless the fact that today any group wishing to make a political claim automatically starts to refer to itself as a "community" reveals the legitimacy that communities (as opposed to individual citizens) are accorded in American life.

The last two essay in Part III fly in the face of this trend. Both might be subtitled "Two cheers for anomie". Richard Sennett, a long-time critic of the repressive aspects of communities, documents the dangers and limits of community politics as it was practiced in New York during the 1970s. The excerpt reproduced here as Chapter 14, from Sennett's *The Fall of the Public Man*, was published in 1976 and draws on the diaries of an astute young lawyer, Mario M. Cuomo, who later became the governor of New York State.

Iris Marion Young, a feminist philosopher, takes as her starting point in Chapter 15 the critique of liberal individualism and the celebration of community empowerment that came out of the new social movements of the late 1960s. Yet Young is wary of the potential contradiction between communal solidarity and the value she places on the toleration of difference. She thus makes the case for seeing in the public life of cities an alternative vision of democracy that avoids both the pitfalls of liberal universalism and the repressive potential of communitarianism.

Notes

1. Robert Park, "The City," in Richard Sennett (ed.) *Classic Essays on the Culture of Cities* (Englewood Cliffs, NJ: Prentice-Hall, 1969), p. 126. Originally published in the *American Journal of Sociology*, vol. xx, 1916.
2. E. B. White, *Here is New York* (New York, Harper and Row, 1949), p. 128.
3. Here again Lewis Mumford, who stood outside the mainstream of social thought, provides a useful exception.
4. See, for example, St. Clair Drake and Horace Clayton, *Black Metropolis* (New York: Harcourt Brace and World, 1945).
5. Morris Janowitz, *The Community Press in an Urban Setting: The Social Elements of Urbanism* (University of Chicago Press, 1952).
6. See Gerald Suttles, *The Social Order of the Slum* (University of Chicago Press, 1968); and *The Social Construction of Communities* (University of Chicago Press, 1972).
7. Claude Fischer, "Toward a Subcultural Theory of Urbanism", *American Journal of Sociology*, vol. 80 (May 1975), pp. 1319–41, and *The Urban Experience* (New York: Harcourt Brace Jovanovich, 1976).
8. Herbert Gans, *The Urban Villagers* (New York: Free Press, 1962). The phrase "urban village" is now so ubiquitous we sometimes for-

get that it is a deliberate oxymoron. The term has been used in a great many ways, some of which of Gans would hardly approve of. Stephen Steinberg has recently noted the title has been something of a rorschach test in urban studies: people see in it what they want to see!

11 Urbanism and Suburbanism as Ways of Life: A Reevaluation of Definitions*

Herbert J. Gans

The contemporary sociological conception of cities and of urban life is based largely on the work of the Chicago School and its summary statement in Louis Wirth's essay "Urbanism as a Way of Life."[1] In that paper, Wirth developed a "minimum sociological definition of the city" as "a relatively large, dense and permanent settlement of socially heterogeneous individuals." From these prerequisites, he then deduced the major outlines of the urban way of life. As he saw it, number, density, and heterogeneity created a social structure in which primary-group relationships were inevitably replaced by secondary contacts that were impersonal, segmental, superficial, transitory, and often predatory in nature. As a result, the city dweller became anonymous, isolated, secular, relativistic, rational, and sophisticated. In order to function in an urban society, he or she was forced to combine with others to organize corporations, voluntary associations, representative forms of government, and the impersonal mass media of communications. These replaced the primary groups and the integrated way of life found in rural and other preindustrial settlements.

Wirth's paper has become a classic in urban sociology, and most texts have followed faithfully his definition and description.[2] In recent years, however, a considerable number of studies and essays have questioned his formulations.[3] In addition, a number of changes have taken place in cities

---

* Reprinted from Herbert J. Gans, *People, Plans and Policies* (New York: Columbia University Press and Russell Sage Foundation, 1991).

since the article was published in 1938, notably the exodus of white residents to low- and medium-priced houses in the suburbs and the decentralization of industry. The evidence from these studies and the changes in American cities suggest that Wirth's statement must be revised.

There is yet another and more important reason for such a revision. Despite its title and intent, Wirth's paper deals with urban–industrial society, rather than with the city. This is evident from his approach. Like other urban sociologists, Wirth based his analysis on a comparison of settlement types, but unlike his colleagues, who pursued urban–rural comparisons, Wirth contrasted the city to the folk society. Thus, he compared settlement types of preindustrial and industrial society. This allowed him to include in his theory of urbanism the entire range of modern institutions which are not found in the folk society, even though many such groups (for example, voluntary associations) are by no means exclusively urban. Moreover, Wirth's conception of the city dweller as depersonalized, atomized, and susceptible to mass movements suggests that his paper is based on, and contributes to, the theory of the mass society.

Many of Wirth's conclusions may be relevant to the understanding of ways of life in modern society. However, since the theory argues that all of society is now urban, his analysis does not distinguish ways of life in the city from those in other settlements within modern society. In Wirth's time, the comparison of urban and preurban settlement types was still fruitful, but today, the primary task for urban (or community) sociology seems to me to be the analysis of the similarities and differences between contemporary settlement types.

This paper is an attempt at such an analysis; it limits itself to distinguishing ways of life in the modern city and the modern suburb. A reanalysis of Wirth's conclusions from this perspective suggests that his characterization of the urban way of life applies only – and not too accurately – to the residents of the inner city. The remaining city dwellers, as well as most suburbanites, pursue a different way of life, which I shall call "quasi-primary." This proposition raises some doubt about the mutual exclusiveness of the concepts of city and suburb and leads to a yet broader question: whether settlement concepts and other ecological concepts are useful for explaining ways of life.

THE INNER CITY

Wirth argued that number, density, and heterogeneity had two social consequences which explain the major features of urban life. On the one hand, the crowding of diverse types of people into a small area led to the segregation of homogeneous types of people into separate neighborhoods. On the other hand, the lack of physical distance between city dwellers resulted in social contact between them, which broke down existing social and cultural patterns and encouraged assimilation as well as acculturation – the melting-pot effect. Wirth implied that the melting-pot effect was far more powerful than the tendency toward segregation and concluded that, sooner or later, the pressures engendered by the dominant social, economic, and political institutions of the city would destroy the remaining pockets of primary-group relationships. Eventually, the social system of the city would resemble Tönnies' *Gesellschaft* – a way of life which Wirth considered undesirable.

Because Wirth had come to see the city as the prototype of mass society, and because he examined the city from the distant vantage point of the folk society – from the wrong end of the telescope, so to speak – his view of urban life is not surprising. In addition, Wirth found support for his theory in the empirical work of his Chicago colleagues. As Greer and Kube[4] and Wilensky[5] have pointed out, the Chicago sociologists conducted their most intensive studies in the inner city.[6] At that time, it consisted mainly of slums recently invaded by new waves of European immigrants and rooming-house and skid-row districts, as well as the habitat of Bohemians and well-to-do "Gold Coast" apartment dwellers. Wirth himself studied the Maxwell Street ghetto, a poor inner-city Jewish neighborhood then being dispersed by the acculturation and mobility of its inhabitants.[7] Some of the characteristics of urbanism which Wirth stressed in his essay abounded in these areas.

Wirth's diagnosis of the city as *Gesellschaft* must be questioned on three counts. First, the conclusions derived from a study of the inner city cannot be generalized to the entire urban area. Second, there is as yet not enough evidence to prove – or, admittedly, to deny – that number, density, and heterogeneity result in the social consequences which Wirth proposed. Finally, even if the casual relationship could be verified, it can be shown that a significant proportion of the city's inhabitants were, and are, isolated from these consequences by social structures and cultural patterns which they either brought to the city or developed by living in it. Wirth conceived the urban population as consisting of heterogeneous individuals, torn from past social systems, unable to develop new ones, and therefore prey to social anarchy in the city. While it is true that a not insignificant proportion of the inner-city population was, and still is, made up of unattached individuals,[8] Wirth's formulation ignores the fact that this population consists mainly of relatively homogeneous groups, with social and cultural moorings that shield it fairly effectively from the suggested consequences of number, density, and heterogeneity. This applies even more to the residents of the outer city, who constitute a majority of the total city population.

The social and cultural moorings of the inner-city population are best described by a brief analysis of the five major types of inner-city residents. These are (1) the "cosmopolites"; (2) the unmarried or childless; (3) the "ethnic villagers"; (4) the "deprived"; and (5) the "trapped" and downwardly mobile.

The "cosmopolites" include students, artists, writers, musicians, and entertainers, as well as other intellectuals and professionals. They live in the city in order to be near the special "cultural" facilities that can be located only near the center of the city. Many cosmopolites are unmarried or childless. Others rear children in the city, especially if they have the income to afford the aid of servants and governesses. The less affluent ones may move to the suburbs to raise their children, continuing to live as cosmopolites under considerable handicaps, especially in the lower-middle-class suburbs. Many of the very rich and powerful are also cosmopolites, although they are likely to have at least two residences, one of which is suburban or exurban.

The unmarried or childless must be divided into two subtypes, depending on the permanence or transience of their status. The temporarily unmarried or childless live in the inner city for only a limited time. Young adults may team up to rent an apartment away from their parents and close to job or entertainment opportunities. When they marry, they may move first to an apartment in a transient neighborhood, but if they can afford to do so, they leave for the outer city or the suburbs with the arrival of the first or second child. The permanently unmarried may stay in the inner city for the remainder of their lives, their housing depending on their income.

The "ethnic villagers" are ethnic groups which are found in such inner-city neighborhoods as New York's Lower East Side, living in some ways as they did when they were peasants in European or Puerto Rican villages.[9] Although they reside in the city, they isolate themselves from significant contact with most city facilities, aside from workplaces. Their way of life differs sharply from Wirth's urbanism in its emphasis on kinship and the primary group, the lack of anonymity and secondary-group contacts, the weakness of formal organizations, and the suspicion of anything and anyone outside their neighborhood.

The first two types of live in the inner city by choice; the third is there partly because of necessity, partly because of tradition. The final two types are in the inner city because they have no other choice. One is the "deprived" population: the emotionally disturbed or otherwise handicapped; broken families; and, most important, the poor-white and especially the nonwhite population. These urban dwellers must take the dilapidated housing and blighted neighborhoods to which the housing market relegates them, although among them are some for whom the slum is a hiding place or a temporary stopover to save money for a house in the outer city or the suburbs.[10]

The "trapped" are the people who stay behind when a neighborhood is invaded by nonresidential land uses or lower-status immigrants, because they cannot afford to move or are otherwise bound to their present location.[11] The "downwardly mobile" are a related type; they may have started life in a higher class position, but have been forced down in the socioeconomic hierarchy and in the quality of their accommodation. Many of them are old people, living out their existence on small pensions.

These five types may all live in dense and heterogeneous surroundings; yet they have such diverse ways of life that it is hard to see how density and heterogeneity could exert a common influence. Moreover, all but the last two types are isolated or detached from their neighborhood and thus from the social consequences that Wirth described.

When people who live together have social ties based on criteria other than mere common occupancy, they can set up social barriers, regardless of the physical closeness or the heterogeneity of their neighbors. The ethnic villagers are the best illustration. While a number of ethnic groups are usually found living together in the same neighborhood, they are able to isolate themselves from one another through a variety of social devices. Wirth himself recognized this when he wrote that "two groups can occupy a given area without losing their separate identity because each side is permitted to live its own inner life and each somehow fears or idealizes the other."[12] Although it is true that the children in these areas were often oblivious of the social barriers set up by their parents, at least until adolescence, it is doubtful whether their acculturation can be traced to the melting-pot effect as much as to the pervasive influence of the American culture that flowed into these areas from the outside.[13]

The cosmopolites, the unmarried, and the childless are *detached* from neighborhood life. The cosmopolites possess a distinct subculture which causes them to be uninterested in all but the most superficial contacts with their neighbors, somewhat like the ethnic villagers. The unmarried and childless – who may also be cosmopolites – are detached from the neighborhood because of their life-cycle stage, which frees them from the routine family responsibilities that entail some relationship to the local area. In their choice of residence, the two types are therefore not always concerned about their neighbors or the availability and quality of local community facilities. Even the well-to-do can choose expensive apartments in or near poor neighborhoods, because if they have children, these are sent to special schools and summer camps which effectively isolate them from neighbors. In addition, the childless and unmarried are often transient. Therefore, they tend to live in areas marked by high population turnover, where their own mobility and that of their neighbors creates a universal detachment from the neighborhood.[14]

The deprived and the trapped do seem to be affected by some of the consequences of number, density, and heterogeneity. The deprived population suffers considerably from overcrowding, but this is a consequence of low income, racial discrimination, and other handicaps and cannot be considered an inevitable result of the ecological makeup of the city.[15] Because the deprived have no residential choice, they are also forced to live amid neighbors not of their own choosing, with ways of life different and even contradictory to their own. If familial defenses against the neighborhood climate are weak, as may happen among single-parent families and downwardly mobile people, parents may lose their children to the culture of "the street." The trapped are the unhappy people who remain behind when their more advantaged neighbors move on; they must endure the heterogeneity which results from neighborhood change.

Wirth's description of the urban way of life fits best the transient areas of the inner city. Such areas are typically heterogeneous in population, partly because they are inhabited by transient types who do not require homogeneous neighbors or by deprived people who have no choice or may themselves be qutie mobile. Under conditions of transience and heterogeneity, people interact only in terms of the segmental roles necessary for obtaining local services. Their social relationships may thus display anonymity, impersonality, and superficiality.[16]

The social features of Wirth's concept of urbanism seem, therefore, to be a result of residential instability, rather than of number, density, or heterogeneity. In fact, heterogeneity is itself an effect of residential instability, resulting when the influx of transients causes landlords and realtors to stop acting as gatekeepers – that is, wardens of neighborhood homogeneity.[17] Residential instability is found in all types of settlements, and presumably its social consequences are everywhere similar. These consequences cannot, therefore, be identified with the ways of life of the city.

THE OUTER CITY AND THE SUBURBS

The second effect which Wirth ascribed to number, density, and heterogeneity was the segregation of homogeneous people into distinct neighborhoods[18] on the basis of "place and nature of work, income, racial and ethnic characteristics, social status, custom, habit, taste, and preference and prejudice."[19] This description fits the residential districts of the *outer city*.[20] Although these districts contain the majority of the city's inhabitants, Wirth went into little detail about them. He made it clear, however, that the sociopsychological aspects of urbanism were prevalent there as well.[21]

Because existing neighborhood studies deal primarily with the exotic sections of the inner city, very little is known about the more typical residential neighborhoods of the outer city. However, it is evident that the way of life in these areas bears little resemblance to Wirth's urbanism. Both the studies which question Wirth's formulation and my own observations suggest that the common element in the ways of life of these neighborhoods is best described as *quasi-primary*. I use this term to characterize relationships between neighbors. Whatever the intensity or frequency of these relationships, the interaction is more intimate than a secondary contact, but more guarded than a primary one.[22]

There are actually few secondary relationships, because of the isolation of residential neighborhoods from economic institutions and workplaces. Even shopkeepers, store managers, and other local functionaries who live in the area are treated as acquaintances or friends, unless they are of a vastly different social status or are forced by their corporate employers to treat their customers as economic units.[23] Voluntary associations attract only a minority of the population. Morever, much of the organizational activity is of a sociable nature, and it is often difficult to accomplish the association's "business" because of the members' preference for sociability. Thus, it would appear that interactions in organizations, or between neighbors generally, do not fit the secondary-relationship model of urban life. As anyone who has lived in these neighborhoods knows, there is little anonymity, impersonality, or privacy.[24] In fact, American cities have sometimes been described as collections of small towns.[25] There is some truth to this description, especially if the city is compared with the actual small town, rather than with the romantic construct of antiurban critics.[26]

Postwar suburbia represents the most contemporary version of the quasi-primary way of life. Owing to increases in real income and the encouragement of homeownership provided by the F.H.A., families in the lower middle class and upper working class can now live in modern single-family homes in low-density subdivisions, an opportunity previously available only to the upper and upper-middle classes.[27]

The popular literature of the 1950s described the new suburbs as communities in which conformity, homogeneity, and other-direction are unusually rampant.[28] The implication is that the move from city to suburb initiates a new way of life which causes considerable behavior and personality change in previous urbanites. My research in Levittown, New Jersey, suggests, however, that the move from the city to this predominantly lower-middle-class suburb does not result in any major behavioral changes for most people. Moreover, the changes which do occur reflect the move from the social isolation of a transient city or suburban apartment building to the quasi-primary life of a neighborhood of single-family homes. Also, many of the people whose life has changed report that the changes were intended. They existed as aspirations before the move or as reasons for it. In other words, the suburb itself creates few changes in ways of life.[29]

A COMPARISON OF CITY AND SUBURB

If outer-urban and suburban areas are similar in that the way of life in both is quasi-primary, and if urban residents who move out to the suburbs do not undergo any significant changes in behavior, it is fair to argue that the differences in ways of life between the two types of settlements

have been overestimated. Yet the fact remains that a variety
of physical and demographic differences exist between the
city and the suburb. However, upon closer examination,
many of these differences turn out to be either spurious or
of little significance for the way of life of the inhabitants.[30]
The differences between the residential areas of cities and
suburbs which have been cited most frequently are:

1. Suburbs are more likely to be dormitories.
2. They are further away from the work and play facilities
   of the central business districts.
3. They are newer and more modern than city residential
   areas and are designed for the automobile rather than
   for pedestrian and mass-transit forms of movement.
4. They are built up with single-family rather than
   multifamily structures and are therefore less dense.
5. Their populations are more homogeneous.
6. Their populations differ demographically: they are
   younger; more of them are married; they have higher
   incomes; and they hold proportionately more white-collar
   jobs.[31]

Most urban neighborhoods are as much dormitories as the
suburbs. Only in a few older inner-city areas are factories
and offices still located in the middle of residential blocks,
and even here many of the employees do not live in the
neighborhood.

The fact that the suburbs are farther from the central
business district is often true only in terms of distance, not
travel time. Moreover, most people make relatively little use
of downtown facilities, other than workplaces.[32] Many downtown stores seem to hold their greatest attraction for the
upper-middle class;[33] the same is probably true of typically
urban entertainment facilities. Teenagers and young adults
may take their dates to first-run movie theaters, but the
museums, concert halls, and lecture rooms attract mainly
upper-middle-class ticket buyers, many of them suburban.[34]

The suburban reliance on the train and the automobile
has given rise to an imaginative folklore about the consequences of commuting an alcohol consumption, sex life,
and parental duties. Many of these conclusions are, however, drawn from selected high-income suburbs and exurbs

and reflect job tensions in such hectic occupations as advertising and show business more than the effects of residence.[35] It is true that the upper-middle-class housewife must become a chauffeur in order to expose her children to the proper educational facilities, but such differences as walking to the corner drugstore and driving to its suburban equivalent seem to me of little emotional, social, or cultural import.[36] In addition, the continuing shrinkage in the number of mass-transit users suggests that even in the city many younger people are now living a wholly auto-based way of life.

The fact that suburbs are smaller is primarily a function of political boundaries drawn long before the communities were suburban. This affects the kinds of political issues which develop and provides somewhat greater opportunity for citizen participation. Even so, in the suburbs as in the city, the minority who participate routinely are the professional politicians, the economically concerned businesspeople, lawyers, and salespeople, and the ideologically motivated middle- and upper-middle-class people with better than average education.

The social consequences of differences in density and house type also seem overrated. Single-family houses in quiet streets facilitate the supervision of children; this is one reason why middle-class parents who want to keep an eye on their children move to the suburbs. House type also has some effects on relationships between neighbors, insofar as there are more opportunities for visual contact between adjacent homeowners than between people on different floors of an apartment house. However, if occupants' characteristics are also held constant, the differences in actual social contact are less marked. Homogeneity of residents turns out to be more important than proximity as a determinant of sociability. If the population is heterogeneous, there is little social contact between neighbors, either on apartment-house floors or in single-family-house blocks; if people are homogeneous, there is likely to be considerable social contact in both house types. One need only contrast the apartment house located in a transient, heterogeneous neighborhood and exactly the same structure in a neighborhood occupied by a single ethnic group. The former is a lonely, anonymous building; the latter, a bustling microsociety. I have observed similar patterns in suburban areas: on blocks where people are homogeneous, they socialize; where they are heterogeneous, they do little more than exchange polite greetings.[37]

Suburbs are usually described as being more homogeneous in house type than the city, but if they are compared to the outer city, the differences are small. Most inhabitants of the outer city, other than well-to-do homeowners, live on blocks of uniform structures as well; for example, the endless streets of row houses in Philadelphia and Baltimore or of two-story duplexes and six-flat apartment houses in Chicago. They differ from the new suburbs only in that they were erected through more primitive methods of mass production. Suburbs are, of course, more predominantly areas of owner-occupied single homes, though in the outer districts of most American cities homeownership is also extremely high.

Demographically, suburbs as a whole are clearly more homogeneous than cities as a whole, though probably not more so than outer cities. However, people do not live in cities or suburbs as a whole, but in specific neighborhoods. An analysis of ways of life would require a determination of the degree of population homogeneity within the boundaries of areas defined as neighborhoods by residents' social contacts. Such an analysis would no doubt indicate that many neighborhoods in the city as well as the suburbs are homogeneous. Neighborhood homogeneity is actually a result of factors having little or nothing to do with the house type, density, or location of the area relative to the city limits. Brand new neighborhoods are more homogeneous than older ones, because they have not yet experienced resident turnover, which frequently results in population heterogeneity. Neighborhoods of low- and medium-priced housing are usually less homogeneous than those with expensive dwellings because they attract families who have reached the peak of occupation and residential mobility, as well as young families who are just starting their climb and will eventually move to neighborhoods of higher status. The latter, being accessible only to high-income people, are therefore more homogeneous with respect to other resident characteristics as well. Moreover, such areas have the economic and political power to slow down or prevent invasion.

The demographic differences between cities and suburbs cannot be questioned, especially since the suburbs have attracted a large number of middle-class child-rearing families. The differences are, however, much reduced if suburbs are compared only with the outer city. In addition, a detailed comparison of suburban and outer-city residential areas would show that neighborhoods with the same kind of people can be found in the city as well as the suburbs. Once again, the age of the area and the cost of housing are more important determinants of demographic characteristics than the location of the area with respect to the city limits.

CHARACTERISTICS, SOCIAL ORGANIZATION AND ECOLOGY

The preceding sections of this chapter may be summarized in three propositions:

1. As concerns ways of life, the inner city must be distinguished from the outer city and the suburbs; and the latter two exhibit a way of life bearing little resemblance to Wirth's urbanism.
2. Even in the inner city, ways of life resemble Wirth's description only to a limited extent. Moreover, economic condition, cultural characteristics, life-cycle stage, and residential instability explain ways of life more satisfactorily than number, density, or heterogeneity.
3. Physical and other differences between city and suburb are often spurious or without much meaning for ways of life.

These propositions suggest that the concepts "urban" and "suburban" are neither mutually exclusive nor especially relevant for understanding ways of life. They – and number, density, and heterogeneity as well – are ecological concepts which describe human adaptation to the environment. However, they are not sufficient to explain social phenomena, because these phenomena cannot be understood solely as the consequences of ecological processes. Therefore, other explanations must be considered.

Ecological explanations of social life are most applicable if the subjects under study lack the ability of *make choices,* be they plants, animals, or human beings. Thus, if there is a housing shortage, people will live almost anywhere, and under extreme conditions of no choice, as in a disaster, married and single, old and young, middle and working class, stable and transient will be found side by side in whatever accommodations are available. At that time, their ways of life represent an almost direct adaptation to the environment. If the supply of housing and of neighborhoods is such that alternatives are available, however, people will make choices, and if the housing market is responsive, they can even make and satisfy explicit *demands*.

Choices and demands do not develop independently or at random; they are functions of the roles people play in the social system. These can best be understood in terms of the *characteristics* of the people involved; that is, characteristics can be used as indices to choices and demands made in the roles that constitute ways of life. Although many characteristics affect the choices and demands people make with respect to housing and neighborhoods, the most important ones seem to be *class* – in all its economic, social, and cultural ramifications – and *life-cycle stage*.[38] If people have an opportunity to choose, these two characteristics will go far in explaining the kinds of housing and neighborhood they will occupy and the ways of life they will try to establish within them.

Many of the previous assertions about ways of life in cities and suburbs can be analyzed in terms of class and life-cycle characteristics. Thus, in the inner city, the unmarried and childless live as they do, detached from neighborhood, because of their life-cycle stage; the cosmopolites, because of a combination of life-cycle stage and a distinctive but class-based subculture. The way of life of the deprived and trapped can be explained by low socioeconomic level and related handicaps. The quasi-primary way of life is associated with the family stage of the life cycle and the norms of child-rearing and parental role found in the upper working class, the lower-middle class, and the noncosmopolite portions of the upper-middle and upper classes.

The attributes of the so-called suburban way of life can also be understood largely in terms of these characteristics. Postwar suburbia is nothing more than a highly visible showcase for the ways of life of young, upper-working- class and lower-middle-class people. Ktsanes and Reissman have aptly described it as "new homes for old values."[39] Much of the descriptive and critical writing about suburbia assumes that as long as the new suburbanites lived in the city, they behaved like upper-middle-class cosmopolites and that suburban living has mysteriously transformed them.[40] The critics fail to see that the behavior and personality patterns ascribed to suburbia are in reality those of class and age.[41] These patterns could have been found among the new suburbanites when they still lived in the city and could now be observed among their peers who still reside there – if the latter were as visible to critics and researchers as are the suburbanites.

Needless to say, the concept of "characteristics" cannot explain all aspects of ways of life, among either urban or suburban residents. Some aspects must be explained by concepts of social organization that are independent of characteristics. For example, some features of the quasi-primary way of life are independent of class and age, because they evolve from the roles and situations created by joint and adjacent occupancy of land and dwellings. Likewise, residential instability is a universal process which has a number of invariate consequences. In each case, however, the way in which people react varies with their characteristics. So it is with ecological processes. Thus, there are undoubtedly differences between ways of life in urban and suburban settlements which remain after behavior patterns based on residents' characteristics have been analyzed and which must therefore be attributed to features of the settlement.[42]

Characteristics do not explain the causes of behavior, however; rather, they are clues to socially created and culturally defined roles, choices, and demands. A causal analysis must trace them to the larger social, economic, and political systems which determine the situations in which roles are played and the cultural content of choices and demands, as well as the opportunities for their achievement.[43] These systems determine income distributions, educational and occupational opportunities, and, in turn, fertility patterns and child-rearing methods, as well as the entire range of consumer behavior. Thus, a complete analysis of the way of life of the deprived residents of the inner city cannot stop at indicating the influence of low income, lack of education, or family instability. These must be related to such conditions as the urban economy's "need" for low-wage workers and the housing-market practices which restrict residential choice. The urban economy is in turn shaped by national economic and social systems, as well as by local and regional ecological processes. Some phenomena can be explained exclusively by reference to these ecological processes. However, it must also be recognized that as human beings have gained greater control over the natural environment, they have been able to free themselves from many of the determining and limiting effects of that environment. Thus, changes in local transportation technology, the ability of industries to be footloose, and the relative affluence of American society have given ever-larger numbers of people increasing amounts of residential choice. The greater the amount of choice available, the more important the concept of characteristics becomes in understanding behavior.

Consequently, the study of ways of life in communities must begin with an analysis of characteristics. If characteristics are dealt with first and held constant, we may be able to discover which behavior patterns can be attributed to features of the settlement and its natural environment.[44] Only then will it be possible to discover to what extent city and suburb are independent – rather than dependent or intervening – variables in the explanation of ways of life.

This kind of analysis might help to reconcile the ecological point of view with the behavioral and cultural one and possibly put an end to the conflict between conceptual positions which insist on one explanation or the other.[45] Both explanations have some relevance, and future research and theory must clarify the role of each in the analysis of ways of life in various types of settlement.[46] Another important rationale for this approach is its usefulness for applied sociology; for example, city planning. Planners can recommend changes in the spatial and physical arrangements of the city. Frequently, they seek to achieve social goals or to change social conditions through physical solutions, having been attracted to ecological explanations because these relate behavior to phenomena which they can affect. For example, many planners tend to agree with Wirth's formulations because they stress number and density, over which the planner has some control. If the undesirable social conditions of the inner city could be traced to these two factors, the planner could propose large-scale clearance projects which would reduce the size of the urban population and lower residential densities. Experience with public housing projects has, however, made it apparent that low densities, new buildings, or modern site plans do not eliminate antisocial or self-destructive behavior. The analysis of characteristics will call attention to the fact that this behavior is lodged in the deprivations of low socioeconomic status and racial discrimination and that it can be changed only through the removal of these deprivations. Conversely, if such an analysis suggests residues of behavior that can be attributed to ecological processes or physical aspects of housing and neighborhoods, the planner can recommend physical changes that can rally affect behavior.

A REEVALUATION OF DEFINITIONS

The argument presented here has implications for the sociological definition of the city. Such a definition relates ways of life to environmental features of the city qua settlement type. But if ways of life do not coincide with settlement types, and if these ways are functions of class and life-cycle stage rather than of the ecological attributes of the settlement, a sociological definition of the city cannot be formulated.[47] Concepts such as "city" and "suburb" allow us to distinguish settlement types from each other physically and demographically, but the ecological processes and conditions which they synthesize have no direct or invariate consequences for ways of life. The sociologist cannot, therefore, speak of an urban or suburban way of life.

CONCLUSION

Many of the descriptive statements made here are as time bound as Wirth's.[48] In the 1940s Wirth concluded that some form of urbanism would eventually predominate in all settlement types. He was, however, writing during a time of immigrant acculturation and at the end of a serious depression, an era of minimal choice. Today, it is apparent that high-density, heterogeneous surroundings are for most people a temporary place of residence; other than for the Park Avenue or Greenwich Village cosmopolites, they are a result of necessity, rather than choice. As soon as they can afford to do so, most Americans head for the single-family house and the quasi-primary way of life of the low-density neighborhood, in the outer city or the suburbs.[49]

Changes in the national economy and in government housing policy can affect many of the variables that make up housing supply and demand. For example, urban sprawl may eventually outdistance the ability of present and proposed transportation systems to move workers into the city; further industrial decentralization can forestall it and alter the entire relationship between work and residence. The expansion of urban-renewal activities can perhaps lure a significant number of cosmopolites back from the suburbs, while a drastic change in renewal policy might begin to ameliorate the housing conditions of the deprived population. A serious depression could once again make America a nation of doubled-up tenants.

These events will affect housing supply and residential choice; they will frustrate, but not suppress, demands for the quasi-primary way of life. However, changes in the national economy, society, and culture can affect people's characteristics – family size, educational level, and various other concomitants of life-cycle stage and class. These in turn will stimulate changes in demands and choices. The rising number of college graduates, for example, is likely to increase the cosmopolite ranks. This might in turn create a new set of city dwellers, although it will probably do no more than encourage the development of cosmopolite facilities in some suburban areas.

The current revival of interest in urban sociology and in community studies, as well as the sociologist's increasing curiosity about city planning, suggests that data may soon be available to formulate a more adequate theory of the relationship between settlements and the ways of life within

188 *Urbanism and Suburbanism as Ways of Life*

them. The speculations presented in this essay are intended to raise questions; they can be answered only by more systematic data collection and theorizing.

POSTSCRIPT[50]

When I reread this essay again after many years, I was struck by how much the first sentence remains largely true. While no single school, including the ecological school, is now dominant in urban sociology, Louis Wirth's "Urbanism as a Way of Life" remains the most often cited article and probably the most often read one as well. It still supplies the simplest and seemingly most accurate definition of the city, and a rationale, not to mention an outline, for studying urban sociology – all the research and writing questioning Wirth's ideas notwithstanding. In fact, although over half of all Americans now live in the suburbs, urban sociology courses remain resolutely urban, although often because they deal with the urban sociology of the poor and the minorities who remain stuck in the city. Whatever the merit of that approach (which I use myself) we still do not have a sociology of the suburbs or even a respectable sociological literature on suburbia.

I pointed out in my article, originally published in 1962, that it was as time bound as Wirth's, and I was by and large right. Even though I seem to have predicted the yuppies in my penultimate paragraph, I did not consider the possibility that someday suburbia would be the majority form of residence, and that it would then be inhabited by people of all ages and households of all types, rather than mainly young families with young children. I did mention the decentralization of industry, but did not think that it might one day become a flood. Now, about two-thirds or more of those living in the suburbs also work there, and even fewer than a third need to come to the city's central business district, except perhaps for high culture, since museums and concert halls have by and large not decentralized (yet). Professional sports teams have, however, even if they are still called by the name of the city nearest to where they play.

I should also have thought about the possibility that when the suburbs became more popular, the mainly urban essayists and intellectuals who criticized them – and by implication their middle-American residents – for undue conformity, homogeneity, and other sociocultural diseases would have to end the suburban critique. This they did, shortly after I published this article, but they found new targets with which to continue the cultural class war. Such targets are always available, however, beginning and still ending with television viewing and television programming.

Having underestimated the extent of the suburban move, I also failed to consider the likelihood of a city inhabited increasingly by the very rich and poor. Nor did I consider that black ghettos would also be found in what I called the outer city, even if they are ghettos of the black working class and lower middle class more than of the black poor, and are thus not altogether different than when they were inhabited by the white working and lower middle classes. It did not even occur to me that housing might one day become expensive, so that most American home buyers could no longer afford either a new or a secondhand single-family house, that suburbia would be filling up with row houses and condominiums – and that the major housing problem of the poor was the inability to pay high rents, which was one cause of the tragic increase in homelessness exacted by the Reagan administration on the poor, the cities, and even many suburbs.

Actually, my prediction of the yuppies was partly luck, for while I expected more young people to come into the inner city after college, some having done so already in the 1950s, I did not expect the large number who came and for whom old neighborhoods near the central business district and elsewhere were gentrified. They have come largely because of the dramatic increase in *professional* service employment in the central business districts of many cities, although because they spend so much time on the streets and in expensive "boutiques," their visibility is greater than their actual number. Moreover, that number could decline sharply in the 1990s, not only because when they marry and have children many move to the suburbs, but also because if the boom times in professional service employment end, their number – and visibility – will shrink quickly and considerably.

I could list other ways in which the 1962 article was time bound; for example, it paid no more attention than Wirth's article to the various political battles – about race, or class, or just property values – that take place in cities and suburbs, and thus could not consider that as all resources became scarcer, these battles would increase in number and intensity. Still, in its basic conception, the article remains accurate as I write this postscript in the spring of 1990. The basic differences are not between city and suburb, but between the inner city and the rest of the metropolitan area, and the major reasons are more or less as I stated them.

Even the five types of inner city residents can still be found, if not solely in the inner city, in the poorer parts of the outer city as well. I should have begun my list of types with those who are in the city by necessity, especially the poor; also, some of my labels seem a bit archaic now, notably because the people who are in the city mainly because of its high culture facilities – and whom I called cosmopolites – have been joined by the aforementioned yuppies. The ethnic villages are now largely *barrios* or Southeast Asian areas, because the white ethnic villages left over from the European immigration are mainly in the outer city and to a lesser extent in the suburbs. (In New York, Bensonhurst, Canarsie, and Howard Beach are among the best known at the start of the 1990s, though unfortunately for tragic reasons.)

Most of the inner city ethnic enclaves were either displaced by an enlarged central business district, were gentrified, or became slums for a later wave of immigrants. Thus, a part of New York's Jewish Lower East Side became a middle-class Jewish area, another is being gentrified for young people, and the rest of it became Loisada, which is the "Puerto Ricanization" of the old neighborhood name. Likewise, New York's Little Italy has become part of the rapidly growing Chinatown, although so far many of the retail stores remain Italian; they are restaurants, food stores and giftshops for the Italians who come back for a visit from the suburbs. Meanwhile, Chinese immigration has been so large that most Chinese now live in Queens, the proto-typical outer city borough.

From here on in, writing about the cities will be even more time bound, because America is now part of the world economy, and what economic changes will affect it, and its cities, will vary and be unpredictable. This may lengthen the life of Wirth's classic article even further, because it transcends economic conditions and thus provides a seemingly timeless definition of the city that is never totally inaccurate. It may even become a bit more accurate as, in growing metropolitan areas, areas we now call suburbs become larger in population, higher in density, and more diverse in population.

Notes

1. Louis Wirth, "Urbanism as a Way of life," *American Journal of Sociology*, vol. (July 1938), pp. 1–24; reprinted in Paul Hatt and Alber J. Reiss, Jr (eds), *Cities and Society* (Glencoe, Ill.: Free Press, 1957), pp. 46–64.
2. Richard Dewey, "The Rural – Urban Continuum: Real but Relatively Unimportant," *American Journal of Sociology* (July 1960), 66:60–66.
3. I shall not attempt to summarize these studies, for this task has already been performed by Dewey, Reiss, Wilensky, and others. The studies include: Morris Axelrod, "Urban Structure and Social Participation," *American Sociological Review* (February 1956), 21:13–18; Dewey, "The Rural – Urban Continuum," William H. Form et al., "The Compatibility of Alternative Approaches to the Delimitation of Urban Sub-areas," *American Sociological Review* (August 1954), 19:434–440; Herbert J. Gans, *The Urban Villagers* (New York: Free Press of Glencoe, 1962); Scott Greer, "Urbanism Reconsidered: A Comparative Study of Local Areas in a Metropolis," *American Sociological Review* (February 1956), 21:19–25; Scott Greer and Ella Kube, "Urbanism and Social Structure: A Los Angeles Study," in Marvin B. Sussman, ed., *Community Structure and Analysis* (New York: Crowell, 1959), pp. 93–112; Morris Janowitz, *The Community Press in an Urban Setting* (Glencoe, Ill.: Free Press, 1952); Albert J. Reiss, Jr., "An Analysis of Urban Phenomena," in Robert M. Fisher, ed., *The Metropolis in Modern Life* (Garden City, N.Y.: Doubleday, 1955), pp. 41–49; Albert J. Reiss, Jr., "Rural – Urban and Status Differences in Interpersonal Contacts," *American Journal of Sociology* (September 1959), 65:182–195; John R. Seeley, "The Slum: Its Nature, Use, and Users," *Journal of the American Institute of Planners* (February 1959),

25:7–14; Joel Smith, William Form, and Gregory Stone, "Local Intimacy in a Middle-Sized City," *American Journal of Sociology* (November 1954), 60:276–284; Gregory P. Stone, "City Shoppers and Urban Identification: Observations on the Social Psychology of City Life," *American Journal of Sociology* (July 1954), 60:36–45; William F. Whyte, *Street Corner Society* (Chicago: University of Chicago Press, 1955); Harold L. Wilensky and Charles Lebeaux, *Industrial Society and Social Welfare* (New York: Russell Sage Foundation, 1958); Michael Young and Peter Willmott, *Family and Kinship in East London* (London: Routledge and Kegan Paul, 1957).

4. Greer and Kube, "Urbanism and Social Structure," p. 112.
5. Wilensky and Lebeaux, "Industrial Society," p. 121.
6. By the *inner city* I mean the transient residential areas, the Gold Coasts and the slums that generally surround the central business district, although in some communities they may continue for miles beyond that district. The *outer city* includes the stable residential areas that house the working- and middle-class tenant and owner. The *suburbs* I conceive as the latest and most modern ring of the outer city, distinguished from it only by yet lower densities and by the often irrelevant fact of the ring's location outside the city limits.
7. Louis Wirth, *The Ghetto* (Chicago: University of Chicago Press, 1928).
8. Arnold M. Rose, "Living Arrangements of Unattached Persons," *American Sociological Review* (August 1947), 12:429–435.
9. Gans, *Urban Villagers*.
10. Seeley, "The Slum."
11. *Ibid.* The trapped are not very visible, but I suspect that they are a significant element in what Raymond Vernon has described as the "gray areas" of the city in his *Changing Economic Function of the Central City* (New York: Committee on Economic Development, Supplementary Paper No. 1, January 1959).
12. Wirth, *The Ghetto*, p. 283.
13. If the melting pot had resulted from propinquity and high density, one would have expected second-generation Italians, Irish, Jews, Greeks, and Slavs to have developed a single "pan-ethnic culture," consisting of a synthesis of the cultural patterns of the propinquitous national groups.
14. The corporation transients, who provide a new source of residential instability to the suburb, differ from city transients. Since they are raising families, they want to integrate themselves into neighborhood life and are usually able to do so, mainly because they tend to move into similar types of communities wherever they go. See William H. Whyte, Jr., *The Organization Man* (New York: Simon & Schuster, 1956), and Wilensky and Lebeaux, "Industrial Society."
15. The negative social consequences of overcrowding are a result of high room and floor density, not of the land coverage and population density which Wirth discussed. Park Avenue residents live under conditions of high land density, but do not seem to suffer from overcrowding.

16. Whether or not these social phenomena have the psychological consequences Wirth suggested depends on the people who live in the area. Those who are detached from the neighborhood by choice are probably immune, but those who depend on the neighborhood for their social relationships – the unattached individuals, for example – may suffer greatly from loneliness.

17. Needless to say, residential instability must ultimately be traced to the fact that, as Wirth pointed out, the city and its economy attract transient – and, depending on the sources of outmigration, heterogeneous – people. However, this is a characteristic of urban – industrial society, not of the city specifically.

18. By neighborhoods or residential districts I mean areas demarcated from others by distinctive physical boundaries or by social characteristics, some of which may be perceived only by the residents. However, these areas are not necessarily socially self-sufficient or culturally distinctive.

19. Wirth, "Urbanism as a Way of Life," p. 56.

20. For the definition of *outer city*, see note 6.

21. Wirth, "Urbanism as a Way of Life," p. 56.

22. Because neighborly relations are not quite primary and not quite secondary, they can also become *pseudo-primary*, that is, secondary ones disguised with false affect to make them appear primary. Critics have often described suburban life in this fashion, although the actual prevalence of pseudo-primary relationships has not been studied systematically in cities or suburbs.

23. Stone, "City Shoppers."

24. These neighborhoods cannot, however, be considered as urban folk societies. People go out of the area for many of their friendships, and their allegiance to the neighborhood is neither intense nor all-encompassing. Janowitz has aptly described the relationship between residents and neighborhoods as one of "limited liability." "The Community Press" ch. 7.

25. Were I not arguing that ecological concepts cannot double as sociological ones, this way of life might best be described as small-townish.

26. Arthur J. Vidich and Joseph Bensman, *Small Town in Mass Society: Class, Power and Religion in a Rural Community* (Princeton, N.J.: Princeton University Press, 1958).

27. Harold Wattel, "Levittown: A Suburban Community," in William M. Dobriner, ed., *The Suburban Community* (New York: Putnam, 1958), pp. 287–313.

28. Bennett Berger, *Working Class Suburb: A Study of Auto Workers in Suburbia* (Berkeley: University of California Press, 1960). Also Vernon, *Changing Economic Function of the Central City.*

29. Berger, *Working Class Suburb.*

30. Wattel, "Levittown" They may, of course, be significant for the welfare of the total metropolitan area.

31. Otis Dudley Duncan and Albert J. Reiss, Jr., *Social Characteristics of Rural and Urban Communities, 1950* (New York: Wiley, 1956), p. 131.

32. Donald L. Foley, "The Use of Local Facilities in a Metropolis," in Hatt and Reiss, *Cities and Societies*, pp. 237–247. Also see Christen T. Jonassen, *The Shopping Center versus Downtown* (Columbus: Bureau of Business Research, Ohio State University, 1955).
33. Jonassen, "The Shopping Center," pp. 91–92.
34. A 1958 study of New York theatergoers showed a median income of close to $10,000, and 35 percent were reported as living in the suburbs. That year, the median U.S. family income was $5087. John Enders, *Profile of the Theater Market* (New York: Playbill, undated and unpaged).
35. A. C. Spectorsky, *The Exurbanites* (Philadelphia: Lippincott, 1955).
36. I am thinking here of adults; teenagers do suffer from the lack of informal meeting places within walking or bicycling distance.
37. Herbert J. Gans, "Planning and Social Life: Friendship and Neighbor Relations in Suburban Communities," *Journal of the American Institute of Planners* (May 1961), 27:134–140.
38. These must be defined in dynamic terms. Thus, class includes also the process of social mobility; the stage in the life cycle, the processes of socialization and aging.
39. Thomas Ktsanes and Leonard Reissman, "Suburbia: New Homes for Old Values," *Social Problems* (Winter 1959–1960), 7:187–194.
40. Leonard J. Duhl, "Mental Health and Community Planning," in *Planning 1955* (Chicago: American Society of Planning Officials, 1956), pp. 31–39; Erich Fromm, *The Sane Society* (New York: Rinehart, 1955), pp. 154–162; David Riesman, "The Suburban Sadness," in Dobriner, *The Suburban Community*, pp. 375–408; W. Whyte, *The Organization Man.*
41. William M. Dobriner, "Introduction: Theory and Research in the Sociology of the Suburbs," in Dobriner, *The Suburban Community*, pp. xiii–xxviii.
42. Sylvia Fleis Fava, "Contrasts in Neighboring: New York City and a Suburban Community," in Dobriner, *The Suburban Community*, pp. 122–131.
43. This formulation may answer some of Duncan and Schnore's objections to sociopsychological and cultural explanations of community ways of life. Otis Dudley Duncan and Leo F. Schnore, "Cultural, Behavioral and Ecological Perspectives in the Study of Social Organization," *American Journal of Sociology* (September 1959), 65:132–155.
44. The ecologically oriented researchers who developed the Shevsky – Bell social-area analysis scale have worked on the assumption that "social differences between the populations of urban neighborhoods can conveniently be summarized into differences of economic level, family characteristics and ethnicity." Wendell Bell and Maryanne T. Force, "Urban Neighborhood Types and Participation in Formal Associations," *American Sociological Review* (February 1956), 21:25–34. However, they have equated "urbanization" with a concept of life-cycle stage by using family characteristics to define the index of urbanization, *Ibid.* Also see Scott Greer, "The Social Struc-

ture and Political Process of Suburbia," *American Sociological Review* (August 1960), 25:514–526, and Greer and Kube, "Urbanism and Social Structure." In fact, Bell has identified suburbanism with familism: Wendell Bell, "Social Choice, Life Styles and Suburban Residence," in Dobriner, *The Suburban Community*, pp. 225–247.

45. Duncan and Schnore, "Cultural, Behavioral and Ecological Perspectives."

46. Dobriner, "Introduction," in Dobriner, *The Suburban Community*, p. xxii.

47. Because of the distinctiveness of the ways of life found in the inner city, some writers propose definitions that refer only to these ways, ignoring those found in the outer city. For example, popular writers sometimes identify "urban" with "urbanity," that is, "cosmopolitanism." However, such a definition ignores the other ways of life found in the inner city. Moreover, I have tried to show that these ways have few common elements and that the ecological features of the inner city have little or no influence in shaping them.

48. Even more than Wirth's they are based on data and impressions gathered in the large eastern and midwestern cities of the United States.

49. Personal discussions with European planners and sociologists suggest that many European apartment dwellers have similar preferences, although economic conditions, high building costs, and the scarcity of land make it impossible for them to achieve their desires.

50. Editor's note: This postscript by the author was added to the 1991 edition of *People Plans and Policies* (New York: Columbia University Press and the Russell Sage Foundation).

51. Editor's note: for more on the urban/suburban shifts of recent decades, see Fishman, Chapter 23 of this volume.

12 Race, Ethnicity and New Forms of Urban Community*

Joseph Bensman and Arthur J. Vidich

The dominant tradition in the study of the community has focused upon the decline or the eclipse of the community. Classical sociologists tended to conceptualize in many different ways two basic polar types of communities. These conceptualizations included community versus society, folk versus urban communities, *Gemeinschaft* versus *Gesellschaft*, mechanical versus organic societies and sacred versus secular societies. In doing so they usually focused on the deep sense of emotional commitment of person-to-person and the strong sense of identity that existed in the isolated, small rural community compared with the rationality, impersonality, isolation and anomie – that is, normlessness – of the urban society. Moreover they pointed to the decline of older forms of emotional expression as the isolated, spatially distinct ecological community was overpowered by large-scale urbanism, industrialization, mass institutions and centralized bureaucracies. To a large extent this overall focus reflects an underlying reality: rural society has been deeply penetrated by the institutions of urban, industrial society. However this has not meant that the community has disappeared.

To the contrary, because of a basic reconstitution of social structure supporting and constraining personal and social life in urban society the forms of community have radically changed. The historic folk societies developed their central characteristics because they were spatially isolated from other societies and because they were small. Their separation from other societies and the resultant density of internal

* Originally published in Bensman and Vidich (eds), *Metropolitan Communities: New Forms of Urban Sub-Communities* (New York: Franklin Watts, 1975). The present version has been slightly reedited by Arthur Vidich.

Joseph Bensman and Arthur J. Vidich 197

personal relations allowed them to develop distinctive cultures
that supported and reinforced the individual, even as that individual was submerged in and by this community culture.
What is important here is that the spatial isolation of
the community allowed for the development of distinctive
communities and created cultural, organizational, ceremonial
and ritual limits on the behavior of the community members. Those limits provided cultural and objective bases for
their activities. Thus individuals were not plagued by the
problem of choice because little choice was allowed, and
conflicts in value were limited because the primitive community tended to have an overarching hierarchy of values.
As a result a person was permitted few choices, and so had
few opportunities to be an "individual" making a choice.
He or she could not experience him- or herself as having a
strong sense of his or her own individuality and subjectivity.
The growth of the metropolis, the gigantic city, destroyed
the territorial limitations placed upon individuals. They were
exposed to vast varieties of stimuli, values, choices and
cultures, so that in fact few external limits were placed on
them. In theory the absence of such limits might (as was
conjectured in classical theories) cause a sense of normlessness, anxiety, alienation and indecision, and could lead some
individuals to the point of suicide or other forms of extreme pathology. At the same time, for others who were
strong enough to profit from the variety of values, cultures
and choices offered by the city, the absence of limits could
lead to a sense of freedom, liberation and opportunity.
Despite the negative theories of urbanism, and despite
the fact that cities and their residents have many problems, it is clear that cities and urban areas have survived
and continue to grow. At least up to now, the existence of
urban problems and pathologies has not constituted a limit
on urban growth. We suggest that the reason why cities
have flourished, even though they provide little sense of
spatial limits and order for the human personality, is that
within the urban area city dwellers have constructed communities that serve the personal and psychological functions once supplied by the isolated rural community.
But these new urban communities are voluntary in nature,
based on a choice of dwelling within the framework of

selected values, institutions and cultures rather than on residential space per se. Here the locality where one lives is less an accident of birth than an individual choice. Thus selection of place of residence is based on the known characteristics – ethnic, class, cultural or social – of a neighborhood. Of course income patterns of residential segregation and the sense of being accepted or excluded by a neighborhood are elements in that choice, but this means that the choices that others make in part determine the choice that an individual makes. However those who make such choices create their own neighborhoods and by their selection of activities in the city-at-large, and by their patterns of consumption and preference, create an almost infinite variety of communities.

Not only are crime, ethnic tension and conflict generic problems of the process of urbanization, but responses to them represent new bases for community organization and reorganization. Thus we point to the recreation of ethnic communities, both at a neighborhood level and at larger institutional and organizational levels. The politicization of ethnic and class communities *in a direct and open form* is a recent trend in American urban life.

The new politicization of the community has been aided and abetted by the creation of administrative communities that are a product of philanthropic activity, federal and municipal legislation and a new activism on the part of ethnics, youth and the new and old middle classes.

The urban environment, simply because of its total size and the size of its institutional components, permits the development of both total communities and institutional communities whose particular culture and preferred or required behavioral style become the basis of a characteristic way of life. The dominance of a neighborhood by one institution can create a countercommunity whose raison d'être may well be its opposition to an organization, institution, another group or the government.

Beyond this, individuals in their pursuit of a single value or a cluster of values may organize activities, institutions and ways of life that, in their inclusiveness and commitment, become communities. Thus a single value, voluntarily accepted, may provide a fabric and texture of life that permit almost any variety and range of the total human experience. These newer forms of community need not be based on spatial isolation: they can be based, in addition to adherence to common values, on availability of transportation, communication and effectiveness of organization.

From the oldest civilizations onward, the city has been the site of diverse ethnic populations and communities. In the United States, ethnic interpenetration has been more extreme than in most areas of the world because the entire development of the country has been based upon successive waves of immigrants. As members of each ethnic wave achieved mobility and dominance, more immigrants poured into the cities to become the new lower classes.

The port and industrial city has always been the first point of entry, and sizable numbers of immigrants, especially in the twentieth century, have settled in cities. As a result ethnic communities of all varieties and ages have emerged in urban areas. Initially they tend to concentrate in ghetto communities, occupying successively the same ghettos from which older immigrants have been displaced or have moved out as they achieved economic success and residential mobility. Some ethnic groups have clung to their areas of original settlement and have become successful there. In other cases, where the number of immigrants is relatively small and they do not come in waves, the problem of establishing an ethnic community is difficult and does not necessarily result in a pattern of concentrated settlement. Immigrants from a relatively progressive industrial society may bypass the older ethnic ghettos and create more advanced ghettos. Some groups are unable to bring with them the skills, wealth and status they held in their place of origin. Status and skills are not necessarily transferable from one society to another because of differences in technology, culture and status systems. Their possessors may be declassed with respect to American society but retain their prestige and status within their own ethnic community. Those who can maintain their skills, wealth and prestige may easily be accepted at comparable class levels.

Other groups have struggled to maintain their culture in their patterns of settlement, often creating a minority culture that may be more unified and concentrated that it

was in their homeland. Among some ethnic groups, conflicts emerge between earlier and later immigrants in the
same group. Most ghetto areas, however, are occupied by
a plurality of ethnic groups whose struggle for common
space can be a source of interethnic problems.

In urban areas where there are well-defined centers of
ethnic concentration the different ethnic groups within a
center may vary widely in density. In fact there is an uneven flow of people from one area to another, and rarely is
one area exclusively occupied by a single ethnic or class
group. Since the mix of given neighborhoods is continuously changing, ethnic "boundaries" are never permanent,
and legal and administrative attempts to fix such boundaries on the basis of residence are negated by the continuous process of ethnic movement within the city. As a result
successive attempts to redefine administrative districts –
whether school, health, election, police, sanitation or fire
department – seldom reflect current reality and will sooner
or later atomize a given residential area.

Any particular neighborhood or public space, then, may
be jointly occupied by several ethnic and class groups.
Members of such communities within the neighborhood may
sometimes be virtually unaware of the cooccupancy. When
they are aware of it, the result may be either ethnic cooperation against external threats or neighborhood conflict.
Also, such ethnic and class mixtures may include social
isolates who belong to no community or who belong to
another community outside the neighborhood.

The effect of these class and ethnic mixtures and of the
fluidity of boundaries can give the city a great deal of its
variety, charm, freedom and looseness. On the other hand
it can become the source of tension and friction.

In medieval times cities were walled enclosures designed
to protect their inhabitants from attack, "rural" crime and
banditry. Later, when they emerged from feudal or state
control into self-government, civic associations or guilds of
magistrates set up specialized police agencies to provide
for the orderly conduct of civic life. As urban populations
grew, especially by the influx of peasants, city life became
more dangerous. Some personal protection was afforded by
architecture: the private home was built like a fortress,

frequently surrounded by a wall. Windows were shuttered and a central gateway was guarded by a concierge or doorman. The streets, however, were unsafe, and the upper classes often traveled in groups, with armed guards. Thus private police services were available. The development of municipal police forces in the middle of the nineteenth century came relatively late in the history of cities.

To a large extent, however, peace and order within the city were dependent on the civic pride and loyalty of its citizens. But this was always threatened by the influx of large numbers of outsiders, usually peasants and the rural disenfranchised. In the United States, over the years, every minority group that has settled in the cities has produced a high percentage of delinquents, criminals and other deviants, especially among the children of immigrants.

At present the newcomers to American cities are primarily blacks, chicanos and Puerto Ricans. Disturbed by the poverty, the dislocation, the "anomie" of the city, they respond in ways that parallel the response of earlier immigrant groups. Their problems are exacerbated by lack of economic opportunity – of unskilled and semiskilled jobs in a highly industrialized economy; by the general belief that a society should provide equality of opportunity for all its citizens; and by the fact that these groups have known intense discrimination and exploitation in their rural past.

Both political protest and individual acts of violence are intensified by the easy availability and low cost of mass-produced lethal hand weapons. This has once again made crime, "law and order" and "safety on the streets" an issue in city life, an issue particularly salient in black, white and Puerto Rican urban neighborhoods. It has developed at a time when police forces, while highly organized, appear to be inadequate to the task of providing protection for urban citizens. As a result residents of many neighborhoods have organized to protest not only the inadequacy of the police but steps taken by welfare, correctional and social-work agencies to bring into their neighborhoods prisoners and ex-prisoners, addicts and ex-addicts, welfare recipients and low-cost housing projects.

These protest movements have often led to the organization of nongovernmental civic associations, which in effect organize new communities out of mere population aggregates. At the same time dogs, private policemen and doormen have been revived as instruments of self-protection, and new ingenious ways of locking and sealing residences have been devised (accounting for a boom in the lock industry). New patterns of architecture, housing and transportation are designed to promote safety and security – an interesting revival of the medieval city-as-fortress pattern.

Ethnic and class conflicts, however, go far beyond the issues of crime and safety. Whites in the slum and ghetto areas attempt to resist the expansion of the black, chicano and Puerto Rican ghettos, especially when it is the product of administrative action by municipal government. Particular resistance is focused upon the creation of low-cost housing projects in middle- and lower-middle-class neighborhoods. In suburbia the problem expresses itself in resistance to changes in zoning regulations, which would permit working-class residents of all ethnic groups to enjoy the advantages of suburban life. When whole cities, such as Newark, become minority-group cities there are conflicts over how much state aid for welfare, housing and schools is needed to overcome problems that, by virtue of the populations, are basically ethnic.

In other cities a struggle occurs within various ethnic centers for the control of municipal institutions and agencies, especially those focused on the ghetto. Characteristically, city institutions have been dominated by older ethnic groups that have become acculturated to urban life. New arrivals thus feel left out in the face of municipal governments and institutions that are alien to their culture, their felt needs and their policy and patronage aspirations. In response they demand community control of municipal institutions. These demands go far beyond the purely political: they are struggles over patronage, life-styles and the distribution of political and economic resources. Quite frequently they activate the older ethnic groups and force them to organize political countercommunities to defend their established advantages. The effect of this activity is to intensify the conflict between old and new ethnic groups. But the ensuing struggles do not produce simple linear gains and losses for a particular group. Temporary and partial victories are often reversed,

and defeats lead to intensified hostilities and a renewal of
ethnic identities. Ethnic assertiveness is a permanent part
of the urban scene.

Political conflict arises as the city develops because of
the very nature of urban government and planning. As the
city grows, municipal governments are forced to make vast
and broad decisions affecting the way of life and the ethnic
and class distribution of its populace. Thus the location of
a subway, an apartment complex, an urban-renewal project
or the construction of a department store can all become
the basis for conflict and for the political organization of a
community.

The tendency to politicize urban communities is in part
a result of a new activism based on social science. Groups
previously unorganized and unaware of their opportunities
for political action have discovered new possibilities. Youth
has learned, at the level of local politics and government,
the power inherent in their numbers. Whenever a group
becomes concentrated ecologically, new potentialities for
organization and activity are revealed.

In the past traditional political machines organized these
"minority" groups, but the machines were not mechanisms
for the expression of minority-group claims and grievances.
Today a new awareness on the part of all groups has resulted in special-interest-group political machines organized
by ethnic- or class-oriented politicians. This direct organization of specialized constituencies is a major innovation in
American politics.

Thus when we speak of "defensive and conflict communities," we mean more than simply concentrations of an
ethnic population in a single neighborhood – more than
the struggle for jobs and for control of the organizations
and institutions that administer a given area. We mean communities whose struggles have brought about the development of a self-conscious organization of ethnic groups with
specific ideologies, loyalties, political organizations and programs. These result in the creation and recreation of ethnic identities and the construction of self-conscious ethnic
communities that extend beyond any territorial base, but
which are often organized on the basis of neighborhood
or locality.

In some cases the construction of an ethnic community in this nonterritorial sense precedes the development of neighborhood communities. Thus the civil-rights movement, black militancy and nationalism arose in response to Supreme Court decisions and national civil-rights legislation. Only later did it become localized, as blacks attempted to implement the specific rights ensuing from these decisions. Their demands for community control, jobs and the end of discrimination and exploitation produced resistance among white ethnic communities as well as in white-dominated social, economic and political institutions and agencies. This reaction and resistance forced blacks to further ideologize their claims and to organize themselves at the level of the community. Such community organization was assisted by programs of community control and was supported by private foundations (such as the Ford Foundation), by the federal government under the aegis of the Office of Economic Opportunity and by municipal governments in a wide range of community-action programs.

The development of black community-action programs – together with fear of race riots, loss of control over governmental institutions, loss of jobs and the incursion of blacks into previously white ethnic territory – caused whites to organize new neighborhood-action groups and other organizations not based on territory. In some cases these organizations were entirely new to a given ethnic group. Thus white ethnics have become militant in ways that are totally untypical of previous community organizations. In other cases older ethnic organizations were given new vitality and interest. The Chinese, at least in San Francisco, have organized themselves to resist school busing in ways not essentially different from those of Caucasian resisters.

All groups appear to follow the strategy of the Jews, who were the first group to organize themselves self-consciously and militantly against discrimination and defamation, and who worked out detailed strategies and organizations to preserve an ethnic identity and culture. But the communities created from the 1960s to the present are much more overtly political and militant than were the strategies and organizations of ethnic groups in earlier periods. In the past, ethnic groups used nonpolitical organizations to present their claims, or veiled their claims when they used political institutions. At present, ethnic and racial issues are nakedly politicized and result in direct ethnic confrontation. The development of such political communities is not smooth or linear. The emergence of new ethnic communities frequently results in political struggles within the ethnic community – over ethnic or community policy and over control of the ethnic community itself. To the extent that the parties to these troubles lack political background and experience, the internal struggles may be divisive and violent, not unlike the internal struggles of new nations as they emerge from colonialism. The development of political communities thus depends on the emergence of a viable public opinion, trust in the new community leadership and institutions, self-restraint by the new leaders and ultimately the establishment of legitimacy of the new institutions in their own community. This is an ongoing process, but one that usually take decades, if not longer, to accomplish.

While there is some tendency to think of communities as emerging naturally out of the growth of commerce and trade, some early cities were created by administrative fiat, with courts, military fortifications, religious and administration centers set up in a fixed locality. (This of course was also true of later cities – for example Washington, DC.) In addition the location of administration centers in some neighborhoods of established cities gave these centers the characteristics of the populations that were attracted to them. Yet the new kinds of communities that emerged by legislation and administrative action in the Kennedy and Johnson administrations were quite different from these earlier ones. Here the attempt was made to organize political and administrative communities in areas of the black ghetto where the indigenous populations were politically and administratively unorganized. The Economic Opportunity Act of 1964 resulted in the creation of over 2000 community-action projects. Private philanthropy and private organizations have also helped to create neighborhood, and at times city-wide, planning organizations aimed at urban renewal, development and long-term planning. Municipal governments have created neighborhood-planning advisory boards drawing from, and sometimes creating, a neighborhood leadership corps. In the Model Cities program also, local leadership was coopted into centralized and decentralized governmental administrative bodies.

These programs have had multiple consequences, and the ultimate results are not yet clear. First of all, whole new populations have been drawn into the planning and government of localities. As a result neighborhoods have become political jurisdictions quite different from established political practice in local urban politics. Traditional governmental jurisdiction, as well as old-style party machines, has frequently been bypassed. At times the new leaders have become independent of their administrative creators and have used their new positions to confront and combat their original sponsors. At other times the apathy of the coopted leadership has paralyzed the actions of the sponsoring agency. At still other times conflict within community groups, together with a lack of experience in political action, have splintered and fragmented the communities, preventing the functioning of traditional political machinery while not creating an effective substitute machinery. Much of the new leadership corps is self-selected within a certain neighborhood. Thus in some areas a new black leadership has emerged; in others a new middle-class local leadership.

In addition, commitment to national politics and issues has had peculiar and unanticipated effects on the politics of local communities. "New-style" political leaders have drawn the youthful members of the middle and upper-middle classes into politics. At different times this group has focused on such issues as control of the atom bomb, the war on poverty, civil rights, the war in Vietnam, ecology and the quality of life. With the death, defeat or failure of candidates and the loss of salience of issues, the new political groups have often thrown themselves into local politics. They have participated in "reform" politics and have joined planning and community boards. Quite often they have been at odds with, or have bypassed, established party and political machinery, frequently rendering that machinery inoperative. At the same time this new "government by amateurs" has not always been able to organize itself into a coherent, all-embracing political machine. As a result the new local politics has often emasculated the older machine politics without creating workable alternatives.

The overall effect of this new participation has been to politicize communities and create new ones, especially in areas once dominated by political machines and governmental agencies where residents have been apathetic or where agencies were unable or unwilling to respond to changes in the local population. These new action and community groups are a significant development in the American city, and the full effect of their activities remains to be seen.

At a different level, ongoing social organizations and institutions have become the basis for new communities. In a metropolitan area a single organization can be so large that its very operation creates a community. Some of these are total institutions whose members are isolated from the outside population, such as prisons, mental institutions, detention centers, drug rehabilitation centers and even monasteries. Other institutions, because of their size, cultural and administrative separateness, technological specialization and spatial separateness, can create a specialized type of community with a distinctive culture. These include hospitals, universities, cultural centers and central organizational headquarters. Finally, some formally organized institutions become centers for community action on the basis of their self-selected specialization. Thus a day-care center, a local cultural center or a community center can become the basis of an organized community.

On the other hand countercommunities can develop from opposition to such institutions, especially to prisons, detention centers, hospitals, universities or religious organizations. A countercommunity can be temporary, organized to resist the policy of a particular institution, or it can itself become institutionalized and a basis of community organization. The number of total, semitotal and countercommunities in this country is unknown and almost unaccountable, and yet they remain one of the central organizing modes of urban life today. The values upon which they organize themselves are as diverse as the values upon which individuals base their lives. Regardless of their basis, these voluntary, one-dimensional communities permit the urbanite to escape from the tyranny of residential space restrictions and provide a range of activity and liberation that enables him or her to make the most of the advantages of urban life. All forms of human expression are capable of being institutionalized and communalized in a metropolitan area where the population density is great enough to supply the requisite number of members.

13 Private, Parochial and Public Social Orders: The Problem of Crime and Incivility in Urban Communities*
Albert Hunter

INTRODUCTION

The purpose of this chapter is to analyze the nature of social control in urban neighborhoods by recasting the central polarities of *gemeinschaft* and *gesellschaft*, community and society. The analysis is both theoretically and empirically eclectic, but it is committed to an *institutional* approach, what Ralph Turner (1980), in referring to Morris Janowitz's recent work, has called the "forgotten paradigm" of American sociology. The explication more finely differentiates among types of social orders, their corresponding forms of social control, and as well their interdependence and mutual limits. The approach is diametrically opposed to more evolutionary grand theories, which simply see community being "eroded," "eclipsed," or "effaced" by the modern social order. Rather, the different forms of social order and social control are seen to mutually coexist, and given varying conditions, new and different combinations will be dynamically constructed.

I will first distinguish among the three levels or types of social order – the private, the parochial, and the public. I will then apply these to a grounded analysis of the nature of crime and incivility within urban communities.[1] Finally I will explore the mutually interacting and limiting

---

* Reprinted from G. Suttles and M. Zald (eds), *The Challenge of Social Control* (Norwood, NJ: Ablex Publishers, 1985).

mechanisms of social control specific to each of these three social orders.

The Institutional Approach to Social Order and Social Control

Social control, in its original and more generic meaning, is concerned with the capacity for "self-regulation" by social groups (Janowitz, 1978), and its institutional analysis stresses both normative and structural components. The normative component includes the standards and values for assessing appropriate and deviant behavior, while the structural component includes the patterned distribution of resources within a social group that may be utilized to sanction the behaviors of its members. This generic conception of social control is at odds with the more narrow, specific use of the concept to refer to coercion or force. The generic conception is analytically more powerful for it allows one to distinguish among different forms of social control, of which coercion is only one, and also to account for historical and situational variations in the forms of social control. By emphasizing "self-regulation," social control becomes an inherent part of the structure and the process of social groups, rather than the episodic actions engaged in by singular institutions (Erickson, 1966). Simply put, to the degree that social order exists, social control exists.

The institutional approach to social control remains uncommitted to either a reified cultural or a deterministic structural perspective. Neither sentiments and beliefs nor resources of power and property are alone given casual priority. As Stinchcombe (1968) has observed, an institutional approach requires that one search at the point of correlation between values *and* power, for order and control emerge from the intersection of both cultural constraints and material conditions.

PRIVATE, PAROCHIAL, AND PUBLIC SOCIAL ORDERS

Three different social orders – the private, the parochial, and the public – are easily distinguished as qualitatively distinct, ideal types. Operationally, one may pursue the question of whether or not each can be treated as a variable, assessing the degree of "privateness", "parochialness", or "publicness" of specific social phenomena. A focus upon these three, and especially the parochial, is particularly useful in organizing data that bear on the problem of social control in contemporary urban communities. In differentiating among these three orders I will isolate three dimensions: the substance and form of their basic social bond, their institutional locus, and their characteristic spatial and physical domain.

Basic Social Bond

Differences in the basic social bonds among these three social orders owes much to the discussion of Edward Shils (1975) in his seminal work, "Primordial, Personal, Sacred, and Civil Ties".[2] First, the three social orders may be arrayed along a continuum of decreasing affect or sentiment from the private to the parochial to the public. The civil tie, in marked contrast to the personal, is affectively neutral or reserved, and furthermore it is most universal, most formal, and according to Goffman (1971), most ritualized. By contrast, the personal tie is more often seen as a uniquely constructed and emergent social bond negotiated among participants (Strauss, 1978).

The parochial bond, in turn is intermediate in affect and sentiment, and in its degree of variability or uniformity. Furthermore, mutual knowledge of particular others with whom one interacts within each type of social bond decreases from private, to parochial, to public. The combined cognitive and affective components are adequately expressed in the social typology of intimate, acquaintance, and stranger.

The structural positions or statuses defined by these three bonds within the three social orders are, respectively, friend, neighbor, and fellow citizen. Each of these statuses implies its structural equivalent in dyadic interaction: friend to friend, neighbor to neighbor and citizen to citizen; and each also implies a larger collective unit of which it is part: a group of friends or kin, a local community, and the state.

The dyadic bonds of each of these social orders is shaped or given form by this overarching collective unit, and in turn each dyadic relationship is mediated through and by the collective unit. Though "friendship" is celebrated as a uniquely emergent and particularistic form of interaction, it is, except in rare circumstances, embedded within a network that is significant in supporting or thwarting the dyadic bond (Rubin, 1983). The neighboring role, as Keller (1968) has shown, is variable from neighborhood to neighborhood; and similarly, both Goffman's (1963) analysis of *Behavior in Public Places*, and Lofland's (1973) observations on the *World of Strangers* suggest that the fragile world of public encounters among citizens is embedded within a pattern of civility or mutually acknowledged rights among equals.

For each of these dyadic relationships in the three social orders there is an important normative asymmetry with respect to the ratio of rights to duties for both interpersonal encounters, and in relationships between the individual and the collective. Within the private order of friendship and kinship obligations are far greater than the claims to rights within the collective, or from others. As friend or kin one is expected to honor an extraordinarily wide range of obligations without question. For co-residents of a community the ratio of rights to duties is more evenly balanced, as a calculus of "limited liability" produces a more balanced sense of mutual obligation and distributive justice. However, within the public order, the ratio of rights to duties is skewed more in the directtion of public rights over public duty. Whether phrased in the calculus of the "tragedy of the commons" or the "free rider problem" of the logic of collective action (Olson, 1971), duties to the public collective and one's fellow citizens have waned in proportion to one's civil rights within the state. This latter shift is a direct outgrowth of the extension of citizenship as Marshall (1964) notes, from civil to economic rights, and the related rise of the welfare state (Janowitz, 1978). While one is increasingly entitled to enjoy the expanded rights of a civil society, obligations to others and the collective are increasingly limited and defined as voluntary. This asymmetry is associated with the increasingly economic and pecuniary nature of the exchange of citizen rights and duties (exchange of taxes for governmental services). This is balanced somewhat in the link of the individual to the state, but decreasingly balanced in the dyadic links among fellow citizens. Where the private order relies upon the exchange of sentiment the parochial order upon the exchange of voluntary labor, the public order is increasingly defined in terms of the cost/benefit ratio of a cash nexus where personal profit in social exchanges between citizens results from rights (benefits) being greater than duties (costs).

Institutional Locus

Following the conception of institutions as the correlation of power and values we can more readily locate and define the institutions of the private, parochial, and public social orders. The private order of friends is found in both informal and more formal primary groups where the values of sentiment, social support, and esteem are the essential resources of the social order and the basis of social control. The giving or withholding of these values in varying frequencies of face-to-face interaction establish the varying power arrangements within groups. These can be empirically observed in case studies of primary groups such as Whyte's *Street Corner Society* (1955), and sociometric models and survey studies of interpersonal friendship networks (Hunter, 1983; Fischer, 1982). The institutions of kinship similarly operate within the private social order. As functions increasingly move out of the family and the private social order, its social support function looms ever more central (Lasch, 1977). The power arrangements of gender and age, rooted in traditional authority, serve to structure this private order, but they are decreasing in significance as more egalitarian mutual ties of socioemotional support become the basis of power and exchange.

The parochial social order is based on the local interpersonal networks and interlocking of local institutions that serve the diurnal and sustenance needs of the residential community – the local stores, schools, churches, and voluntary associations of various kinds. The values of the parochial order are twofold (1) providing mutual aid and sustenance support, and (2) the differential distribution of local community status, or reputation, and power (Barber, 1961). Power arrangements within a community are to be found in the interlocking of local institutional leaders – local businessman, religious leaders, directors and board members of local voluntary organizations, etc. (Laumann, *et al.*, 1978). The key commodity of exchange within the parochial order is voluntary labor, for as Janowitz (1978) notes, the parochial order of "limited liability" is the core of voluntarism in American society.

The institutional base of public order is found preeminently in the formal, bureaucratic agencies of the state. The values of efficacy, efficiency, and equity in the democratic welfare state center upon the delivery of public goods and services to meet citizens' demands. In sharp contrast with the private and parochial orders, the public order is ultimately structured by the state's claim to a legitimate monopoly of the use of coercion, force, and violence (Weber, 1978). The legitimacy of this claim to a monopoly of coercion is at the crux of the contemporary asymmetry between citizen rights and duties in the public order. The calculus of legitimacy is questioned to the degree that this monopoly by the state is seen by some as either capricious, selective, inequitable, or ineffective. The calculus of distributive justice shifts from the simple exchange between self and collectivity in the realm of public safety to a more complex pluralistic distributive justice of comparative advantage among competing groups. It is in this sense that inequality in the provision of citizenship rights creates the conditions for eroding a sense of individual duty to the public collective.

To the degree that coercion or violence are used by institutions of the private, and especially the parochial order, they undermine the social control mechanisms of the rational legal public order. A civil society cannot tolerate the systematic use of violence by private and parochial social orders, even when they are used for legitimate ends. This is, in fact, one of the major points of conflict between these three social orders.

The Spatial Domain

Each of the three social orders is associated with a characteristic spatial distribution and physical locus. Much social theory assumes away the spatial aspect of social phenomena, or treats it as a ubiquitous and unvarying condition.[3] Either way, it is too seldom directly incorporated into social theories, as an explicit set of variables, as cause or consequence. I suggest that an adequate understanding of these three social orders, their processes of social control, and their mutual interdependence requires an explicit consideration of their characteristic spatial domains.

The spatial structure of the private social order is defined by two extremes of the metropolitan environment, the household, and the metropolitan-wide network of personal relations that link these private nodes. As Fischer (1977) and Wellman and Leighton (1979) have found in their recent research, the physical distribution of friendship is seldom constrained to physical proximity, as in the neighborhood, but is widely distributed throughout the metropolitan field. To focus solely upon the household, the dwelling, or similar micro-level physical units is to miss this important more expansive spatial characteristic of the private social order. The metropolitan-wide spatial network of the private order is especially important for the mutual interaction between the private and the public orders. It is this characteristic that most often brings these two social orders into contact, and raises problems for their different mechanisms of social control.

To focus upon the household alternatively highlights the point of contact between the private and the parochial social orders. As people move outside of their dwellings they are most immediately entering the physical domain of the parochial social order. However, whether or not they are entering a parochial social order depends upon the strength of that social order, and the operation of its mechanisms of social control. By definition, the parochial social order is necessarily based upon the physical proximity of neigh-dwellers, co-habitants of a common area sharing a common fate. These parochial social orders are well documented in the classic case studies by Gans (*Urban Villagers*, 1962) and Suttles (his "segmental" *Social Order of the Slum*, 1968). In both, the dense networks of personal knowledge and trust, held together in interlocking local institutions, result in spatial and social boundaries that can be used to define insiders who are mutually accountable to one another, while outsiders have more limited rights within the community. Because it moves out of the household, the parochial social order is often defined as but another variant of the public order over and against the private social order. However, this parochial order is qualitatively distinct from the public order. It is not a world of citizen strangers, and rarely are the operations of formal agents of social control observed or central to its operations. The parochial social order leaves unresolved the problems of public order in a civil society.

The spatial domain of the public order is not simply a residual of places left over after extracting the private order of households, and the parochial order of neighborhoods; neither is it, to go to the other extreme, ubiquitous within the legal territorial boundaries of a given government or state. The spatial domain of the public order is characteristically found at the points of intersection and interpenetration of other social orders. It is found preeminently at those locations where people are most likely to be interacting solely as citizens. That is not to say that the interactants are not sometimes operating simultaneously within other social orders, for the public order is often the point where individuals from different social orders meet, where social worlds collide. Public places – the streets, the sidewalks – are public domains that often link private and parochial worlds (Jacobs, 1961; Lofland, 1973, 1983). Public places such as nodes, areas, and paths – downtowns, parks and subways (Lynch, 1960) – to the degree that they "belong" to no one, are not parts of private and parochial orders, therefore belong equally to everyone. Their use then is considered the legitimate right of all as citizens of the state. This is the spatial domain of the public order, and as with private and parochial orders, it is difficult to delineate without mutual reference to the others. We will now explore the nature of "disorder" within these three social orders, specifically, the question of crime and incivility in urban neighborhoods and how the three social orders interact in their attempts at social control.

CRIME AND INCIVILITY IN LOCAL COMMUNITIES

The concern with crime over the past decade has by and large centered upon rising rates of victimization from violent crime committed in urban areas throughout the nation, especially in public places by strangers. This is exemplified clearly by the slogan "crime in the streets." The emphasis upon crime has in turn spawned a "safety industry" both public and private, the former exemplified by the rapid rise (and fall) of the Law Enforcement Assistance Administration (LEAA) of the Federal Department of Justice, and the latter in numerous "target hardening" devices for the home, ranging from relatively inexpensive locks to elaborate burglar alarm systems. The rising "fear of crime" far outstrips any objective measure of the rising "rate of crime." The absence of specific correlations between actual victimization and fear has been noted by numerous researchers (DuBow, 1978). For example, the elderly have the highest fear level but the lowest rate of victimization, while teenagers have the lowest fear level and the highest victimization, and women are more fearful but less victimized than men.

Furthermore, the fear of specific victimizations is far different from the most likely victimization. Most assaults, murders, and rapes occur in the home to victims who know their assailant; and yet, most fear is expressed in settings and situations where the crime is committed by a stranger in public places. Biderman *et al.* (1967) have summarized these findings most succinctly, "fear of crime is the fear of strangers."

Given this definition of the problem, it follows that attention should focus upon the public order and the institution most clearly concerned with social control in the public arena – the police. LEAA then poured money into police technology and social science research in an attempt to increase the efficiency of police practices. However, this narrowly focused conception of "social control" abandoned a rich sociological tradition and misspecified both its problem and solution. As Wilson (1968) among others has noted, the primary function of the police is to maintain a *semblance* of public order, not to "catch criminals." As such, the police are primarily a reactive instrument of social control, responding to "calls for service." By asking who calls, for what service, and why, the issue of social control may be broadened beyond the narrowly defined problem of efficient police practice.

However, even in studies which have looked at these questions (Reiss, 1971), analyses have remained narrowly focused on police practice although answers to the problem of social control were suggested in the data. These studies noted that police often had to "waste time" with such "noncriminal complaints" as family disputes, teenagers hanging out on the corner, drunks in hallways, and various acts of vandalism. If a high proportion of police activity is geared to such disruptions of the social order it is in part for two reasons: (1) these acts are much more frequent than "serious crimes" no matter what the "serious crime rate" may be; and (2) these are the disruptions of the social order that are of sufficient concern and visibility to local residents to prompt them to call the police for service.

Findings such as these suggested a slightly different question than previous research; namely, "What is it that people fear?" In both field interviews and surveys, the answer became clear: though people express a general fear of "serious" criminal victimization, when asked when and where they are most fearful, the answer came in terms of those ubiquitous signs in the environment that suggested a more pervasive loss of social order what I have called "symbols of incivility" (Hunter, 1978). It is these numerous "petty assaults" against the social order that produce an "urban unease" (Wilson, 1975) which is then translated into "fear." Most often, these assaults on the public order are either anonymous (graffiti, vandalism) or perpetrated by strangers . . .

It is apparent, therefore, that the rising fear and concern about crime is experientially rooted in a more pervasive experience than the more narrow question of serious crime and police practices. Once again, Biderman *et al.* (1967) have summarized it best: "We have found that attitudes of citizens regarding crime are less affected by their past victimization than by their ideas about what is going on in their community – fears about a weakening of social controls on which they feel their safety and the broader fabric of social life is ultimately dependent."

The Intersection and Disarticulation of Private, Parochial and Public Social Control

Disruption of the social order may emanate from any one of our three social orders, the private, the parochial, or the public. However, the resulting attempts at social control are likely to emerge not simply within a given social order, but as well from one or both of the remaining social orders. When family violence spills into the streets, or rival ethnic street gangs from nearby neighborhoods clash, then the public agents of social control, the police, are likely to be called on to restore order. There is a built in asymmetry in this process that is related to the increasing expansion of the state (Marshall 1964; Meyer and Hannan, 1979; Janowitz, 1978); namely, that the institutions of public social control, specifically the police and the criminal justice system, have both claimed and increasingly become defined as the final or "ultimate" source of social control. This asymmetry is the joint outcome of state expansion of the rights of citizenship to demand increasing protection of person and property from violence, and in Weber's terms, the state's claim to the monopoly of that violence.

However, given the bureaucratic organization of state structures with their emphasis upon efficiency, and given increasing fiscal constraints faced by state structures at all levels but especially by municipal governments (Clark, 1981; O'Conner, 1973), the police are increasingly limited in their capacity to satisfy the increasing demands for their services. The potential for a crisis of legitimacy has prompted a search for alternative solutions to the problem of social control by shifting the focus to other social orders, one of the results of which is what may be labelled "the rediscovery of community" (Hunter, 1979; Hunter, 1985). The parochial and private social orders are "enlisted," and often nourished with state resources, in an attempt to counteract the prevailing sense of disorder on the streets of urban neighborhoods.

Although the breakdown of the private order of the family is often mentioned by both social analysts and local residents as the cause of urban disorder, two qualifications have to be noted. The first is that crimes of passion (murder, assault, and rape) occur precisely within the private social order where affect is highest, and few people propose a public or parochial solution to this problem. Second, the major perpetrators of some of the serious crimes and most of the "incivilities" are teenagers. However, this does not necessarily imply a breakdown of the family, for adolescence is traditionally the age at which one's interests, activities, and interactions move outside of the nuclear family into the wider community (Erickson, 1968). The failure to deal adequately with adolescents therefore reflects more of a break in the link between parochial and private social orders than a break down of the private social order itself. It is the interlocking institutions of the local community that have generally provided for social control of teenagers – the schools, churches, YMCAs, athletic leagues, and the like (Zald, 1970).

Many of the activities of the parochial order that support these local institutions, as we have seen, rely upon the voluntary contribution and labor of one's fellow neighbors. However, such voluntary activity is difficult to elicit and maintain in the face of increasing expectation that the state should provide many of these services. Rising social disorder in urban communities would therefore appear to be more the result of a disarticulation with the parochial order than a failure of the state to provide social control in the public order. Yet, because of state expansion there is a greater expectation on the part of citizens for state actions for social control, a social control the state is inadequately equipped to provide because of its own formal restraints.

The solution to the dilemma is not for the state to engage in direct social control, that is, to attempt to increase its efficiency in catching criminals; but rather, for the state to increasingly support stronger parochial orders what will engage in social control activities in conjunction with the state and the private order. This is the solution that is, in fact, emerging in many urban areas throughout the nation. For example, local community organizations in urban neighborhoods are often explicitly concerned in their activities about social control and "doing something" about crime. When asked what they are doing the typical responses include: cleaning up garbage and litter in the streets, getting rid of eyesores and abandoned buildings, developing youth centers, and sponsoring more direct programs such as Block Watch, Operation I.D., or Whistlestop (Podolefsky and DuBow, 1979). In short, the definition of social disorder and proposed solutions again focus on the parochial and public orders and their institutional interlinkage to deal with the ubiquitous symbols of incivility.

The ultimate success of a variety of local crime control programs appears to depend upon whether or not they are embedded in ongoing community organizations. As federal agencies in conjunction with local police departments attempt to establish such programs as citizen patrols, Block Watch, and Whistlestop, the continued success of these programs requires the structure of a larger community organization to provide for voluntary recruitment and sustained participation. People join local community organizations as "quasigovernments"; that is, they pay taxes or dues to a democratic territorial collective, offer labor and services, and, in turn, expect the organization to provide for a multifacted set of concerns and interests both internally in organizing the activities of one's neighbors, and externally in relationship with outside actors and agencies (Taub *et al.*, 1977; Davidson, 1979). Such organizations most often include or interlock with other local institutions such as schools, churches, and local businesses. As a structural embodiment of the parochial social order, the social control activities of such organizations are precisely those that the police require to more effectively perform their function of social control in the public arena. The parochial order can operate most effectively in the realm of surveillance, a limited form of mutual assistance that the police are inadequately staffed to perform and a function that feeds into the police authority to exercise coercion and their responsibility to face danger. In short, the parochial and the public social orders are functionally different, each is limited, and yet they are mutually interdependent upon one another. One should note also that local organizations and parochial institutions are also mutually interdependent with a number of state agents other than the police in maintaining the parochial and the public order. For example, building departments that enforce housing codes, school administrators that enforce discipline in and around schools, and street and sanitation departments that deal with the *semblance* of a *physical* social order.

Similarly, the private social order provides a basic bond that is limited in its social control activities in the public arena, for it operates at best as a segmented and limited network of personal trust. However, the linking of these networks through parochial institutions such as schools, churches, and local organizations enables these parochial institutions to mobilize the powerful social control of the interpersonal bond.

The private, the parochial, and the public social orders cannot maintain social order throughout a society without a mutual interdependence. Each is limited in the functions and activities it can perform, and it is precisely at those limits that the other social orders come into play. The problem of social disorder is more a function of the disarticulation among these social orders than it is due to the failure to any one of them. A civil society, that provides both for safety *from*, strangers and safety *for* strangers, requires an acknowledgement of the intrinsic limits, and a recognition of the need for better articulation among the private, the parochial, and the public social orders.

Notes

1. The analysis draws from and is "grounded in" research recently completed at the Center for Urban Affairs and Policy Research at Northwestern University. "The Reactions to Crime Project." This was a five year, multimethodological study of both individual and collective reactions to crime in four urban neighborhoods in each of three cities – Philadelphia, Chicago, and San Francisco. The data come from both neighborhood and city-wide surveys, and from year-long fieldwork and participant observation in each of the 12 neighborhoods. (See Skogan *et al.*, 1982).

2. First, I am in effect, using Shils's discussion of "personal" and "civil" ties, but I am not, for the purposes at hand, dealing with the "primordial" or the "sacred." Furthermore, in spite of the usual linkage of Gemeinschaft to the primordial ties of blood and land, the "parochial" social order is not necessarily considered a *primordial* type, especially in discussions of contemporary urban neighborhoods (See Suttles, 1972). Secondly, I incorporate both friend and kin within my discussion of the "private" social order.

3. There are two major exceptions to this observation. First are the
micro theories of personal interaction such as Goffman's (1971)
analysis of the "staging" of everyday public life, and Sommer's (1969)
analysis of personal space, and second are the more macro theories
in urban sociology from the early human ecologists of the Chicago
School (Park and Burgess, 1924) to more contemporary political
economists such as Castells (1977) and Harvey (1973).

References

Barber, B. (1961). "Family status, local-community status, and social
stratification: Three types of social ranking." *Pacific Sociological Re-
view, IV* (1) 3–10.
Biderman, A. D., Johnson, L. A., Intyre, J. M. & Weir, A. (1967). Re-
port on a Pilot Study in the District of Columbia on Victimization
and Attitudes Toward Law Enforcement, Field Surveys I National
Commission on Law Enforcement and Administration of Justice.
Washington, DC: US Government Printing Office.
Castells, M. (1977). *The urban question.* Cambridge, MA: MIT Press.
Clark, T. N. (ed.). (1981) *Urban policy analysis.* Beverly Hills, CA: Sage.
Davidson, J. L. (1979). *Political partnerships.* Beverly Hills, CA: Sage.
DuBow, F. (1978). "Reactions to Crime: A Critical Review of the Lit-
erature". Evanston, IL: Center for Urban Affairs and Policy Research,
Northwestern University.
Erikson, K. T. (1966). *Wayward puritans: A study in the sociology of de-
viance.* New York: Wiley.
Erikson, E. H. (1968). *Identity, youth and crisis.* New York:W. W. Norton.
Fischer, C. S. (1977). *Networks and places: Social relations in the urban
setting.* New York: Free Press.
Fischer, C. S. (1982). *To dwell among friends: Personal networks in town
and city.* Chicago: University of Chicago Press.
Gans, H. J. (1962). *The urban villagers: Group and class in the life of
Italian-Americans.* New York: Free Press.
Goffman, E. (1963). *Behavior in public places.* New York: The Free Press.
Goffman, E. (1971). *Relations in public: Microstudies of the public order.*
New York: Basic Books.
Harvey, D. (1973). *Social justice and the city.* Baltimore: John Hopkins
University Press.
Hunter, A. (1978). "Symbols of Incivility: Social Disorder and Fear of
Crime in Urban Neighborhoods." Evanston, IL: Reactions to Crime
Project, Center for Urban Affairs and Policy Research, Northwestern
University.
Hunter, A. (1979). "The urban neighborhood: Its analytical and social
contexts." *Urban Affairs Quarterly, 14* (3), 267–288.
Hunter, A. (1983). "Friends and Associates: Informal and Formal Status
Structures of Community Elites." Evanston, IL: Center for Urban Affairs
and Policy Research, Northwestern University.

224   *Private, Parochial and Public Social Orders*

Hunter, A. (1985). "The meaning of community in community mental health." *Journal of Community Psychology*, (forthcoming).
Jacobs, J. (1961). *The death and life of great American cities.* New York: Random House.
Janowitz, M. (1978). *The last half-century: Societal change and politics in America.* Chicago: University of Chicago Press.
Keller, S. I. (1968). *The urban neighborhood: A sociological perspective.* New York: Random House.
Lasch, C. (1977). *Haven in a heartless world: The family besieged.* New York: Basic Books.
Laumann, E. O., Galaskiewicz, J. & Marsden, P. V. (1978). Community structure and interorganizational linkages. *Annual Review of Sociology, 4,* 455–84.
Lofland, L. H. (1973). *A world of strangers: Order and action in urban public space.* New York: Basic Books.
Lofland, L. H. (1983). "Understanding urban life: The Chicago legacy." *Urban Life, 11* (4), 491–511.
Lynch, K. (1960) (1975). *The image of the city.* Cambridge, MA: MIT Press.
Marshall, T. H. (1964). *Class, citizenship and social development.* Garden City: Doubleday.
Meyer, J. W. & Hannan, M. T. (1979). *National development and the world system.* Chicago: University of Chicago Press.
O'Connor, J. (1973). *The fiscal crisis of the state.* New York: St. Martin's Press.
Olson, M. (1971). *The logic of collective action: Public goods and the theory of groups.* Cambridge, MA: Harvard University Press.
Park, R. E. & Burgess, E. W. (1924). *Introduction to the science of sociology* (2nd. ed.). Chicago: University of Chicago Press.
Podolefsky, A. & DuBow, F. (1979). "Citizen Participation in Collective Responses to Crime." Evanston: IL: Center for Urban Affairs and Policy Research, Northwestern University.
Reiss, A. J. (1971). *The police and the public.* New Haven, CT: Yale university Press.
Rubin, L. B. (1983). *Intimate strangers.* New York: Harper and Row.
Shils, E. A. (1975). *Center and periphery: Essays in macrosociology.* Chicago: University of Chicago Press.
Skogan, W. G. *et al.* (1982). "Executive Summary: The Reactions to Crime Project." Evanston, IL: The Center for Urban Affairs and Policy Research, Northwestern University.
Sommer, R. (1969). *Personal space: The behavioral basis of design,* Englewood Cliffs, NJ: Prentice-Hall.
Stinchcombe, A. L. (1968). *Constructing social theories.* New York: Harcourt, Brace and World.
Strauss, A. L. (1978). *Negiotations: Varieties, contexts, processes, and social order,* p. 275. San Francisco: Jossey-Bass.
Suttles, G. D. (1968). *The social order of the slum.* Chicago: University of Chicago Press.
Suttles, G. D. (1972). *The social construction of communities.* Chicago: University of Chicago Press.

Taub, R. P., Surgeon, G. P., Lindholm, S., Otti, P. B. & Bridges, A. (1977). Urban voluntary associations, locality based and externally induced. *American Journal of Sociology*, 83, 425–442.

Turner, R. H. (1980). The forgotten paradigm? *Contemporary Sociology*, 9 (5), 609–612.

Weber, M. (1978). *Economy and society*. Berkeley: University of California Press.

Wellman, B. & Leighton, B. (1979). "Networks, neighborhoods, and communities: Approaches to the study of the community question." *Urban Affairs Quarterly*, 14, 363–390.

Whyte, W. F. (1955). *Street corner society*. Chicago: University of Chicago Press.

Wilson, J. Q. (1968). *Varieties of police behavior: The management of law and order in eight communities*. Cambridge, MA: Harvard University Press.

Wilson, J. Q. (1975). *Thinking about crime*. New York: Basic Books.

Zald, M. N. (1970). *Organizational change: The political economy of the YMCA*. Chicago: University of Chicago Press.

14 Community Becomes Uncivilized*
Richard Sennett

Ever since the work of Camillo Sitte a century ago, city planners have committed themselves to the building or preservation of community territory in the city as a social goal. Sitte was the leader of the first generation of urbanists to revolt against the monumental scale of Baron Haussmann's planning for Paris. Sitte was a Pre-Raphaelite of cities, arguing that only when the scale and functions of urban life returned to the simplicities of the late medieval era would people find the kind of mutual support and direct contact with each other which makes the city a valuable environment. Today we would dismiss this idealization of the medieval town as an escapist romance, but it is curious how the essentials of the first urban Pre-Raphaelite's vision has come to dominate the modern urbanist's imagination. Or rather, the belief in small-scale community has become ever more powerful an ideal. Whereas Sitte, or in an allied way the visionaries of the "garden city" in England, imagined community relations to transpire within a properly designed city, today planners have largely given up hope on properly designing the city as a whole – because they have come to recognize both their own limits of knowledge and their lack of political clout. They instead have enshrined working at a community level, against whatever interests of money and politics dominate the shaping of the whole city. Sitte's generation conceived of community within the city; today's urbanist conceives of community against the city.

The thread between Sitte's generation and our own is an assumption about impersonality, as it is experienced in the city, which makes face-to-face contacts in a territorial community seem so important. This assumption is that imper-

* Reprinted from Richard Sennett, *The Fall of Public Man* (New York: Alfred A. Knopf, 1976).

sonality is a summation, a result, a tangible effect of all
the worst evils of industrial capitalism. The belief that
impersonality manifests the ills of capitalism is so prevalent among the public at large as well as among urban
planners that it is worth looking at the idea in some detail, for it leads to a bizarre end.

Industrial capitalism, we all know, divorces the man at
work from the work he does, for he does not control his
own labor, but rather must sell it. Therefore, we all know,
the fundamental problem of capitalism is dissociation, called
variously alienation, non-cathectic activity, and the like;
division, separation, isolation are the governing images which
express this evil. Any situation which puts a distance between people must therefore reinforce, if it does not directly result from, capitalistic forces of dissociation. The
very idea of the unknown can modulate into seeming one
form of the problem of capitalism; just as man is distant
from his work, he is distant from his fellows. A crowd would
be a prime example; crowds are bad because people are
unknown to one another. Once this modulation occurs –
and it has a consistency in emotional terms if not in pure
logic – then to overcome the unknown, to erase differences
between people, seems to be a matter of overcoming part
of the basic illness of capitalism. To erase this strangerhood,
you try to make intimate and local the scale of human
experience – that is, you make local territory morally sacred.
It is celebration of the ghetto.

Now precisely what gets lost in this celebration is the
idea that people grow only by processes of encountering
the unknown. Things and persons which are strange may
upset familiar ideas and received truths; unfamiliar terrain
serves a positive function in the life of a human being. The
function it serves is to accustom the human being to take
risks. Love of the ghetto, especially the middle-class ghetto,
denies the person a chance to enrich his perceptions, his
experience, and learn that most valuable of all human lessons,
the ability to call the established conditions of his life into
question.

Of course, the capitalist system does dissociate man from
his work. But it is important to see the ways in which this
system, like any other, controls not only the ideas of those

who are its defenders, but shapes the imagination of those
who are in revolt against its evils. All too often, what is
"self-evidently wrong" about a social system is self-evident
precisely because the critique fits nicely into, and does little
damage to, the system as a whole. In this case, the celebration of territorial community against the evils of impersonal, capitalist urbanism quite comfortably fits into the
larger system, because it leads to a logic of local defense
against the outside world, rather than a challenge to the
workings of that world. When a community "fights" city
hall on these terms, it fights to be left alone, to be exempted
or shielded from the political process, rather than to change
the political process itself. And this is why the emotional
logic of community, beginning as a resistance to the evils
of modern capitalism, winds up at a bizarre kind of
depoliticized withdrawal; the system remains intact, but
maybe we can get it to leave our piece of turf untouched.

But, it might be argued, you are too idealistic: sheer
survival in a harsh world is a virtue. If people can reasonably do no more than defend their local communities, then
why criticize this – especially as the public world of that
larger city is so empty and uninhabitable? What I want to
do in the following pages is show that we have no choice
but to try to make that larger world habitable; the reason
is that, given the terms of personality which have developed in the modern period, the experience of other people's
personalities in an intimate communal territory is itself a
destructive process. Modern community seems to be about
fraternity in a dead, hostile world; it is in fact all too often
an experience of fratricide. Furthermore, these terms of
personality which govern face-to-face relationships in a community are likely to cut down the desire of people to experience those jolts which might occur in a more unfamiliar
terrain. These jolts are necessary to a human being to give
him that sense of tentativeness about his own beliefs which
every civilized person must have. The destruction of a city
of ghettoes is both a political and a psychological necessity.

Perhaps I put the matter so strongly because I and many
other writers in the New Left during the last decade so
erroneously believed that the rebuilding of local community was the starting point for politically rebuilding the

larger society. Ours could be called "experiential fallacy": if in direct experience there were radical changes in belief and behavior, then the people so altered would gradually collectivize this experience, bringing light and change to others.

Today, the patronizing and upper-class character of this belief in intra- as interpersonal change is excruciatingly clear. Even if the idea of building a community sharing intimately new forms of experience had been initiated by the oppressed, or sustained by them, I think the results would have come to the same dead end. For what is wrong about the notion of building a community against the world is that it assumes that the very terms of intimate experience would indeed permit people to create a new kind of sociability, based on the sharing of their feelings.

BARRICADES BUILT AROUND A COMMUNITY

The larger society, of which radical community organizers form an unwitting part, has focused attention on small-scale community life in two ways. It has first done so practically, and second, ideologically.

The real estate ideas of Baron Haussmann in the last century were based on homogenization. New districts in the city were to be of a single class, and in the old central city rich and poor were to be isolated from each other. This was the beginning of "single function" urban development. Each space in the city does a particular job, and the city itself is atomized. In the American middle-class suburbs of the 1950s, single-function planning reached an extreme instance; houses were built en bloc in vast numbers, with the services for families in those houses located somewhere else: a "community center," an "educational park," a shopping center, a hospital "campus." Large-scale planners in the rest of the world were quick to deride the emptiness, tastelessness, and the like of these suburban tracts, and at the same time have blithely proceeded to build in the same manner. Take settlements as diverse as the new city of Brasília in Brazil, Levittown, Pennsylvania, and the Euston Center in London, and you will find the results of planning in which one-space, one-function is the operant principle. In Brasília, it is building by building, in Levittown it is zone by zone, in Euston Center it is horizontal level by horizontal level. Although these planning ideas may be profitable to put into practice – for there is a single and coherent investment in a known quantity – they are not practical to use. For one thing, if the functional needs of the localized area change historically, the space cannot respond; it can only be used for its original purpose, or be abandoned, or be prematurely destroyed and remade. The difficulties of Brasília are well known in this respect, but the process has a larger dimension than single plans which fail. Think, for instance, of what a city of atoms, with a space for each class to live, for each race to live, for each class and race to work, means for attempts at racial or class integration, either in education or in leisure: displacement and invasion must become the actual experiences involved in the supposed experience of intergroup rapprochement. Whether such forced mixings would ever work in racialist or highly class-segregated societies is an open question; the point is that a city map of single-functions, single-spaces makes all such problems worse.

The atomizing of the city has put a practical end to an essential component of public space: the overlay of function in a single territory, which creates complexities of experience on that turf. The American urbanist Howard Saalmon once wrote that the planning effort Haussmann initiated put an end to the modal urban scene: the interweaving of the necessities of work, of child nurturance, of adult sociability, and of impersonal encounter in and around a single house. Saalmon had in mind the preindustrial urban households in which shops, offices, and living quarters were located in the same building, but the rebuke is just in terms of the larger city as well. To destroy the multiplicity of function in it and so design that usages of space cannot change as the users of it change, is rational only in terms of initial investment.

Part of the ultimate cost which has to be reckoned in this destruction of public space is the paradoxical emphasis on community it creates. For even as the atomizing of the city makes it difficult, say, for mothers or fathers watching their children at play also to work, this same erasure sets up a hunger for human contact. In American suburbs, this hunger is met by resort to voluntary associations; under cover of engaging in a common task, or pursuing a single experience, people get a chance to overcome the wounds of geography imposed by the planners of their communities. Thus, among people who tell researchers they are areligious, there are found an enormous number who belong to suburban churches; thus, as the post-World War II baby boom ends, many of the parents who now have adult children continue to belong to parent–teacher associations. A long and essentially fruitless debate among American urbanists has gone on in the last two decades about whether the suburbs are "real" communities or not; the important thing is that the issue is raised at all, that community has become a problem of people's minds. For the terms of modern urban development make community contact itself seem an answer to the social death of the city. These patterns of urban development have not aroused a desire to remake the city itself in a new image: "alternatives" – that is, flight – is the response.

We know from the history of public life in the 19th Century that the decline in this realm was matched by a contradictory and painful growth in the terms of its opposite number – the psychological sphere. The forces that caused the decline of the one encouraged the rise of the other. The attempts to create community in cities are attempts to make psychological values into social relations. The real measure of what the imbalance of impersonal and psychological life has done to community relations thus lies beyond the fact that the search for community life has become compulsive; it lies also in the expectations people harbor in the desire they have for close, open relations face to face with other people in the same territory.

The larger society has shaped these expectations in an ideological as well as a practical way. It has done so through the images of crowds. For these images have come to be distinct in people's minds from images of community: in fact, community and crowd seem now to be antithetical. The bourgeois man in the crowd developed in the last century a shield of silence around himself. He did so out of fear. This fear was to some extent a matter of class, but it was not only that. A more undifferentiated anxiety about not knowing what to expect, about being violated in public, led him to try to isolate himself through silence when in this public milieu. Unlike his *ancien régime* counterpart, who also knew the anxiety of crowd life, he did not try to control and order his sociability in public; rather he tried to erase it, so that the bourgeois on the street was in a crowd but not of it.

The imagery of crowds regnant today is in one way an extension of this 19th Century idea of isolation. The works of Lyn Lofland and Erving Goffman have explored in great detail, for instance, the rituals by which strangers on crowded streets give each other little clues of reassurance which leave each person in isolation at the same time: you drop your eyes rather than stare at a stranger as a way of reassuring him you are safe; you engage in the pedestrian ballets of moving out of each other's way, so that each of you has a straight channel in which to walk; if you must talk to a stranger, you begin by excusing yourself; and so forth. This behavior can be observed even in the relaxed crowds at sporting events or political rallies.

But, in another way, modern images of the crowd have so extended the 19th Century fear that a wholly new principle of dealing with, and thinking about, crowds has appeared. It is that the crowd is the mode in which the most venal passions of man are not spontaneously expressed; the crowd is man the animal let off his leash. This image of the crowd has come to have an explicit class character: the people actively expressing their feelings in crowds are seen usually as the *Lumpenproletariat*, the under-classes, or dangerous social misfits. In the urban riots in Paris in the late 1960's, as in the urban riots in American cities in the same decade, the conservative press and its audience would describe the "bad" students and the "bad" blacks as stirring up crowd sentiments, and these were, in the first case and in the words of *Figaro*, "students from destitute or broken homes," and in the second case and in the words of the then Vice-President, "nothing but drunken bums." Thus danger from below and danger from the vocal crowd become united; but this conjunction itself will not quite explain the fear of spontaneous feelings unleashed which seem to make the crowd into a monster. Respectable people who voice these fears are not talking in a racialist way only about poor bad blacks who have more spontaneity; investigators in the wake of the American riots often found people who criticized the rabble ending up with the rueful comment that anyone might go out of control in a crowd. In this case, the crowd appears as a cause of vicious spontaneity, as well as the medium in which a vicious class expresses itself.

The literature of the social sciences offers instances of this fear of spontaneous crowd violence, exemplified in greater depth than popular feeling, but still within the same orbit. The discipline of social psychology itself dates back to the work of Gustave Le Bon, who at the beginning of this century used the transformations crowds were supposed to cause in individual feelings, making an ordinary upright citizen into a monster, as his prime example of how the "psychology" of a human being depended on whether he was considered as a single creature or considered as part of a social group. The crowd unleashed spontaneous violence in its members, which none of them would exhibit in their ordinary dealings with other people. Le Bon made no scientific claims for his view, but a group of animal experimenters with a similar outlook have. These experimenters, working with rats, proclaim that a "behavior sink" is induced in rats when they are crowded together in the laboratory. The rats, supposedly, become terribly vicious, each defending its territory against all comers; crowding is supposed to induce a kind of psychotic frenzy. These scientific claims turn out to be rather paltry, whether or not one believes one can infer human behavior from the behavior of other animals. Although psychotic during the day, crowded rats, like all other rats, sleep huddled as close together at night as possible; stray rats who can't snuggle are insomniacs. Few other animals respond to crowding in the same way; caged rats do not respond to crowding – which for all they know is permanent – the way rats in their own habitats do; and so on. What is important about this "scientific" theory of crowding is not its defects, but the cultural suppositions which led the researchers involved to expand a very peculiar situation into a general metaphor of the psychological evils of crowds. What is implicitly affirmed is that only a simple, clearly demarcated space, with contact between very few individuals, keeps order.

Modern images of crowds have consequences for modern ideas of community. In the more simplified environment there will be order, because individuals know other individuals, and each knows his territorial place. Your neighbors will know if you go out on a spontaneous rampage, whereas in a crowd no one knows you. In other words, community has a surveillance function. But how could it also be a place where people are open and free with each other? It is exactly this contradiction which creates the peculiar roles played out in modern community life, roles in which people are attempting at once to be emotionally open with each other and to control each other. The result of this contradiction is that the experience of local community life, seemingly an exercise in fraternity in a hostile milieu, often becomes an exercise in fratricide.

Fratricide has two meanings. It first and directly means that brothers turn on each other. They reveal themselves to each other, they have mutual expectations based on those self-disclosures, and they find each other wanting. Fratricide secondly means that this mentality is turned toward the world. We are a community; we are being real; the outside world is not responding to us in terms of who we are; therefore something is wrong with it; it has failed us; therefore we will have nothing to do with it. These processes are in fact the same rhythm of disclosure, disappointment, and isolation.

When this rhythm of community began to be heard in the last century, it was still as in large hall. The conflicts in the Dreyfus Affair, the fights over who really belonged to the radical left, were still governed by a sense of large issues at stake. The logic of a gemeinschaft community will push it over time into becoming more and more local in its terms. That is what has happened in the last half century. Community has become both emotional withdrawal from society and a territorial barricade within the city. The warfare between psyche and society has acquired a real geographical focus, one replacing the older, behavioral balance between public and private. This new geography is communal versus urban; the territory of warm feeling versus the territory of impersonal blankness.

BARRICADES BUILT FROM WITHIN

It is instructive to look at a case of this withdrawal from the outside world, in a neighborhood where initially no one wanted the process to occur. I have in mind the Forest Hills dispute in New York, little known outside the city but immensely disruptive within it. For in Forest Hills a community group took form to pursue exclusively political goals, and gradually evolved into a self-enclosed refuge. The psychological transactions between people in the community became more important than challenge to the operating procedures of the city. In one way, the Forest Hills affair has a direct relationship to the Dreyfus Affair; for in both, community gradually took form around a collective personality whose care and feeding became the main business of the people in the community. But this modern communal struggle shows also the cumulative effects of the atomizing of the city.

Forest Hills is a middle-class, mostly Jewish section of the borough of Queens, threatened a few years ago with the influx of black families through a housing project New York City planned to build in the area. Thanks to a journal kept by a city mediator, Mario Cuomo, during the course of the dispute over this housing, it is possible to follow step by step the response of the citizens to this event. The history of the Forest Hills dispute began in a nearby community, Corona. This working-class Italian neighborhood in the middle 1960s waged a bitter struggle with the city, first to prevent a low-income housing project from being built, and then to scale down the size of a school the city proposed. At long last the Corona residents, with Cuomo as their lawyer, forced the city to abandon its original plans.

From this struggle the people of Forest Hills largely held aloof. "It," the poor black and his culture, didn't seem likely to happen to them. They were as well a community of well-educated, liberal voters, the kind of citizens that had looked with favor on the civil rights movement. Then "it" struck Forest Hills too – a plan of the city that would locate 840 units of low-income housing in three twenty-four-story towers in the midst of this area of private homes and small apartment buildings.

Now the middle-class Jews encountered what the work-ing-class Italians had faced. The city hearings were farces; in one, for example, a board member who was absent sent a subordinate to cast his vote and read a statement sum-marizing his "reactions" to the issues the community had raised. As an exercise in omniscience, such behavior con-vinced Forest Hills, as it had Corona, that politicians and their commissions didn't care what the people of the affected neighborhoods thought.

For the people of Forest Hills, recognition by the city that they had legitimate objections was especially import-ant. We are not racist bigots, they insisted; slum families have a high incidence of crime; we are afraid for our own children; physically our neighborhood will be destroyed.

The more concerned the people of Forest Hills became, the closer the city machinery of community consultation, Board of Estimate hearing, and the like moved the project toward completion – indifferent to the complaints of the residents. Finally, all the legal formalities were completed, and building began. The residents resorted to the one re-source they had left: the media. They staged publicity demonstrations; the residents hounded Mayor Lindsay even down to Florida, where he was campaigning for the Demo-cratic presidential nomination, waving hostile signs at his rallies and following him around in view of television cameras.

This publicity campaign scared City Hall. As the con-flict between the city and the neighborhood became in-creasingly complex, Mayor Lindsay assigned Mario Cuomo the role of fact finder and independent judge. Cuomo re-solved to set down as precisely as possible what people said, and how they behaved; this record is all the more valu-able, perhaps, because it is straightforward, innocent of any theory of what was happening.[1]

What happened to Cuomo was in a way quite simple. He observed, talked, and debated; he drew up a compro-mise favorable to Forest Hills. The compromise was reluc-tantly adopted by the Mayor and then by the responsible governmental group, the Board of Estimate. But these prac-tical gains had by that time ceased to matter to the com-munity. In the same way that the Dreyfus combatants passed from a political drama to conflict for the sake of the community, the people in this racial–class dispute passed across that line; in the wake of that passage, results obtained through normal political channels felt meaningless. The community became the implacable defender of each member's integrity. It asserted its legitimacy in defiance of the politicians and the bureaucracy, not by maintaining that the community had legally inviolate rights, but by acting as if only the people of the community, the Jews of Forest Hills, knew what it is to suffer; only the people in the community could judge the moral worth of public housing; resistance to the people of the community was immoral and probably anti-Semitic.

The stigma placed on those enrolled in welfare has strong class origins in addition to racial ones. Thus in New York City the Forest Hills housing project aroused few people in the black community in its favor, because many middle-class blacks had themselves little desire to have welfare families as neighbors. The Forest Hills group was aware of this, and occasionally made use of working-class black antipathy to those on welfare to bolster their own case. But those who actively supported the project – mostly upper-class blacks and whites – did so in a way that reinforced the rage the community felt at first against the bungling of the city government.

On June 14, 1972, Cuomo, listening to a coalition spokesman for the city groups favoring the project, noted: "For the most part they're not residents of the community and aren't immediately affected . . . it's easier for these groups to operate from high 'moral principle precepts.'" The supporters appear to be people who can judge morally without having to experience the lower-class intruders; whatever they say must be fraudulent because this relation of appearance to reality is obviously a fraud. Therefore, the suffering community came to think of itself as an island of morality. What Cuomo noticed among the Jews of Forest Hills, the observer of Paris in the 1890's saw among anti-Semites like Drumont: the world being corrupt and blind, only we count.[2]

At the early stages of the conflict, however, such feelings as "nobody understands us" were often manipulated appearances, consciously exaggerated. For in the beginning people in the community were thinking about a specific goal – how to end the project. They played a role of moral outrage to win specific concessions from the city.

On July 12, 1972, Cuomo had, for instance, a meeting with Jerry Birbach, one of the Forest Hills leaders; Birbach announced that unless the project was changed to meet his demands, Birbach would sell his own house to a black man, and then organize a massive emigration of the whites, "tearing down in his wake the whole community." Is Cuomo horrified? Not really, for he knows Birbach, who speaks with ferocious conviction, doesn't mean it. "The approach had been plotted out carefully," Cuomo notes. "Birbach was going to start by coming on strong."[3]

On September 14 Cuomo records the way the ruse of "sandbagging" works. A community group had gotten word to the Mayor that it could accept a compromise in the dispute if the Mayor would first commit himself to it; the community group then would work covertly on the other members of a board on which the Mayor sits to get them to vote against the compromise. In this way, the Mayor would be tricked into supporting something that no one else supported; he would appear isolated and extreme; he would be humiliated. "It was," Cuomo concludes, "a classic case of fraud in the inducement, but then almost everybody actively engaged in the political game-playing appears to regard that kind of tactic as permissible if not *de rigueur*." Then Cuomo reflects on what he has just said: "That kind of sophistication is disheartening but increasingly it appears naïve to believe it could be any other way."[4]

If the game-playing were only a matter of frauds and deceits, an observer might well conclude that it was high time the fact finder lost his naïveté. Fraud and deception are classic weapons in the political arsenal. Indeed, a contemporary theory of urban structure advanced by the political scientist Norton Long argues that without such games the fabric of the city would break apart. In "The City as an Ecology of Games," Norton Long writes, "The games and their players mesh in their particular pursuits to bring about overall results; the territorial system is fed and ordered." By this, Long does not mean to say that players like Birbach are conscious that their frauds do good; self-interest, as Hobbes once wrote, makes men blind to what lies beyond personal desires. Long's concept of the ecology of games asserts that a balancing of power in the city is what these informal ploys bring. Long views the city as a state of equilibrium produced by conflict; his concept of the city resembles Locke's view of society at large. The city's inhabitants, says Long, "are rational within limited areas and, pursuing the ends of these areas, accomplish socially functional ends."[5]

Theories of this sort attempt to define role-playing within a community in relation to the powers-that-be outside it. Moral postures, masks of intransigence, and the like are adjusted to fit how much the community has accomplished its ends in the world. What is peculiar about modern community roles, however, is that the masks, supposedly only the means to power, become ends in themselves. The reason is that people are disposed by the very terms of personality which have come to rule modern society to believe that an appearance is an absolute reality. When a group of people are brought together for political purposes, forge some common stances for themselves, and then begin to behave on the basis of that common appearance, they gradually begin to believe in, to cling to, to defend the posture itself. It is on the way to becoming a real definition of who they are, rather than a position taken in a game for power. For powerless groups challenging an institution of power like New York City, the only wearable masks at first are moral ones. It would be unreal, of course, to treat these cries of moral outrage as insincere; that is not the point. Most community groups that begin to fight on this basis use their own genuine moral outrage as a way of legitimating themselves. What happens is that the codes of belief which reign in modern society gradually induce them to believe that this outrage is so precious it can never be compromised or even slaked by real action, because it has become a definition of who they are as a collective person. At this point, politics is replaced by psychology.

There are many other names for this phenomenon – rule by rhetoric, ideological senility – and often these names are invoked as criticisms by people who really want to decry the legitimate demands of the groups themselves. What is malign in the process is not the political demands, but the way in which the cultural terms of personality can take hold of an assertive group and gradually lead the group into thinking of itself as an emotional collectivity. At that point the face turned to the outer world becomes rigid, and the community embarks on an internal course which becomes ever more destructive.

In the Forest Hills affair, the change took about three months. By the middle of September, in the words of the diarist, people were beginning to "believe what they had earlier pretended to believe." Unlike the Dreyfus Affair, there was no single event, or small groups of events, which served as catalyst. The experience of sharing their anger had rather imperceptibly accustomed more and more people to think of this exhibition as a sort of communion with each other. Sharing anger became a way of talking within the community, and anybody who would not share this feeling was suspect.

A preview of this came to Cuomo through the Gordons and the Sterns, two couples who came to see him on June 13. Gordon was a retired schoolteacher and came prepared with a full set of lecture notes. "He tried to be coolly professional in his delivery but before long he was caught up in his own fear and would end up literally screaming at me." Cuomo tells us, "There was no devil's advocate role possible with him; any probing question that appeared contradictory to his position was pure 'devil' and no advocate. . . . He finished up in a crescendo – 'My wife will be mugged and raped and you ask me to be reasonable.' "[6]

In June, he also caught a glimpse of the ethnic terms which will frame these common sentiments. On June 19, a delegation of community women visited Cuomo. They began with a monotonously familiar theme: people who have not "worked for it should not be given 'expensive apartments.' " But their subsequent arguments were rather more striking. They told Cuomo they had been "conspired against by an anti-Jewish mayor"; they told him they were angry at the Italians of Corona for fending off the blacks. They felt as though, once again, the Jew was society's victim.[7]

Jewish paranoia? Ethnic isolation? It is a question of asking what these words mean.

The ethnic dimensions of people's lives are peculiarly susceptible to community processes through which a collective personality is projected. A mask of anger, turned toward a world which has in the past denied the needs of ethnics, becomes a rigid mask, and questions of solidarity and betrayal become painfully confused. It is true that among western European and American urbanites, ethnicity is being discovered as a new, more "meaningful" principle of group life than class principles. Ethnic revolts by bourgeois people against the outer world can be rather comfortably integrated into that world; the people involved get to be angry, implacable, and cohesive; the system gets to go on much as before. The reason ethnicity is so perfect a vehicle for modern community roles is that ethnicity concerns the recovery in emotional terms of a life which cannot be recovered in political, demographic, and above all religious terms. Bourgeois ethnicity is the recovery of personality traits of a lost culture, not of the culture itself.

Forest Hills, like so many other sections of New York, is Jewish in the sense that the people in it, both now and in the past, are Jews and used to be Jewish. Yiddish is no longer heard and the Yiddish newspapers are gone. A few kosher butchers exist because kosher poultry is the only fresh-killed poultry to be had in the city, but few people keep kosher. Few Jews below the age of fifty can write or speak a sentence of their own in Hebrew, although the words of the services may be known by rote. Among older New York Jews there were, up to a few years ago, great efforts to act contrary to all stereotypes of Jews – not to talk loudly, not to seem "clannish," not to behave aggressively at work or in school – all of which, of course, is to take the stereotypes immensely seriously. The Yiddish word *yenta* originally meant a person who was both aggressively gross and stupid; among Jews now in their twenties, it is used to refer to anyone who acts "Jewish." This sanitizing of ethnicity is an experience most ethnic groups in America have experienced, whether upwardly mobile or not. Language, food habits, customs of family deference – all were ambivalent matters, if not outright shameful.

The central experience lost, however, was religious, most of the European and Asian immigrants being, at the point of immigration, peasants or villagers who were strongly devout. When an ethnic group now becomes conscious of itself anew, the customs may be revived, but his heart is missing. The shell of custom around this faith is renewed in order to define a sense of particular and warm association with others. People feel close to each other because as Jews, as Italians, as Japanese in America they share "the same outlook" without sharing, if it can be put this way, "the same inlook" – religious faith – from which mores and customs of the past originated.

How does this sense of community, of sharing the shell of "outlook" and perception, become activated? The simplest way is through resisting attacks from the outside; inside, when an attack on a group becomes modulated in the group's mind to an attack on its culture, people believe they can rely on each other only. What does an ethnic community share when it comes under attack? Don't be ashamed of being Jewish, people in Forest Hills said, stand up and defend yourself; be angry. But if sharing an ethnic identity is sharing an impulse, who is this collective person, this angry Jew? He is angry. If he ceases to be angry, does he cease to be Jewish? It is a perverse tautology. Reviving the ethnic shell without its center of belief, what people have to share is their desire to feel something with other people. Community on these terms is a state of being rather than believing. It maintains itself only by internal passion and external withdrawal.

So it should not be surprising when Cuomo reports about the women of Forest Hills who began early to perceive an ethnic threat that, like the men, like the leaders, they "simply refused to listen – let alone believe" when he would correct errors of fact in their presentations. Were they to operate as a group open to give-and-take with him, they would lose that momentary strength of feeling committed to one another, fraternal, united, and pure, by virtue of being under attack as Jews.

Cuomo gives us an eloquent description of this rigidification in describing a meeting he attended on September 21:

> The Forest Hills community is convinced that their principal weapon now, as it has been for the past few months,

is to persuade the City fathers and the public-at-large
that it is impossible to expect tolerance and acceptance
on the part of the community. To do this they exaggerate their force and resistance. *And what is initially in part
a pose then communicates itself and feeds on itself and eventually the illusion becomes reality.* Yesterday the hundred or
so Forest Hills residents who screamed and stomped, cried
and shouted, *believed what they had earlier pretended to
believe.*[8]

By the end of September, as they became more solidly and
emotionally together, people in Forest Hills began to regard the world outside Forest Hills with resignation. "Wait
for a miracle," they said – the miracle that the slate of
past actions would be wiped clean, and "no project, no way"
would come to pass. In the meantime, expose the actual
mechanisms of power as frauds. Since real power in a city
is always a matter of give-and-take, actual offers from the
government began to seem tainted and unclean to the community because these were only partial concessions. The
only true power the community could imagine was total
gratification – everything is a non-negotiable demand – and
such gratification can never be. The community naturally
turned against the instruments of power, the commissions,
the formal hearings, etc., to destroy these mechanisms,
hoping to show the world that they were phony and morally inauthentic. Believing they were false, the community
would have nothing to do with them; otherwise it would
compromise its own reason for being. The ironic conclusion
of the Forest Hills affair was that bureaucratic inefficiency
tied up the project for a long time, and the city's mediator
Mario Cuomo, whom people in Forest Hills distrusted as
an outsider, turned out to be the most effective spokesman
for their interests.[9]

A withdrawal from political wheeling-and-dealing because
you want to preserve communal solidarity must inevitably
confuse the line between solidarity and betrayal. In this
particular community, being against any compromise was
taken to mean that someone was unashamed of being Jewish. In my own walks around the community at the time, I
frequently heard people talking about being for Israel and

being against any compromise over the local housing project as the same thing. At meetings people were continually tested for the steadfastness and implacability of their feelings, and those who leaned toward a settlement were taken to be fatally flawed in their morality. Indeed, the Jewish Defense League (a group of militants) scrawled on the business windows of one of these "compromisers" the motto "Never Again!" – a code phrase intimating that a desire to accept a settlement was the same spirit as that of passively walking into the Nazi death camps.

This pleasant, quiet community made itself into a ghetto, built its own walls. Its members acted as though they had a corner on the market of moral outrage. In no sense is the substance of conflict in this community like the substance of ideological conflicts. But the process of conflict is the same, as the taking of a position becomes gradually the taking on of a rigid, symbolic, collective self. Closer in time and place, the black community movements of the 1960s, challengers to the middle class, ended by building similar walls, as each of the different factions involved in disputes on tactics or long-range plans gradually came to see itself as a single legitimate voice of "the people." Outsiders, other blacks no less than whites, were to keep away.

THE HUMANE COSTS OF COMMUNITY

Anthropologists have a term for one aspect of territorial, communitarian rigidity. They call it pseudo-speciation, by which they mean that a tribe will act as though it is the only assemblage of human beings who are really human. The other tribes are lesser, are not as human. But if modern community processes were cast simply into this anthropological framework, something essential about the process would be lost. The growth of this intolerance is not a product of overweening pride, arrogance, or group self-assurance. It is a much more fragile and self-doubting process, in which the community exists only by a continual hyping-up of emotions. The reason for this hysteria is, in turn, not a matter of the innate destructiveness of man unleashed in the act of solidarity, but precisely that the terms of culture have come to be so arranged that, without some forcing and prodding, real social bonds seem so unnatural.

In a society of atomized social spaces, people are always afraid that they will be cut off from each other. The materials this culture offers people to use to "connect" with other people are unstable symbols of impulse and intention. Because the symbols are so problematic in character, it is inevitable that the people who use them are at the same time always going to have to test their strength. How far can you go, how much of a sense of community can you feel? People are going to have to equate real feeling with extreme feeling. In the Age of Reason, people gave themselves over to emotional displays which would be considered embarrassing in a modern playhouse or bar. To weep in the theater, however, had a meaning in and of itself, no matter who you were. Whereas the emotion experienced in a modern fraternal group is part and parcel of declaring what kind of person you are, and who is your brother. Now the dramatic displays of feeling become signals to others that you are "for real," and also, by whipping you up to a fever pitch, convince you yourself that you are "for real."

Let us sum up the fire urban planners play with so carelessly when they talk about building a sense of community at a local level in the city, as opposed to reawakening meaningful public space and public life in the city as a whole.

One need not be a believer in omnipresent conspiracy to perceive that this struggle for community solidarity serves a stabilizing function in terms of the larger political structures of the society. Just as charismatic experience becomes a deflection from dealing with those political structures, the attempt to form community deflects attention from those structures. The storms and stresses of fratricide are system-maintaining. Again, as with charismatic experience, it is all too easy now to confuse personal passion in society with the disordering of society. In fact the reverse is the case: the more people are plunged into these passions of community, the more the basic institutions of social order are untouched. To speak of questions of personal motivation in politics as seductive – either in charismatic leadership or in forming the basis of communal feeling – is not to speak of a metaphor but of a systematic structural fact. People in struggling to be a community become ever more absorbed in each other's feelings, and ever more withdrawn from an understanding of, let alone a challenge to, the institutions of power so very willing to have "local participation" and "local involvement."

Most so-called progressive town planning has aimed at a very peculiar kind of decentralization. Local units, garden suburbs, town or neighborhood councils are formed; the aim is formal local powers of control, but there is no real power that these localities in fact have. In a highly interdependent economy, local decision about local matters is an illusion. The result of these well-intentioned efforts at decentralization produces community rhythms, if not as extreme as the crisis in Forest Hills, depressingly similar in structure. Every urban planner will have experienced these local fights in which people, thinking they have in fact power to change something in the community, become engaged in intense struggle about who "really" speaks for the community. These struggles so engage people in matters of internal identity, solidarity, or dominance that when the real moments of power negotiation do come, and the community must turn toward the larger structures of city and state which have actual power, the community is so absorbed in itself that it is deaf to the outside, or exhausted, or fragmented.

A society which fears impersonality encourages fantasies of collective life that are parochial in nature. Who "we" are becomes a highly selective act of imagination: one's immediate neighbors, co-workers in the office, one's family. Identifying with people one doesn't know, people who are strangers but who may share one's ethnic interests, family problems, or religion, becomes hard. Impersonal ethnic ties, no less than impersonal ties of class, don't really make a bond; one feels one has to know others as persons to use "we" in describing one's relations to them. The more local the imagination, the greater becomes the number of social interests and issues for which the psychological logic is: we won't get involved, we won't let this violate us. It is not indifference; it is refusal, a willed constriction of experience the common self can permit. To think of this localization in narrowly political terms is to lose some of the force of the phenomenon; basically what is at issue is the degree of risk-taking a person is willing to engage in. The more local his sense of a self he can share with others, the fewer risks he is willing to take.

The refusal to deal with, absorb, and exploit reality outside the parochial scale is in one sense a universal human desire, being a simple fear of the unknown. Community feeling formed by the sharing of impulses has the special role of reinforcing the fear of the unknown, converting claustrophobia into an ethical principle.

The term *Gemeinschaft* meant, originally, the full disclosure of feeling to others; historically it has come at the same time to mean a community of people. These two taken together make *Gemeinschaft*, a special social group in which open emotional relations are possible as opposed to groups in which partial, mechanical, or emotionally indifferent ones prevail. Any community, we have noted, is in some degree built on fantasy. What is distinctive about the modern *Gemeinschaft* community is that the fantasy people share is that they have the same impulse life, the same motivational structure. In Forest Hills, for example, anger showed you were proud to be a Jew.

Impulse and collective life now joined, the fratricidal rhythm is ready to begin. If people have new impulses, the community will then shatter; they will not be sharing the same feelings; the person who changes "betrays" the community; individual deviation threatens the strength of the whole; people have therefore to be watched and tested. Distrust and solidarity, seemingly so opposed, are united. The absence, misunderstanding, or indifference of the world outside the community is interpreted in the same way. Since fraternal feelings are immediate and strongly felt, how can others not understand, why don't they respond in kind, why won't the world bend to emotional desires? The answer to these questions can only be that the world outside the community is less real, less authentic than the life within. The consequence of that answer is not a challenge to the outside, but a dismissal of it, a turning away, into the watchful sharing with others who "understand." This is the peculiar sectarianism of a secular society. It is the result of converting the immediate experience of sharing with others into a social principle. Unfortunately, large-scale forces in society may psychologically be kept at a distance, but do not therefore go away.

Finally, modern *Gemeinschaft* is a state of feeling "bigger" than action. The only actions the community undertakes are those of emotional housekeeping, purifying the community of those who really don't belong because they don't feel as the others do. The community cannot take in, absorb, and enlarge itself from the outside because then it will become impure. Thus a collective personality comes to be set against the very essence of sociability – exchange – and a psychological community becomes at war with societal complexity.

Urban planners have yet to learn a profound truth which conservative writers have perceived but have put to the wrong uses. It is that people can be sociable only when they have some protection from each other; without barriers, boundaries, without the mutual distance which is the essence of impersonality, people are destructive. It is so not because "the nature of man" is malevolent – the conservative error – but because the sum effect of the culture spawned by modern capitalism and secularism makes fratricide logical when people use intimate relations as a basis for social relations.

The real problem with town planning now is not what to do, but what to avoid. Despite the alarms sounding from social psychology laboratories, human beings have potentially a real genius for group life under crowded conditions. The art of planning town squares is not arcane; it has been practiced with great success for centuries, usually without formally trained architects. Historically, the dead public life and perverted community life which afflicts Western bourgeois society is something of an anomaly. The question is how to recognize symptoms of our peculiar disease, symptoms which lie as much in current notions of what humane scale and good community are as in the false notions we have of impersonality per se as a moral evil. In short, when town planning seeks to improve the quality of life by making it more intimate, the planner's very sense of humanity creates the very sterility he should seek to avoid.

Notes

1. Now in published form: Mario Cuomo, *Forest Hills Diary*, with a preface by Jimmy Breslin and an afterword by Richard Sennett (New York: Random House, 1974). The analysis that follows is a reworking of the afterword appearing in that book.
2. Ibid., p. 61.
3. Ibid., pp. 103 ff.
4. Ibid., pp. 128–9.
5. Norton Long, "The Local Community as an Ecology of Games," in Edward Banfield (ed.), *Urban Government*, revised edn (New York: Free Press, 1969), p. 469.
6. Cuomo, op. cit., pp. 56 ff.
7. Ibid., pp. 67 ff.
8. Ibid., p. 134.
9. Ibid., pp. 147–9.

15 City Life and Difference*
Iris Marion Young

> The tolerance, the room for great differences among neighbors – differences that often go far deeper than differences in color – which are possible and normal in intensely urban life, but which are so foreign to suburbs and pseudosuburbs, are possible and normal only when streets of great cities have built-in equipment allowing strangers to dwell in peace together on civilized but essentially dignified and reserved terms.
>
> Jane Jacobs[1]

One important purpose of critical normative theory is to offer an alternative vision of social relations which, in the words of Marcuse, "conceptualizes the stuff of which the experienced world consists ... with a view to its possibilities, in the light of their actual limitation, suppression, and denial".[2] Such a positive normative vision can inspire hope and imagination that motivate action for social change. It also provides some of the reflective distance necessary for the criticism of existing social circumstances.

Many philosophers and political theorists criticize welfare capitalist society for being atomistic, depoliticized, fostering self-regarding interest-group pluralism and bureaucratic domination. The most common alternative vision offered by such critics is an ideal of community. Spurred by appeals to community as an alternative to liberal individualism made by Michael Sandel, Alasdair MacIntyre, and others, in recent years political theorists have debated the virtues and vices of communitarianism as opposed to liberalism.[3] Many socialists, anarchists, feminists, and others critical of welfare capitalist society formulate their vision of a society free from domination and oppression in terms of an ideal of community. Much of this discussion would lead

* Reprinted from Iris Marion Young, *Justice and the Politics of Difference* (Princeton, NJ: Princeton University Press, 1990).

250

us to think that liberal individualism and communitarianism exhaust the possibilities for conceiving social relations.

I share many of the communitarian criticisms of welfare capitalist liberal democratic theory and society. I shall argue however that the ideal of community fails to offer an appropriate alternative vision of a democratic polity. This ideal expresses a desire for the fusion of subjects with one another which in practice operates to exclude those with whom the group does not identify. The ideal of community denies and represses social difference, the fact that the polity cannot be thought of as a unity in which all participants share a common experience and common values. In its privileging of face-to-face relations, moreover, the ideal of community denies difference in the form of the temporal and spatial distancing that characterizes social process.

As an alternative to the ideal of community, I propose an ideal of city life as a vision of social relations affirming group difference. As a normative ideal, city life instantiates social relations of difference without exclusion. Different groups dwell in the city alongside one another, of necessity interacting in city spaces. If city politics is to be democratic and not dominated by the point of view of one group, it must be a politics that takes account of and provides voice for the different groups that dwell together in the city without forming a community.

City life as an openness to unassimilated otherness, however, represents only an unrealized social ideal. Many social injustices exist in today's cities. Cities and the people in them are relatively powerless before the domination of corporate capital and state bureaucracy. Privatized decision-making processes in cities and towns reproduce and exacerbate inequalities and oppressions. They also produce or reinforce segregations and exclusions within cities and between cities and towns, which contribute to exploitation, marginalization, and cultural imperialism.

Many democratic theorists respond to these ills of city life by calls for the creation of decentralized autonomous communities where people exercise local control over their lives and neighborhoods on a human scale. Such calls for local autonomy reproduce the problems of exclusion that the ideal of community poses.

THE OPPOSITION BETWEEN INDIVIDUALISM AND COMMUNITY

Critics of liberalism frequently invoke a conception of community as an alternative to the individualism and abstract formalism they attribute to liberalism.[4] They reject the image of persons as separate and self-contained atoms, each with the same formal rights, rights to keep others out, separate. For such writers, the ideal of community evokes the absence of the self-interested competitiveness of modern society. In this ideal, critics of liberalism find an alternative to the abstract, formal methodology of liberalism. Existing in community with others entails more than merely respecting their rights; it entails attending to and sharing in the particularity of their needs and interests.

In his rightly celebrated critique of Rawls, for example, Michael Sandel argues that liberalism's emphasis on the primacy of justice presupposes a conception of the self as an antecedent unity existing prior to its desires and goals, whole unto itself, separated and bounded.[5] This is an unreal and incoherent conception of the self, he argues. It would be better replaced by a conception of the self as the product of an identity it shares with others, of values and goals that are not external and willed, as liberalism would have it, but constitutive of the self. This constitutive conception of the self is expressed by the concept of community.

Benjamin Barber[6] also uses the idea of community to evoke a vision of social life that does not conceive of the person as an atomistic, separated individual. Liberal political theory represents individuals as occupying private and separate spaces, as propelled only by their own private desires. This is a consumer-oriented conception of human nature, in which social and political relations can be understood only as goods instrumental to the achievement of individual desires, and not as intrinsic goods. This atomistic conception generates of political theory that presumes conflict and competition as characteristic modes of interaction. Like Sandel, Barber appeals to an ideal of community to invoke a conception of the person as socially constituted, actively oriented toward affirming relations of mutuality, rather than oriented solely toward satisfying private needs and desires.[7]

I share these critiques of liberalism. Liberal social ontology has no place for a concept of social groups. I have characterized a social group as the relational outcome of interactions, meanings, and affinities according to which people identify one another. The self is indeed a product of social relations in profound and often contradictory ways. A person's social group identities, moreover, are in some meaningful sense shared with others of the group.

I have also criticized liberalism's consumer-oriented presuppositions about human nature, and agree with Barber that these lead to an instrumentalist understanding of the function of politics. With Barber and other new republican theorists, I too reject the privatization of politics in liberal pluralist processes, and call for the institution of democratic publics. I think, however, that all these criticisms of liberalism can and should be made without embracing community as a political ideal.

Too often contemporary discussion of these issues sets up an exhaustive dichotomy between individualism and community. Community appears in the oppositions individualism/community, separated self/shared self, private/public. But like most such terms, individualism and community have a common logic underlying their polarity, which makes it possible for them to define each other negatively. Each entails a denial of difference and a desire to bring multiplicity and heterogeneity into unity, though in opposing ways. Liberal individualism denies difference by positing the self as a solid, self-sufficient unity, not defined by anything or anyone other than itself. Its formalistic ethic of rights also denies difference by bringing all such separated individuals under a common measure of rights. Proponents of community, on the other hand, deny difference by positing fusion rather than separation as the social ideal. They conceive the social subject as a relation of unity or mutuality composed by identification and symmetry among individuals within a totality. Communitarianism represents an urge to see persons in unity with one another in a shared whole.

For many writers, the rejection of individualism logically entails the assertion of community, and conversely any rejection of community entails that one necessarily supports individualism. In their discussion of a debate between Jean Elshtain and Barbara Ehrenreich, for example, Harry Boyte and Sara Evans[8] claim that Ehrenreich promotes individualism because she rejects the appeal to community that Elshtain makes. Recent accounts of the debate among political theorists generated by communitarian critiques of Rawls all couch that debate in terms of a dichotomy between liberal individualism and community, suggesting that these two categories are indeed mutually exclusive and exhaust all possible social ontologies and conceptions of the self.[9] Thus even when the discussants recognize the totalizing and circular character of this debate, and seek to take a position outside its terms, they tend to slide into affirming one or the other "side" of the dichotomy because that dichotomy, like the dichotomy a/not-a, is conceived as exhausting all logical possibilities.

THE ROUSSEAUIST DREAM

The ideal of community expresses a longing for harmony among persons, for consensus and mutual understanding, for what Foucault calls the Rousseauist dream of

> a transparent society, visible and legible in each of its parts, the dream of there no longer existing any zones of darkness, zones established by the privileges of royal power or the prerogative of some corporation, zones of disorder. It was the dream that each individual, whatever position he occupied, might be able to see the whole of society, that men's hearts should communicate, their vision be unobstructed by obstacles, and that the opinion of all reign over each.[10]

Whether expressed as shared subjectivity or common consciousness, or as relations of mutuality and reciprocity, the ideal of community denies, devalues, or represses the ontological difference of subjects, and seeks to dissolve social inexhaustibility into the comfort of a self-enclosed whole.

Sandel is explicit about defining community as shared subjectivity. The difference between his own constitutive meaning of community and the instrumental and sentimental meanings he finds in Rawls is precisely that in constitutive community subjects share a common self-understanding.[11] He is also explicit about social transparency as the meaning and goal of community:

> And in so far as our constitutive self-understandings comprehend a wider subject than the individual alone, whether a family or tribe or city or class or nation or people, to this extent they define a community in the constitutive sense. And what marks such a community is not merely a spirit of benevolence, or the prevalence of communitarian values, or even certain 'shared final ends' alone, but a common vocabulary of discourse and a background of implicit practices and understandings within which the opacity of the participants is reduced if never finally dissolved. In so far as justice depends for its pre-eminence on the separatedness or boundedness of persons in the cognitive sense, its priority would diminish as that opacity faded and this community deepened.[12]

Barber also takes shared subjectivity as the meaning of community. Through political participation individuals confront one another and adjust their wants and desires, creating a "common ordering of individual needs and wants into a single vision of the future in which all can share." Strong democracy seeks to reach a "creative consensus" which through common talk and common work creates a "common consciousness and political judgment".[13]

Some theorists of community, on the other hand, replace commonness in the meaning of community with mutuality and reciprocity, the recognition by each individual of the individuality of all the others.[14] Seyla Benhabib, for example, regards a standpoint that emphasizes the commonness of persons as that of an ethic of rights and justice of the sort that Rawls represents, which she calls the standpoint of the "generalized other." Moral theory must also express a complementary point of view what Benhabib calls the standpoint of the "concrete other." Benhabib refers to this as a vision of a community of needs and solidarity, in contrast with the community of rights and entitlements envisaged by liberalism:

The standpoint of the "concrete other," by contrast, requires us to view each and every rational being as an individual with a concrete history, identity, and affective-emotional constitution. In assuming this standpoint, we abstract from what constitutes our commonality and seek to understand the distinctiveness of the other. We seek to comprehend the needs of the other, their motivations, what they search for, and what they desire. Our relation to the other is governed by the norm of *complementary reciprocity*: each is entitled to expect and to assume from the other forms of behavior through which the other feels recognized and confirmed as a concrete, individual being with specific needs, talents, and capacities. . . . The moral categories that accompany such interactions are those of responsibility, bonding, and sharing. The corresponding moral feelings are those of love, care, sympathy, and solidarity, and the vision of community is one of needs and solidarity.[15]

Despite the apparent divergence of Sandel's and Barber's language of shared subjectivity and Benhabib's language of complementary reciprocity, I think all three express a similar ideal of social relations as the *copresence of subjects*.[16] Whether expressed as common consciousness or as mutual understanding, the ideal is one of the transparency of subjects to one another. In this ideal each understands the others and recognizes the others in the same way that they understand themselves, and all recognize that the others understand them as they understand themselves. This ideal thus submits to what Derrida calls the metaphysics of presence, which seeks to collapse the temporal difference inherent in language and experience into a totality that can be comprehended in one view. This ideal of community denies the ontological difference within and between subjects.

In community persons cease to be other, opaque, not understood, and instead become mutually sympathetic, understanding one another as they understand themselves, fused. Such an ideal of the transparency of subjects to one another denies the difference, or basic asymmetry, of subjects. As Hegel first brought out and Sartre's analysis deepened, persons necessarily transcend one another because subjectivity is negativity. The regard of the other is always objectifying.

Other persons never see the world from my perspective, and in witnessing the other's objective grasp of my body, actions, and words, I am always faced with an experience of myself different from the one I have.

This mutual intersubjective transcendence, of course, makes sharing between us possible, a fact that Sartre notices less than Hegel. The sharing, however, is never complete mutual understanding and reciprocity. Sharing, moreover, is fragile. At the next moment the other person may understand my words differently from the way I meant them, or carry my actions to consequences I do not intend. The same difference that makes sharing between us possible also makes misunderstanding, rejection, withdrawal, and conflict always possible conditions of social being.

Because the subject is not a unity, it cannot be present to itself, know itself. I do not always know what I mean, need, want, desire, because meanings, needs, and desires do not arise from an origin in some transparent ego. Often I express my desire in gesture or tone of voice, without meaning to do so. Consciousness, speech, expressiveness, are possible only if the subject always surpasses itself, and is thus necessarily unable to comprehend itself. Subjects all have multiple desires that do not cohere; they attach layers of meanings to objects without always being aware of each layer or the connections between them. Consequently, any individual subject is a play of difference that cannot be completely comprehended.

If the subject is heterogeneous process, never fully present to itself, then it follows that subjects cannot make themselves transparent, wholly present to one another. Consequently the subject also eludes sympathetic comprehension by others. I cannot understand others as they understand themselves, because they do not completely understand themselves. Indeed, because the meanings and desires they express may outrun their own awareness or intention, I may understand their words or actions more fully than they.

The ideal of community expresses a desire for social wholeness, symmetry, a security and solid identity which is objectified because affirmed by others unambiguously. This is an understandable dream, but a dream nevertheless, and, as I shall now argue, one with serious political consequences.

PRIVILEGING FACE-TO-FACE RELATIONS

The ideal of community as a pure copresence of subjects to one another receives political expression in a vision of political life that privileges local face-to-face direct democracy. Critics of welfare capitalist society repeatedly invoke such a model of small group relations as a political ideal. The anarchist tradition expresses these values most systematically, but they retain their form in other political soils as well. This model of politics as founded in face-to-face relations poses as the alternative to the impersonality, alienation, commodification, and bureaucratization of governance in existing mass societies.

> The incarnation of this project is the immediate, indeed unmediated, community that enters so profoundly into the fashioning of our humanity. This is the community in which we genuinely encounter each other, the public world that is only a bare step above our private world, in short, our towns, neighborhoods, and municipalities.[17]

Several problems arise when a community that privileges face-to-face relations is taken as the ideal of the polity. The ideal presumes a myth of unmediated social relations, and wrongly identifies mediation with alienation. It denies difference in the sense of temporal and spatial distancing. It implies a model of the good society as consisting of decentralized small units which is both unrealistic and politically undesirable, and which avoids the political question of just relations among such decentralized communities.

As the above quotation indicates, theorists of community privilege face-to-face relations because they conceive them as *immediate*. Immediacy is better than mediation because immediate relations have the purity and security longed for in the Rousseauist dream: we are transparent to one another, purely copresent in the same time and space, close enough to touch, and nothing comes between us to obstruct our vision of one another.

This ideal of the immediate copresence of subjects, however, is a metaphysical illusion. Even face-to-face relations between two people is mediated by voice and gesture, spacing and temporality. As soon as a third person enters the interaction the possibility arises of the relations between the first two being mediated through the third, and so on. The mediation of relations among persons by the speech and actions of other persons is a fundamental condition of sociality. The richness, creativity, diversity, and potential of a society expand with growth in the scope and means of its media, linking persons across time and distance. The greater the time and distance, however, the greater the number of persons who stand between other persons.

I am not arguing that there is no difference between small groups in which persons relate to one another face-to-face and other social relations, nor am I denying a unique value to such face-to-face groups. Just as the intimacy of living with a few others in the same household has unique dimensions that are humanly valuable, so existing with others in communities of mutual regard has specific characteristics of warmth and sharing that are humanly valuable. There is no question either that bureaucratized, capitalist, patriarchal society discourages and destroys such communities of mutual friendship, just as it pressures and fragments families. A vision of the good society surely should include institutional arrangements that nurture the specific experience of mutual friendship which only relatively small groups interacting in a plurality of contexts can produce. But recognizing the value and specificity of such face-to-face relations is different from privileging them and positing them as a model for the institutional relations of a whole society.

In my view, a model of the good society as composed of decentralized, economically self-sufficient, face-to-face communities functioning as autonomous political entities does not purify politics, as its proponents think, but rather avoids politics. First, it is wildly utopian. To bring it into being would require dismantling the urban character of modern society, a gargantuan overhaul of living space, workplaces, places of trade and commerce. A model of a transformed society must begin from the material structures that are given to us at this time in history, and in the United States those are large-scale industry and urban centers.

More importantly, however, this model of the good society as usually articulated leaves completely unaddressed the question of how such small communities relate to one another. Frequently the ideal projects a level of self-sufficiency and decentralization which suggests that proponents envision few relations among these communities except occasional friendly visits. Surely it is unrealistic, however, to assume that such decentralized communities need not engage in extensive relations of exchange of resources, goods, and culture.

Proponents frequently privilege face-to-face relations in reaction to the alienation and domination produced by huge, faceless bureaucracies and corporations, whose actions and decisions affect most people, but are out of their control. Appeals to community envision more local and direct control. A more participatory democratic society should indeed encourage active publics at the local levels of neighborhood and workplace. But the important political question is how relations among these locales can be organized so as to foster justice and minimize domination and oppression. Invoking a mystical ideal of community does not address this question, but rather obscures it. Politics must be conceived as a relationship of strangers who do not understand one another in a subjective and immediate sense, relating across time and distance.

UNDESIRABLE POLITICAL CONSEQUENCES OF THE IDEAL OF COMMUNITY

I have argued that the ideal of community denies the difference between subjects and the social differentiation of temporal and spatial distancing. The most serious political consequence of the desire for community, or for copresence and mutual identification with others, is that if often operates to exclude or oppress those experienced as different. Commitment to an ideal of community tends to value and enforce homogeneity.[18]

In ordinary speech in the United States, the term community refers to the people with whom one identifies in a specific locale. It refers to neighborhood, church, schools. It also carries connotations of ethnicity, race, and other group identifications. For most people, insofar as they consider themselves members of communities at all, a community is a group that shares specific heritage – a common self-identification, a common culture and set of norms. Self-identification as a member of such a community also often occurs as an oppositional differentiation from other groups, who are feared, despised, or at best devalued. Persons feel a sense of mutual identification only with some persons, feel in community only with those, and fear the difference others confront them with because they identify with a different culture, history, and point of view on the world. The ideal of community, I suggest, validates and reinforces the fear and aversion some social groups exhibit toward others. If community is a positive norm, that is, if existing together with others in relations of mutual understanding and reciprocity is the goal, then it is understandable that we exclude and avoid those with whom we do not or cannot identify.

Richard Sennett[19] discusses how a "myth of community" operates perpetually in American society to produce and implicitly legitimate racist and classist behavior and policy. In many towns, suburbs, and neighborhoods people do have an image of their locale as one in which people all know one another, have the same values and life-style, and relate with feelings of mutuality and love. In modern American society such an image is almost always false; while there may be a dominant group with a distinct set of values and life style, within any locale one can usually find deviant individuals and groups. Yet the myth of community operates strongly to produce defensive exclusionary behavior: pressuring the Black family that buys a house on the block to leave, beating up the Black youths who come into "our" neighborhood, zoning against the construction of multiunit dwellings.

The exclusionary consequences of valuing community, moreover, are not restricted to bigots and conservatives. Many radical political organizations founder on the desire for community. Too often people in groups working for social change take mutual friendship to be a goal of the group, and thus judge themselves wanting as a group when they do not achieve such commonality.[20] Such a desire for community often channels energy away from the political goals of the group, and also produces a clique atmosphere which keeps groups small and turns potential members away.

Mutual identification as an implicit group ideal can reproduce a homogeneity that usually conflicts with the organization's stated commitment to diversity. In recent years most socialist and feminist organizations, for example, have taken racial, class, age, and sexual diversity as an important criterion according to which the success of political organizations should be evaluated. To the degree that they take mutual understanding and identification as a goal, they may be deflected from this goal of diversity.

The exclusionary implications of a desire for face-to-face relations of mutual identification and sharing present a problem for movements asserting positive group difference. I argue that the effort of oppressed groups to reclaim their group identity, and to form with one another bonds of positive cultural affirmation around their group specificity, constitutes an important resistance to the oppression of cultural imperialism. It shifts the meaning of difference from otherness and exclusion to variation and specificity, and forces dominant groups to acknowledge their own group specificity. But does not such affirmation of group identity itself express an ideal of community, and is it not subject to exclusionary impulses?

Some social movements asserting positive group difference have found through painful confrontation that an urge to unity and mutual identification does indeed have exclusionary implications. Feminist efforts to create women's spaces and women's culture, for example, have often assumed the perspective of only a particular subgroup of women – white, or middle class, or lesbian, or straight – thus implicitly excluding or rendering invisible those women among them with differing identifications and experiences.[21] Similar problems arise for any movement of group identification, because in our society most people have multiple group identifications, and thus group differences cut across every social group.

These arguments against community are not arguments against the political project of constructing and affirming a positive group identity and relations of group solidarity, as a means of confronting cultural imperialism and discovering things about oneself and others with whom one feels an affinity. Critique of the ideal of community, however, reveals that even in such group-specific contexts affinity cannot mean the transparency of selves to one another. If in their zeal to affirm a positive meaning of group specificity people seek or try to enforce a strong sense of mutual identification, they are likely to reproduce exclusions similar to those they confront. Those affirming the specificity of a group affinity should at the same time recognize and affirm the group and individual differences within the group.

CITY LIFE AS A NORMATIVE IDEAL

Appeals to community are usually antiurban. Much sociological literature diagnoses modern history as a movement to the dangerous bureaucratized *Gesellschaft* from the manageable and safe *Gemeinschaft*, nostalgically reconstructed as a world of lost origins.[22] Many others follow Rousseau in romanticizing the ancient *polis* and the medieval Swiss *Bürger*, deploring the commerce, disorder, and unmanageable mass character of the modern city.[23] Throughout the modern period, the city has often been decried as embodying immorality, artificiality, disorder, and danger – as the site of treasonous conspiracies, illicit sex, crime, deviance, and disease.[24] The typical image of the modern city finds it expressing all the disvalues that a reinstantiation of community would eliminate.

Yet urbanity is the horizon of the modern, not to mention the postmodern, condition. Contemporary political theory must accept urbanity as a material given for those who live in advanced industrial societies. Urban relations define the lives not only of those who live in the huge metropolises, but also of those who live in suburbs and large towns. Our social life is structured by vast networks of temporal and spatial mediation among persons, so that nearly everyone depends on the activities of seen and unseen strangers who mediate between oneself and one's associates, between oneself and one's objects of desire. Urbanites find themselves relating geographically to increasingly large regions, thinking little of traveling seventy miles to work or an hour's drive for an evening's entertainment. Most people frequently and casually encounter strangers in their daily activities. The material surroundings and structures available to us define and presuppose urban relationships. The very size of populations in our society and most other nations of the world, coupled with a continuing sense of national or ethnic identity with millions of other people, supports the conclusion that a vision of dismantling the city is hopelessly utopian.

Starting from the given of modern urbanlife is not simply necessary, moreover; it is desirable. Even for many of those who decry the alienation, bureaucratization, and mass character of capitalist patriarchal society, city life exerts a powerful attraction. Modern literature, art, and film have celebrated city life, its energy, and cultural diversity, technological complexity, and the multiplicity of its activities. Even many of the most staunch proponents of decentralized community love to show visiting friends around the Boston or San Francisco or New York in or near which they live, climbing up towers to see the glitter of lights and sampling the fare at the best ethnic restaurants.

I propose to construct a normative ideal of city life as an alternative to both the ideal of community and the liberal individualism it criticizes as asocial. By "city life" I mean a form of social relations which I define as the being together of strangers. In the city persons and groups interact within spaces and institutions they all experience themselves as belonging to, but without those interactions dissolving into unity or commonness. City life is composed of clusters of people with affinities – families, social group networks, voluntary associations, neighborhood networks, a vast array of small "communities." City dwellers frequently venture beyond such familiar enclaves, however, to the more open public of politics, commerce, and festival, where strangers meet and interact. City dwelling situates one's own identity and activity in relation to a horizon of a vast variety of other activities, and the awareness of these unknown, unfamiliar activities affects the conditions of one's own.

City life is a vast, even infinite, economic network of production, distribution, transportation, exchange, communication, service provision, and amusement. City dwellers depend on the mediation of thousands of other people and vast organizational resources in order to accomplish their individual ends. City dwellers are thus together, bound to one another, in what should be and sometimes is a single polity. Their being together entails some common problems and common interests, but they do not create a community of shared final ends, of mutual identification and reciprocity.

A normative ideal of city life must begin with our given experience of cities, and look there for the virtues of this form of social relations. Defining an ideal as unrealized possibilities of the actual, I extrapolate from that experience four such virtues.

Social Differentiation Without Exclusion

City life in urban mass society is not inconsistent with supportive social networks and subcultural communities. Indeed, for many it is their necessary condition. In the city social group differences flourish. Modernization theory predicted a decline in local, ethnic, and other group affiliations as universalist state institutions touch people's lives more directly and as people encounter many others with identifications and life styles different from their own. There is considerable evidence, however, that group differences are often reinforced by city life, and that the city even encourages the formation of new social group affinities.[25] Deviant or minority groups find in the city both a cover of anonymity and a critical mass unavailable in the smaller town. It is hard to imagine the formation of gay or lesbian group affinities, for example, without the conditions of the modern city.[26] While city dwelling as opposed to rural life has changed the lives and self-concepts of Chicanos, to take another example, city life encourages group identification and a desire for cultural nationalism at the same time that it may dissolve some traditional practices or promote assimilation to Anglo language and values.[27] In actual cities many people express violent aversions to members of groups with which they do not identify. More than those who live in small towns, however, they tend to recognize social group difference as a given, something they must live with.[28]

In the ideal of city life freedom leads to group differentiation, to the formation of affinity groups, but this social and spatial differentiation of groups is without exclusion.

The urban ideal expresses difference as a side-by-side particularity neither reducible to identity nor completely other. In this ideal groups do not stand in relations of inclusions and exclusion, but overlap and intermingle without becoming homogeneous. Though city life as we now experience it has many borders and exclusions, even our actual experience of the city also gives hints of what differentiation without exclusion can be. Many city neighborhoods have a distinct ethnic identity, but members of other groups also dwell in them. In the good city one crosses from one distinct neighborhood to another without knowing precisely where one ended and the other began. In the normative ideal of city life, borders are open and undecidable.

Variety

The interfusion of groups in the city occurs partly because of the multiuse differentiation of social space. What makes urban spaces interesting, draws people out in public to them, gives people pleasure and excitement, is the diversity of activities they support. When stores, restaurants, bars, clubs, parks, and offices are sprinkled among residences, people have a neighborly feeling about their neighborhood, they go out and encounter one another on the streets and chat. They have a sense of their neighborhood as a "spot" or "place," because of that bar's distinctive clientele, or the citywide reputation of the pizzas at that restaurant. Both business people and residents tend to have more commitment to and care for such neighborhoods than they do for single-use neighborhoods. Multifunctional streets, parks, and neighborhoods are also much safer than single-use functionalized spaces because people are out on the streets during most hours, and have a commitment to the place.[29]

Eroticism

City life also instantiates difference as the erotic, in the wide sense of an attraction to the other, the pleasure and excitement of being drawn out of one's secure routine to encounter the novel, strange, and surprising.[30] The erotic dimension of the city has always been an aspect of its fearfulness, for it holds out the possibility that one will lose one's identity, will fall. But we also take pleasure in being open to and interested in people we experience as different. We spend a Sunday afternoon walking through Chinatown, or checking out this week's eccentric players in the park. We look for restaurants, stores, and clubs with something new for us, a new ethnic food, a different atmosphere, a different crowd of people. We walk through sections of the city that we experience as having unique characters which are not ours, where people from diverse places mingle and then go home.

The erotic attraction here is precisely the obverse of community. In the ideal of community people feel affirmed because those with whom they share experiences, perceptions, and goals recognize and are recognized by them; one sees oneself reflected in the others. There is another kind of pleasure, however, in coming to encounter a subjectivity, a set of meanings, that is different, unfamiliar. One takes pleasure in being drawn out of oneself to understand that there are other meanings, practices, perspectives on the city, and that one could learn or experience something more and different by interacting with them.

The city's eroticism also derives from the aesthetics of its material being: the bright and colored lights, the grandeur of its buildings, the juxtaposition of architecture of different times, styles, and purposes. City space offers delights and surprises. Walk around the corner, or over a few blocks, and you encounter a different spatial mood, a new play of sight and sound, and new interactive movement. The erotic meaning of the city arises from its social and spatial inexhaustibility. A place of many places, the city folds over on itself in so many layers and relationships that it is incomprehensible. One cannot "take it in," one never feels as though there is nothing new and interesting to explore, no new and interesting people to meet.

Publicity

Political theorists who extol the value of community often construe the public as a realm of unity and mutual understanding, but this does not cohere with our actual experience of public spaces. Because by definition a public space is a place accessible to anyone, where anyone can participate and witness, in entering the public one always risks encountering those who are different, those who identify with different groups and have different opinions or different forms of life. The group diversity of the city is most often apparent in public spaces. This helps account for their vitality and excitement. Cities provide important public spaces – streets, parks, and plazas – where people stand and sit together, interact and mingle, or simply witness one another, without becoming unified in a community of "shared final ends."

Politics, the critical activity of raising issues and deciding how institutional and social relations should be organized, crucially depends on the existence of spaces and forums to which everyone has access. In such public spaces people encounter other people, meanings, expressions, issues, which they may not understand or with which they do not identify. The force of public demonstrations, for example, often consists in bringing to people who pass through public spaces those issues, demands, and people they might otherwise avoid. As a normative ideal, city life provides public places and forums where anyone can speak and anyone can listen.

Because city life is a being together of strangers, diverse and overlapping neighbors, social justice cannot issue from the institution of an Enlightenment universal public. On the contrary, social justice in the city requires the realization of a politics of difference. This politics lays down institutional and ideological means for recognizing and affirming diverse social groups by giving political representation to these group, and celebrating their distinctive characteristics and cultures. In the unoppressive city people open to unassimilated otherness. We all have our familiar relations and affinities, the people to whom we feel close and with whom we share daily life. These familial and social groups open onto a public in which all participate, and that public must be open and accessible to all. Contrary to the communitarian tradition, however, that public cannot be conceived as a unity transcending group differences, nor as entailing complete mutual understanding. In public life the differences remain unassimilated, but each participating group acknowledges and is open to listening to the others. The public is heterogeneous, plural, and playful, a place where people witness and appreciate diverse cultural expressions that they do not share and do not fully understand.

Notes

1. Jone Jacobs, *The Death and Life of Great American Cities* (New York: Random House, 1961).
2. Herbert Marcuse, *One-Dimensional Man* (Boston: Beacon, 1964), p. 7.
3. Amy Gutmann, "Communitarian Critics of Liberalism," *Philosophy and Public Affairs*, vol. 14 (summer 1985), pp. 308–22; H. N. Hirsch, "The Threnody of Liberalism: Constitutional Liberty and the Renewal of Community," *Political Theory*, vol. 14 (August 1986), pp. 423–49; Allen Buchanan, "Assessing the Communitarian Critique of Liberalism," *Ethics*, vol. 99. (July 1989), pp. 852–82.
4. Robert Paul Wolff, *The Poverty of Liberalism* (Boston: Beacon, 1968); Christian Bay, *Strategies for Political Emancipation* (Notre Dame: University of Notre dame Press, 1981).
5. Michael Sandel, *Liberalism and the Limits of Justice* (Cambridge University Press, 1982).
6. Benjamin Barber, *Strong Democracy* (Berkeley and Los Angeles: University of California Press, 1984).
7. Martha Ackelsberg, "Communities, Resistance and Women's Activism," in Ann Bookman and Sandra Morgen (eds), *Women and the Politics of Empowerment* (Philadelphia: Temple University Press, 1988).
8. Harry Boyte and Sara M. Evans, "Strategies in Search of America: Cultural Radicalism, Populism, and Democratic Culture," *Socialist Review* (May–August 1984), pp. 73–100.
9. Drucilla Cornell, "Two Lectures on the Normative Dimensions of Community in the Law," *Tennessee law Review*, vol. 54 (winter 1987), pp. 327–43.
10. Michel Foucault, *Power/Knowledge* (New York: Pantheon, 1980).
11. Michael Sandel, *Liberalism and the Limits of Justice* (Cambridge University Press, 1982), pp. 62–3, 173.
12. Ibid., pp. 172–3.
13. Benjamin Barber, *Strong Democracy* (Berkeley and Los Angeles: University of California Press, 1984).
14. Drucilla Cornell, "Two Lectures on the Normative and Dimensions of Community in the Law," *Tennessee Law Review*, vol. 54 (Winter 1987), pp. 327–43.
15. Seyla Benhabib, *Critique, Norm and Utopia* (New York: Columbia University Press, 1986), p. 341.
16. Jacques Derrida, *Of Grammatology* (Baltimore: Johns Hopkins University Press, 1976), pp. 137–9.
17. Murray Bookchin, *The Rise of Urbanization and the Decline of Citizenship* (San Francisco: Sierra Club Books, 1987), p. 267; Peter Manicas,

The Death of the State (New York: Putnam, 1974), pp. 246-50; Christian Bay, *Strategies for Political Emancipation* (Notre Dame: University of Notre Dame Press, 1981), chaps 5 and 6; Charles Taylor, "The Nature and Scope of Distributive Justice," in *Philosophy and the Human Sciences* (Cambridge University Press, 1985), pp. 27-8.

18. H. N. Hirsch, "The Threnody of Liberalism: Constitutional Liberty and the Renewal of Community," *Political Theory*, vol. 14 (August 1986), pp. 423-49.

19. Richard Sennett, *The Fall of Public Man* (New York: Random House, 1974), chap. 2.

20. Jane Mansbridge, *Beyond Adversarial Democracy* (New York: Basic Books, 1980), chap. 21; Wini Breines, *Community and Organization in the New Left: 1962-1968* (South Hadley, Mass: Bergin, 1982).

21. Elizabeth V. Spelman, *The Inessential Woman* (Boston: Beacon, 1989).

22. Maurice Stein, *The Eclipse of Community* (Princeton University Press, 1960); Robert A. Nisbet, *The Quest for Community* (New York: Oxford University Press, 1953).

23. Charles Ellison, "Rousseau and the Modern City: The Politics of Speech and Dress," *Political Theory*, vol. 13 (November 1985), pp. 497-534; Richard Sennett, *The Fall of Public Man*, op. cit., chaps 7-10.

24. George Mosse, *Nationalism and Sexuality* (New York: Fertig, 1985), pp. 32-3, 137-43; Sander L. Gilman, *Difference and Pathology: Stereotypes of Sexuality, Race, and Madness* (Ithaca: Cornell University Press, 1985), p. 214.

25. Claude Fischer, *To Dwell Among Friends: Personal Networks in Town and City* (University of Chicago Press, 1982), pp. 206-30; Joseph Rothschild, *Ethnopolitics* (New York: Columbia University Press, 1981).

26. Joseph D'Emilio, *Sexual Politics, Sexual Communities* (University of Chicago Press, 1983).

27. Martin Sanchez Jankowski, *City Bound: Urban Life and Political Attitudes among Chicano Youth* (Albuquerque: University of New Mexico Press, 1986).

28. Claude Fischer, *To Dwell Among Friends: Personal Networks in Town and City* (University of Chicago Press, 1982), pp. 206-40.

29. Jane Jacobs, *The Death and Life of Great American Cities* (New York: Random House, 1961), chap. 8; Richard Sennett, *The Fall of Public Man*, op. cit., chap. 4; William Whyte, *City: Rediscovering the Center* (New York: Doubleday, 1981).

30. Roland Barthes, "Semiology and the Urban," in M. Gottdiener and Alexandros P. Lagopoulos (eds), *The City and the Sign: An Introduction to Urban Semiotics* (New York: Columbia University Press, 1986).

Part IV

Social Relations and Public Places

16 Introduction
Philip Kasinitz

Even if you had important business, you'd probably forget
it all as soon as you stepped into the street. This is the
one place people don't show themselves because they have
to, where they aren't driven by necessary and commercial interest that embraces the whole of St Petersburg. . . .
The Nevsky is the common meeting ground and communications line of St Petersburg. No directory or information bureau will furnish such correct information as the
Nevsky. Omniscient Nevsky Prospect! How swift the phantasmagoria that develops here in the course of a single
day! How many metamorphoses it goes through within
twenty-four hours!

>   Nikolai Gogol, "Nevsky Prospect", 1835.[1]

The presence of a large number of public places is one of
the most notable characteristics of cities. Physical spaces
in which strangers can come together to meet, communicate, transact business or just enjoy the sight and sound of
each other are at the very core of the urban experience. It
is in public that one feels the "pulse" of the modern city.
As Raymond Williams writes:

> I have felt it again and again: the great buildings of civi-
> lization; the meeting-places; the libraries and theaters,
> the towers and domes; and often more moving than these,
> the houses, the streets, the press and excitement of so
> many people, with so many purposes. I have stood in many
> cities and felt this pulse . . . this identifiable and moving
> quality: the center, the activity, the light.[2]

At the more abstract level, the concept of a "public sphere"
is also used indicate that arena of social life to which access
is theoretically open to all enfranchised members of the
community. This notion is vital to modern politics. From
its origins in the Athenian agora, the idea of democracy
has, at least at the metaphoric level, long been associated

with a physical location of face-to-face communication. In practice, however, many of the world's great public spaces – Gogol's Nevsky Prospect, for example – have been created by societies that were far from democratic. As Bonnie Menes Kahn reminds us, rich cosmopolitan public life often comes about in places where popular participation in government is quite limited, and the political participation of the masses has, at times, been the enemy of tolerance and pluralism – compare the Vienna of the mid-nineteenth century with the Vienna of the early 1930s![3]

While public spaces are, in theory, those that guarantee free access to all members of the community,[4] they are not spaces in which people are free to act in any way they please. Quite the opposite: public places usually have their own distinct social rules, norms and dynamics. One cannot behave in the street the way one does in one's home. As Jukes notes, "streets are a means of communication. Like other media they have their codes and conventions . . ."[5] Without a knowledge of these shared codes and willingness to abide by them, the simplest forms of public life become impossible. As Erving Goffman writes:

> City streets, even in times which defame them, provide a setting where mutual trust is routinely displayed among strangers. Voluntary coordination of action is achieved in which each of the two parties has a conception of how matters ought to be handled between them, the two conceptions agree, each party believes that this agreement exists and each appreciates that this knowledge about the agreement is possessed by the other. In brief, structural prerequisites for rule by convention are found. Avoidance of collision is one example of the consequences.[6]

Thus public life often requires a degree of artificiality, sociability, tolerance, formality and perhaps even repression. Contemporary Americans tend to view with humor, if not horror, the elaborate social rituals of public behavior of our Victorian predecessors. Yet, as Goffman's work shows, the rules governing our own behavior in public places may be no less elaborate, even though we are usually only marginally aware of these rules until they have been violated.[7]

Today, in many cities the structure of public life often seems to be eroding. In the central cities poverty and homelessness can blur the line between the private and public realms, as the private lives of the destitute spill out into public spaces.[8] In some places crime and incivility discourage many people from fully participating in public life, while in others the political and architectural measures taken to reduce crime effectively prevent the possibility of meaningful public interaction. Suburbs – which have now become the dominant settlement pattern in the United States and Canada – are notably rich in private spaces and poor in public ones. By the postwar era even the layout of American homes – spacious back yards and "decks" replacing front porches and stoops – had come to express a turning away from the street and towards controllable domesticity. In recent decades suburban innovations in privatizing space, from gated communities to nighttime curfews, have become common in many cities as well.

Yet if public spaces are in decline, many Americans seem to miss them. It is interesting to note that "strip" style suburban shopping centers, spaces designed to discourage any activity other than commerce, have in recent decades been largely replaced by shopping malls than often attempt to look like indoor, climate-controlled versions of downtown streets.[9] In the cities retail malls patterned after the nineteenth-century arcades and located in "historic" settings have become the centerpieces of numerous efforts to attract suburbanites and tourists back downtown.[10] Of course sustained encounters with urban differences are more difficult than a quick visit to a downtown mall or a promenade along a "hot" strip of sidewalk cafes in a gentrifying area. Whether America's interest in a revival of public life will go beyond the occasional tourist and retailing excursion remains to be seen.

Jeff Weintraub, in an essay prepared for this volume (Chapter 17), discusses the various social and political meanings of the concept of "public." Differentiating the literal use of "public space," meaning the realm of face-to-face interaction and sociability, from the metaphoric political meanings of the term, he points to the source of much of the confusion implied by the notion of "public realm".

Picking up similar themes, in Chapter 18 Michael Walzer differentiates between what he terms "single-minded" and "open-minded" public spaces and reminds us of the broad political and cultural consensus that is required for public spaces to operate.

The remaining chapter, in this part deal with relations in public in contemporary American cities. Elijah's Anderson's "Street Etiquette and Street Wisdom" (Chapter 19) is taken from his book, *Streetwise*. In this ethnography Anderson examines two adjacent neighborhoods in a northeastern US city. "Northton" and the "Village" (pseudonyms) were both built in the nineteenth century to house industrial workers. While the Village was originally the slightly more middle class of the two, by the early twentieth century both areas were home to predominantly working-class, "ethnic" whites. Both received a large influx of African Americans during the 1930s and 1940s; by 1950 nearly half of the people living in the Village and over three quarters of those in Northton were black. The decline in local industry after 1960 left many residents of the area in poverty. At the same time, however, economic opportunities and new housing options opened up for some African Americans in the wake of the civil-rights movement. Upwardly mobile blacks left the area in droves, taking many local institutions with them but leaving behind their less fortunate neighbors. In Northton the population declined sharply and the neighborhood was increasingly beset by the problems of concentrated poverty and crime.

The Village developed differently. Starting in the late 1950s the architecturally appealing area attracted several waves of bohemian white immigrants: self-described "liberals" attracted by the racially integrated neighborhood in the 1950s, counterculture members and antiwar activists during the late 1960s, and somewhat more affluent younger whites – "yuppies" to their detractors – during the late 1970s and 1980s. While each of these groups disapproved of aspects of the others' life-styles, all found themselves bound together by the difficulties of living on the border of an increasingly violent ghetto.

Despite their different histories, Northton and the Village are inextricably connected to each other. The

neighborhoods are so near to each other that residents share
mass-transportation and commercial facilities and often have
to walk through each other's "turf." In Chapter 19 Anderson
addresses what happens when worlds collide, sometimes literally, on the city streets. His depiction of the rules and
codes by which these disparate groups share public space
are in many ways reminiscent of Goffman and of Jacobs'
"sidewalk ballet." Yet to Jacobs' harmonious picture of self-
regulating street life Anderson adds the discordant notes
of racial and gender divisions as well as the pervasive fear
of crime. To navigate comfortably through this landscape,
he argues, requires "street wisdom": a frame of mind that
is part sociological imagination, part effective use of stereotypes and part willful self-delusion.

Political authorities must also respond to the perception
of danger in the streets. In no large city has the privatization of public space and public functions progressed further
than in Los Angeles. This is, in part, a consequence of the
city's history and its automotive infrastructure. Yet in "Fortress Los Angeles" (Chapter 20, an excerpt from a longer
article with the same title) Mike Davis maintains that elite
attempts at social control have gone far beyond the technical necessities of an auto-friendly environment. Davis argues
that Los Angeles has used architecture, urban planning and
an aggressive police force to effectively "militarize" large
sections of the city and to criminalize much of the public
activity of the poor.[11] Particularly striking is his comparison of the ideology behind Frederick Law Olmstead's nineteenth-century parks and the regulation of public life in
contemporary Los Angeles, as seen in the "clean-up" of
MacArthur Park.

Fred Siegel, a writer with a very different ideological perspective than Davis, also uses urban parks as the centerpiece
for a discussion of public space in the city (Chapter 21).
Taking as his text the renovation of New York's Bryant Park
and the surrounding 42nd Street area, Siegel disapproves
of both the anarchic, "anything goes" attitude he identifies
with Richard Sennett (and would probably see in Davis)
and those who would abandon urban public space entirely
in favor of expressways and suburbs. He sees in New York's
"business improvement districts" a model for securing public-

private cooperation in maintaining urban amenities. Some have criticized this approach for abandoning the universalistic principals implied by the idea of public space. Others note that the "business improvement district" works best in those areas that already have substantial private investment: a solution more appropriate to 42nd Street than to central Harlem. Nevertheless Siegel sees in them one way that local government might use private resources in an effort to reestablish a notion of the public good.

Notes

1. Nikolai Gogol, "Nevsky Prospect" translated by Bertrice Scott, (London: Lindsay Drummond, 1945). Quoted in Marshall Berman, *All that is Solid Melts into Air* (New York: Simon and Schuster, 1982), p. 196.
2. Raymond Williams, *The Country and the City* (New York: Oxford University Press, 1973), p. 5.
3. Bonnie Menes Kahn, *Cosmopolitan Culture: The Gilt-Edged Dream of the Tolerant City* (New York: Atheneum, 1987).
4. Indeed public spaces may serve to define who "the community" is for political purposes, by graphically demonstrating who is included and who is excluded! Consider the many "public" spaces that have historically excluded women, for example.
5. Peter Jukes, *A Shout in the Street* (Berkeley: Universtiy of California Press, 1990), p. xiv.
6. Erving Goffman, *Relations in Public* (New York: Harper and Row, 1973), p. 17.
7. Erving Goffman, *Behavior in Public Places* (New York: Free Press, 1963), and *Relations in Public* (New York: Free Press, 1963).
8. See for example, Kim Hopper and Ellen Baxter, *Private Lives/Public Spaces* (New York: The Community Service Society of New York, 1981).
9. This leads to an interesting legal debate now unfolding in the United States. Does one have freedom of speech in a shopping mall? A citizen clearly has a right to demonstrate or petition on a public thoroughfare. He or she does not have the right to do so in a store. But what about in the "food court" of a shopping mall – a privately owned space designed to look like a public space? What if that is the only real meeting space in the community? Court rulings on this matter have thus far been ambiguous.
   It is also interesting to note that while many suburbanites have essentially given up on the idea of public space in favor of their rich private spaces, one group – teenagers – has persisted in making even the most unlikely settings the scene of lively peer-group socia-

bility. Nothing could be less conducive to long-lingering social interaction than a convenience-store parking lot, yet for many American teens it is as much a meeting place as the fountain in a town square might be for their Mediterranean counterparts!

10. In some cases – Faneuil Hall in Boston, South Street Seaport in New York, Harbor Place in Baltimore – these efforts have been far more successful than originally predicted.

11. It should be noted that this article was written before the Rodney King beating and the subsequent trials and riot focused national attention on the relations between the police and racial minorities in Los Angeles.

17 Varieties and Vicissitudes of Public Space*

Jeff Weintraub

> The better constituted the state, the more public affairs outweigh private ones in the minds of citizens.... In a well-conducted city, everyone rushes to the assemblies. Under a bad government, no one cares to take even a step to attend them: no one takes an interest in what is done there, since it is predictable that the general will won't prevail, and so finally domestic concerns absorb everything.
>
> Rousseau, *The Social Contract*, 1754.

> The tolerance, the room for great differences among neighbors – differences that often go far deeper than differences in color – which are possible and normal in intensely urban life, but which are so foreign to suburbs and pseudosuburbs, are possible and normal only when streets of great cities have built-in equipment allowing strangers to dwell in peace together on civilized but essentially dignified and reserved terms. Lowly, unpurposeful and random as they may appear, sidewalk contacts are the small change from which a city's wealth of public life may grow.
>
> Jane Jacobs, *The Death and Life of Great American Cities*, 1961.

Both of these striking passages are quoted often, but rarely, I think, in the same places. This is a pity, because when taken in juxtaposition they have the advantage of capturing two powerful, influential, yet curiously disparate images of "public life," and of the public space in which it can thrive. Rousseau's is a characteristically extreme formulation of a much more widespread conception that ties

---

* Published for the first time in this volume.

"public" life to the practice of citizenship. The citizens who "rush" to the public space of the assembly do so to engage in self-conscious collective deliberation and decision concerning common – that is, public – affairs. When we venture into Jane Jacobs's public space, on the other hand, we enter what Roger Scruton has aptly termed "a sphere of broad and largely unplanned encounter,"[1] of fluid sociability among strangers and near-strangers. The "wealth" of the public life to which it contributes lies not in self-determination or collective action, but in the multistranded liveliness and spontaneity arising from the ongoing intercourse of heterogeneous individuals and groups that can maintain a civilized coexistence. Its function is not so much to express or generate solidarity as, ideally, to make diversity agreeable[2] – or at least manageable. It may be that both these forms, or aspects, of public life are valuable and ought to be encouraged; and some might argue that, in the right circumstances, they can be complementary. But it is clear that they differ in their defining characteristics, requirements and implications.

It would be easy to multiply further examples, but these two are probably sufficient to convey the essential point: any discussion of public space should begin by recognizing, and trying to clarify, the multiple and ambiguous character of its subject matter. If the phenomena evoked by these different images, and the issues they raise, were *entirely* disconnected, then it might not be terribly difficult to sort them out; but matters are not as simple as that, either. Rather the problem of public space covers a variety of subjects that are analytically distinct but at the same time subtly – often confusingly – overlapping and intertwined.

This situation is not really surprising given that each of the two terms combined in the phrase "public space" is itself multifaceted and conceptually slippery. Space, when used in this context, can be concrete, metaphorical or a range of possibilities in between.[3] It may refer, most straightforwardly, to physical space, and to the variety of ways that this is configured, for example by a city's built environment. Or it can mean interactional and experiential space – which is physically patterned, to be sure, but also defined and mediated by social conventions, controls and symbolic demarcations. Or, most abstractly, space is a term of art in conceptual schemas framed by topological metaphors – as with Hannah Arendt's powerful conception of public space (or the public realm: *öffentliche Raum*) as a distinctive field of action that can emerge whenever human beings act and deliberate in concert.[4] In the modern polity, public space in this sense has no specific location and is structured much more by institutions, parties and movements than by physical boundaries; the processes by which groups and issues make their way into (or are excluded from) this public space, or by which publics are created and maintained, usually have more to do with the uses of organization and mass communication than with the literal congregation of citizens in the physical space of the *agora* or forum. On the other hand, even if the participants in these processes are dispersed, they act in a variety of physical settings whose spatial arrangement continues to be significant. (And public assembly in its primordially physical sense – manifested in marches, demonstrations, mass meetings, collective celebrations and crowd actions – has hardly become obsolete or politically irrelevant either.) In fact it is rarely profitable to consider social and physical space in total isolation from each other, and the patterns of interplay between them are manifold and often intricate.[5]

However, negotiating the ambiguities of space is not my prime concern here. The more important source of difficulty, and the one upon which I will focus in this chapter, lies in the complexity and ambiguity of the term public – or, more precisely, of the public/private *distinction* in which any notion of public is necessarily (if at times implicitly) embedded.[6]

PUBLIC AND PRIVATE: USES AND CONFUSIONS OF A GRAND DICHOTOMY

The distinction between public and private has been a central and characteristic preoccupation of Western thought since classical antiquity, and has long served as a point of entry into some of the key issues of social and political analysis, of moral and political debate, and of the ordering of everyday life. In Norberto Bobbio's useful phrase, the public/private distinction stands out as one of the "grand dichotomies" of Western thought, in the sense of a binary opposition that is used to subsume a wide range of other important distinctions, and which attempts (more or less successfully) to dichotomize the social universe in a comprehensive and sharply demarcated way.[7] In recent decades different versions of this distinction have attained new or renewed prominence in a wide range of disciplines and areas of inquiry, from public-choice economics to social history and feminist scholarship.

However it is important to grasp that the different sets of people who use these terms mean very different things by them. The expanding literature on the problem of public goods, which takes its lead from neoclassical economics, is addressing a quite different subject from the public sphere of discussion and political action delineated by Jürgen Habermas or Hannah Arendt, not to mention the public life of sociability charted by Philippe Ariès or Richard Sennett. What do the current debates over privatization, largely concerning whether governmental functions should be taken over by corporations, have to do with the world explored by Ariès and Duby's multivolume *History of Private Life* (1987–90) – families, sexuality, modes of intimacy and obligation – or with the way that privacy has emerged as a central concept in the controversy over abortion rights?

Unfortunately the widespread invocation of the notions of public and private is not always informed by a careful consideration of the meaning and implications of the concepts themselves. And, even where there is sensitivity to these issues, those who draw on one or another version of the public/private distinction are rarely attentive to, or even clearly aware of, the wider range of alternative frameworks within which it is employed. For example, many discussions take for granted that distinguishing public from private is equivalent to establishing the boundary of the political – though even here it makes a considerable difference whether the political is conceived in terms of the administrative state or of the public sphere. But the public/private distinction is also used as a conceptual framework for demarcating other important boundaries: between the private worlds of intimacy and the family and the public worlds of sociability or economic life; between the inner privacy of the individual self and the "interaction order" of Erving Goffman's *Relations in Public* (1963); and so on in rich (and overlapping) profusion.

The public/private distinction, in short, is not unitary, but protean. It comprises not a single paired opposition, but a complex family of them, neither mutually reducible nor wholly unrelated. These different usages do not simply point to different phenomena; often they rest on different underlying images of the social world, are driven by different concerns, generate different problematics and raise very different issues. It is all too common for these different fields of discourse to operate in mutual isolation, or to generate confusion when their categories are casually or unreflectively blended. This chapter will undertake an initial venture inclarification by delineating what I see as four major organizing types of public/private distinction that operate under the surface of current discussion (political as well as scholarly), and will attempt to elucidate the theoretical imagery and presuppositions that inform each one. I think in doing so I can clarify the ways that people talk past each other – and confuse themselves – on these issues and also suggest the potentially useful elements in each of these perspectives.

These different distinctions emerge, to put it another way, from different (often implicit or only partly conscious) theoretical languages or universes of discourse. While the analysis of public and private can usefully be informed by a number of these approaches, the result is most likely to be fruitful cross-fertilization and reasoned contestation – as opposed to the prevailing conceptual confusion – if it starts with a clear grasp of the differences between them. Not only is this essential to avoid missing the point of arguments that employ the categories of public and private; it can also help us reflect with conceptual self-awareness about how far the concerns of these different perspectives can or should be synthesized. Some of these differences simply express variations in terminology, and could be cleared up (or reconciled) conceptually without requiring any very agonized choices. But to a considerable degree they also reflect deeper differences in both theoretical and ideological commitments, in sociological assumptions and/or in sociohistorical context. To bring some intelligible order into the discussion, its complexity needs to be acknowledged and the roots of this complexity need to be elucidated.[8]

PUBLIC AND PRIVATE: SOME BASIC ORIENTATIONS

We can begin by reminding ourselves that any notion of public or private makes sense only as one element in a paired opposition – whether the contrast is being used as an analytical device to address a specific problem or being advanced as a comprehensive model of social structure. To understand what public, or private, means within a given framework, we need to know with what it is being contrasted (explicitly or implicitly) and upon what basis the contrast is being drawn.

At the deepest and most general level, lying behind all the different forms of public/private distinction are (at least) two fundamental and analytically quite distinct kinds of imagery in terms of which private can be contrasted with public:

- What is hidden or withdrawn versus what is open or revealed.
- What is individual, or pertains only to an individual, versus what is collective, or affects the interests of a collectivity of individuals. This individual/collective distinction can, by extension, take the form of a distinction between part and whole (of some social collectivity).[9]

We might refer to these two underlying criteria as "visibility" (audibility being one component) and "collectivity." The two may blur into each other in specific cases, and can also be combined in various ways, but the difference in principle is clear enough. When an individual is described as pursuing his or her private interest rather than the public interest – or a group is described as pursuing a special interest rather than the public interest – the implication is not necessarily that they are doing it in secret. The criterion involved is the second one: the private is the particular.

One especially pure application of this criterion is perhaps the way in which economists use the term public good to mean an indivisible collective benefit – that is, one that is *essentially* collective; the question of visibility is irrelevant here. Likewise the basis for using the term public to describe the actions and agents of the state (so that public/ private = state/nonstate) lies in the state's claim to be responsible for the general interests and affairs of a politically organized collectivity (or at least its ability to monopolize them) as opposed to private – that is, merely particular – interests. Treating the state as the locus of the public *may* be combined with arguments for the openness or publicity of state actions; but it has been at least as common to claim that, in order to advance the public interest, rulers must maintain state secrets and have recourse to the *arcana imperii*. As for the first criterion, visibility, its basic thrust is too evident to require much explication. Its specific instances, however, can be sociologically quite subtle and even paradoxical.[10] The use of the term privacy usually signals the invocation of this criterion, since it generally concerns things that we are able and/or entitled to keep hidden, sheltered or withdrawn from others. (There may also be things that we are required to keep hidden from others, such as our "private parts," so that having sex or urinating in public is frowned on in many cultures.)[11]

There are a number of ways in which each of these underlying criteria can be conceived, and a number of ways in which they can be combined, to produce the various concrete versions of the public/private distinction. The range of permutations is sufficiently formidable to prevent my attempting to list all the ways in which public and private are listed in current discourse. But it may be worth reemphasizing the cautionary point that there is no necessary connection between the notions of public and political; while this should be obvious (as I hope the discussion this far has made clear), it is often overlooked that there are many varieties of public/private distinction that have litttle or nothing to do – directly, at all events – with politics. For example, when Clifford Geertz insists, as he does frequently, "that human thought is both social and public,"[12] he is using the language of post-Wittensteinian analytical philosophy to express the idea that thought is essentially intersubjective rather than something that happens entirely in the individual head, that it relies on collectively elaborated media such as language and cultural symbolism.[13] This quite significant conception of public applies to politics no more than to any other human activity.

I will not pursue this particular example any further, since in one respect it leads away from the main thrust of my discussion. The kind of argument being made by Geertz is that all human action necessarily has an element that is, in a certain sense, public. More often, however, public and private are used to distinguish different *kinds* of human action – and, beyond that, the different realms of social life, or the different physical and social spaces, in which they occur; and these are the sorts of arguments upon which I want to focus. The following are, I think, the four major ways in which these distinctions are currently drawn in social analysis (I remind the reader that this list is not meant to be exhaustive):

1. The liberal-economistic model, dominant in most public-policy analysis and in the work of people such as Mancur Olson or Thomas Schelling (and so on), which sees the public/private distinction primarily in terms of the distinction between state administration and the market economy.
2. The republican-virtue (and classical) approach, which sees the public realm in terms of political community and citizenship, analytically distinct from *both* the market and the administrative state.
3. The approach, exemplified for example by the work of Ariès (and other figures in social history and anthropology), which sees the public realm as a sphere of fluid and polymorphous sociability, and tires to analyze the cultural and dramatic conventions that make it possible. (This approach might almost be called dramaturgic, if that term were not so ambiguous.)
4. A tendency, which has recently become important in certain kinds of economic history and feminist analysis, to conceive of the distinction between private and public in terms of the distinction between the family and the market economy (with the latter becoming the public realm).

Now let me elaborate.

Liberalism: The Market and the State

This is the framework into which terms such as public sector and private sector usually fit, and which structures the great bulk of what is called public-policy debate. the assumptions of neoclassical economics tend to dominate,[14] which is to say – putting the matter into a grander theoretical perspective – the assumptions of utilitarian liberalism.[15] They are embodied in a characteristic, if not always explicit, image of social reality (which, like most such images, has both descriptive and normative dimensions): that what exists in society are individuals pursuing their self-interest more or less efficiently (that is, "rationally," in the peculiar sense this term is used in utilitarian liberalism); voluntary (particularly contractual) relations between individuals; and the state. Thus in practice the distinction between public and private – between the public sector and the private sector – usually means the distinction between governmental and nongovernmental, with the implication that this distinction should be as clearly and sharply dichotomous as possible. The field of the nongovernmental is conceived essentially in terms of the market. It is therefore not surprising that the use of the public/private distinction within this framework has characteristically involved a preoccupation with questions of *jurisdiction*, and especially with demarcating the sphere of the public authority of the state from the sphere of formally voluntary relations between private individuals. These questions of jurisdiction tend predominantly to boil down to disputes about whether particular activities or services should be left to the market or be subject to government intervention, usually conceived in terms of administrative regulation backed by coercive force.

To put it another way, this orientation defines public/private issues as having to do with the balance between individuals and contractually created organizations on the one hand and state action on the other. The fact that these disputes may often be quite bitter should not conceal the fact that both sides are operating within a common universe of discourse, drawing different conclusions from the same premises. They are simply replicating the two classic answers to the problem of order as posed by utilitarian liberalism.[16] Locke and Adam Smith on the one hand and Hobbes and Bentham on the other might be taken as the most distinguished representatives of the two poles within this universe of discourse: the side that leans toward a natural harmonization of selfish interests, whose grand theoretical achievement is the theory of the market; and the more technocratic, social-engineering side, which posits the need for a coercive agency standing outside society (epitomized by Hobbes's Leviathan), that maintains order by manipulating the structure of rewards and punishments within which individuals pursue their rational interests. Given the underlying assumptions, the invisible hand of the market and what Alfred Chandler calls the "visible hand" of administrative regulation[17] are the two key solutions. The pervasiveness of this dichotomous model is brought out by the way it is replicated when the second pole is represented, not by the state, but by the private government of the business firm; again, the alternatives, as captured in the title of an influential book by Oliver Williamson, are *Markets and Hierarchies* (1975).

This theoretical tendency is of course highly imperialistic, and its influence extends well beyond its core stronghold in neoclassical economics. Important examples from attempts to generalize this perspective range from Anthony Downs' *An Economic Theory of Democracy* (1957) to the work of Gary Becker and the exchange theory of Peter Blau; and its inroads throughout the social sciences are registered by the alarming vogue of what is currently being termed rational-choice theory.[18] (Along the same lines, a good deal of analytical Marxism is essentially a branch of utilitarian liberalism, even where the Marxist part of the package has not gradually disintegrated – the intellectual trajectory of Jon Elster is instructive here.) Its limitations are brought out, from the inside, by two currently prominent writers: the first does it unintentionally, the other quite self-consciously.

The first is Mancur Olson, whose core argument was set out in *The Logic of Collective Action* (1971). What he argues is that rational actors will never engage in collective action

– due to the "free-rider" problem – unless subjected to coercion and selective incentives. Workers submit to coercion by unions for the same reason that Hobbes' men in the state of nature submit to the sovereign: it is the only way they can pursue their egoistic interests, which they are incapable of pursuing cooperatively. Actually what Olson shows is that these premises render many forms of collective action – and particularly collective self-determination – incomprehensible. The premises are too narrow and the dichotomous framework is too restricted.

A writer who starts within this framework and deliberately works through to its limits is Albert Hirschman, particularly in *Exit, Voice, and Loyalty* (1970). "Exit" – which exercises an indirect pressure on the operation of "firms, organizations, and states" – is the only option of the rational individual of liberal theory. But that is inadequate as a mechanism to keep the world going. There is also a need for "voice," which means participation in making decisions about matters of common concern. And for voice to work requires some degree of "loyalty." Within the framework that Hirschman starts from, voice is an imported category and loyalty an essentially residual one; thus both are only thinly fleshed out. But they point the way to the problematic of the next perspective, which focuses on the problem of citizenship.

Citizenship: From the Polis to the Public Sphere

Here the public realm is the realm of political community based on citizenship: at the heart of public life is a process of active participation in collective decision-making, carried out within a framework of fundamental solidarity and equality. The key point is that this whole realm of activity, and the problematic it generates, are essentially invisible within the framework of the first perspective.

In a sense public means political in both this perspective and that in the subsection above. But these are very different meanings of political. Above, political or public authority meant the administrative state. Here politics means a world of discussion, debate, deliberation, collective decision-

making and action in concert. In this context it makes sense
to speak not only of public jurisdiction and public interest,
but also of public life.

These two notions of public as political become clearer
if we grasp their historical roots and the social contexts
from which they emerged.[19] Both derive originally from
classical antiquity. The words public and private were originally Roman, the concepts Greco-Roman. Their dual register
stems in part from the fateful circumstance that the Roman
empire took over much of the political language of the
Roman republic (including such terms as public and even
citizen) but shaded their meanings rather differently. A great
deal of the conceptual vocabulary of Western social, political and moral discourse has thus been shaped by two
interconnected but distinctive legacies, those of ancient republicanism and of the Roman empire – the latter being
conveyed, above all, by the massive influence of Roman
law, not only on jurisprudence but on the categories of more
than a thousand years of Western social and political
philosophy.

The result is that there are two basic models of the public
realm drawn from antiquity:

- The self-governing polis or republic (*res publica*, literally
  "public thing") from which we inherit a notion of politics as *citizenship*, in which individuals, in their capacity
  as citizens, participate in an ongoing process of conscious
  collective self-determination.
- The Roman empire, from which we get the notion of
  sovereignty: of a centralized, unified and omnipotent
  apparatus of rule that stands above the society and
  governs it through the enactment and administration
  of laws. The public power of the sovereign rules over
  and, in principle, on behalf of a society of private and
  politically passive individuals who are bearers of rights
  granted to them and guaranteed by the sovereign. This
  conception of the public/private distinction permeates,
  for example, Roman (imperial) law.[20]

Many of the ambiguities in our thinking about politics
stem from the fact that both of these underlying images have a significant presence in modern thought.

Compared with the main patterns of political thought developed in other civilizations, both are distinctive in the sharpness of the line they draw between public and private. In many other respects, however, their presuppositions and implications are profoundly different.

If we examine the origins of systematic political reflection in other civilizations, and in other periods of Western history as well, the most common pattern is for political thought to take one or another form of monarchy as its main point of reference; and the notion of politics centered on the model of sovereignty accords with this general tendency. In such a context the key issues for discourse and sophisticated theorizing about politics center on the problem of rulership or, to use the more Roman term, domination – its nature, its modes, its justifications, its limits. This kind of theorizing takes for granted, in its underlying premises, the separation between rulers and ruled (whether it takes the side of the rulers or the ruled). Classical moral and political philosophy, however, was profoundly marked by the fact that it took as its point of departure a fundamentally different, and rather more exceptional, model of politics, one based on a process of collective decision making by a body of citizens united in a community (albeit, of course, a restricted and exclusive community). Thus the central image of political action as we find it in Aristotle is not domination and compliance (or resistance) but participation in collective self-determination; Aristotle's classic definition of the citizen is one who is capable *both* of ruling and of being ruled. The appropriate sphere for domination is within the private realm of the household, which is structured by relationships of "natural" *in*equality: between master and slave, parent and child, husband and wife.

What separates the problematic of citizenship, in any strong sense of the term, from the conceptual framework of liberal-social theory is that the practice of citizenship is inseparable from active participation in a decision-making *community* maintained by solidarity and the exercise of (what used to be called) republican virtue. But since liberalism is too often counterposed nowadays to an undifferentiated communitarianism, it is also important to emphasize that membership in community does not necessarily constitute citizenship. Citizenship entails participation in a particular *kind* of community (which I have elsewhere called "willed community"):[21] one marked by, among other things, fundamental equality and the consideration and resolution of public issues through conscious, collective decision-making.

Both the notion of citizenship and the notion of sovereignty went into eclipse in the middle ages, for reasons that are understandable. For one thing, neither of them is compatible with the feudal system of rule, based on a web of personal dependent ties and the absence of any significant distinction between public and private authority. The same can be said of the customary communities of mediaeval *Gemeinschaft*. As has frequently been stressed, a society of this sort really does not have a differentiated public *or* private realm. In such a context the distinction does not make sense.

A significant part of the development of modernity concerns the gradual rediscovery of these notions and the attempt to realize and institutionalize them – and sometimes, in a move that would have puzzled the ancients, to combine them. Behind this process lie three grand historical transformations, whose complex interconnections need not trouble us here.

First, the development of modern civil society, which is the seedbed of liberalism. "Civil society" is, of course, another historically complex and multivalent term; but I do not want to enter into the relevant controversies at this point so I will simply state my own position. Following Hegel's guide, I will use civil society to refer to the social world of self-interested individualism, competition, impersonality and contractual relationships – centered on the market – that, as thinkers in the early modern West slowly came to recognize, seemed somehow able to run itself. Liberalism is the philosophy of civil society, and frequently its apology. Its tendency is to reduce society to civil society (in the case of rational-choice theory, for example, to collapse both politics and community into the market).

Second, the recovery of the notion of sovereignty, to complement the notion of the atomistic liberal individual.

The rediscovery of sovereignty was obviously connected in its initial stages to the gradual reassertion of royal power, to the multifaceted "recovery" of Roman law that often accompanied it, and particularly to the era of absolutism.[22] To restate a point emphasized earlier, the liberal conception of the public/private distinction turns fundamentally on the separation between the administrative state and civil society – one dichotomy being mapped onto the other. It has difficulty dealing with other aspects of social life.

Third, the recovery of the notion of citizenship. This followed a different route from the rediscovery of sovereignty, beginning with the reemergence of the self-governing city in the later middle ages and the rebirth of civic consciousness that this made possible. From this perspective the public realm is above all a realm of participatory self-determination, deliberation and conscious cooperation among equals, the logic of which is distinct from those of *both* civil society and the administrative state.

Tocqueville's conception of "political society," Arendt's conception of the "public realm," and Habermas's conception of the "public sphere" represent some of the more significant efforts to characterize and theorize this sphere of social life.[23] It is worth emphasizing one larger implication that emerges from all three of these analyses: attempts to use the public/private distinction as a dichotomous model to capture the overall pattern of social life in a society – as opposed to using one or another version for specific and carefully specified purposes – are likely to be inherently misleading because the procrustean dualism of their categories will tend to blank out important phenomena. Thus, just as the public realm (and politics) cannot be reduced to the state, the realm of social life outside the state (and its control) cannot simply be identified as private. The conceptual limitations of the public/private dichotomy in this connection are emphasized in Habermas's deliberately paradoxical formulation that "the bourgeois public sphere may be conceived above all as the sphere of private people [who have] come together as a public" (outside and even against the state) to discuss and debate matters of common concern.[24] Similarly, the fact that political society, though it coexists with both civil society and the state, is not reducible to either lies behind an equally paradoxical observation of Tocqueville's that is really central to his argument in *The Old Regime and the French Revolution*: that, precisely as the centralized and bureaucratized French state achieved its apotheosis, *political* life was smothered and suppressed.[25]

In short these two notions of public – and the two versions of the public/private distinction in which they are embedded – rest on crucially different images of politics and society, and a good deal of modern thought reflects the tension between them. However they far from exhaust the significant discussion of public and private. In particular, neither addresses the conditions for the "wealth of public life" in the form celebrated by Jane Jacobs; this vision of public life belongs to the realm of discourse that links it neither to the state nor to citizenship, but to sociability.

Public Life as Sociability

This is the notion of public we have in mind when we speak of Mediterranean (but not American) cities having a rich public life. It is what Ariès means when he says that, in the society of the old regime, "life was lived in public," and the intense privatization of the family and intimate relations, with their sharp separation from an impersonal public realm, had not yet occurred. The key point is that public in this sense has nothing to do, necessarily, with collective decision making (let alone the state). The key to it is not solidarity or obligation, but sociability.

The work of Philippe Ariès, beginning with *Centuries of Childhood* (1962),[26] forms an outstanding starting-point for the exploration of this world. The significance of Ariès' analysis in this respect is often missed because of the misimpression that he is recounting *simply* an isolated history of the family. Instead he is developing – admittedly in a discursive and far from analytically rigorous way – a sweeping interpretation of the transformations in the texture of Western society from the old regime to the modern era. In this connection the emergence of the modern family can be understood only in the context of the changing *relationship* between the family and the broader web of communal ties and sociability. The heart of the story, therefore, really lies in Ariès' reconstruction of the public life of the society of the old regime and its gradual decay. The decay of the older public world and the emergence of the modern family (along with other relationships committed to creating islands of privacy and intense intimacy) form a mutually reinforcing process. The result is a drastic transformation of the relationship between the public and private realms, and of the character of each. For Ariès (to put words in his mouth), modern civil society represents not the private realm but the new public realm; the private realm is the realm of personal life, above all of domesticity. "The progress of the concept of the family followed the progress of private life, of domesticity."[27]

This notion of the public realm, then, sees it as a realm of sociability, mediated by conventions that allow diversity and social distance to be maintained despite physical proximity. It is a picture of a world more disorderly and yet in some ways more stable, less intimate but also less impersonal than our own (if we happen to be middle-class North Americans and North-West Europeans). Huizinga is trying to capture some of the same phenomena, but striking a more somber note, when he observes in *The Waning of the Middle Ages* that "all things in life were of a proud and cruel publicity."[28] The great and the small, the rich and the poor were jumbled together more casually and promiscuously than today; both ostentation and wretchedness were less embarrassed. Ariès' brilliant, though unsystematic, depiction of this world is probably aided by the fact that he was something of a conservative with a real sympathy for the old regime. But the insights to be derived from this conceptual framework do not depend on ideological attitude. For example, Lawrence Stone's 1979 book on *The Family, Sex, and Marriage in England 1500–1800* draws very powerfully on Ariès despite the fact that Stone, unlike Ariès, believes in "progress" (a little excessively for my taste) and is firmly convinced of the relative wretchedness of the past. I have chosen to use Ariès as a touchstone for identifying this version of the public/private distinction,[29] but the project of delineating the public world of sociability and tracing its transformations is not, of course, peculiar to Ariès. It now informs an enormous range of work in the social history and historical sociology of the family – some of it inspired by Ariès, some of it running parallel to, or intersecting with, his work. And many of the issues he is dealing with would be immediately recognizable to readers of anthropological investigations in many non-Western (or even Mediterranean) cultures. Thus it is not surprising that, if one looks for them, one will find many of the same themes in the work of the better social historians influenced by interpretive anthropology – the treatment of everyday ritual and popular culture by Natalie Davis and Robert Darnton are good examples – as well as those *Annales* historians who have returned to the reconstruction of *mentalités*.

However it has to be said that people not concerned with these particular lines of historiographic investigation, even if they are aware of these bodies of work, have often failed to address the more general theoretical challenges they raise for social and political analysis. It might help to point out – at least this is what I would argue – that Ariès, Norbert Elias and Foucault were all, in different ways, exploring the same broad historico-theoretical terrain: the triumph of privacy and discipline in the modern West. The composite picture of the historical transformation of Western societies that has emerged from these different lines of research emphasizes, albeit in very different ways, the breakdown of the older public realm of polymorphous sociability and, with it, the increasingly sharp polarization of social life between an increasingly impersonal public realm (of the market, the modern state and bureaucratic organization) and a private realm of increasingly intense intimacy and emotionality (the modern family, romantic love and so on). As Elias puts it:

> In other words, with the advance of civilization the lives of human beings are increasingly split between an intimate and a public sphere, between secret and public behavior.

And this split is taken so much for granted, becomes so compulsive a habit, that it is hardly perceived in consciousness.[30]

In short, one of the most salient forms (or versions, or variants) of the public/private distinction in modern culture (in both thought and practice) is that which demarcates the private realm of personal life from the public realm of *Gesellschaft* (epitomized by the market and bureaucratically administered formal organization). The contrast between the personal, emotionally intense and intimate domain of family, friendship and the primary group and the impersonal, severely instrumental domain of the market and formal institutions is in fact widely experienced – one need only think about the evidence of popular culture – as one of the great divides of modern life.[31] But historically these two poles emerge together, to a great extent in dialectical tension with each other; and the sharpness of the split between them is one of the defining characteristics of modernity. This perspective can help us make sense of the emergence of a whole range of different forms of private relationship that are distinctive to modern society and that are simultaneously defined in opposition to the logic of *Gesellschaft*: for example the modern notion of anti-instrumental friendship based exclusively on sympathy and affection; or the ideal of romantic marriage and the emotionally bonded child-centered family with its cult of the economically useless but emotionally "priceless child."[32] Ariès sums up his view of this process with this striking remark:

> It is not individualism which has triumphed, but the family. But this family has advanced in proportion as sociability has retreated. It is as if the modern family had sought to take the place of the old social relationships (as these gradually defaulted) in order to preserve mankind from an unbearable moral solitude.[33]

A similar vision is expressed, in more general terms, in these formulations by Peter Berger and his coauthors in *The Homeless Mind* (1974, pp. 183–6):

All the major public institutions of modern society have become 'abstract'. . . . There are also discontents specifically derived from the pluralization of social life-worlds. Generally, these discontents can be subsumed under the heading of 'homelessness'. . . . Modern society's 'solution' to these discontents has been, as we have seen, the creation of the private sphere as a distinctive and largely segregated sector of social life, along with the dichotomization of the individual's societal involvements between the private and the public spheres. The private sphere has served as a kind of balancing mechanism providing meanings and meaningful activities to compensate for the discontents brought about by the large structures of modern society.[34]

This is not necessarily a happy solution. One implication of this process – and here Ariès' reflections converge in an interesting way with the concerns of Philip Slater, the brilliant outlaw Parsonian sociologist[35] – is the possibility that the emotional "overloading" of the domain of intimate relations will develop in tandem with the increasing emotional emptiness and isolation of an inhospitable public domain. Not that many of us would want to abandon the satisfactions of intimate life or the advantages of impersonal institutions: they are, at least potentially, among the benefits of modernity. But if they confront us as sharply dichotomized and exclusive alternatives, they add up to an unsatisfactory prospect. Once again part of the solution, both theoretical and practical, may lie in complexification: in the existence and vitality of a sphere of public life, in the sense of sociability, that can mediate between the particularistic intimacies of private life and extreme impersonality and instrumentalism of *Gesellschaft*. As a number of the writers represented in the present volume have suggested, this "wealth of public life" has been, at its best, one of the characteristic achievements of the successful cosmopolitan city.

The analysis of sociability thus ought to be a central concern in thinking about city life; and, as Jane Jacobs (1961) brought home powerfully in her account of the "intricate ballet" of the streets, this form of public life has its own distinctive conditions of vitality and fragility.

Of the types we have examined so far, it is probably the most closely and essentially tied to the spatial organization of social life. Its domain lies, after all, in the public space of street, park and plaza – but also of neighborhood and bar and café. Its character and possibilities are influenced by the ways that the configurations of physical space facilitate, channel and block the flow of everyday movement and activity. This aspect of Jane Jacobs' legacy is especially well represented by William H. Whyte's long-term project to investigate the ways that the shape of urban space can enhance the vitality of public life.[36] On the other hand it is also clear that the requirements of successful public space are never only physical. Two of the most influential and evocative ethnographic accounts of urban sociability, William Foote Whyte's *Street Corner Society* (1943) and Herbert Gans' *The Urban Villagers* (1962), dealt with ethnic enclaves whose sense of neighborhood was culturally as well as physically based. The context of ethnic community helped to maintain – though by itself it can never guarantee – the background conditions of basic trust, security, predictability and a sense of shared conventions against which the spontaneity of public life can develop.

These background conditions are even more important if the public space is to do its more ambitious work of allowing more diverse individuals and groups "to dwell in peace together on civilized but essentially dignified and reserved terms" (Jacobs, 1961). The characteristic virtue of this form of public space, which it both requires and reinforces, is civility[37] – which is a matter of codes and conventions, no less important for being largely implicit. Once established as a pattern (and it comes in a variety of socio-historical forms) civility can be resilient; but, as Fred Siegel argues in Chapter 21 of this volume, it also begins to unravel if put under excessive strain. Or, if different groups start out with enough mutual fear, hostility or incomprehension, it is unlikely to emerge in the first place. And this leaves out of the account the fact that successful public space relies on a range of political and economic resources – including such mundane matters as policing, trash collection and street cleaning – which it does not itself provide. Even in its most physically situated form the

public space of sociability emerges from a complex interplay of spatial and social arrangements.

All these qualifications point to a larger reservation. The
face-to-face interaction of the neighborhood – where Jacobs'
vision is at its strongest and most illuminating – is not
sufficient by itself to tie a city together, to manage the relations between its different groups and interests, and to
make it work. But Jacobs and much of the work she has
inspired have found it difficult to deal with the processes
that connect the world of neighborhood sociability to these
larger arenas – which have profound effects on the character and viability of the small-scale arenas themselves. Nor
is this only a question of scale. The success or failure of
cities requires a range of decisions, actions and policies that
cannot emerge from the flow of everyday sociability alone.
Their terrain is a different sort of public space, that of the
political. If this public space cannot generate and maintain a political community capable of collective decision
and collective action, then the crucial tasks will have to be
addressed by authority and administration from above – or
they may not get done at all. An analysis of the public life
of cities that cannot effectively deal with the political is
necessarily truncated.

In any event it is clear that a notion of the public
sphere of sociability, along the lines developed especially
by Ariès and Elias, is not only of historical interest but
ought to be employed in the analysis of contemporary societies. Doing so would require that this conception of the
public sphere be more explicitly elaborated and theoretically refined so as to increase its analytical flexibility, and
so that its interplay with other forms of public life can be
systematically explored. Probably the most ambitious and
comprehensive effort along these lines has been that of
Richard Sennett, most notably in *The Fall of Public Man*
(1978).[38] Sennett insists on the need to link the study of
the great cosmopolitan city to a theoretically informed analysis of sociability – one that addresses the interplay between
the spatial organization of cities and long-term socio-
historical processes – and further attempts to link the analysis
of sociability to a vision of the political. Whether or not
the success of Sennett's project has fully matched its

ambition, it underlines the need for further efforts to theorize more fully this notion of public space, and to integrate it more systematically into the comprehensive analysis of modern societies.

Sennett, like Ariès, sees in the decay of sociability a threatening dialectic between "dead public space" and a pathological over-investment in intimate life – with the additional side effect that community comes to be disastrously misconceived as intimacy writ large, which renders it both exclusivistic and ultimately unworkable. Here is the way that Ariès sums up some of the key themes we have been discussing:

> My central theme will be that when the city (and, earlier, the rural community) deteriorated and lost its vitality, the role of the family expanded like a hypertrophied cell (Ariès, 1977, p. 227).

> Thus, the separation of space into work areas and living areas corresponds to the division of life into a public sector and private sector. The family falls within the private sector (ibid., p. 230).

> These [the family and the café] were the only two exceptions to the modern system of surveillance and order which came to include all social behavior (ibid., p. 232).

> In the so-called post-industrial age of the mid-twentieth century, the public sector of the nineteenth century collapsed and people thought they could fill the void by extending the private, family sector. They thus demanded that the family see to all their needs. . . . Although people today often claim that the family is undergoing a crisis, this is not, properly speaking, an accurate description of what is happening. Rather, we are witnessing the inability of the family to fulfill all the many functions with which it has been invested, no doubt temporarily, during the past half-century (ibid., pp. 234–5).

Before leaving this section I will, like Ariès, step back from the family and focus on the larger problem of sociability. What needs to be stressed again about this version of the

public/private distinction is that it entails a very different
conception of public space from that of the civic perspective in the subsection above. (The two *may* be combinable,
but they are analytically distinct.) This is a space of heterogeneous coexistence, not of inclusive solidarity or conscious
collective action; a space of symbolic display, of the complex blending of practical motives with interaction ritual
and personal ties, of physical proximity coexisting with social
distance – and *not* a space (to use the Habermasian phrase),
of 'discourse oriented to achieving consensus by communi-
cative means' to address common concerns. In the last section of this chapter I will return to consider some
implications of these differences.

Feminism: Private/Public as Family/Civil Society

The split between public and private life has been a
central organizing theme in feminist scholarship – as
well as semischolarly debates – for the last several
decades.[39] And, as one might expect, the concerns driving
this scholarship have led to some sharp reformulations
of the terms in which the public/private distinction is
considered. This by now too rich and diverse a field of
discourse to characterize in a short space. Rather than
attempt anything like a comprehensive overview of feminist
treatments of the public/private distinction, therefore, I
will focus on delineating a few of the distinctive themes
they have introduced to the discussion and their implications for some issues we have already encountered.

On the whole, in general one can say that the characteristic tendency in most branches of feminist scholarship is
to focus on the family as the private realm, so that the
formulation domestic/public is often used almost inter-
changeably with private/public. To that extent a number
of feminist approaches have something in common with the
perspective just discussed, and often shade into it in practice, but – and here one has to speak cautiously because
of the range of positions in feminist argument – the implications tend to be different. While the private sphere tends
to be that of intimacy and the family, as in the subsection
above, the conception of the public sphere is often quite

different. The ideological and normative concerns driving the analysis also tend to be different – though they are themselves far from uniform.

One further general point is worth making. I think it is fair to say that, for the perspectives in the first two subsections, the real conceptual interest is usually in defining "public," and "private" is, to some extent, a residual category. Here, however, the conceptual starting point is the private sphere, conceived as the family, and if anything it is "public" that is treated as a residual category. In this respect the perspective in the third subsection is intermediate between those in the first and second, on the one hand, and most feminist approaches on the other.

The domestic/public framework was first elaborated by a set of writers in the overlapping categories of feminist anthropology and Marxist (or, more broadly, socialist) feminism. One of the earliest influential formulations along these lines appears to have been that of the anthropologist Michelle Zimbalist Rosaldo.[40] Her orienting framework, which opposes the private or domestic sphere to the public sphere of extrafamilial economic and political activity, recurs with remarkable frequency in subsequent work. The point is, of course, that in all known societies (some would say most) this social division is asymmetric in gender terms, and the domestic sphere is disproportionately (to use a nineteenth century American phrase) a "woman's sphere." While the arguments discussed in the previous section tend to focus on the ways that many of the characteristically modern forms of public/private division cut through the lives of both men and women, feminists have tended to emphasize the ways that these public/private divisions are gender-linked in terms of both social structure and ideology.

Feminists have tended to make (at least) three overlapping, though not precisely identical, points. One is that the conceptual orientations of much social and political theory have ignored this sphere or treated it as trivial. The second is that that the public/private distinction itself is often deeply gendered, and in almost uniformly invidious ways. It very often plays a role in ideologies that purport to assign men and women to different spheres of social life on the basis of their "natural" characteristics, and thus to confine women to positions of inferiority. The third is that, by classifying institutions such as the family as "private," the public/private distinction often serves to shield abuse and domination within these relationships from political scrutiny or legal redress.

This version of the public/private distinction took a wide range of feminist scholarship by storm, since it appeared to speak to a dimension of gender relations that was at once deeply consequential, apparently universal and highly nuanced. A good many feminist writers treated the public/private distinction as an essential key to understanding women's oppression, and in some cases tended to forget that there were important versions of the public/private distinction that could not be mapped directly onto a female/male opposition.[41] A number of reconsiderations in the course of the 1980s have brought a more troubled and ambivalent attitude toward the use of the public/private distinction as conceptual tool. Some have argued that to accept that women have indeed always been confined to the private realm is to repeat ideologies of male domination rather than criticizing them, and that the reality has almost always been more complex.[42] There has also been an increasing recognition of the complexity of the public/private distinction itself, as well as an increasing diversity in the ways it is approached.

One way or another, one of the significant contributions of feminist treatments of the public/private distinction has been to greatly extend the range of people who are aware of the insights to be gained by linking the private to the family – rather than, say, to the market or the isolated individual. In a sense, however, it is odd that this perspective had to be recovered, since it is, so to speak, the one with which Western social and political theory began. In Aristotle, for example, the distinction between private and public is fundamentally that between the household (the *oikos*) and the political community – with the household seen as a realm of both particularistic ties and of "natural" inequality. The public space of the *polis*, on the other hand, is a sphere of wider engagement and fundamental equality in the practice of citizenship. Men (or at least citizens) have the ability to move between these two realms; and one of the bases of the citizens' public, civic personality is their private personalities as heads of households. On the other hand, women (like children and slaves) belong "naturally," and exclusively, in private life. Variations on this model have remained influential in political theory for the subsequent 2500 years. In the last several centuries, however, it has been overlaid and usually displaced by the alternative frameworks we have been examining.[43]

The road back to family as the private realm seems to have had a dual route: one, as noted, from feminist anthropology, the other from "the unhappy marriage of Marxism and feminism."[44] Since many feminist writers have had to grapple with Marxism at some point in their intellectual formation, one key question was how to deal with the fact that most formulations of the all-important "mode of production" relegated the household (and the women in it) to a minor role. The formulation of the domestic/public framework helped provide a theoretical emancipation from the more rigid Marxist frameworks.[45] On the other hand, in relation to the alternative forms of public/private distinction I have been outlining so far, this move also leads back to – and highlights – the analytical difficulties surrounding the treatment of civil society in all these discussions. Once one adopts the standpoint of the family and looks out, it seems very peculiar to treat civil society as the private sphere.

Since there has only recently been much traffic between feminist writing and mainstream political theory (let alone public-choice economics!), it took some time for this problem to be faced explicitly and systematically. One of the first people to do so was Carole Pateman (who might be said to have a foot in each camp). Since "domestic life is . . . paradigmatically private for feminists," she notes, it is civil society that is the public realm. The historic liberal formulation of the public/private distinction in terms of the division between state and civil society has the effect of mystifying certain crucial facts about social life. "Precisely because liberalism conceptualizes civil society in abstraction from ascriptive domestic life, the latter remains `forgotten' in theoretical discussions. The separation between private and public is thus re-established as a division *within* civil society itself, within the world of men."[46] That is, the supposedly private realm of civil society as well as the public realm of politics are populated largely by male heads of household (as with Locke) or male wage workers (as with much of Marxism), and so on. The truly privatized realm of the family is hidden behind them. Thus women "disappear" theoretically along with the domestic sphere.[47] This is not, however, a benign neglect. Its result is to exclude women (on the basis of their "naturally" private character), from both of the spheres in which men have increasingly claimed equality and agency in the modern world, as independent actors in civil society and as citizens in the political community. On the other hand the private realm to which this ideology confines women continues in fact to be regarded (as Aristotle regarded it) as appropriately a realm of male authority and female subordination.

Breaking the taken-for-granted identification between civil society and the private side of the public/private dichotomy is therefore a key requirement for a feminist rethinking of a wide range of social and political theory. And overcoming the gendered and invidious separation between the private sphere of the family and the rest of social life is a key practical task for women's emancipation. One of the strengths of Pateman's analysis is that it confronts directly the essential ambiguity of the public/private distinction itself – and the importance of this ambiguity. In this respect, however, it remains relatively unusual, despite the broad appeal of Pateman's recent writings. It is striking that most feminist writing (there are important exceptions) continues to treat the public/private dichotomy as a binary opposition – or, rather, as a shifting cluster of binary oppositions.

Once the social world has been split along domestic/public lines, the next question is how the public realm is defined. To this question there is no uniform answer; and most of the time, as I noted earlier, the public side of the division tends to be an undifferentiated or grabbag residual category.[48] One move to give the public realm a more concrete content involved the convergence, via the influence of Engels' book on *The Family, Private*

Property, and the State (1884), of the domestic/public framework with a Marxist-feminist discussion stressing the articulation between the mode of production and the mode
of reproduction. One effect of the triumph of capitalist
commodity production (as people from a number of theoretical perspectives have been pointing out for a long time)
is to sharpen, in many respects, the institutional separation between work and home. Only the production of ex-
change-value (disproportionately by men) in the market
economy is considered real work, as opposed to the production of use-values and emotional management (disproportionately by women) in the home. Thus while in the
discussion of preindustrial societies the public realm often
remains an undifferentiated residual category, in terms of
modern society the effective conception of the public realm
is essentially the market economy. A typical example (of
many) would be Karen Sacks's distinction (following Engels)
between the "private *domestic* labor of women" and "public
or wage labor."[49] At this point the attentive reader will have
noticed that, as our discussion of the public/private distinction has moved from the liberal-economistic formulation to the Marxist-feminist formulation, the market economy
has migrated from the heart of the private sector to the
heart of the public realm.

I have focused on this particular approach not because
it is in any way predominant (or even as widely supported
as it once was), but because it constituted the most sharply
defined solution within feminism to the problem of formulating a binary public/private dichotomy that included a
concrete picture of both poles. However, while this is a
solution it is not an entirely adequate one. Apart from flat-
tening out the complexity of past and present societies, it
may be quite misleading as a guide to action. As Jean Elshtain
has pointed out in a series of sharp criticisms, the way in
which this literature formulates the public/private distinction has the effect of conflating public in the sense of the
market economy with public in the quite different sense of
politics (in the form of citizenship). Thus while the family
has been rescued from theoretical invisibility, the end result
is that the civic public realm is blanked out as thoroughly
as in the utilitarian liberal perspective.

Elshtain has argued that the same urge for simplification lies behind potentially dangerous tendencies in some
varieties of feminist argument to call for eliminating the
separation between public and private.[50] (These tendencies,
which were once fueled by Maoist fantasies, are now more
likely to be informed by deconstruction or by the type of
radical feminism represented by Catharine MacKinnon.)
Similar arguments have been made by other writers whose
viewpoints are in other respects very different from Elshtain;
one important example – among a number that could be
mentioned – is Nancy Fraser, who is one of the current
feminist writers most perceptively sensitive to the complexities
of the public/private distinction and to the need – both
theoretical and practical – for complexification rather than
simplification.[51]

These criticisms seem to me well taken. But the problem they point to is not merely a problem of Marxist
feminism. Rather, as I have already hinted more than
once, it reflects the sort of difficulty that any attempt at
a dichotomous public/private distinction will eventually
encounter. When used as a simple model of social life,
it will always prove inadequate – both theoretically and
normatively – to the complexity of modern societies.

THE TWO CITIES

My primary purpose has been to establish the historical and theoretical ambiguity of the public/private distinction; to delineate some of the more important of the
multiplicity of ways in which this distinction is used; and
to bring out some of the implications of this multiplicity.
I hope this has been accomplished. Now I will return to
the problem of public space with which the chapter began.

One of the disconcerting features of discussing the
public space of cities is that the city is simultaneously
an object of theoretical analysis and the metaphorical
source of many of the key concepts of Western social
and political theory. So let me end by drawing on the
dual character of the city as both social fact and evocative
symbol. If we compare the notions of "the public" of,

for example, Hannah Arendt in *The Human Condition* (1958) and Philippe Ariès in "The Family and the City," (1977), I think one could say that a certain image of the city lies in the background of each. But they are very different cities. Arendt's city is, of course, the polis; it is a self-governing political community whose common affairs are in the hands of its citizens, which both allows and requires that they deliberate explicitly about collective outcomes. (As the Romans would have put it, her city is not just *urbs*, which means a city as physical agglomeration, but *civitas*.) Now, the Greeks of Aristotle's time were already familiar with an alternative image of the city, and it was Babylon: the world-city defined by the interconnected facts that it was enormous, heterogeneous and unfree (that is, not self-governing). Size is not necessarily the essential point. The central point about Babylon was that it was *not* a political community; and since its heterogeneous multitudes were not called upon to be citizens, they could remain in apolitical coexistence, and each could do as he or she wished without the occasion to deliberate with his or her neighbors. In short, this is the city, not as polis, but as cosmopolis – by this I mean "cosmopolis" not in the Stoic or Kantian sense of the ideal unity of mankind, but in the sense of Haroun al-Rashid's Baghdad or of "Paris, the capital of the nineteenth century."[52]

Now, cosmopolis is not the only alternative to the polis as an image of city life, but by its extreme opposition it highlights some of the key issues. Cosmopolis has often been decried, but it has also exercised a certain charm. Its charms are those of diversity, of openness, of "street life," and of the tolerable (though often not happy) coexistence of groups that mingle without joining; but they are not necessarily – are not usually – the charms of active citizenship. Can the advantages of polis and cosmopolis be combined? Perhaps, but the route to answering that question must lie through developing ways to understand both of the types of public space they represent.

Notes

My thanks to Phil Kasinitz for his editorial comments and stimulating conversation.

1. Scruton, 1987, p. 13.
2. To borrow another phrase, slightly out of context, from Scruton, (ibid., p. 23). A remark by Philippe Ariès (in his Introduction to vol. III of Ariès and Duby, 1987–90), brings out the same implication of this particular meaning of public: "I am here using the word 'public' as it is used in 'public park' or 'public place', to denote a place where people who do not know each other can meet and enjoy each other's company" (p. 9).
3. In an analogous way, a market can be either a specific place or an abstract system of relationships; however the ambiguities involved with the notion of space are much more extensive and consequential, since so many of the concepts used in social analysis are themselves shaped by spatial metaphors.
4. Her most systematic discussion of these concepts is in Arendt, *The Human Condition* (1958).
5. Most of the essays in this volume address aspects of this subject, explicitly or in effect.
6. The present chapter draws extensively on my arguments in The Theory and Politics of the Public/Private Distinction (Weintraub, 1990). A revised version of that paper serves as the introductory essay in Weintraub, and Krishan Kumar (eds), 1994.
7. Norberto Bobbio, 1989.
8. For a recent effort along these lines, see Benn and Gaus, 1983.
9. This refinement was suggested to me by Paul Starr. Starr makes use of some of the ideas I am presenting here in his essay on "The Meaning of Privatization" (included in Kamerman and Kahn, 1989).
10. Take, for example, the sociologically quite fascinating notion of acting "discreetly" – that is, acting in a way that is not really hidden but also not flaunted, so that it is known but not officially "visible" – which every culture develops in its own unique way.
11. In the work of Erving Goffman practically all activity carried out in the presence of others constitutes "behavior in public place"; the domain of the private is restricted to the backstage, where we prepare to enact our roles in social interaction.
12. Geertz, "The Impact of the Concept of Culture on the Concept of Man," in Geertz, 1973, p. 45.
13. Terminology aside, this is of course a crucial Durkheimian insight, partly reinvented by Wittgenstein – as Ernest Gellner is fond of pointing out.
14. This is brought out quite well by Robert Bell in *The Culture of Policy Deliberations* (1985).
15. "Liberalism" is another contested and ambiguous term; any usage is potentially controversial, and this is not the place for a lengthy

justification of the one employed here. Let me just note that I have specified "utilitarian liberalism" to make it clear that I am not addressing the Kantian strain in liberalism, whose approach to the public/private distinction is somewhat different — in ways that would merit a separate discussion.

16. I am drawing here on the well-known argument of Elie Halévy in *The Growth of Philosophic Radicalism* (1972). Decades of criticism and historiographic revisionism — especially work on the Scottish Enlightenment of the eighteenth century — have made clear the need for extensive refinements in the Halévy/Parsons argument; but they have not, I think, refuted this crucial insight.

17. Alfred D. Chandler, Jr, 1977.

18. For an overview of both the multidisciplinary influence of this perspective and some important lines of criticism, see the useful collection edited by Jane Mansbridge, *Beyond Self-Interest* (1990).

19. I have developed the argument that follows more fully in Weintraub, forthcoming, particularly in chapter 3.

20. It is distilled in a crucial formulation that appears, identically worded, in the first chapter of each of the two sections of the *Corpus Juris Civilis*, the great compilation of Roman law issued in the name of the Emperor Justinian in 533–4: "Public law is that which regards the condition of the Roman commonwealth, private, that which pertains to the interests of single individuals" (*Publicum jus est, quod ad statum rei Romanae spectat, privatum, quod ad singulorum utilitatem pertinet*).

21. See Weintraub, forthcoming, particularly chapters 1 and 2.

22. On this subject, see for example Poggi, 1978, and Strayer, 1970. On the "recovery" or "reception" of Roman law and its significance, the commanding treatment is still to be found in the work of Otto Gierke; see, for example the portion of *Das Deutsche Genossenschaftsrecht* translated by F. W. Maitland as *Political Theories of the Middle Age* (Gierke, 1987).

    To avoid any ambiguity on this point, the *word* "sovereign" does not come to us from antiquity. It is of later origin and its different variants - the Old-French *souverein*, the Spanish *soberano* and so on - appear to be derived from the mediaeval-Latin *superanus* (at least, this is the tentative suggestion of the *Oxford English Dictionary*). But the *concept* is characteristically Roman, and the increasing importance of this terminology, from the later middle ages onward, is part of the process that Gierke describes as "the resuscitation and further development of the classical idea of Sovereignty" (Gierke, 1987, p. 92). To employ one of Gierke's favorite formulations, sovereignty is a quintessentially "ancient–modern" concept, as opposed to a "properly mediaeval" one.

23. For the arguments behind these remarks, see my discussions in Weintraub, 1986, and chapters 7–8 of Weintraub, forthcoming.

24. Habermas, 1989, p. 26. (This was originally published in 1962 as *Strukturwandel der Öffentlichkeit*, but only translated into English in 1989. A condensed version of the argument can be found in Habermas's encyclopedia article on "The Public Sphere" – Habermas, 1974.

25. Tocqueville's insight is further confirmed by the historical experience of state-socialist regimes, where the hypertrophy of the state (based on public control of the economy) was accompanied by the atrophy of public life in the sense of citizenship and participation. Ironically the Jacobin approach to citizenship, carried on and intensified by Leninism, which aims at having the public entirely submerge the private through the continuous mobilization of civic virtue, tends to yield the same ultimate result (as Tocqueville also understood). Maoism attempted the most hyper-Jacobin intensification of participation and public virtue – and wound up, perhaps, most thoroughly burning out. In general the attempt by these regimes to politicize everything in society has led, in the long or short run, to massive depoliticization and a retreat to the privacy of personal relations (when these are not themselves under direct assault, as in periods of "high" totalitarianism, such as the 1930s in the Soviet Union, the Cultural Revolution in China or Cambodia under the Khmer Rouge).

26. A slightly misleading translation of his title, which is more literally *The Child and Family Life in the Old Régime.*

27. Ariès, 1962, p. 375.

28. Huizinga, 1954 p. 9 (". . .*von einer prunkenden und grausamen Öffentlichkeit*": translation slightly altered to make it more literal).

29. Quite late in his life, in his Introduction to vol. III of *A History of Private Life*, Ariès observes with charming nonchalance that, until he entered on that collaborative project and discovered with surprise that his colleagues all associated the distinction public/private with the distinction state/nonstate, the idea had barely occurred to him – not for any deeply considered reasons, but because he was profoundly uninterested in "political history" (Ariès and Duby, 1987–90, p. 9). This was one of those fruitful oversights that sometimes help a scholar develop a distinctive vision.

30. Elias, 1978, vol. I, p. 190.

31. I have borrowed the last phrase from Allan Silver's useful and insightful essay, "'Two Different Sorts of Commerce': Friendship and Strangership in Civil Society" (in Weintraub and Kumar, 1994).

32. To borrow the expression of Viviana Zelizer in *Pricing the Priceless Child* (1985).

33. Ariès, 1962, p. 406.

34. To be precise, among the perspectives that explore this distinctively modern polarization of private and public life along personal/impersonal lines, there are really *two* broad theoretical currents. The first, which might be termed a more eighteenth-century approach (drawing especially on the Scottish Enlightenment and Georg Simmel), emphasizes the ways in which the impersonal structures

of *Gesellschaft*, paradoxically, create a space for and enable the emergence of this new realm of anti-instrumental private life (for example by reducing the need to seek vital resources and physical protection through one's personal ties). This is the position represented by Silver in his essay cited above. Then there is a more nineteenth-century approach, which emphasizes the ways in which these new forms of personal relations emerge, at least in part, in reaction *against* the world of *Gesellschaft* (as we have come to call it since Tönnies). This perspective has taken on a range of forms (left and right, conservative, Marxian, romantic and so on); contemporary examples would include not only Ariès and Peter Berger but also Eli Zaretsky, Christopher Lasch, Philip Slater and Richard Sennett.

35. Slater, of course, synthesized Parsons with Freud (a Freud closer to the version of the British object-relations psychoanalysts than the one Parsons had already ingested) to produce a radical critique of modern society. He is a powerful influence behind the work of Nancy Chodorow and – I assume independently – behind Hannah Pitkin's feminist reading of Machiavelli in *Fortune Is a Woman*, (1984), so he can serve to illustrate some of the bridges that connect the concerns of Ariès and Elias with those of feminist scholars, whom I will discuss in the next subsection.

36. See Whyte, 1980 and 1988.

37. Not that far removed, either etymologically or conceptually, from urbanity – as Michael Walzer's essay on public space brings out nicely (see chapter 18).

38. Elaborated somewhat unsystematically in *The Conscience of the Eye* (Sennett, 1990).

39. For a number of key formulations, see two of the landmark essay collections of the 1970s: Michelle Zimbalist Rosaldo and Louise Lamphere (eds), *Woman, Culture, and Society* (1974) and Rayna Reiter (ed.), *Toward an Anthropology of Women* (1975).

40. Michelle Zimbalist Rosaldo, "Women, Culture, and Society: A Theoretical Overview", in Rosaldo and Lamphere, 1974.

41. Both these characteristics are exemplified by an otherwise quite useful collection of essays by feminist sociologists: Eva Gamarnikow *et al.* (eds), *The Public and the Private* (1983).

42. One important recent collection that focuses on this theme is Dorothy O. Helly and Susan M. Reverby, *Gendered Domains: Rethinking Public and Private in Women's History* (1992). (In 1980 Michelle Rosaldo wrote a reflective essay reconsidering her original argument, "The Use and Abuse of Anthropology: Reflections on Feminism and Cross-Cultural Understanding." In the end, however, she essentially restates the original domestic/public distinction, while acknowledging the complexity and diversity of the ways it is socially institutionalized.)

43. As one of the first prominent figures in post-1960s feminism whose starting-point included an active engagement with classical political thought, Jean Elshtain, was one of the first to address this legacy and its problematic in *Public Man, Private Woman* (1981).

44. Hartmann, 1981.

45. Another extremely important step in this direction was Gayle Rubin's formulation of the notion of the "sex/gender system" in "The Traffic in Women: Notes on the 'Political Economy' of Sex" (1975). A third influential statement of this sort was Sherry Ortner's "Is Female to Male as Nature is to Culture?" (1974); unfortunately, despite raising some thought-provoking questions, this formulation is considerably more problematic than the other two (since the universal and cross-cultural answer to her central question is *not* uniformly "yes").

46. Carole Pateman, 1983, *Ben and G. F. Gaus, eds. Public and Private in Social Life* pp. 284–5.

47. By denying the attribution of "private" to civil society, transferring it to the domestic sphere, yet continuing to recognize the need to distinguish between civil society and politics, Pateman moves (not entirely explicitly) to a tripartite model. By an interesting parallel, Hannah Arendt also applies a tripartite model to modern society, and also does so because she does not want to recognize civil society as the private sphere. Instead she marks it off as the sphere of the "social." This is ironic since Arendt can hardly be termed a feminist thinker, and her ideal involves precisely the kind of rigid division between the private sphere of the household and the public realm of political community (along with a devaluation of the former) that Pateman would like to overcome. But Arendt's classification brings out, from another direction, the abiguities involved in fitting civil society into any dichotomous public/private distinction.

48. One nice illustrative example would be Rayna Reiter's (perceptive but analytically diffuse) 1975 essay on "Men and Women in the South of France: Public and Private Domains". The private domain is defined by the household and kinship relationships; the public domain comprehends the economy, politics, open (versus enclosed) physical spaces – and so on.

49. Sacks, 1975.

50. Elshtain, 1981, p. 256: "The basic notions of public and private do not move as guiding orientations through Marxist feminist literature – at least not as such. Rather, in most (but not all) cases public and private are recast into spheres of production and reproduction respectively. In this recasting the meaning of public and private is remarkably transformed."

51. See, in particular, Fraser 1987 and 1992.

52. One of the disconcerting secrets of the history of great cosmopolitan cities, which is brought out nicely by Bonnie Menes Kahn's charming and stimulating book-length essay on *Cosmopolitan Culture* (1987), is that very often they flourish most successfully in a political context of (relatively) benign despotism – Vienna being, perhaps, an especially poignant example.

316   *Varieties and Vicissitudes of Public Space*

References

Arendt, Hannah (1958) *The Human Condition* (University of Chicago Press).
Ariès, Philippe (1962) *Centuries of Childhood: A Social History of Family Life* (New York: Vintage) [*L'Enfant et la vie familiale sous l'Ancien Régime*, Paris, 1960].
Ariès, Philippe (1977) "The Family and the City," in Alice S. Rossi *et al.* (eds), *The Family* (New York: Norton) [originally an issue of *Daedalus*].
Ariès, Philippe and Georges Duby *et al.* (eds) (1987–90) *A History of Private Life*, 4 vols (Cambridge, MA: Harvard University Press).
Becker, Gary (1976) *The Economic Approach to Human Behavior* (University of Chicago Press).
Bell, Robert (1985) *The Culture of Policy Deliberations* (New Brunswick: Rutgers University Press).
Benhabib, Seyla and Drucilla Cornell (eds) (1987) *Feminism as Critique* (Minneapolis: University of Minnesota Press).
Benn, S. I. and G. F. Gaus (eds) (1983) *Public and Private in Social Life* (London: Croom Helm).
Berger, Peter, Brigitte Berger and Hansfried Kellner (1974) *The Homeless Mind: Modernization and Consciousness* (New York: Vintage).
Blau, Peter (1964) *Exchange and Power in Social Life* (New York: Wiley).
Bobbio, Norberto (1989) *Democracy and Dictatorship* (Minneapolis: University of Minnesota Press).
Calhoun, Craig (ed.) (1992) *Habermas and the Public Sphere* (Cambridge, MA: MIT Press).
Chandler, Alfred D., Jr (1977) *The Visible Hand: The Managerial Revolution in American Business* (Cambridge: Harvard University Press).
Downs, Anthony (1957) *An Economic Theory of Democracy* (New York: Harper & Row).
Elias, Norbert (1978, 1982) *The Civilizing Process*, 2 vols (New York: Pantheon).
Elshtain, Jean Bethke (1981) *Public Man, Private Woman* (Princeton University Press).
Engels, Friedrich (1972) [1982] *The Origin of the Family, Private Life and the State* (New York: International).
Fraser, Nancy (1987) "What's Critical about Critical Theory?: The Case of Habermas and Gender," in Benhabib and Cornell (eds), 1987.
Fraser, Nancy (1992) "Rethinking the Public Sphere: A Contribution to the Critique of Actually Existing Democracy," in Craig Calhoun (ed.), 1992.
Gamarnikow, Eva *et al.* (eds) (1983) *The Public and the Private* (London: Heinemann).
Gans, Herbert J. (1962) *The Urban Villagers* (New York: Free Press).
Geertz, Clifford (1973) *The Interpretation of Cultures* (New York: Basic Books).
Gierke, Otto (1987) *Political Theories of the Middle Age*, translated by F. W. Maitland (Cambridge University Press).

Glazer, Nathan and Mark Lilla (eds) (1987) *The Public Face of Architecture: Civic Culture and Public Spaces* (New York: Free Press).

Goffman, Erving (1963) *Behavior in Public Places: Notes on the Social Organization of Gatherings* (New York: Free Press).

Goffman, Erving (1971) *Relations in Public: Microstudies of the Public Order* (New York: Basic Books).

Habermas, Jürgen (1974) "The Public Sphere," *New German Critique*, vol. I, no. 3 (fall, pp. 49–55) [originally published in 1964 as an encyclopedia article in *Fischer-Lexikon*].

Habermas, Jürgen (1989) *The Structural Transformation of the Public Sphere: An Inquiry into a Category of Bourgeois Society* (Cambridge, MIT Press) [*Strukturwande] der Öffentlichkeit: Untersuchungen zu einer Kategorie der bürgerlichen Gesellschaft*, Neuwied, Luchterhand, 1962].

Halévy, Elie (1972) *The Growth of Philosophic Radicalism* [1928] (Clifton: Augustus M. Kelley).

Hartmann, Heidi (1981) "The Unhappy Marriage of Marxism and Feminism: Towards a More Progressive Union," in Lydia Sargent (ed.), *Women and Revolution: A Discussion of the Unhappy Marriage of Marxism and Feminism* (Boston: South End Press).

Helly, Dorothy O. and Susan M. Reverby (1992) *Gendered Domains: Rethinking Public and Private in Women's History* (Ithaca: Cornell University Press).

Hirschman, Albert O. (1970) *Exit, Voice, and Loyalty: Responses to Decline in Firms, Organizations, and States* (Cambridge: Harvard University Press).

Huizinga, Johan (1954) *The Waning of the Middle Ages* [1924] (Garden City: Doubleday).

Jacobs, Jane (1961) *The Death and Life of Great American Cities* (New York: Vintage).

Kahn, Bonnie Menes (1987) *Cosmopolitan Culture: The Gilt-Edged Dream of a Tolerant City* (New York: Atheneum).

Kamerman, Sheila B. and Alfred J. Kahn (eds) (1989) *Privatization and the Welfare State* (Princeton University Press).

Mansbridge, Jane J. (1990) *Beyond Self-Interest* (University of Chicago Press).

Olson, Mancur (1971) *The Logic of Collective Action* (Cambridge, MA: Harvard University Press, first edition 1965).

Ortner, Sherry B. (1974) "Is Female to Male as Nature Is to Culture?", in Rosaldo and Lamphere (eds), 1974.

Pateman, Carole (1983) "Feminist Critiques of the Public/Private Dichotomy," in Benn and Gaus (eds), 1983.

Pateman, Carole (1989) *The Disorder of Women: Democracy, Feminism and Political Theory* (Stanford University Press).

Pitkin, Hannah Fenichel (1984) *Fortune Is a Woman: Gender and Politics in the Thought of Niccolò Machiavelli* (Berkeley: University of California Press).

Poggi, Gianfranco (1978) *The Development of the Modern State: A Sociological Introduction* (Stanford University Press).

Reiter, Rayna R. (1975) "Men and Women in the South of France: Public and Private Domains," in Reiter (ed.), 1975.

Reiter, Rayna R. (ed.) (1975) *Toward an Anthropology of Women* (New York: Monthly Review Press).

Rosaldo, Michelle Zimbalist (1974) "Women, Culture, and Society: A Theoretical Overview," in Rosaldo and Lamphere (eds), 1974.

Rosaldo, Michelle Zimbalist (1980) "The Use and Abuse of Anthropology: Reflections on Feminism and Cross-Cultural Understanding," *Signs*, vol. 5, no. 3 (spring), pp. 389–417.

Rosaldo, Michelle Zimbalist and Louise Lamphere (eds) (1974) *Woman, Culture, and Society* (Stanford University Press).

Rousseau, Jean-Jacques (1964) *The First and Second Discourses* (New York: St Martins Press) (1754).

Rubin, Gayle (1975) "The Traffic in Women: Notes on the 'Political Economy' of Sex," in Reiter (ed.), (1975).

Sacks, Karen (1975) "Engels Revisited: Women, the Organization of Production, and Private Property," in Reiter (ed.), (1975).

Schoeman, Ferdinand David (ed.) (1984) *Philosophical Dimensions of Privacy: An Anthology* (Cambridge University Press).

Scruton, Roger (1987), "Public Space and the Classical Vernacular," in Glazer and Lilla (eds), 1987.

Sennett, Richard (1978) *The Fall of Public Man: On the Social Psychology of Capitalism* (New York: Vintage).

Sennett, Richard (1990) *The Conscience of the Eye: The Design and Social Life of Cities* (New York: Knopf).

Silver, Allan (1994) "'Two Different Sorts of Commerce': Friendship and Strangership in Civil Society," in Weintraub and Kumar (eds), 1994.

Slater, Philip (1968) *The Glory of Hera: Greek Mythology and the Greek Family* (Boston: Beacon Press).

Slater, Philip (1970) *The Pursuit of Loneliness: American Culture at the Breaking Point* (Boston: Beacon Press).

Stone, Lawrence (1979) *The Family, Sex and Marriage in England 1500–1800* (New York: Harper & Row).

Strayer, Joseph R. (1970) *On the Medieval Origins of the Modern State* (Princeton University Press).

Tocqueville, Alexis de (1955) *The Old Regime and the French Revolution* (Garden City, NY: Anchor).

Weintraub, Jeff (1986) "Tocqueville's Conception of Political Society," unpublished paper, University of California at San Diego.

Weintraub, Jeff (1990) "The Theory and Politics of the Public/Private Distinction," paper presented at the 1990 annual meeting of the American Political Science Association.

Weintraub, (forthcoming) *Freedom and Community: The Republican Virtue Tradition and the Sociology of Liberty* (Berkeley, University of California Press).

Weintraub, Jeff and Krishan Kumar (eds) (1994) *Public and Private in Thought and Practice: Perspectives on a Grand Dichotomy* (University of Chicago Press).

Whyte, William F. (1943) *Street Corner Society* (University of Chicago Press).

Whyte, William H. (1980) *The Social Life of Small Urban Spaces* (Washington, DC: The Conservation Foundation).

Whyte, William H. (1988) *City: Rediscovering the Center* (New York: Doubleday).

Williamson, Oliver (1975) *Markets and Hierarchies* (New York: Free Press).

Wilson, Thomas and Andrew S. Skinner (eds) (1976) *The Market and the State: Essays in Honour of Adam Smith* (Oxford: Clarendon Press).

Zaretsky, Eli (1986) *Capitalism, the Family, and Personal Life* (New York: Harper & Row).

Zelizer, Viviana (1985) *Pricing the Priceless Child* (New York: Basic Books).

18 Pleasures and Costs of Urbanity*
Michael Walzer

The shape and character of public space is a central issue
in city planning, and it has often been central, too, in political thought, especially on the left. Radical intellectuals
live in cities, think of themselves as city people, imagine
the good society as a large and splendid city. Socialist and
republican politics alike require public spaces in which a
common life can be enacted – and such spaces are available only in cities.

Curiously, the city figured more significantly in the social
criticism of the 1950s and early '60s than in the activist
politics that came later. Civil rights and Vietnam, race and
war overwhelmed our speculations about urbanity and its
physical requirements. Paul and Percival Goodman's
Communitas (cloth 1947, paper 1960) and Jane Jacob's *Life
and Death of Great American Cities* (1961) were much noticed and talked about when they were published and re-
published, but the talk faltered after only a few years. When
Rayner Banham's exuberant defense of Los Angeles appeared
in 1971, there was no equal exuberance displayed in defense
of other cities and alternative urban styles. The left had,
or thought it had, more urgent issues. Yet thinking about
public space and its uses might have helped us, say, to
think about racial integration. Thinking about government
centers, medical centers, and housing projects might have
deepened our understanding of the welfare state and its
discontents. Thinking about freeways, shopping malls, and
suburban homes might have led us to anticipate Reaganite
politics.

Public space is space we share with strangers, people
who aren't our relatives, friends, or work associates. It is

* Reprinted from *Dissent* (Fall 1986).

space for politics, religion, commerce, sport; space for peaceful coexistence and impersonal encounter. Its character expresses and also conditions our public life, civic culture, everyday discourse. We need to talk about this again, and though I have no special expertise, I will try to begin, drawing freely on the Goodmans and Jane Jacobs and also on more recent books by Richard Sennett and Marshall Berman – but on my own experience, too; for cities are, like novels and movies, necessarily subject to lay criticisms. So, too, though less gloriously, are the deurbanized wastelands we have created, even in the midst of the city itself.

We need to distinguish between two kinds of public space. The two probably exist on a continuum, but for the sake of clarity I will draw the line sharply between them. The first is *single-minded* space, designed by planners or entrepreneurs who have only one thing in mind, and used by similarly single-minded citizens. Entering space of this sort we are characteristically in a hurry. The second is *open-minded* space, designed for a variety of uses, including unforeseen and unforeseeable uses, and used by citizens who do different things and are prepared to tolerate, even take an interest, in, things they don't do. When we enter this sort of space, we are characteristically prepared to loiter.

Architects and planners write about single-purpose and multipurpose space, but I want to emphasize "mindedness." It's not only that space serves certain purposes known in advance by its users, but also that its design and character stimulate (or repress) certain qualities of attention, interest, forbearance, and receptivity. We act differently in different sorts of space – in part, to be sure, because of what we are doing there, but also because of what others are doing, because of what it means to be "there," and because of the look and feel of the space itself.

My examples ought to be obvious to anyone who has moved around in cities. Zoned business and residential areas are single-minded, as is the modern dormitory suburb. The central city (as it once was) and also the "quarter" or neighborhood with its own stores and shops and small factories constitute open-minded space. The government center, medical center, cultural center, shopping center are all single-minded; the forum, the square, the courtyard are all open-minded. The highway – Le Corbusier's "machine for traffic" – is single-minded, the city street is open-minded; the green belt is single-minded, the city park or playground is open-minded; the housing project is single-minded, the urban block is open-minded.

We can take the contemporary shopping center, sitting on a highway outside the city, close to the suburbs, as the epitome of single-mindedness (the urban mall, when it is continuous with the surrounding streets, is less so: I will come back to this later). The shopping center is a place to shop, nothing more, and its owners characteristically resist all attempts to use it in other ways. The most revealing example of this resistance is their invocation of the laws against trespass to exclude political activity – leafletting, say, on their "property." They don't want the extra costs of policing such activity, but they also don't want the attention of shoppers diverted from their primary mission. The ideal shopper doesn't take up parking space except when actually shopping. Ideally, the shopper is in and out, or wanders from store to store only in order to stimulate the urge to buy – and does buy in the end. Buying is all; so far as shopper is concerned, this is not a place for conversation or play but only for getting and spending.

Other examples: the fast-food restaurant is single-minded, the café or pub or cafeteria, where people are encouraged to linger, is open-minded; the motel or motor inn is single-minded, the urban hotel, with its public rooms, bars, restaurants, shops, and its ready access to the surrounding streets, is open-minded; the airplane is single-minded, the long-distance train or ship is open-minded: one can write a novel about what happens on trains and ships, but not about what happens on planes. The movie is single-minded compared to the theater; this is less obvious but the point is worth making: theatrical time and space, the intermission, the bar, the lobby, the theater "district" with its restaurants – all this encourages a longer and more varied "evening out" than going to the movies; one more often hurries to a movie and home again. The exhibition center, like most centers, is single-minded (one exhibit at a time) compared to the old urban fairground; the department store or supermarket is single-minded compared to the row of specialty shops – because the row is on the street, and the street is open-minded space.

The square or piazza is the epitome of open-mindedness. Here public space is surrounded by a mix of public and private buildings: government offices, museums, lecture and concert halls, churches, shops, cafés, residences. Some of these have single, some have multiple uses, but joined together they give to the space they enclose and create a vital and receptive quality. In the square itself, people meet, walk, talk, buy and sell, argue about politics, eat lunch, sit over coffee, wait for something to happen.

This is the crucial setting for urbanity: without the square, write the Goodmans, "there is no city. . . . There is no substitute for the spontaneous social conflux whose atoms unite, precisely, as citizens of the city." In fact, of course, they unite in all sorts of other ways, and for reasons that have nothing to do with citizenship – commerce, worship, pleasure, love. That is just the point. They are different people, with different purposes, educated by the space they share to a civil deportment.

The university campus is another model of open-mindedness, with its own squares and courtyards, its varied activities, its in-close housing. I am not sure what the appropriate comparison is here. In the night school and the commuter school this sort of space doesn't exist, and education is a more single-minded experience. Correspondence and television courses provide no space at all. These sorts of institutions and arrangements accommodate people under economic pressure, people in a hurry, and that is certainly a good thing to do. But the accommodation involves a loss of diversity and unexpectedness, of a certain sort of educational loitering.

I don't mean to equate open-minded/single-minded with good/bad. Nothing so simple: we need not be against airplanes or highways or even fast-food restaurants. Single-minded space is sometimes wonderfully convenient; we don't always want to notice or be noticed by other people; we don't always feel capable of civility. At certain times in our lives, at certain times in everyday life, we are and have every right to be single-minded, and we require space that fits our mood or enterprise. But the reiteration of single-mindedness at one public site after another seems to me something that civilized societies should avoid. I can't specify the effects of that reiteration, for the character of city life today has other, though related, causes – among them the causes, which I will come to, of single-mindedness itself.

But open-minded space has in the past been a breeding ground for mutual respect, political solidarity, civil discourse, and it makes sense to suggest that without it all these will be put at risk. Without it, as the Goodmans say, "our city crowds are doomed to be lonely crowds, bored crowds, humanly uncultured crowds."

But why should there be crowds at all? The real alternative to open-minded space is private space, and it is the (genuine) appeal of private space that shapes the contemporary city. Single-mindedness is designed to serve and facilitate privacy; it has no value in itself, and no one ever thought that it did (even the romance of the highway is largely the romance of the private car). The point of single-mindedness is career discipline at one end of our lives and home-boundedness at the other. The home, the crucial setting for privacy, is neither single-minded nor open-minded. Not single-minded, because it is designed to accommodate a variety of activities; cooking, eating, sleeping, loving, quarreling, talking, working, playing, raising children. And not open-minded, because the actual encounters and activities that take place are tightly controlled by the small circle of participants. Home is and ought to be predictable. Perhaps the best word for private space is Richard Sennett's "intimate." Single-mindedness serves intimacy, because it moves us quickly through the public, nonintimate, and unpredictable world.

Open-minded space, by contrast, competes with intimacy because it provides an alternative pattern of activity and encounter. These days it competes less and less successfully. The more privileged we are, the more quickly we move from place to place, the less time we spend in public. The ideal is door-to-door: private airplane, helicopter, limousine. Public space is degraded, first because it is taken to be merely instrumental, then because even the instrument is avoided by those who are able to do so. Think of the waiting rooms of the great 19th-century train stations and then of the way we wait now: the experience has been stripped of all grace and expectation, except for the dim hope that the train will be on time. Single-minded space, without value of its own, tends to run down. Technology advances, fashions change, the affluent depart; ultimately the space is taken over by those to whom society denies the comforts of intimacy, the vagabonds and homeless.

It's not difficult to describe the process by which this happens or to explain its reasons. Indeed, there are too many reasons; the process is overdetermined. What is hard is to suggest how it might be abated or reversed.

(1) *The first reason is cultural* and has to do with the success (or perhaps the development beyond the point of success) of liberal individualism – which is not merely a creed but a state of mind, a certain characterological formation. Increasingly, we conceive of well-being exclusively in terms of the self. The material realization of well-being lies in the personal or domestic accumulation of goods; the moral realization lies in self-understanding and meaningful relationships. Materialism and morality alike lead to the enhanced valuation of intimate space, the setting for private comfort and also for personal or mutual exploration. Public space, by contrast, requires what Sennett calls impersonality and role-playing: civility rather than sincerity. It's a setting for reticence and wit, not for confession. At home you can say to someone you love or hope to love: Sit down, sit down, and tell me *everything*; in the café we tell one another censored stories, artful stories. Liberalism breeds an expansive desire for comfort and closeness, useful commodities and loving persons, while an older republicanism, historically associated with open-minded space, provides us only with monuments and fellow citizens.

(2) *New technologies also enhance* the value of the home – not only labor-saving devices that make housework easier but also, and probably more important, the new communications media. Less housework might mean more time to "go out," but the new media make possible a kind of engagement-with-the-world at home: we don't need to go out at all. We can sit, safe and secure, in our living rooms or family rooms and listen to music, watch the news, see movies, plays, or vaudeville shows, tune in a political debate or a

revivalist preacher or a "talk" show (where famous people, whom we cannot hope to meet, do the talking, and we are free to kibitz), watch national and international athletic competitions – with a better view of the action than the actual spectators have.

Any of these activities, passive though they are, would once have carried us out of intimate space into many different sorts of public space, single-minded and open-minded in different degrees, lobbies and halls and stadiums and parks, and led to encounters (at least, visual encounters) with other people doing similar or different things. The experience is less engaging, I think, when we are homebound, but it is also less trouble, less time-consuming, physically and mentally easier. "Perhaps,' as the Goodmans say, "there are no longer real occasions for social congregation. . . ." Not true, of course: people still go out to concerts, movies, ball games, church services, and I shall want to ask why they do. But they also spend a lot of time "attending" these events, not together but one by one, as a locational series (separately, in their own living rooms) rather than a social congregation. And, increasingly, when they do go out, they travel in their cars, small pieces of intimate space, hurtling along the single-minded highway.

(3) *Shaped by culture and technology* – here the car has been more important than the new communications media – the concepts that have guided city planning and urban redevelopment in the 20th century have been largely single-minded in tendency. The reigning maxim is one site/one purpose: hence the "center" and the "project." "Modernist architecture and planning," writes Marshall Berman in *All That Is Solid Melts Into Air*, "created a modernized version of pastoral: a spatially and socially segmented world – people here, traffic there; work here, homes there; rich here, poor there; barriers of grass and concrete in between. . . ."

Berman's list can be extended: housing, business, manufacture, government, culture, recreation – each has its proper place, cut off from all the others. Open-minded space is equated with urban disorder, the uncertainties of street life, the chaos of the petty-bourgeois economy. All this is to be banished, "We must kill the street," Le Corbusier said, and that is the effect, not yet achieved, of his "radiant city" as of Frank Lloyd Wright's "living city," both of them really anti-cities, organized to serve the private car and the solitary individual.

(4) *The ideological critique of open-minded space* has been paralleled by a social inundation: crowding, overuse, conflict. It would be foolish to deny that the planners and architects have responded, sometimes to real, not ideological, disorders. Economic mobilization and the slow advance of democracy (at least, of democratic manners and a superficial "equality of condition") bring more and more people into available public space. And, what may be more important, they bring increasingly diverse kinds of people, from different classes and ethnic groups, into the same public space. Open-mindedness implies a tolerance for diversity, but in the past this has most commonly been a diversity of function and only within limits a diversity of people.

Lovers of urbanity celebrate the city's chaotic mix, but it is wise to notice that many of the most celebrated examples of urban space "belong" to quite specific groups of people. The forum and the piazza were places first of all for male citizens; universities are segregated cities of the young; neighborhoods are often ethnically homogeneous (like one of Jane Jacobs's favorite neighborhoods, the Italian North End of Boston); streets and parks are someone's "turf," cafés and bars are most interesting when they are taken over by particular groups of writers, actors, journalists, and so on. Insofar as this sort of possession ceases to be possible, or ceases to be secure, the space deteriorates. The unpredictability of open-mindedness becomes threatening. There is more difference, more tension and potential conflict, than people want to cope with.

Jane Jacobs has described how a successful street is self-policing. An unsuccessful street, by contrast, always seems inadequately policed, dangerous, a place to avoid. The same is true for parks, playgrounds, waiting rooms, lobbies. Without regular and confident users, they become settings for social, sexual, and political deviance: derelicts, criminals, "hippies," political and religious sectarians, adolescent gangs. All these belong, no doubt, to the urban mix, but if they are too prominent within it, ordinary men and women will flee as soon as they can into private and controlled worlds.

Their flight carries them through single-minded space, which is subject to a similar deterioration and can come to feel equally dangerous. But single-mindedness is, at least, transitional and instrumental: we aim only to be in and out and have no high hopes of conversation or engagement along the way. So we avoid urbanity, move between the instrumental and the intimate, give up those areas of public life where civility is necessary but increasingly difficult.

(5) *What we might think of as the mass consumption of open-minded space* strains and sometimes overwhelms its financial base. Open-mindedness requires public subsidy. This can take the form of direct provision (squares, parks, sidewalks) or of maintenance and control. Sometimes it requires planning – if only to undo the effects of previous plans. Market provision is also possible, as in the case of the café (though the café is dependent on the sidewalk) or the row of shops. But enterprises of this sort don't seem profit-maximizing, and may require entrepreneurs who themselves enjoy the public life they facilitate. They are often bought out by national chains whose local managers are not trained for a similar enjoyment. Under contemporary conditions, it appears that commerce favors single-mindedness, which is easier to invest in and capitalize on, and which represents a more profitable use of increasingly high-priced land. Alternative uses and possibilities are uneconomic, rather like political speeches in a shopping center (agitation is only appropriate at the government center where taxpayers foot the bill). There is no obvious entrepreneurial interest in reproducing the civility of the old street and square (or, say, the spaciousness and dignity of the old waiting room) – except, perhaps, as luxury goods, like the first-class bar in a 747.

The truth is that open-minded space depends upon police, street-cleaners, waiters, conductors, gardeners, supervisors of all sorts, *whose wages it doesn't pay*. These people have to be paid out of tax money, and there is less and less willingness to pay enough of them. We try to accommodate ourselves to the supermarket model, where service personnel are reduced to a minimum. But that reduction is deadly for open-minded space: one can't strike up a conversation at the check-out counter or "hang around" in a parking lot. If there is to be room for conversation and for hanging around, it must be, so to speak, room with amenities.

An overabundance of reasons – cultural, technological, ideological, social, and economic – and all of them seem to point in the same direction: toward single-mindedness on the one hand and intimacy on the other. But this can't be, and obviously isn't, the whole story. Life at home requires, if only for contrast, an extramural life; it is too much of a strain on intimacy when intimacy is all there is. Once, perhaps, it was in the interest of women to raise the walls high around the home, and to emphasize the coziness and comfort of domesticity, for they were largely excluded from public activities outside. But the success of the feminist movement, if it is successful, ought to lead to a new demand for space outside the home. Affluence breeds a similar demand: how often can one redecorate the living room? There is bound to be growing pressure from people with time and money on their hands for interesting things to do as well as for (or even instead of) domestic enhancements: holidays, travel, evenings out, "social congregations" of different sorts, places to see and be seen. People will continue to want to rub shoulders even if they are leery of actual encounters.

Certain sorts of single-minded space can meet this pressure – in their different ways, for example, shopping centers and cultural centers. But settings of this sort are most successful if they open out on alternative spaces or slowly come to accommodate alternative uses. The new urban malls are a nice example of the adaptation of the "center" to a genuine urbanity – though they have mostly been successful only on dramatic sites, like the Boston or Baltimore waterfronts. In any case, success points strongly to the appeal of open-minded space, with its easy access to many different sorts of activity, the sense it conveys of things to do and time to waste, and the security generated by consistent use over the span of day and night.

What has made all this possible is an interesting combination of entrepreneurial activity, local politics, planning and antiplanning – a market/political process that liberals and leftists committed to the city would do well to study. What isn't yet clear is the extent to which success, where it has occurred, depends upon exclusion, in this case by price (especially from the in-close housing that has sprung up around the new malls).

The real test is to make such arrangements work in more ordinary neighborhoods – or, in the absence of the mall, to rehabilitate the street. It would be a great achievement to provide urbanity only as a luxury good, and chiefly for a homogeneous but transient population of upwardly mobile young professionals. The more appropriate homogeneity for a democratic city is the residential district, shaped over the years by ethnicity or interest. Years ago, Percival Goodman argued in *Dissent* against the construction of Lincoln Center. The buildings planned for the Center, he suggested should be scattered across the city, strengthening its different parts. I suppose there are counterarguments. Certainly, Lincoln Center is very convenient for cultural commuters from New Jersey; it is hardly necessary to register the (alarming) fact that one is in Manhattan. And lots of people do come, creating, at least at certain fixed times, a nice liveliness.

Cities, indeed, need centers, but only insofar as these accommodate diverse kinds of enterprises and activities. Otherwise, they need decentering, for the sake of diversity. It is probably better that a cultural palace be located near a church, a government office building, a good café, an apartment house, and so on, than that it be adjacent to another palace – better at least for the residents of the city. If open-minded space is good for the people called "yuppies," then it is probably good for the rest of us. But are there enough of the rest of us, living in more or less stable neighborhoods, eager for the pleasures and ready to pay the costs of urbanity?

19 Street Etiquette and Street Wisdom*

Elijah Anderson

The streets have a peculiar definition in the Village community. Usually pedestrians can walk there undisturbed. Often they seem peaceful. Always they have an elegant air, with mature trees, wrought-iron fences, and solid architecture reminiscent of pre-war comfort and ease. But in the minds of current residents the streets are dangerous and volatile. Lives may be lost there. Muggings occur with some regularity. Cars are broken into for tape decks and other valuables. Occasionally people suffer seemingly meaningless verbal or even physical assaults. For these reasons residents develop a certain ambivalence toward their neighborhood. On the one hand, they know they should distrust it, and they do. But on the other hand, distrusting the area and the people who use it requires tremendous energy. To resolve this problem, they tentatively come to terms with the public areas through trial and error, using them cautiously at first and only slowly developing a measure of trust.

How dangerous an area seems depends on how familiar one is with the neighborhood and what one can take for granted. Villagers often use the euphemism "tricky." Depending on how long they have lived here and how "urban" they are, the streets may seem manageable or unmanageable.

Most people in the Village, because of their social class as well as the cultural history of the community (which includes a legacy of nonviolence), shy away from arming themselves with guns, knives, and other weapons. A more common "defense" is simply avoiding the streets. Many whites and middle-income blacks use them as infrequently as they can, particularly at night.

---

* Reprinted from Elijah Anderson, *Streetwise* (Chicago: University of Chicago Press, 1990).

Because public interactions generally matter for only a few crucial seconds, people are conditioned to rapid scrutiny of the looks, speech, public behavior, gender, and color of those sharing the environment. The central strategy in maintaining safety on the streets is to avoid strange black males. The public awareness is color-coded: white skin denotes civility, law-abidingness, and trustworthiness, while black skin is strongly associated with poverty, crime, incivility, and distrust. Thus an unknown young black male is readily deferred to. If he asks for anything, he must be handled quickly and summarily. If he is persistent, help must be summoned.

This simplistic racial interpretation of crime creates a "we/they" dichotomy between whites and blacks. Yet here again the underlying issue is class. One may argue that the average mugger is primarily concerned with the trouble or ease of taking his victim's property and only secondarily with race or with the distant consequences of his actions. It is significant, then, that the dominant working conception in the black community at large is that the area is being overrun by well-to-do whites. Not only do the perpetrators of crime often view anonymous whites as invaders but, perhaps more important, they see them as "people who got something" and who are inexperienced in the "ways of the streets."

Middle-income blacks in the Village, who also are among the "haves," often share a victim mentality with middle-income whites and appear just as distrustful of black strangers. Believing they are immune to the charge of racism, Village blacks make some of the same remarks as whites do, sometimes voicing even more incisive observations concerning "street blacks" and black criminality.

That middle-class whites and blacks have similar concerns suggests a social commonality and shared moral community, allowing people the limited sense that all residents of the neighborhood have comparable problems with street navigation. But this assumption ultimately breaks down, affecting neighborhood trust and the social integrity of the community. For in fact the experiences and problems on the streets of a person with dark skin are very different from those of a white person, for several reasons.

First, whereas the law-abiding black possesses a kind of protective coloration, the white man or woman has none. This defense allows the black person to claim street wisdom, which the white person generally does not find it easy to do.

Second, there is a felt deterrent to black-on-black crime because the victim may recognize his assailant later. This possibility may cause the potential mugger, for a crucial instant, to think twice before robbing another black person. Not only may the victim "bump into" his assailant again, but there is a chance he will try to "take care of him" personally. Many a mugger would not like to carry such a burden, especially when there are so many "inexperienced" whites around who may be assumed, however erroneously, to be easier to rob, unlikely to recognize their assailant, and certainly less likely to retaliate.

Finally, the white male does not represent the same threat in the public arena, making him, and by implication whites generally, feel especially vulnerable and undermining respect for his defensive capabilities. Perhaps in response to this cultural truth, some white men take a generalized exaggerated, protective posture toward white women in the presence of "threatening" black males. One young black man described this scene:

> One evening I was walking down the street and this older white lady was at the middle of the block, and I was walking toward her. It was just me and her. Then all of a sudden this young white man runs across the street and just stands between me and this lady. He just kept watching me, and I stared him down. When I passed him. I turned and kept on looking at him. I know he thought I was gon' mess with that woman or something.

This deliberate confrontation is rare on Village streets. Rather, whites and middle-class blacks are skilled in the art of avoidance, using their eyes, ears, and bodies to navigate safely. Although this seems to work for the residents, however, it vitiates comity between the races. One class of people is conditioned to see itself as law-abiding and culturally superior while viewing the other as a socially bruised underclass inclined to criminality. This perspective creates social distance and racial stereotyping, to which middle-income blacks are especially sensitive. Further, it makes even liberal whites vulnerable to the charge of racism.

Although such prejudice is at work in the Village community, there is a deceptive appearance of an effortlessly ordered and racially tolerant public space. All individuals walking the streets, whether white or black, must negotiate their passage with others they encounter. There are essentially two ways of doing this. One is to formulate a set of rules and apply them in every situation, employing what I call "street etiquette." This requires only a generalized perception of the people one encounters, based on the most superficial characteristics. Because it represents a crude set of guidelines, street etiquette makes the streets feel somewhat comfortable to the user, but it may be a security blanket rather than a real practical help. For many it becomes a learning tool.

Pedestrians who go beyond the simplistic rules of street etiquette develop a kind of "street wisdom," a more sophisticated approach. Those who acquire this sophistication realize that the public environment does not always respond to a formal set of rules rigidly applied to all problems. So they develop coping strategies for different situations, tailoring their responses to each unique event. By doing so they develop a "conception of self" in public that in itself provides some safety; in effect, they learn how to behave on the streets.

STREET ETIQUETTE

A set of informal rules has emerged among residents and other users of the public spaces of the Village. These rules allow members of diverse groups orderly passage with the promise of security, or at least a minimum of trouble and conflict. The rules are applied in specific circumstances, particularly when people feel threatened. Public etiquette is initiated where the jurisdiction of formal agents of social control ends and personal responsibility is sensed to begin. Because crime is a central issue to most residents, their concern for safety leads them to expand great effort in getting to know their immediate area. Potential and actual street crime inspires the social process of mental note taking, which lays a foundation for trust among strangers, dictated by the situation and proceeding by repeated face-to-face encounters. It works to form the basis of public community within the immediate neighborhood.

The process begins something like this. One person sees another walking down the street alone, with another person, or perhaps with a few others. Those seen might be getting out of an unusual car, riding a ten-speed bicycle, walking a dog, strolling on the grounds of a dwelling in the neighborhood, or simply crossing the street at the light or leaving a store carrying groceries. The sight of people engaging in such everyday activities helps to convey what may be interpreted as the usual picture of public life – what residents take for granted.

Skin color, gender, age, dress, and comportment are important markers that characterize and define the area. Depending on the observer's biases, such as specific markers can become the most important characteristics determining the status of those being watched, superseding other meaningful attributes. However, the most important aspect of the situation is simply that the observer takes mental note of the other person: a significant social contact, though usually not a reciprocal one, is made. The person seen, and the category he or she is believed to represent, comes to be considered an ordinary part of the environment.

Although the initial observation is important, it is not the crucial element in "knowing about" others and feeling comfortable. Rather, it helps determine the social context for any other meaningful interactions, whether unilateral or bilateral. It gives users of the streets a sense of whom to expect where and when, and it allows them to adjust their plans accordingly.

The significance of the initial encounter is contingent upon subsequent meetings and interactions. If the person is never seen again, the encounter gradually loses significance. But if the observer sees the person again or meets others who are similar, the initial impression may become stronger and might develop into a theory about that category of people, a working conception of a social type. The strength of such impressions – nurtured and supported through repeated encounters, observations, and talk with other residents – gradually builds.

Background information and knowledge may provide a basis for social connection. A stranger may be seen in one context, then in another, then in a third. In time the observer might say to himself, "I know that person." Certainly he does know the person, if only by sight. He has noticed him many times in various neighborhood contexts, and with each successive encounter he has become increasingly familiar with him and the class he has come to represent. Probably the two are not yet speaking, though they may have exchanged looks that establish the minimal basis for trust. If asked directly, the observer might say, "Yeah, I've seen him around." In this way strangers may know each other and obtain a degree of territorial communion without ever speaking a word. It is quite possible that they will never reach speaking terms.

But there are circumstances where the social gap between visual and verbal interaction in public is pressed and the relationship between incomplete strangers is required to go further. People sometimes feel silly continually passing others they know well by sight without speaking to them. They may resolve their discomfort by greeting to them or by contrived avoidance. If they choose to speak, they may commit themselves to a series of obligatory greetings.

Introductions may also occur when two people who have seen each other in the neighborhood for some time happen to meet in a different part of town; there, despite some awkwardness, they may feel constrained to greet each other like long-lost friends. Perhaps they had not yet reached the point of speaking but had only warily acknowledged one another with knowing looks, or even with the customary offensive/defensive scowl used on the street for keeping strangers at a distance. After this meeting, previously distant Villagers may begin to speak regularly on the neighborhood streets. In this way trust can be established between strangers, who may then come to know each other in limited ways or very well.

Just the fact of their regular presence offers a sense of security, or at least continuity, to their neighbors. Thus,

many people walk the streets with a confidence that belies
their serious concerns. They use those they "know" as buffers
against danger. Although they may still be strangers, they
feel they can call on each other as allies when neighborhoods
crises emerge, when they would otherwise be seriously short
of help, or when they must protect themselves or their loved
ones. For example, during emergencies such as house fires,
street crimes in which someone clearly needs help, or some
other event where partial strangers have an opportunity to
gather and compare notes with neighbors who seemed out
of reach before, they may first provide help and only then
reach out a hand and introduce themselves, saying, "Hello,
my name is . . ."

This invisible but assumed network of reserve relationships binds together the residents and regular users of the
public spaces of the Village. However, the person-specific
designations that Villagers make every day are not always
conducive to the flourishing of "ideal-typical gemeinschaft"
relations. On the contrary, mental note taking like that
described above also allows neighbors *not* to become involved in indiscriminate social exchange. For example, lower-
income black people are often observed closely by whites
who use the streets, perhaps primarily because they remain
exotic and sometimes dangerous to many Villagers. Many
whites may wish to get closer to the blacks, but for complicated reasons having to do with local history, class etiquette, and lingering racism, they normally maintain their
established social distance. Most residents want social contact
only with others of their own social class. In public they
note the speech patterns of lower-class blacks. They pay
attention to how "they" walk and how "they" treat their
children, absorbing everything and shaping and reshap-
ing their notions. It is not unusual to see whites, particularly women, observing the ways lower-income black women
handle their children in public. The following field note
illustrates this:

On a Saturday morning in May at approximately 11:00,
a young black woman was managing a little girl of three,
a boy of about five, and a small baby in a stroller. They
were standing at Linden Avenue and Cherry Street in the

Village, waiting for the bus. Two young white women and a middle-aged black man, apparently from the Village, were waiting for the bus too.

The two small children began to fight over a toy. The older child won, and the smaller one began to have a temper tantrum. She wailed and stamped. Her face contorted, the mother cursed at the children, yelling obscenities at them and trying to get them to behave themselves. The white women paid "civil inattention," their actions and words belying their interest. As the woman spanked the three-year-old, one of the white women visibly cringed, as if to say to her friend and anyone else caring to pay attention, "Oh! What a way to treat your child!" Meanwhile, the other white woman didn't say a word. The black man, in silence, simply observed the performance. The woman continued to berate the children. She clearly had her hands full. Finally the bus arrived.

Such critiques are not for the black woman's benefit, nor are they always made openly. Whereas in the gemeinschaft type of community people may become quite openly involved with the lives of their neighbors, trading favors and various kinds of help without keeping an account of who owes what to whom, Villagers generally avoid the responsibilities and social obligations that emerge from deeper forms of interpersonal involvement. Instead of intervening in either a helpful or a critical way, the two white women chose to strengthen the bond between them – their shared values – and to distance themselves from this other "element" of the public community.

TALK

In the Village, as in various neighborhoods of the city, young black males are carefully observed. They are often blamed for crimes when no contrary evidence is available. However, neighborly talk about crime becomes a problem when the age, ethnicity, or other defining attributes of the assailant and victim are introduced. In the Village, the all-too-easy dichotomizing by race into criminal and victim categories is complicated by the friendly, even intimate, relations between some blacks and whites. Neighbors bound by the dominant Village ideology of racial harmony and tolerance risk offending some members of their audience when they make broad racial remarks. Hence neighbors tread lightly except when they forget themselves or presume they are in "safe" company and can speak freely.

There are many times when whites educate other whites who believe their prejudices are generally shared. A thirty-year-old white man who grew up in an Irish working-class section of the city had this to say:

> I had a small gathering at my house just the other night. Tommy Jones, Charlie, Dave and some women. Well, Dave started in talking about crime in the streets. And he started to talk about "niggers." And I just said to him. "Whoa, whoa, man. I don't allow that kind of talk in my house. If you want to talk like that, you gotta go outside, or go somewhere else." And I meant it. Yeah, I meant it. You should have seen the look on his face. Well, he didn't use that word no more.

Patterns of information exchange develop where neighbors talk to each other with different degrees of frankness about the alleged or actual attributes of assailants and victims. For instance a white person might tell his black neighbor a story in which the assailant was believed to be black, but he might politely omit race if he thinks the black neighbor will be offended.

As neighbors come to know one another, fewer offenses are likely to occur; identifications with certain social circles become known, and information exchanges can proceed by neighborhood-specific code words in which race need not be overtly stated but is subtly expressed. For instance, a young couple moving in from the suburbs learn from an upstairs neighbor that the reason Mrs. Legget (white) walks with a cane is not just that she is eight-five years old. Until a few years ago, she took her regular afternoon walks unaided by the thick wooden stick she now relies on. One afternoonshe was knocked to the pavement by a "couple of kids" outside Mr Chow's, the neighborhood market where

black high-school students stop for candy and soda and
congregate on their way home from school. In the scuffle,
Mrs Legget's purse was taken. The police took her to the
hospital, and it was discovered that she had a broken hip.

Since her injury, Mrs Legget's gait is less steady. She
still takes her walks, but now she goes out earlier and avoids
Mr Chow's at the time school lets out. When the new couple
ask her about the mugging, she is unwilling to describe
the "kids" who knocked her down. She only smiles and
gestures toward the small, low-slung cloth bag in which
she now carries her valuables. "This one is mug-proof, they
tell me," she says, a playful glimmer in her eye. It is a
poignant lesson for the young couple. Purse straps should
be worn across the chest bandolier style, not carelessly hooked
over the arm, and perhaps Mr Chow's is worth avoiding at
3:00 in the afternoon. As time goes by the young couple
will come to understand the special meaning of the term
"kids," which Villagers, particularly whites, often use in
stories about street muggings to mean "black kids."

Through neighborly talk, inhabitants of the Village provide new arrivals, as well as established residents, with rules
concerning the use of sidewalks at different times of day.
Newcomers learn the schedule of the nearby black high
school, enabling them to avoid the well-traveled north–south
streets when the high-school students are there in force.
They slowly learn how the racial and age composition of
the clientele at Mr Chow's varies with time of day, so they
can choose safer hours, "working around" those they view
as threatening. In addition, they come to recognize other
Villagers and frequent visitors from Northton, though they
may not always be conscious of the process. The more general color-coding that people in racially segregated areas
apply goes through a refinement process because of the
heterogeneous makeup of the Village.

When neighbors tell horror stories from the next block
over, the shape of the tale and the characteristics of the
actors depend on the values that the storyteller and his
audience share. In this sense a general moral community is
forged each time neighbors get together and talk about
crime. A we/they dichotomy often becomes explicit, and a
community perspective of "decent" people is articulated:

While casually sitting in their backyard, Adam and Lisa (a newly arrived white professional couple; he is an architect, she is a schoolteacher) and I were discussing their upcoming vacation to California. They were concerned about their house and wanted me to keep an eye on things. They lamented having to be so worried about break-ins but conceded that the Village was "not the suburbs." "If we have a break-in, they wouldn't know what to take; they wouldn't know the value of our things. I just worry about my Sony," Adam said with a laugh. From his tone of voice, his glance, and his nod toward Northton, it was clear that the would-be intruders, at least in his mind, were poor, ignorant, and black.

Coded or not, the collective definitions of "safe," "harmless," "trustworthy," "bad," "dangerous," and "hostile" become part of the Village perspective. Reports of personal experiences, including "close calls" and "horror stories," initiate and affirm neighborhood communion. At social gatherings, dinner parties, and the like, middle-class white Villagers mingle with other city dwellers and exchange stories about urban living. Conversation invariably turns to life in their neighborhoods – particularly its more forbidding aspects. Middle-class people commiserate, casting themselves and others they identify with in the role of victim. Recent stickups, rapes, burglaries, and harassment are subjects that get their attention, and they take note of where certain kinds of trouble are likely to occur and in what circumstances.

This type of communication enables residents to learn more about the streets, adding to what they have gleaned from experience. Though initially superficial, this information and the mental maps it helps form let strangers and residents of various life-styles and backgrounds navigate the Village streets with a reserve of social knowledge and a "working conception," a coherent picture, of local street life.

Neighborhood talk also affirms the belief that "city people" are somehow special, deserving commendation for tolerating the problems of being middle class in an environment that must be shared with the working class and the poor. "I'm convinced," one middle-class woman said while out on her porch fertilizing the geraniums, "that city people are just so much more ingenious." (She was discussing a friend who had moved out to one of the city's posh suburbs.) "We *have* to be," she concluded matter-of-factly.

PASSING BEHAVIOR

Even the deceptively simple decision to pass a stranger on the street involves a set of mental calculations. Is it day or night? Are there other people around? Is the stranger a child, a woman, a white man, a teenager, or a black man? And each participant's actions must be matched to the actions and cues of the other. The following field note illustrates how well tuned strangers can be to each other and how capable of subtle gestural communication:

It is about 11:00 on a cold December morning after a snowfall. Outside, the only sound is the scrape of an elderly white woman's snow shovel on the oil-soaked ice of her front walk. Her house is on a corner in the residential heart of the Village, at an intersection that stands deserted between morning and afternoon rush hours. A truck pulls up directly across from the old lady's house. Before long the silence is split by the buzz of two tree surgeons' gasoline-powered saws. She leans on her shovel, watches for a while, then turns and goes inside. A middle-aged white man in a beige overcoat approaches the site. His collar is turned up against the cold, his chin buried within, and he wears a Russian-style fur-trimmed hat. His hands are sunk in his coat pockets. In his hard-soled shoes he hurries allong this east–west street approaching the intersection, slipping a bit, having to watch each step on the icy sidewalk. He crosses the north–south street and continues westward.

A young black male, dressed in a way many Villagers call "streetish" (white high-top sneakers with loose laces, tongues flopping out from under creased gabardine slacks, which drag and soak up oily water; navy blue "air force" parka trimmed with matted fake fur, hood up, arms dangling at the sides) is walking up ahead on the same side of the street. He turns around briefly to check who is coming up behind him. The white man keeps his eye on the treacherous sidewalk, brow furrowed, displaying a look of concern and determination. The young black man moves with a certain aplomb, walking rather slowly. From the two men's different paces it is obvious to both that either the young black man must speed up, the older white man must slow down, or they must pass on the otherwise deserted sidewalk.

The young black man slows up ever so slightly and shifts to the outside edge of the sidewalk. The white man takes the cue and drifts to the right while continuing his forward motion. Thus in five or six steps (and with no obvious lateral motion that might be construed as avoidance), he maximizes the lateral distance between himself and the man he must pass. What a minute ago appeared to be a single-file formation, with the white man ten steps behind, has suddenly become side-by-side, and yet neither participant ever appeared to step sideways at all.

In this intricate "ballet," to use Jane Jacobs's term (1961), the movements are patterned to minimize tension and allay fears and yet not openly express a breach of trust between the two parties. This "good behavior" is more conspicuous on the relatively well-defended east–west streets of the Village, where many white professionals tend to cluster and where blacks and whites often encounter each other. Such smooth gestural communication is most evident between blacks and whites traveling alone, especially during hours when the sidewalks are deserted. White Villagers' fears seem to run highest then, for that is when the opportunity for harrassment or mugging is greatest.

However, black male strangers confront problems of street navigation in similar ways. This field note illustrates some of the rules city dwellers must internalize:

At 3:00 Sunday morning I parked my car one street over from my home. To get to my front door I now had to walk to the corner, turn up the street to another corner, turn again and walk about fifty yards. It was a misty morning, and the streets were exceptionally quiet. Before leaving the car, I found my door key. Then, sitting in the parked car with the lights out, I looked up and down the street at the high bushes, at the shadows. After determining it was safe I got out of the car, holding the key, and walked to the first corner. As I moved down the street I heard a man's heavy footsteps behind me. I looked back and saw a dark figure in a trench coat. I slowed down, and he continued past me. I said nothing, but I very consciously allowed him to get in front of me. Now I was left with the choice of walking about five feet behind the stranger or of crossing the street, going out of my way, and walking parallel to him on the other side. I chose to cross the street.

All these actions fall in line with rules of etiquette designed to deal with such public encounters. First, before I left the safety of my car I did everything possible to ensure speedy entrance into my home. I turned off the car lights, looked in every direction and took my house key in hand. Second, I immediately looked back when I heard footsteps so that I could assess the person approaching. Next, I determined that the stranger could be a mugger in search of a victim – one of many possible identities, but naturally the one that concerned the most. I knew that at night it is important to defer to strangers by giving them room, so I established distance between us by dropping back after he passed me. Further, providing for the possibility that he was simply a pedestrian on his way home, I crossed the street to allow him clear and safe passage, a norm that would have been violated had I continued to follow close behind him.

When I reached the corner, after walking parallel to the stranger for a block, I waited until he had crossed the next street and had moved on ahead. Then I crossed to his side of the street; I was now about thirty yards behind him, and we were now walking away from each other at right angles. We moved farther and farther apart. He looked back. Our eyes met. I continued to look over my shoulder until I reached my door, unlocked it, and entered. We both continued to follow certain rules of the street. We did not cross the street simultaneously, which might have caused our paths to cross a second time. We both continued to "watch our backs" until the other stranger was no longer a threat.

In this situation skin color was important. I believe the man on the street distrusted me in part because I was black, and I distrusted him for the same reason. Further, we were both able-bodied and young. Although we were cautious toward each other, in a sense we were well matched. This is not the case when lone women meet strangers.

A woman being approached from behind by a strange man, especially a young black man, would be more likely to cross the street so that he could pass on the opposite side. If he gave any sign of following her, she might head for the middle of the street, perhaps at a slight run toward a "safe spot." She might call for help, or she might detour from her initial travel plan and approach a store or a well-lit porch where she might feel secure.

In numerous situations like those described above, a law-abiding, streetwise black man, in an attempt to put the white woman at ease, might cross the street or simply try to avoid encountering her at all. There are times when such men – any male who seems to be "safe" will do – serve women of any color as protective company on an otherwise lonely and forbidding street.

This quasi "with" is initiated by the woman, usually as she closely follows the man ahead of her "piggyback" style. Although the woman is fully aware of the nature of the relationship, the man is usually not, though he may pick up on it in the face of danger or demonstrable threat. The existence of this "with," loose and extended as it may be, gives comfort and promises aid in case of trouble, and it thereby serves to ward off real danger. Or at least the participants believe it does.

EYE WORK

Many blacks perceive whites as tense or hostile to them in public. They pay attention to the amount of eye contact given. In general, black males get far less time in this regard than do white males. Whites tend not to "hold" the eyes of a black person. It is more common for black and white strangers to meet each other's eyes for only a few seconds, and then to avert their gaze abruptly. Such behavior seems to say, "I am aware of your presence," and no more. Women especially feel that eye contact invites unwanted advances, but some white men feel the same and want to be clear about what they intend. This eye work is a way to maintain distance, mainly for safety and social purposes. Consistent with this, some blacks are very surprised to find a white person who holds their eyes longer than is normal according to the rules of the public sphere. As one middle-aged white female resident commented:

> Just this morning, I saw a [black] guy when I went over to Mr Chow's to get some milk at 7.15. You always greet people you see at 7.15, and I looked at him and smiled. And he said "Hello" or "Good morning" or something. I smiled again. It was clear that he saw this as surprising.

Many people, particularly those who see themselves as more economically privileged than others in the community, are careful not to let their eyes stray, in order to avoid an uncomfortable situation. As they walk down the street they pretend not to see other pedestrians, or they look right at them without speaking, a behavior many blacks find offensive.

Moreover, whites of the Village often scowl to keep young blacks at a social and physical distance. As they venture out on the streets of the Village and, to a lesser extent, of Northton, they may plant this look on their faces to ward off others who might mean them harm. Scowling by whites may be compared to gritting by blacks as a coping strategy. At times members of either group make such faces with little regard for circumstances, as if they were dressing for inclement weather. But on the Village streets it does not always storm, and such overcoats repel the sunshine as well as the rain, frustrating many attempts at spontaneous human communication.

MONEY

Naturally, given two adjacent neighborhoods representing "haves" and "have-nots," there is tremendous anxiety about money: how much to carry, how to hold it, how to use it safely in public. As in other aspects of Village life, shared anecdotes and group discussions help newcomers recognize the underlying rules of comportment.

Perhaps the most important point of etiquette with regard to money in public places is to be discreet. For example, at the checkout counter one looks into one's wallet or purse and takes out only enough to cover the charge, being careful that the remaining contents are not on display. Further, one attempts to use only small bills so as not to suggest that one has large ones.

When walking on the streets at night, it is wise to keep some money in a wallet or purse and hide the rest in other parts of one's clothing – some in a jacket pocket, some in the back pocket of one's jeans, maybe even some in a sock. In this one way would not lose everything in a mugging, yet the mugger would get something to appease him.

A final rule, perhaps the most critical, is that in a potentially violent situation it is better to lose one's money than one's life. Thus the person who plans to travel at dangerous times or in dangerous areas should have some money on hand in case of an assault:

It was 9.00 P.M., and the Christmas party had ended. I was among the last to leave. John [a forty-five-year-old professional], the host, had to run an errand and asked if I wanted to go with him. I agreed. While I was waiting, Marsha, John's wife, said in a perfectly serious voice, "Now, John, before you go, do you have $10 just in case you get mugged?" "No, I don't have it, do you?"

Marsha fetched $10 and gave it to John as what was in effect protection money, a kind of consolation prize designed to cool out a prospective mugger. As we walked the three blocks or so on the errand, John said, "We've come two blocks, and it's not so bad." His tone was that of a nervous joke, as though he really half expected to encounter muggers.

The reality of the Village is that residents can make their lives safer by "expecting" certain problems and making plans to cope with them. The mental preparation involved – imagining a bad situation and coming up with the best possible solution, acting it out in one's mind – may well be a valuable tool in learning to behave safely on the streets.

STREET WISDOM

Those who rely on a simplistic etiquette of the streets are likely to continue to be ill at ease, because they tend not to pay close attention to the characteristics that identify a suspect as harmless. Rather, they envelop themselves in a protective shell that wards off both attackers and potential black allies, allowing the master status of male gender and black skin to rule. Such people often display tunnel vision with regard to all strangers except those who appear superficially most like themselves in skin color and dress.

This is a narrow and often unsatisfying way to live and to operate in public, and many of those who cannot get beyond stiff rules of etiquette decide in the end to move to safer, less "tricky" areas. But most people come to realize that street etiquette is only a guide for assessing behavior in public. It is still necessary to develop some strategy for using the etiquette based on one's understanding of the situation.

Once the basic rules of etiquette are mastered and internalized, people can use their observations and experiences to gain insight. In effect, they engage in "field research." In achieving the wisdom that every public trial is unique, they become aware that individuals, not types, define specific events. Street wisdom and street etiquette are comparable to a scalpel and a hatchet. One is capable of cutting extremely fine lines between vitally different organs; the other can only make broader, more brutal strokes.

A person who has found some system for categorizing the denizens of the streets and other public spaces must then learn how to distinguish among them, which requires a continuing set of assessments of, or even guesses about, fellow users. The streetwise individual thus becomes interested in a host of signs, emblems, and symbols that others exhibit in everyday life. Besides learning the "safety signals" a person might display – conservative clothing, a tie, books, a newspaper – he also absorbs the vocabulary and expressions of the street. If he is white, he may learn for the first time to make distinctions among different kinds of black people. He may learn the meaning of certain styles of hats, sweaters, jackets, shoes, and other emblems of the subculture, thus rendering the local environment "safer" and more manageable.

The accuracy of the reading is less important than the sense of security one derives from feeling that one's interpretation is correct. Through the interpretive process, the person contributes to his working conception of the streets. In becoming a self-conscious and sensitive observer, he becomes the author of his own public actions and begins to act rather than simply to react to situations. For instance, one young white woman had on occasion been confronted and asked for "loans" by black girls who appeared to "guard the street" in front of the local high school. One day she decided to turn the tables. Seeing the request coming, she confidently walked up to one of the girls and said, "I'm out of money. Could you spare me fifty cents?" The young blacks were caught off balance and befuddled. The woman went on, feeling victorious. Occasionally she will gratuitously greet strange men, with similar effect.

A primary motivation for acquiring street wisdom is the desire to have the upper hand. It is generally believed that this will ensure safe passage, allowing one to outwit a potential assailant. In this regard a social game may be discerned. Yet it is a serious game, for failing could mean loss of property, injury, or even death. To prevail means simply to get safely to one's destination, and the ones who are most successful are those who are "streetwise." Street wisdom is really street etiquette wisely enacted.

Among the streetwise, there is a common perspective toward street criminals, those who are "out there" and intent on violating law-abiding citizens. The street criminal is assumed to "pick his people," knowing who is vulnerable and who is not, causing some people to think that victimization is far from inevitable. This belief gives them confidence on the streets and allows them to feel a measure of control over their own fate. Indeed, avoiding trouble is often, though not always, within the control of the victim. Thus the victim may be blamed, and the streets may be viewed as yielding and negotiable. Consistent with this working conception of street life and crime, the task is to carry oneself in such a way as to ward off danger and be left alone. A chief resource is one's own person – what one displays about oneself. Most important, one must be careful.

Typically, those generally regarded as streetwise are veterans of the public spaces. They know how to get along with strangers, and they understand how to negotiate the streets. They know whom to trust, whom not to trust, what to say through body language or words. They have learned how to behave effectively in public. Probably the most important consideration is the experience they have gained through encounters with "every kind of stranger." Although one may know about situations through the reports of friends or relatives, this pales in comparison with actual experience. It is often sheer proximity to the dangerous streets that allows a person to gain street wisdom and formulate some effective theory of the public spaces. As one navigates there is a certain edge to one's demeanor, for the streetwise person is both wary of others and sensitive to the subtleties that could salvage safety out of danger.

The longer people live in this locale, having to confront problems on the streets and public spaces every day, the greater chance they have to develop a sense of what to do without seriously compromising themselves. Further, the longer they are in the area, the more likely they are to develop contacts who might come to their aid, allowing them to move more boldly.

This self-consciousness makes people likely to be alert and sensitive to the nuances of the environment. More important, they will project their ease and self-assurance to those they meet, giving them the chance to affect the interaction positively. For example, the person who is "streetdumb," relying for guidance on the most superficial signs, may pay too much attention to skin color and become needlessly tense just because the person approaching is black. A streetwise white who meets a black person will probably just go about his or her business. In both cases the black person will pick up the "vibe" being projected – in the first instance fear and hostility, in the second case comfort and a sense of commonality. There are obviously times when the "vibe" itself could tip the balance in creating the subsequent interaction.

CRISIS AND ADAPTATION

Sometimes the balance tips severely, and the whole neighborhood reacts with shock and alarm. A wave of fear surges through the community when violent crimes are reported by the media or are spread by word of mouth through the usually peaceful Village. One February a young woman, a new mother, was stabbed and left for dead in her home on one of the well-traveled north–south streets. Her month-old baby was unharmed, but it was weeks before the mother, recuperating in the hospital, remembered she had recently given birth. Word of how the stabbing occurred spread up and down the blocks of the Village. Neighbors said the woman often went out her back door to take out the garbage or call in the dog. But to uninitiated newcomers, the brick streets and large yards seem deceptively peaceful. Crises like these leave in their wake a deeper understanding of the "openness" that characterizes this quaint area of the city.

They also separate those who survive by brittle etiquette from those who – despite increased temporary precautions – can continue to see strangers as individuals. Less than half a block away from the scene of the attack, in a building facing an east–west street, a friend of the young mother was overcome with fear. Her husband was scheduled to go out of town the week after the vicious attack on her friend. She was so frightened that he had to arrange for a neighbor to "baby-sit" with his wife and children at night while he was away.

Security all over the Village was tightened for a time. People who used to go in and out, feeding the birds, shoveling walks, visiting their neighbors and friends, no longer came and went so carelessly. As the news traveled, fear rippled out from the young victim's immediate neighbors to affect behavior in other parts of the Village. One young black man reported that after the attack he was greeted with suspicious stares on his way to Mr Chow's. "Everyone's looking over their shoulder suddenly," he said. "All black people are suspects."

"It makes you stop and wonder about living here," said one young mother shortly after the stabbing became the main item of conversation. "I've never lived in such a dangerous neighborhood. I run upstairs and leave my back door open sometimes. Like today, I got both kids and took them upstairs, and all of a sudden I said, 'Oh, no! I left the door unlocked!' and I just stopped what I was doing and ran downstairs to lock it." This kind of fear-induced behavior occurs as neighbors work out their group perspective on what is possible, if not probable, in the aftermath of such a crime.

Violence causes residents to tense up and begin taking defensive action again. They may feel uncomfortable around strangers on the streets, particularly after dark. They become especially suspicious of black males. An interview with a young black man from the area sheds some light on how residents react to neighborhood blacks shortly after a violent incident:

> People come out of the door and they're scared. So when they see blacks on the streets they try to get away. Even ones who live right next door. All of a sudden they change attitudes toward each other. They're very suspicious. The guy that killed that lady and her husband down on Thirty-fourth in the Village, he from the Empire [gang]. He tried to rape the lady right in front of the husband – he stabbed the husband and killed him. He'll get the electric chair now; they gave him the death penalty. They caught him comin' out. Wouldn't been so bad, the cops got another call to next door to where he did it at. She was screamin' and the cops heard and came around to the door.
>
> After that happened, you could feel the vibes from whites. When things like that happen, things get very tense between blacks and whites. And you can feel it in the way they look at you, 'cause they think you might be the one who might do the crime. Everytime they see a black they don't trust 'em. Should stay in their own neighborhood.
>
> That's the Village. They paranoid.

In time the fear recedes. Through successive documentations and neighborhood gossip, Villagers slowly return to some level of complacency, an acceptance of the risks of living in the city. Familiar people on the streets are "mapped" and associated with their old places, much as veteran Villagers have mapped them before. Streets, parks, and playgrounds are again made theirs. When these mental notations remain reliable and undisturbed for a time, a kind of "peace" returns. More and more can be taken for granted. Night excursions become more common. Children may be given a longer tether. Villagers gather and talk about the more pleasant aspects of neighborhood life. But they know, and are often reminded, that the peace is precarious, for events can suddenly shake their confidence again. Mr Chow's gets robbed, or the Co-op, or someone is mugged in broad daylight.

One mugging was especially disturbing, for the victim was a pillar of stability, familiar on the streets. Mrs Legget, the eighty-five-year-old white woman, was mugged *again*. As she took her usual afternoon walk, coming down one of the well-traveled north–south streets to her own east–west street, at the intersection near Mr Chow's, several black girls approached her and demanded her money, which Mrs Legget gave them. News of this crime reverberated throughout the neighborhood. People were shocked, particularly those from the middle-income white and black communities, but also those from other enclaves of the Village. Who would do such a thing? What sort of person would steal from an eighty-five-year-old lady? She was quite defenseless, with her frail body, failing eyesight, and disarming wit. She has been walking the neighborhood streets for years and is the sort of person "everybody knows" – at least by sight.

Neighbors identify with Mrs Legget. They are aware of her plight and sympathize with her, even if they do not know her personally. Anyone who does any amount of walking in the neighborhood remembers "that frail old lady with a cane." She is a reference point by which many Villagers gauge their own security. If she can walk the streets, then others, visibly stronger (if less streetwise), can feel capable of maintaining the same rights of passage. Mrs Legget's freedom of movement stood as a symbol of safety.

Now residents think, "If they'll do it to Mrs Legget, they'll do it to anybody," and thus the mugging becomes an affront to the whole neighborhood. It transforms an amorphous group into a more consolidated community of "decent people." The neighbors begin to talk and ponder their group position in relation to others, particularly the group from which the muggers are thought to originate, the black youths of Northton, the Village, and other ghetto areas of the city.

People became more circumspect again after the attack on Mrs Legget. Her daily public presence implied that law-abiding residents had at least partial hegemony over some of the streets during the daylight hours. After the attack, Villagers' plans for taking public transportation became more elaborate. One young woman, a tenant in the apartment building where Mrs. Legget has lived for twenty years, changed her plans to take the city bus home from the Greyhound bus terminal. Instead, she drove her car and paid to park it near the terminal, thus assuring herself of door-to-door transportation for her nighttime return from out of town. "There's a lot of crime going on right now," she told a friend. She was embarrassed, for she usually ridicules the block meetings and homeowners' gripes about theft and vandalism. But Mrs. Legget's mugging shook even the firmest believers in street safety.

Yet like the stabbing of the young mother, this incident eventually passed into memory for most Villagers. Time helps people forget even the most perilous incidents. Neighbors talk and socialize about other things. After a period of using the public spaces uneventfully, suspicion and distrust subside, but they never fade completely. Familiarity is rebuilt and a shared trust in the public spaces is gradually restored.

In this way social knowledge of the immediate area becomes assimilated as stories are shared and retold and a more refined group perspective emerges. This rebuilding of trust occurs by testing the public areas through careful walking and greater-than-usual scrutiny of strangers, particularly young black males. But always and inevitably, things gradually return to "normal." Otherwise life would simply require too much energy.

Reference

Jacobs, Jane (1961) *The Death and Life of Great American Cities* (New York: Vintage).

20 Fortress Los Angeles: The Militarization of Urban Space*

Mike Davis

The city bristles with malice. The carefully manicured lawns of the Westside sprout ominous little signs threatening "ARMED RESPONSE!" Wealthier neighborhoods in the canyons and hillsides cower behind walls guarded by gun-toting private police and state-of-the-art electronic surveillance systems. Downtown, a publicly subsidized "urban renaissance" has raised a forbidding corporate citadel, separated from the surrounding poor neighborhoods by battlements and moats. Some of these neighborhoods – predominately black or Latino – have in turn been sealed off by the police with barricades and checkpoints. In Hollywood, architect Frank Gehry has enshrined the siege look in a library that looks like a Foreign Legion fort. In Watts, developer Alexander Haagen has pioneered the totally secure shopping mall, a latter-day Panopticon, a prison of consumerism surrounded by iron-stake fences and motion detectors, overseen by a police substation in a central tower. Meanwhile in Downtown, a spectacular structure that tourists regularly mistake for a hotel is actually a new federal prison.

Welcome to post-liberal Los Angeles, where the defense of luxury has given birth to an arsenal of security systems and an obsession with the policing of social boundaries through architecture. This militarization of city life is increasingly visible everywhere in the built environment of the 1990s. Yet contemporary urban theory has remained oddly silent about its implications. Indeed, the pop apocalypticism of Hollywood movies and pulp science fiction has been more realistic – and politically perceptive –

* Reprinted from Michael Sorkin (ed.), *Variations on a Theme Park* (New York: Hill and Wand, 1990).

in representing the hardening of the urban landscape. Images of prisonlike inner cities (*Escape from New York, Running Man*), high-tech police death squads (*Bladerunner*), sentient skyscrapers (*Die Hard*), and guerrilla warfare in the streets (*Colors*) are not fantasies, but merely extrapolations from the present.

Such stark dystopian visions show how much the obsession with security has supplanted hopes for urban reform and social integration. The dire predictions of Richard Nixon's 1969 National Commission on the Causes and Prevention of Violence have been tragically fulfilled in the social polarizations of the Reagan era.[1] We do indeed now live in "fortress cities" brutally divided into "fortified cells" of affluence and "places of terror" where police battle the criminalized poor. The "Second Civil War" that began during the long hot summers of the late 1960s has been institutionalized in the very structure of urban space. The old liberal attempts at social control, which at least tried to balance repression with reform, have been superseded by open social warfare that pits the interests of the middle class against the welfare of the urban poor. In cities like Los Angeles, on the hard edge of postmodernity, architecture and the police apparatus are being merged to an unprecedented degree.

THE DESTRUCTION OF PUBLIC SPACE

The universal consequence of the crusade to secure the city is the destruction of any truly democratic urban space. The American city is being systematically turned inward. The "public" spaces of the new megastructures and supermalls have supplanted traditional streets and disciplined their spontaneity. Inside malls, office centers, and cultural complexes, public activities are sorted into strictly functional compartments under the gaze of private police forces. This architectural privatization of the physical public sphere, moreover, is complemented by a parallel restructuring of electronic space, as heavily guarded, pay-access databases and subscription cable services expropriate the invisible *agora*. In Los Angeles, for example, the ghetto is defined not only

by its paucity of parks and public amenities, but also by
the fact that it is not wired into any of the key information
circuits. In contrast, the affluent Westside is plugged – often
at public expense – into dense networks of educational and
cultural media.

In either guise, architectural or electronic, this polarization marks the decline of urban liberalism, and with it
the end of what might be called the Olmstedian vision of
public space in America. Frederick Law Olmsted, the father
of Central Park, conceived public landscapes and parks as
social safety-valves, *mixing* classes and ethnicities in common (bourgeois) recreations and pleasures: "No one who
has closely observed the conduct of the people who visit
[Central] Park," he wrote, "can doubt that it exercises a
distinctly harmonizing and refining influence upon the most
unfortunate and most lawless classes of the city – an influence favorable to courtesy, self-control, and temperance."[2]

This reformist ideal of public space as the emollient of
class struggle is now as obsolete as Rooseveltian nostrums
of full employment and an Economic Bill of Rights. As for
the mixing of classes, contemporary urban America is more
like Victorian England than the New York of Walt Whitman
or Fiorello La Guardia. In Los Angeles – once a paradise
of free beaches, luxurious parks, and "cruising strips" –
genuinely democratic space is virtually extinct. The pleasure domes of the elite Westside rely upon the social im-
prisonment of a third-world service proletariat in increasingly
repressive ghettos and barrios. In a city of several million
aspiring immigrants (where Spanish-surname children are
now almost two-thirds of the school-age population), public amenities are shrinking radically, libraries and playgrounds are closing, parks are falling derelict, and streets
are growing ever more desolate and dangerous.

Here, as in other American cities, municipal policy has
taken its lead from the security offensive and the middle-
class demand for increased spatial and social insulation.
Taxes previously targeted for traditional public spaces and
recreational facilities have been redirected to support corporate redevelopment projects. A pliant city government –
in the case of Los Angeles, one ironically professing to represent a liberal biracial coalition – has collaborated in

privatizing public space and subsidizing new exclusive enclaves (benignly called "urban villages"). The celebratory
language used to describe contemporary Los Angeles – "urban
renaissance," "city of the future," and so on – is only a
triumphal gloss laid over the brutalization of its inner-city
neighborhoods and the stark divisions of class and race
represented in its built environment. Urban form obediently
follows repressive function. Los Angeles, as always in the
vanguard, offers an especially disturbing guide to the emerging liaisons between urban architecture and the police state.

FORBIDDEN CITY

Los Angeles's first spatial militarist was the legendary General Harrison Gray Otis, proprietor of the *Times* and implacable foe of organized labor. In the 1890s, after locking
out his union printers and announcing a crusade for "industrial freedom," Otis retreated into a new *Times* building
designed as a fortress with grim turrets and battlements
crowned by a bellicose bronze eagle. To emphasize his trucu-
lence, he later had a small, functional cannon installed on
the hood of his Packard touring car. Not surprisingly, this
display of aggression produced a response in kind. On October 1, 1910, the heavily fortified *Times* headquarters – the
command-post of the open shop on the West Coast – was destroyed in a catastrophic explosion, blamed on union saboteurs.
    Eighty years later, the martial spirit of General Otis
pervades the design of Los Angeles's new Downtown, whose
skyscrapers march from Bunker Hill down the Figueroa
corridor. Two billion dollars of public tax subsidies have
enticed big banks and corporate headquarters back to a
central city they almost abandoned in the 1960s. Into a
waiting grid, cleared of tenement housing by the city's
powerful and largely unaccountable redevelopment agency,
local developers and offshore investors (increasingly Japanese) have planted a series of block-square complexes:
Crocker Center, the Bonaventure Hotel and Shopping Mall,
the World Trade Center, California Plaza, Arco Center, and
so on. With an increasingly dense and self-contained circulation system linking these superblocks, the new financial

district is best conceived as a single, self-referential hyperstructure, a Miesian skyscape of fantastic proportions.

Like similar megalomaniacal complexes tethered to fragmented and desolate downtowns – such as the Renaissance Center in Detroit and the Peachtree and Omni centers in Atlanta – Bunker Hill and the Figueroa corridor have provoked a storm of objections to their abuse of scale and composition, their denigration of street life, and their confiscation of the vital energy of the center, now sequestered within their subterranean concourses or privatized plazas. Sam Hall Kaplan, the former design critic of the *Times*, has vociferously denounced the antistreet bias of redevelopment; in his view, the superimposition of "hermetically sealed fortresses" and random "pieces of suburbia" onto Downtown has "killed the street" and "dammed the rivers of life."[3]

Yet Kaplan's vigorous defense of pedestrian democracy remains grounded in liberal complaints about "bland design" and "elitist planning practices." Like most architectural critics, he rails against the oversights of urban design without conceding a dimension of foresight, and even of deliberate repressive intent. For when Downtown's new "Gold Coast" is seen in relation to other social landscapes in the central city, the "fortress effect" emerges, not as an inadvertent failure of design, but as an explicit – and, in its own terms, successful – socio-spatial strategy.

The goals of this strategy may be summarized as a double repression: to obliterate all connection with Downtown's past and to prevent any dynamic association with the non-Anglo urbanism of its future. Los Angeles is unusual among major urban centers in having preserved, however negligently, most of its Beaux Arts commercial core. Yet the city chose to transplant – at immense public cost – the entire corporate and financial district from around Broadway and Spring Street to Bunker Hill, a half-dozen blocks further west.

The underlying logic of this operation is revealing. In other cities, developers have tried to harmonize the new cityscape and the old, exploiting the latter's historic buildings to create gentrified zones (Faneuil Market, Ghirardelli Square, and so on) as supports to middle-class residential colonization. But Downtown Los Angeles's redevelopers

considered property values in the old Broadway core as irreversibly eroded by the area's status as the hub of public
transportation primarily used by black and Mexican poor.
In the wake of the 1965 Watts Rebellion, whose fires burned
to within a few blocks of the old Downtown, resegregated
spatial security became the paramount concern. The 1960–
64 "Centropolis" masterplan, which had envisioned the renewal of the old core, was unceremoniously scrapped.
Meanwhile the Los Angeles Police Department (LAPD)
abetted the flight of business from the Broadway – Spring
Street area to the fortified redoubts of Bunker Hill by spreading scare literature about the "imminent gang invasion" by
black teenagers."[4]

To emphasize the "security" of the new Downtown, virtually all the traditional pedestrian links to the old center,
including the famous Angels' Flight funicular railroad, were
removed. The Harbor Freeway and the regraded palisades
of Bunker Hill further cut off the new financial core from
the poor immigrant neighborhoods that surround it on every
side. Along the base of California Plaza (home of the Museum of Contemporary Art), Hill Street functions as the
stark boundary separating the luxury of Bunker Hill from
the chaotic life of Broadway, now the primary shopping
and entertainment street for Latino immigrants. Because
gentrifiers now have their eye on the northern end of the
Broadway corridor (redubbed Bunker Hill East), the redevelopment agency promises to restore pedestrian access
to the Hill in the 1990s. This, of course, only dramatizes
the current bias against any spatial interaction between old
and new, poor and rich – except in the framework of
gentrification. Although a few white-collar types sometimes
venture into the Grand Central Market – a popular em-
porium of tropical produce and fresh foods – Latino shoppers or Saturday *flaneurs* never ascend to the upscale
precincts above Hill Street. The occasional appearance of
a destitute street nomad in Broadway Plaza or in front of
the Museum of Contemporary Art sets off a quiet panic, as
video cameras turn on their mounts and security guards
adjust their belts.

Photographs of the old Downtown in its 1940s prime show
crowds of Anglo, black, and Mexican shoppers of all ages

and classes. The contemporary Downtown "renaissance" renders such heterogeneity virtually impossible. It is intended not just to "kill the street" as Kaplan feared, but to "kill the crowd," to eliminate that democratic mixture that Olmsted believed was America's antidote to European class polarization. The new Downtown is designed to ensure a seamless continuum of middle-class work, consumption, and recreation, insulated from the city's "unsavory" streets. Ramparts and battlements, reflective glass and elevated pedways, are tropes in an architectural language warning off the underclass Other. Although architectural critics are usually blind to this militarized syntax, urban pariah groups – whether young black men, poor Latino immigrants, or elderly homeless white females – read the signs immediately.

Extreme thought it may seem, Bunker Hill is only one local expression of the national movement toward "defensible" urban centers. Cities of all sizes are rushing to apply and profit from a formula that links together clustered development, social homogeneity, and a perception of security. As an article in *Urban Land* magazine on "how to overcome fear of crime in downtowns" advised:

> A downtown can be designed and developed to make visitors feel that it – or a significant portion of it – is attractive and the type of place that "respectable people" like themselves tend to frequent. . . . A core downtown area that is compact, densely developed and multifunctional, [with] offices and housing for middle- and upper-income residents . . . can assure a high percentage of "respectable," law-abiding pedestrians. Such an attractive redeveloped core area would also be large enough to affect the downtown's overall image.[5]

MEAN STREETS

This strategic armoring of the city against the poor is especially obvious at street level. In his famous study of the "social life of small urban spaces," William Whyte points out that the quality of any urban environment can be measured, first of all, by whether there are convenient, comfortable places for pedestrians to sit. This maxim has been warmly taken to heart by designers of the high corporate precincts of Bunker Hill and its adjacent "urban villages." As part of the city's policy of subsidizing the white-collar residential colonization of Downtown, tens of millions of dollars of tax revenue have been invested in the creation of attractive, "soft" environments in favored areas. Planners envision a succession of opulent piazzas, fountains, public art, exotic shrubbery, and comfortable street furniture along a ten-block pedestrian corridor from Bunker Hill to South Park. Brochures sell Downtown's "livability" with idyllic representations of office workers and affluent tourists sipping cappuccino and listening to free jazz concerts in the terraced gardens of California Plaza and Grand Hope Park.

In stark contrast, a few blocks away, the city is engaged in a relentless struggle to make the streets as unlivable as possible for the homeless and the poor. The persistence of thousands of street people on the fringes of Bunker Hill and the Civic Center tarnishes the image of designer living Downtown and betrays the laboriously constructed illusion of an urban "renaissance." City Hall has retaliated with its own version of low-intensity warfare.

Although city leaders periodically propose schemes for removing indigents *en masse* – deporting them to a poor farm on the edge of the desert, confining them in camps in the mountains, or interning them on derelict ferries in the harbor – such "final solutions" have been blocked by council members' fears of the displacement of the homeless into their districts. Instead the city, self-consciously adopting the idiom of cold war, has promoted the "containment" (the official term) of the homeless in Skid Row, along Fifth Street, systematically transforming the neighborhood into an outdoor poorhouse. But this containment strategy breeds its own vicious cycle of contradiction. By condensing the mass of the desperate and helpless together in such a small space, and denying adequate housing, official policy has transformed Skid Row into probably the most dangerous ten square blocks in the world. Every night on Skid Row is Friday the 13th, and, unsurprisingly, many of the homeless seek to escape the area during the night at all costs, searching safer niches in other parts of Downtown. The city in turn tightens the noose with increased police harassment and ingenious design deterrents.

One of the simplest but most mean-spirited of these deterrents is the Rapid Transit District's new barrel-shaped bus bench, which offers a minimal surface for uncomfortable sitting while making sleeping impossible. Such "bumproof" benches are being widely introduced on the periphery of Skid Row. Another invention is the aggressive deployment of outdoor sprinklers. Several years ago the city opened a Skid Row Park; to ensure that the park could not be used for overnight camping, overhead sprinklers were programmed to drench unsuspecting sleepers at random times during the night. The system was immediately copied by local merchants to drive the homeless away from (public) storefront sidewalks. Meanwhile Downtown restaurants and markets have built baroque enclosures to protect their refuse from the homeless. Although no one in Los Angeles has yet proposed adding cyanide to the garbage, as was suggested in Phoenix a few years back, one popular seafood restaurant has spent $12,000 to build the ultimate bag-lady-proof trash cage: three-quarter-inch steel rod with alloy locks and vicious out-turned spikes to safeguard moldering fishheads and stale french fries.

Public toilets, however, have become the real frontline of the city's war on the homeless. Los Angeles, as a matter of deliberate policy, has fewer public lavatories than any other major North American city. On the advice of the Los Angeles police, who now sit on the "design board" of at least one major Downtown project, the redevelopment agency bulldozed the few remaining public toilets on Skid Row. Agency planners then considered whether to include a "freestanding public toilet" in their design for the upscale South Park residential development; agency chairman Jim Wood later admitted that the decision not to build the toilet was a "policy decision and not a design decision." The agency preferred the alternative of "quasi-public restrooms" – toilets in restaurants, art galleries, and office buildings – which can be made available selectively to tourists and white-collar workers while being denied to vagrants and other unsuitables. The same logic has inspired the city's transportation planners to exclude toilets from their designs for Los Angeles's new subway system.[6]

Bereft of toilets, the Downtown badlands east of Hill Street also lack outside water sources for drinking or washing. A common and troubling sight these days is the homeless men – many of them young refugees from El Salvador – washing, swimming, even drinking from the sewer effluent that flows down the concrete channel of the Los Angeles River on the eastern edge of Downtown. The city's public health department has made no effort to post warning signs in Spanish or to mobilize alternative clean-water sources.

In those areas where Downtown professionals must cross paths with the homeless or the working poor – such as the zone of gentrification along Broadway just sought of the Civic Center – extraordinary precautions have been taken to ensure the physical separation of the different classes. The redevelopment agency, for example, again brought in the police to help design "twenty-four-hour, state-of-the-art security" for the two new parking structures that serve the *Los Angeles Times* headquarters and the Ronald Reagan State Office Building. In contrast with the mean streets outside, both parking structures incorporate beautifully landscaped microparks, and one even boasts a food court, picnic area, and historical exhibit. Both structures are intended to function as "confidence-building" circulation systems that allow white-collar workers to walk from car to office, or from car to boutique, with minimum exposure to the public street. The Broadway-Spring Center, in particular, which links the two local hubs of gentrification (the Reagan Building and the proposed Grand Central Square) has been warmly praised by architectural critics for adding greenery and art to parking. It also adds a considerable dose of menace – armed guards, locked gates, and ubiquitous security cameras – to scare away the homeless and the poor.

The cold war on the streets of Downtown is ever escalating. The police, lobbied by Downtown merchants and developers, have broken up every attempt by the homeless and their allies to create safe havens or self-governed encampments. "Justiceville," founded by homeless activist Ted Hayes, was roughly dispersed; when its inhabitants attempted to find refuge at Venice Beach, they were arrested at the behest of the local council member (a renowned environmentalist) and sent back to Skid Row. The city's own brief

experiment with legalized camping – a grudging response
to a series of deaths from exposure during the cold winter
of 1987 – was abruptly terminated after only four months
to make way for the construction of a transit maintenance
yard. Current policy seems to involve perverse play upon
the famous irony about the equal rights of the rich and
poor to sleep in the rough. As the former head of the city
planning commission explained, in the City of the Angels
it is not against the law to sleep on the street per se –
"only to erect any sort of protective shelter."[7] To enforce
this proscription against "cardboard condos," the police
periodically sweep the Nickel, tearing down shelters, con-
fiscating possessions, and arresting resisters. Such cynical
repression has turned the majority of the homeless into urban
bedouins. They are visible all over Downtown, pushing their
few pathetic possessions in stolen shopping carts, always
fugitive, always in motion, pressed between the official policy
of containment and the inhumanity of Downtown streets.

SEQUESTERING THE POOR

An insidious spatial logic also regulates the lives of Los
Angeles's working poor. Just across the moat of the Harbor
Freeway, west of Bunker Hill, likes the MacArthur Park
district – once upon a time the city's wealthiest
neighborhood. Although frequently characterized as a no-
man's-land awaiting resurrection by developers, the district
is, in fact, home to the largest Central American community
in the United States. In the congested streets bordering the
park, a hundred thousand Salvadorans and Guatemalas,
including a large community of Mayan-speakers, crowd into
tenements and boarding houses barely adequate for a fourth
as many people. Every morning at 6 A.M. this Latino
Bantustan dispatches armies of sewing *operadoras*, dishwash-
ers, and janitors to turn the wheels of the Downtown economy.
But because MacArthur Park is midway between Downtown
and the famous Miracle Mile, it too will soon fall to redevelopment's bulldozers.

Hungry to exploit the lower land prices in the district, a
powerful coterie of developers, represented by a famous

ex-councilman and the former president of the planning commission, has won official approval for their vision of "Central City West": literally, a second Downtown comprising 25 million square feet of new office and retail space. Although local politicians have insisted upon a significant quota of low-income replacement housing, such a palliative will hardly compensate for the large-scale population displacement sure to follow the construction of the new skyscrapers and yuppified "urban villages." In the meantime, Korean capital, seeking *lebensraum* for Los Angeles's burgeoning Koreatown, is also pushing into the MacArthur Park area, uprooting tenements to construct heavily fortified condominiums and office complexes. Other Asian and European speculators are counting on the new Metrorail station, across from the park, to become a magnet for new investment in the district.

The recent intrusion of so many powerful interests into the area has put increasing pressure upon the police to "take back the streets" from what is usually represented as an occupying army of drug-dealers, illegal immigrants, and homicidal homeboys. Thus in the summer of 1990 the LAPD announced a massive operation to "retake crime-plagued MacArthur Park" and surrounding neighborhoods "street by street, alley by alley." While the area is undoubtedly a major drug market, principally for drive-in Anglo commuters, the police have focused not only on addict–dealers and gang members, but also on the industrious sidewalk vendors who have made the circumference of the park an exuberant swap meet. Thus Mayan women selling such local staples as tropical fruit, baby clothes, and roach spray have been rounded up in the same sweeps as alleged "narcoterrorists."[8] (Similar dragnets in other Southern California communities have focused on Latino day-laborers congregated at streetcorner "slave markets.")

By criminalizing every attempt by the poor – whether the Skid Row homeless or MacArthur Park venders – to use public space for survival purposes, law-enforcement agencies have abolished the last informal safety-net separating misery from catastrophe. (Few third-world cities are so pitiless.) At the same time, the police, encouraged by local businessmen and property owners, are taking the first, tentative steps toward criminalizing entire inner-city communities. The "war" on drugs and gangs again has been the pretext for the LAPD's novel, and disturbing, experiments with community blockades. A large section of the Pico-Union neighborhood, just south of MacArthur Park, has been quarantined since the summer of 1989; "Narcotics Enforcement Area" barriers restrict entry to residents "on legitimate business only." Inspired by the positive response of older residents and local politicians, the police have subsequently franchised "Operation Cul-de-Sac" to other low-income Latino and black neighborhoods.

Thus in November 1989 (as the Berlin Wall was being demolished), the Devonshire Division of the LAPD closed off a "drug-ridden" twelve-block section of the northern San Fernando Valley. To control circulation within this largely Latino neighborhood, the police convinced apartment owners to finance the construction of a permanent guard station. Twenty miles to the south, a square mile of the mixed black and Latino Central-Avalon community has also been converted into Narcotic Enforcement turf with concrete roadblocks. Given the popularity of these quarantines – save amongst the ghetto youth against whom they are directed – it is possible that a majority of the inner city may eventually be partitioned into police-regulated "no-go" areas.

The official rhetoric of the contemporary war against the urban underclasses resounds with comparisons to the War in Vietnam a generation ago. The LAPD's community blockades evoke the infamous policy of quarantining suspect populations in "strategic hamlets." But an even more ominous emulation is the reconstruction of Los Angeles's public housing projects as "defensible spaces." Deep in the Mekong Delta of the Watts–Willowbrook ghetto, for example, the Imperial Courts Housing Project has been fortified with chain-link fencing, 'Restricted Entry' signs, obligatory identity passes – and a substation of the LAPD. Visitors are stopped and frisked, the police routinely order residents back into their apartments at night, and domestic life is subjected to constant police scrutiny. For public-housing tenants and inhabitants of narcotic-enforcement zones, the loss of freedom is the price of "security."

Notes

1. National Committee on the Causes and Prevention of Violence, *To Establish Justice, To Ensure Domestic Tranquility*, final report (Washington DC: USGPO, 1969).
2. Quoted in John F. Kasson, *Amusing the Million* (New York: Hill and Wang, 1978), p. 15.
3. *Los Angeles Times*, 4 November 1978.
4. Ibid., 24 December 1972.
5. N. David Milder, "Crime and Downtown Revitalization," *Urban Land*, September 1987, p. 18.
6. Tom Chorneau, "Quandry Over a Park Restroom," *Downtown News*, 25 August 1986.
7. See "Cold Snap's Tool at 5 as Its Iciest Night Arrives," *Los Angeles Times*, 29 December 1988.
8. Ibid., 17 June 1990.

21 Reclaiming Our Public Spaces*
Fred Siegel

Public space is both the glory and shame of New York. New Yorkers glory in the liveliness of our sidewalks and plazas, the vitality that sets us apart from other big cities where reliance on the automobile has reduced the streets to a mere means of getting about. Our shame is that we've allowed fear and filth to subvert one of our most important assets.

The slow subversion of civility in New York's public spaces has caused even diehard New York loyalists, black and white, to think about what was once unthinkable – leaving. This is not merely a passing phase, a response to the economic downturn. Rather, it is a long-term trend that actually intensified during the boom of the 1980s. In a December 1991 *New York Times* survey, more than half the adult residents polled said they had plans to leave. The *Times* also found that pessimism about the city's future, which is closely tied to the sense of social breakdown, has been increasing steadily since 1985.

Traditionally, the Big Apple's boosters have thought of themselves as tart yet tender, driven yet tolerant and compassionate. That self-conception was long reflected in their regard to city spaces. New Yorkers saw their own relentless energy reflected in what Jane Jacobs described as the "intricate ballet" of the streets. New York's dynamic diversity – its mix of touts and tribes, characters and con men – gave total strangers a shared satisfaction in watching the drama of daily life unfold in our parks and plazas. For many, the public character of their private selves was revealed in the pleasure they took in being described as "streetwise."

Contemptuous of conformity, New Yorkers were happy to draw on the energy of "the street," even as they were

---

* Reprinted from *The City Journal*, vol. 2, no. 2 (Spring 1992).

wary of being drawn too deeply into the depravity they some-times glimpsed. That balance between pride in being part of the action and prudence in interacting with strangers has been unsettled by the sense of menace that now too often pervades our public places.

Jane Jacobs, whose 1961 book, *The Death and Life of Great American Cities*, has set the terms for discussion of public space ever since, argued that "lowly, unpurposeful, and random as they may appear, sidewalk contacts are the small change from which a city's wealth of public life may grow. . . . The tolerance, the room for great differences among neighbors, are possible and normal only when the streets of great cities have built-in equipment allowing strangers to dwell in peace together on civilized but essentially dignified and reserved terms." New York's reputation for rudeness notwithstanding, there was much to the image of a street ballet in which thousands of individuals rushed past each other, guided by the unspoken assumptions of an urban choreography. But the grace of the ballet has too often been replaced by something resembling roller derby. This new "in your face" assault on what were once widely shared sensibilities is symbolized by the bold-letter T-shirts: "It's a — thing – you wouldn't understand" (the blank is filled in with the name of the preferred ethnic group).

New Yorkers understand that entering public places leaves them open to what have become the indignities of everyday interaction. Walking in the park outside city hall, the New Yorker faces an aesthetic assault in the form of mounds of swirling garbage. In the East Village and on Upper Broad-way, "thieves' markets" set up by predatory peddlers block the sidewalks. On nearly every street, homeless men pan-handle aggressively, often "rough tailing" passersby. Even those who drive must pay a toll to not-so-subtle shakedown artists, the "squeegie men." Writer Gil Schwartz tells of picking up his daughter from a play-date: "I told another parent we were moving out of the city. 'Why?' he asked. I quietly took my child, stepped over the wino sleeping in the vestibule, [and left]."

The fear of what nineteenth-century journalists called the "dangerous classes" and Marxists described as the "lumpenproletariat" now directs both private choices and public policy. Individuals organize their days to minimize unpleasant encounters. When I asked a variety of New Yorkers – men and women, black and white – about how they viewed public space in the city, they told me the distress of their daily rounds could be measured by the number of times they were "hassled" between home and work. Not surprisingly, a 1989 Metropolitan Transit Authority survey of subway riders found that nearly half chose to stay home at night rather than contend with the fear, not to mention the crime, associated with public places.

Increasingly, fear has turned the city outside in. Author Michael Davis writes that a "second civil war," which began in the long hot summers of the 1960s, has been institutionalized into the very structure of urban space. For example, the midtown Marriott hotel – well known for its vast interior atrium – has its lobby on the seventh floor, sealed off from the "street people" below in Times Square. Similarly, the new Zeckendorf Tower deliberately cuts itself off from adjacent Union Square Park. The sole entrance to the complex is hidden on 15th Street. On a grander scale, projects like Battery Park City, with their vast internal expanses, effectively create private versions of public space. All of these projects, organized around the concept of "defensible space," illustrate how urban planning, both public and private, is now driven in considerable measure by attempts at "insulation."

Journalist Phil Weiss reports that new buildings in the open city are now "filled with gates, guards, and solid planes [to] funnel you this way and that," so designed to facilitate surveillance. Without such measures, he writes, "in a matter of days drug dealers can take over a public space, even a public space that is privately owned, [and] make it theirs." In Battery Park City, 32 surveillance cameras linked to 28 VCRs monitor the entrances and stairwells of 17 State Street. "New York wasn't supposed to be this way," Weiss writes. "License was one of the reasons you came here."

In the Progressive era, roughly the first two decades of the twentieth century, New York's public places were largely reclaimed from the "dangerous classes." Progressive institutions like the settlement house, sanitation corps, juvenile court, and recreation leagues later made possible the full integration of new immigrants and the victims of industrial society into the mainstream of New York life. Indigenous organizations of the working poor, such as fraternal associations, trade unions, and local churches, played a similar role, channeling personal hostilities into collective action. As the urban poor were assimilated into the working and middle classes, the city became an ocean of passable public behavior with a few islands of incivility. (Today, by contrast, we speak of islands of civility in an ocean of incivility.) Deviance of the most extreme sort was largely confined to skid row and to mental institutions, which, whatever their faults, were an improvement over the earlier practice of simply jailing the mentally ill.

It was the Progressives who built the vast network of public toilets that once allowed New Yorkers to enjoy walking the city in comfort. But we can no longer even maintain what these late-Victorians and their working-class allies once built, as anyone looking for a public toilet can attest.

Beginning roughly a quarter-century ago, the work of the Progressives and their New Deal successors was undone. In a great but now all too obviously failed experiment, the Progressive ideals of integration and uplift that had served the city so well were largely abandoned as repressive mechanisms of middle-class social control. In the great wave of moral deregulation that began in the mid-1960s, the poor and the insane were freed from the fetters of middle-class mores. The "revolution" achieved some important gains: It freed people unjustly imprisoned in mental hospitals, made the police a bit less highhanded, and gave welfare recipients the dignity afforded by due process rights. But like every revolution, it had its victims. In the new climate in which drug use was redefined as a "victimless crime" and purity of legal procedure took precedence over the safety of the community, people who had once been shackled by the inequities of the law found themselves trapped by a pervasive lawlessness. Delivered into the tender mercies of the streets, the most vulnerable among us have suffered immeasurably. Their suffering now overwhelms our public life.

When the police were withdrawn from the neighborhoods and the social workers pulled out of the projects, skid row behavior and a sense of menace extended outward to include larger and larger portions of the city. The attempt to eliminate arbitrary authority resulted in the elimination of almost all stabilizing authority. The upshot, as a woman enraged by the litter in front of her apartment building explained, is that "you feel you're all alone when you ask someone not to drop garbage on the sidewalk."

The collapse of common standards first threatened minority neighborhoods and then spread of ethnic "villages" in the outer boroughs. Cosmopolitan Manhattanites first ignored the problem, then dismissed concerns about it as a not-so-thinly-disguised expression of bigotry. But as decay, disorder, and the greater dangers they portend spread geographically, they spread up the class structure as well. While it was once possible for New Yorkers to enjoy the city by staying out of specific areas, there is now, as one Brooklynite put it, "almost no place to run, no place to hide."

As the fabled images of "tapping feet on 42nd Street" have been displaced by the almost Dickensian despair of New York's suffering street people, the connections between our identities as New Yorkers and our public places have also been severed. Residents now tend to define themselves against their surroundings, and thus against the city that once inspired them. James Bowman's review of Bret Easton Ellis's recent novel *American Psycho* captures the current cynicism. "The book," writes Bowman, "unintentionally poses a new idea for crime fiction" – the murderer who has no problem disposing of bodies "because no one can see them against the background of New York's moral and physical squalor."

Yet all is not lost. There are some signs of renewal and regeneration, and of what, for want of a better term, might be described as nascent neo-Progressivism. Some of the civic spirit of Progressivism, if not its specific policies, is being recreated in efforts to restore and revive one of the city's greatest assets, its parks.

New York's flagship parks were designed after the Civil War by Frederick Law Olmstead, the Mugwump, who saw pleasing public spaces as both a balm for the injuries of industrialization and a means to calm the "rough element of the city." The parks, he hoped, would restore some of the civic "communicativeness" that had been lost in a rapidly growing city of strangers. Olmstead inspired the Progressives, who built on his ideas with the "playground movement," the Outdoor Recreation League, and the movement for children's gardens.

For the Progressives, the parks were an irreplaceable part of a "livable city." In the century between the early 1870s and the early 1960s – the period linking the accomplishments of Olmstead to those of Robert Moses – the parks expanded almost continuously. But in the late 1960s, they came to be viewed as almost the first bit of ballast to be tossed overboard in an emergency. Undercut first by the shift of money into social spending, and then by the budget cuts of the mid-1970s, the city's 26,000 acres of parks and playgrounds were deprived of the funds needed for basic maintenance, let alone long-term capital investment. During the fiscal crisis, staff was cut from 6,200 to 3,850, and morale declined as well.

Ironically, it was precisely because the parks were so vulnerable that they became the focus of new public/private initiatives. For most agencies of the city government, the mid-1970's "crisis of the old order" was little more than a brief, unfortunate interlude of belt-tightening and fiscal reorganization, which resulted in little change in the way the government delivered services. But the parks were different. The first steps were taken under Parks Commissioner Martin Lang when the fiscal crisis hit. Lang encouraged the formation of "Friends of the Parks" organizations and extended help to the community garden groups that had already sprung up. But it was under Gordon Davis's tenure as Parks Commissioner from 1978 through 1983 that restructuring began in earnest.

Davis and his successor, Henry Stern, upgraded the quality of management, spun off the zoological society and golf courses, and reached out to fledgling community organizations concerted with the parks. Davis, who has been described as "the first of the modern parks commissioners," also created the highly visible new post of Central Park administrator in order to decentralize management and provide a focus for local fund-raising. At the same time, Davis was instrumental in joining with the Friends of Central Park to initiate the Central Park Conservancy, a group that was to become a model for community involvement around the city and the country.

In the late 1970s and 1980s, the Conservancy was joined by a number of other organizations dedicated to restoring the democratic promise of New York's parks, playgrounds, and gardens. While both funding and faith in government were declining, these groups initiated public/private partnerships to achieve what the city alone could not. The Central Park Conservancy raised $64 million during the 1980s. Under the leadership of its president, Elizabeth Barlow, who also served as the city's Central Park administrator, the Conservancy was providing more than half of the park's operating funds and underwriting more than half of its workforce. The Conservancy became the model for groups established to support Prospect, Riverside, Flushing Meadows–Corona, Van Cortlandt, and Pelham Bay parks.

Private involvement in the large parks has naturally garnered the most attention. But from the South Bronx to downtown Brooklyn, community groups are increasingly adopting small parks and playgrounds as well. The Neighborhood Open Space Coalition pioneered a grass roots version of the public/private partnership. Just as the Conservancy has taken over from the city the care of trees, laws, and plants, neighborhood groups have taken over abandoned lots and parks, many of which are tiny and have been turned into gardens. Almost a quarter of the city's 1490 parks, mostly the smallest ones, are cared for by community groups in cooperation with the city's Operation Green Thumb. These efforts cultivate character as well as flowers. They catalyze neighborhood energies and can become an emblem of pride for local communities. These are efforts that can only grow in importance during the current recession since the city has already reduced park funding, proportionately, to the lowest levels of the twentieth century.

In the carefully studied case of Central Park, the public/private partnership has produced payoffs in public perception. In 1982, research by William Kornblum and Terry Williams showed that only 56 percent of park users surveyed felt that Central Park was as safe as or safer than two years before. That number jumped to 72 percent in the 1989 survey. In the seven years between the two surveys, reported crime in the park dropped by 59 percent, robberies by 73 percent. The survey was taken before the infamous rape and assault of the Central Park jogger, but nonetheless fear persisted. Despite the improvements, 82 percent of the men and 71 percent of the women questioned in 1989 still said they had "felt victimized, harassed, [or] threatened in the park." The people polled also called for more crime-prevention measures and less liter. A 1988 telephone survey conducted by the Department of Parks and Recreation's Office of Operations Management and Planning likewise found that excessive litter and the absence of visible park employees were high on the list of complaints.

People grew to feel safer in Central Park in part because of the increased number of planned activities, designed on the assumption that good uses will drive out bad. "There is," states the Conservancy's 1990 annual report, "a direct correlation between the volume of park use and the perception of security." But it's more than a matter of perception. Malicious mischief, not to mention crime, Jane Jacobs explained, is most likely to flourish in a "vacuum," that is, when the park has fewer "legitimate" uses.

In the case of smaller parks, Jacobs argued that one way to fill the vacuum is by developing mixed-use neighborhoods, where the interspersion of commercial and residential buildings guarantees an ongoing flow of street life. In recent years, William H. Whyte has applied Jacobs's ideas about mixed-used neighborhoods to the parks and plazas of the center city. Through an almost microscopic study of how small parks and plazas are used, Whyte has shown that public spaces can be almost self-policing if they are in continuous use by ordinary citizens. In *City: Rediscovering the Center*, Whyte argues that "the biggest single obstacle to the provision of better spaces is the undesirables problem." But he argues that measures like ridged benches designed to be impossible to lie down on and high fences designed to make space uninviting are often self-defeating. "Places designed in distrust get what was anticipated," he says. "The best way to handle the problem of undesirables is to make a place attractive to everyone else."

Whyte's ideas have been applied by a new kind of organization – a consulting firm for sick spaces called the Project for Public Space. Begun by Fred Kent in 1975, the project employs "space therapists" whose job is to troubleshoot problem spaces. Architects, Kent says, often approach the design of plazas as a purely aesthetic exercise: They "like to build plazas as settings for their buildings, not as usable space." The project associates approach the problem anthropologically: They observe, record, and analyze spaces, with an eye toward making them hospitable. Often they recommend small, simple changes: Replace fixed benches with movable chairs, for instance, to facilitate conversation and cordiality. The project's microscopic methods have succeeded in reviving a number of "dead" or drug-ridden spaces, like midtown's Exxon Park, by taking down fences, rearranging benches and chairs, and moving in vendors to attract a steady flow of people.

The notable successes of Whyte's acolytes notwithstanding, there are sharp limitations to their "continuous use" model. Jane Jacobs's most original proposal, wrote Lewis Mumford, was to turn the cities' "chronic symptom of disorganization – excessive congestion – into a remedy, by deliberately enlarging the scope of the disease." Jacobs loved the streets but had little use for the parks. They were for her little more than vacuums waiting to be filled by crime. But what, asks Mumford, of the individual who longs to get away from being bumped and scraped by crowds, what of the lone soul who longs to escape the throngs and take a solitary walk in the woods? Is there to be no place in the city for them? Mumford's critique of Jacobs was written thirty years ago, but someone searching for serenity and solitude today would do well to avoid, for instance, the heavily wooded northern sections of Central Park, where solitude can only be pursued by risking robbery or worse.

Beauty is similarly inaccessible in Highbridge Park located in Washington Heights. In what amounts to geographic triage, the more beautiful and remote sections of Highbridge have been given over to hookers, drug dealers, the homeless, and chop shops for stolen cars. Because the park is in an immigrant area where pressing necessities seem to preclude effective community involvement, the people of Washington Heights have settled for using a portion of the park that receives regular police protection.

Whyte's applications of Jacobs's ideas have proven most effective for well-financed midtown plazas, where unconnected individuals come and go casually and where money to support attractive improvements is readily available from corporate proprietors. But a Parks Department already bearing the disproportionate brunt of budget cuts can spare little in the way of programming activity for local parks that lack financial support. And at times it is just as well. For neighborhood parks, congestion can create more conflict than comfort, unless there is a consensus about how the park should be used. Tompkins Square, which has aroused bitter antagonism on the Lower East Side, was, after all, precisely the kind of dense and continuously used space called for by Jacobs and Whyte.

What Whyte's ingenious but limited solutions studiously avoid, and what the homeless crisis has made unavoidable, is the clash of values created around contested spaces. The problems of public space and the homeless have become inextricably intertwined. Last fall, an early-morning survey by the city found two thousand homeless living in parks in Manhattan alone. The controversy surrounding the closing of Tompkins Square Park and the expulsion of its homeless population is too extensive to go into here. But the same problem can be examined in miniature at two other Greenwich Village parks.

Jackson Park is a quarter-acre triangle bounded on two sides by Eighth and Greenwich avenues and blessed with what the *New York Times* describes as "24 pin oak trees" which "form a verdant canopy over a functioning fountain." Beset by homeless addicts, drunks, and all manner of deviants, the park was cleared of undesirables, closed, and given a $1.2 million reconstruction. Fenced in as part of the rebuilding, the reclaimed park is largely maintained by the Friends of Jackson Park, who, with the cooperation of Parks Commissioner Betsy Gotbaum, organize volunteers to pick up litter and lock the park each day at dusk. The Parks Department unlocks the fence in the morning.

The West Village neighborhood bordering Abingdon Square Park and the adjacent Bleecker Street playground tells a different story. "We lost," said Arthur Schwartz, a member of Community Board 2 and a founder of Bring

Back Our Parks (BBOP), who worries that the local parks families depend on are "out of control." On any given night, as many as forty people, many of whom appear to be mentally ill, homeless, transvestite prostitutes, as well as the usual drunks and drug addicts, sleep in the park and use its bathrooms for sex. BBOP members proposed the Jackson Park solution, a fence that could be locked at night. But they were denounced by local activists as "yuppie scum and yuppie speculators," a cry also heard from East Village residents opposed to clearing out Tompkins Square.

"Park cleanup," said Schwartz, a lawyer, "was a way for middle-class families to stay in the city. People wanted to put time, money, and effort into cleaning up and improving the park." But the fencing plan, which Commissioner Gotbaum supported, was opposed by the West Village Committee, an organization founded in the 1950s by Jane Jacobs to oppose Robert Moses's proposed Lower Manhattan Expressway. The organization's initial and effective idealism has curdled into a hostility to change so intense that some members even threatened to vandalize a temporary fence erected as an experiment. One of Schwartz's neighbors warned him, "There are many ways to make this experiment unviable, and many of them involve hand tools."

In the West Village Committee, two of Jacobs's prime concerns came crashing up against each other. On the one hand, as Mumford had noted, "Her ideal city is mainly an organization for the prevention of crime . . . in which each householder, compelled to find both his main occupations and his recreations on the street, will serve as a watchman and policeman." But Jacobs saw the surveillance of neighborly eyes as the best security, and feared the conformity and sterility she associated with planning and imposed regularity. Some of her heirs went further, opposing all efforts to contain disorder as attempts to enforce conformity. Frozen in old animosities, the West Village Committee "prefers the homeless to children," Schwartz says.[16] The upshot, he adds, is that many middle-class families are more likely to flee the city.

The revival of public parks in the 1970s and 1980s was paralleled by another innovation in the management of public space, the Business Improvement District. This experiment in decentralization may be even more important to the city's long-term future. The Bryant Park Business Improvement District played a path-breaking role for BIDs, similar to that played for parks by the Central Park Conservancy.

Bryant Park, located next to the stately main branch of the New York Public Library, has long been a midtown sore spot. As early as the 1920s, *New York Times* accounts described the park as "poorly planned," a "disgrace," and an "eyesore." No other city in the world, the *Times* asserted, "would have tolerated such a park in the heart of the most important district." In 1934, Mayor Fiorello LaGuardia's new Parks Commissioner, Robert Moses, redesigned Bryant with a plan that went against almost everything organizations like the Project for Public Space have subsequently learned about city spaces. Raised four feet above the street, the new park was isolated from the surrounding sidewalks, making it an ideal location for "undesirables." "Bad design," says landscape architect Chris Allen, "contributed to bad uses."[2] By the 1970s the park had become a haven for muggers and marijuana dealers who appreciated its isolation.

In the late 1970s, the Parks Council took the initiative by helping to bring music and art to the park on a part-time basis. Food kiosks, book stalls, and flower stands were introduced, followed by a booth selling discount music and dance tickets. But all this activity made the park safer only during the day. Andrew Heiskell, who was chairman of both Time Inc. and the library board, approached Parks Commissioner Gordon Davis about the need for more fundamental changes. Heiskell brought together people from the library board, the Parks Department, the Parks Council, and other civic groups, with financial support from the Rockefeller Brothers Fund, to create the Bryant Park Restoration Corporation.

The corporation institutionalized the advances initiated by the Parks Council and laid plans for the full-scale redesign of the park. The redesign has been carried out by the Bryant Park Business Improvement District, which was established in 1985. The Grand Central Partnership, a spin-off of the Bryant Park Restoration Corporation, was organized in 1988 to clean up the area around Grand Central Station.

The city has long benefited from local development corporations (LDCs) like those involved in the rehabilitation of Bryant Park, Union Squares, and the Flatbush area of Brooklyn. The LDCs, like the recently developed BIDs, provide supplemental sanitation and security services. Both are involved in what has been described as "neighborhood space management." The crucial difference is that while even effective, well-established LDCs have to scramble for funds, the BIDs, which levy taxes on commercial property owners, are on a far firmer financial footing. In the words of the New York City Department of Business Services, the BIDs "use the city's tax collection power to assess themselves. These funds are... returned in entirety to the BID," so that "the program is one of self-help through self-taxation."[3]

The BIDs vary widely in size and scope, from Grand Street, with a 1991 budget of just $65 000, to the Grand Central Partnership, with a budget of $5 million, a capital improvement program of more than $20 million, and an outreach program for the homeless. What they have in common is an attempt to reclaim public space from the sense of menace that drives shoppers, and eventually store owners and citizens, to the suburbs.

The problem for any business district is that it is forced to deal with wildly overlapping jurisdictions. Take the 14th Street BID, the city's first, for example. It includes 14th Street between First and Sixth avenues as well as the streets adjacent to Union Square. Its area includes parts of five community boards, five sanitation districts, and three police precincts, not to mention several City Council and state legislative districts. The BID, explains Executive Director Joan Talbert, coordinates the city services coming into the area. It functions "like a little city hall," says the owner of a small business in Talbert's BID. "By watching out for the district all the time, it stays on top of the petty problems like crime and litter in a way that city bureaus can't." Another businessman likens the BID to "the cop on the beat and the guy with the broom keeping the streets clean."

The BIDs are not without their critics. Some small businessmen object to paying additional taxes for basic services the city should be providing. Tenants object to provisions which can allow their landlords' assessments to be passed on to them. More fundamentally, despite the fact that each BID is subject to extensive city oversight, critics complain that the BIDs represent a reversion to private, hence potentially unresponsive, government. Property owners, they note, are the largest bloc on the BID boards. These criticisms seem to be strongest in mid-Manhattan; Biederman, the guiding force behind the Bryant Park, Grand Central, and now the 34th street BIDs, has even been accused of being a "mini-Moses." The potential unresponsiveness of BIDs is a legitimate concern, but it's hard to argue that our overcentralized city government, one of a dying breed of command-driven bureaucracies, has been responsive to local needs.

There are still a few writers on public space who revel in the romance of what they describe as the continuous carnival of city street life. One is Professor Richard Sennett, who since the 1960s has been writing on the virtues of anarchic liberty. In his recent book, *The Conscience of the Eye: The Design and Social Life of the Cities*, Sennett urges his readers to "transcend the need for order." The "public realm," he says, "should be gritty and disturbing rather than pleasant." Sennett hopes for what might be described as the experimental life, life as it might be led in a postmodern novel. He writes that "urbanists might learn from modern artists who have experimented with notions of fragmentation and indeterminacy." The irony which escapes him is that the experiment was carried out, the city's Progressive legacy was dismantled, but it was an experiment that failed.

But as those who find the city "disturbing rather than pleasant" decamp – Sennett seems not to be able to find any resting place between the two – his is an increasingly lonely voice. What was once "funky" and "freaky" is now seen more often than not, even by children of the Sixties, as merely repellent. That change of heart suggests the possibility of a new consensus on the problems of public space, a consensus based on the need to respect individuality even while demanding a common standard of behavior.

The decline and partial revitalization of the city's parks and other public places illustrate the intimate connection between the problems of public space and the structure of government. Under the current form of city government, the parks have been "rewarded" for their ingenuity and success by having their allocations cut sharply, while agencies that fail are rewarded with an increased percentage of the budget. Similarly, the crisis of public space is the result in large measure of the city's well-meaning attempt to make the crooked straight by continuously shifting resources away from basic services like sanitation (and until recently street police patrols) and into social services. Here, too, failure has been rewarded. In the midst of the current cutbacks and almost all-pervasive gloom, it is all the more important to tell the story of the Parks Department and the BIDs – examples of how government can be made to work. They demonstrate what might be possible if the rethinking and restructuring they represent is carried out on a wider scale.

Part V

The Future of the City: Space, Race, Class and Politics

22 Introduction
Philip Kasinitz

> It's like a jungle sometimes,
> It makes me wonder
> How I keep from going under.
> (Grandmaster Flash, "The Message", 1982)[1]

In the premodern world only a small minority lived in cities, yet the city and civilization were often considered synonymous. It was taken for granted that the city was the locus of culture. After the industrial revolution a large portion of the population of many societies began to live in cities. Yet the city came to be seen as problematic; it was an object of both sociological study and efforts at social reform.

In the United States today urbanism is once again a minority experience, in both the numerical and sociological senses of the term. About half of all Americans now live in suburbs, less than a third in cities.[2] Urban living is frequently viewed as outside the social mainstream, and in many cases the problems of "the cities" in contemporary America (and increasingly Western Europe) are perceived as being the problems of racial and ethnic minorities.[3] For many Americans the city has also come to symbolize chaos, social breakdown and the lack of civilization: "its like a jungle out there." Indeed at times the city has come to replace the frontier as a symbol of lawlessness, danger and marginality. We call middle-class people moving into poor and working-class areas "urban pioneers," with obvious, unpleasant implications about who gets to play the part of the new "savage Indians."

Early this century Simmel and Park delineated the effects of the breakdown of older forms of community. Along with the dangers of the mass society, they saw in the emerging urban order a new type of human freedom. Yet, in the world of which they wrote, few people were more than a generation or two away from rural or small-town life. If many early-twentieth-century urbanites felt themselves to be

disconnected from their roots and floating above the sources
of their traditions like figures in a Chagall painting, it should
also remembered that, as in a Chagall painting, those traditions remained real, powerful and visible. Today, several
generations further along the modernist trajectory, many
of those traditions have been substantially eroded. To be
sure, community is far from dead. The modern world has
produced entirely new bases for fraternization. Yet most of
these do not require common histories, deeply held common values or even – thanks to electronic communication
– face-to-face interaction. As Vidich and Hughey put it:

> *Caveat emptor* in the marketplace is extended to *caveat
> emptor* in interpersonal relations. Thus, our communities
> become networks of friends, relatives, associated, co-con-
> spirators, co-authors, and collaborators bound to each
> other without regard to spatial proximity, affective feel-
> ings, or life long acquaintance. The golden rule guiding
> each member of such communities is: to each according
> to their needs, tastes and interests and from each according
> to their usefulness.[4]

Group "identity" has become a central focus of late-twentieth-century political life, and the very notion that universalism
in human values is possible, or even desirable, now frequently
comes under attack. The sorts of group identities that have
come to the fore, such as ethnicity, are often those that
claim a deep primordial resonance. Yet the bases upon which
such "imagined communities" are constructed are increasingly symbolic and abstract, and connected only tenuously
with the conditions of people's daily lives.[5]

Recently it has become fashionable to speak of both the
changing physical form of cities and the changing social
bases of human communities as being part of a broader
shift in world culture towards a "postmodern" epoch. The
term postmodernism was first popularized in architecture,
where it referred to the rejection of austere, ahistorical,
Le Corbusier-style modernism in favor of an architecture
abounding in historical references, playfulness and a deep
sense of irony. The use of the term in social theory is a
good deal less precise. In general the condition of postmodernity is said to be marked by a shift away from "faith

in humanly engineered progress," as well as the rejection of the overarching "grand narratives," (particularly the privileged claims of scientific rationality) characteristic of modernity.[6] Analysts of postmodernity emphasize the persistence of a multiplicity of different world-views and the irreducibililty of human difference in the face of the supposedly homogenizing forces of modernism. In contrast to the universalism implied in both liberal individualism and historical materialism, postmodernists point to particularisms of race, gender, nationality and other nonrational forms of human association. "Otherness," they claim, can not be reduced to a mere epiphenomenon of deeper social trends. Further, postmodernists point to the autonomy of the cultural realm and the importance of images, symbols and modes of discourse in shaping the social order. "Aesthetic and cultural practices matter," David Harvey writes, "and the conditions of their production deserve the closest attention."[7] Yet postmodernists also point out the importance of eclecticism in contemporary culture, the juxtaposition of cultural forms from different traditions, brought together across the boundaries of space and time.

Others insist that these trends do not represent a radical break from the modern era. Indeed, they maintain that this so-called postmodernism, far from representing a discontinuity with the modern epoch, is only a description of the latest in the constant stream of change that modernism unleashed.[8] New technologies certainly have created new forms of spatial organization. Just as cities built for the automobile look different from those built for the street car, we should expect an "information economy" to produce different settlement patterns from an industrial economy. New patterns of social solidarity and new forms of community based on taste, interest and other superficial ties are indeed now possible and commonplace. Yet many argue that the forces that have made them so – mass markets, mass communication, the decline in traditional communities – remain quintessentially modern.

Whether we think of our current period as postmodern or simply a higher form of modernism, it does seem clear that the material conditions that gave birth to the spatial, cultural and political form of the modern city are becoming less relevant to how cities are built. Since the industrial revolution the primary force shaping the development of urban communities has been the requirements – social and political requirements as well as technological ones – of industrial production. As fewer and fewer people in the most developed societies actually work in industry,[9] we see the urban form in these societies becoming less and less constrained by these requirements.

We should, however, be careful not to attribute changes in urban social life solely to changes in technology – to slip into the popular cliché that what makes New York different from Los Angeles can be largely explained by the internal combustion engine. Although low-cost, private automotive transportation made possible the decentralized pattern of settlement common in late-twentieth-century North American cities, it did not make it inevitable. While Los Angeles and many other US cities virtually abandoned mass transportation in favor of private automobiles during the postwar era, Japanese and Scandinavian cities continued to invest in new and better mass transit. Since Japan and the Scandinavian countries obviously had the technological capacity to build automobiles and highways, the reasons that they *chose* to continue to build trains and streetcars, while Americans by in large did not, might be explained in terms of politics or perhaps culture, but not in terms of technology.

Once a new technology is adopted, however, it may have long-lasting social consequences. In the United States it is clear that those cities that experienced their largest growth during the heyday of industrial urbanism continue to bear the marks of their industrial pasts, even while they struggle to reorient themselves to new modes of production and new transportation technologies. Newer cities, in contrast, seem to lack not only the physical infrastructure of the dense industrial metropolis, but often lack much of the cultural and institutional infrastructure as well. This has political implications. For example, when comparing industrial (or formerly industrial) US cities such as Pittsburgh and Chicago with postindustrial cities such as Houston and San Diego, one is struck by the fact that the latter are largely devoid of those institutions – strong labor unions, political machines, public cultural and educational facilities – that facilitate, however imperfectly, the participation of working-class people in public life.

The declining significance of industrial production has also facilitated changes in the physical appearance of cities, and made possible the increasingly autonomous role that culture and consumption seem to play in the creation of urban landscapes. As Sharon Zukin notes,

> we sense a difference in how we organize what we see; how the visual consumption of space and time is both speeded up and abstracted from the logic of industrial production, forcing a dislocation of traditional spatial identities and their reconstitution along new lines.[10]

The most significant change in the postwar North American metropolis has been the suburbanization of so much of the population. To be sure, North American cities have always been strikingly decentralized compared with European, Asian or Latin American ones.[11] Yet for the first time the suburbs now seem to be eclipsing central cities economically and politically as well as demographically. While large metropolitan regions have continued to grow, the central places within them have become less important. In many cases jobs and commerce have all followed middle-class residents to suburbia. Corporate headquarters are now often located in small, secondary cities on the outer edge of the metropolitan area,[12] or on suburban campuses along the side of highways.

In his 1990 essay, "Megalopolis Unbound," reprinted in this volume as chapter 23, historian Robert Fishman traces the development of this highly decentralized urban form. In addition to the economic implications Fishman discusses, it should be noted that this new, diffuse pattern of settlement raises important political issues. The fact that middle-class Americans generally now live in different political jurisdictions from poor people has contributed to the erosion of both the fiscal ability and the political will of American cities to provide many public services.[13] Suburbanization means that it is far easier for middle-class people to turn their backs on the poor.

There are also cultural questions raised by the "city of time instead of space." What does it mean to have a culture without physical centers of face-to-face interaction? It may be that, in a world linked by electronic communication and computer-generated "virtual reality," physically central places are, or will soon become, superfluous. Yet it is also interesting to note that while the production and consumption functions of large cities have been effectively decentralized, many of the cultural functions have not. Suburban branches of department stores are common and successful; suburban branches of museums are rare, although in truth few people seem to miss them.

The spatial configuration of inner-city poverty has also changed in recent decades. Once characterized by the exploitation of industrial labor, urban poverty is now marked by the lack of it. As many of the poor have been "deprolitarianized,"[14] large parts of American central cities have been reduced to virtual reservations for redundant populations excluded from the new, information-oriented economy. In chapter 24 Loïc J. D. Wacquant explores these changes in the nature of the urban ghetto. A close collaborator of William Julius Wilson, Wacquant points to the development of a kind of "hyper-ghetto," a new social and spatial form, segregated by both class and race and marked by unprecedented levels of social isolation and violence.

Some have criticized the Wilson–Wacquant thesis for exaggerating the historical novelty of this type of community. The ghetto, they argue, has never had the "golden age" of a mutually supportive multiclass African-American community with which the new ghetto is implicitly compared.[15] Wilson (less so Wacquant) has also been criticized for paying too much attention to the behavioral characteristics of the American "underclass" and not enough to the historical conditions that created it. Yet however we understand its origins, few would deny that the spatial concentration of poverty Wacquant discusses has imposed tremendous hardships on the poor and changed the lives of many other urban Americans. "The Ghetto, the State and the New Capitalist Economy" was originally published in *Dissent* in 1989. The author has added a postscript reflecting on the aftermath of the Los Angeles riot and the 1992 presidential election.

Finally, it should be noted that the decline of central places presumed by both Fishman and Wacquant has not been universal. Many large, central cities, including those some of those struggling to adjust industrial infrastructures to the needs of a postindustrial economy, have shown surprising resilience. Of particular importance is the role that some large cities – New York, London, Tokyo, arguably Miami – have come to play as centers of international commerce and migration.[16] On the other hand this prosperity of "world cities" does not seem to trickle down – indeed their wealth seems to lend itself less to redistribution than was the case in industrial cities.

Contemporary writers rarely address "the city" as a singular entity. Whereas Simmel and Wirth saw the city, however fragmented, as a unitary phenomenon, today's urban sociologists address it in pieces: either as distinct sorts of geographic forms – the ghetto, the suburb, the gentrified neighborhood – or as a locale for "urban" social problems – "urban education," "urban poverty," "urban crime." Italian social theorist Franco Ferrarotti is a welcome exception. In his 1992 essay, "Civil Society as a Polyarchic Form: The City," reprinted in this volume as chapter 25, he takes us back to the question of the city as a distinctive social and political construct. Although drawing primarily on Western European examples, his rethinking of these basic questions reflects many of the same trends examined by Fishman and Wacquant.

Notes

1. Grandmaster Flash, "The Message" Copyright 1982 by Sugar Hill Music Ltd.
2. William Schneider, "The Suburban Century Begins," *The Atlantic*, July 1992, pp. 33–9. Original source of statistics: the 1990 US Census.
3. Indeed in the United States the term "urban" has increasingly come to be used, in phrases such as "urban youth" and even "urban dance music," as a euphemism for African-American.
4. Arthur Vidich and Michael Hughey, "Fraternization and Rationality in Global Perspective," in *Politics, Culture and Society*, vol. 2, no. 2 (winter 1988), p. 246.

5. The term "imagined communities" is borrowed from Benedict
   Anderson's study of nationalism. Anderson points out the striking contradiction between the appearance and reality of the nation
   state. Nations all claim to be ancient, yet we now they are quite
   modern; national identity appears universal yet is based on particular criteria; and nationalism is politically powerful even while
   being philosophically vacuous. Yet Anderson would disagree with
   Vidich and Hughey's implication that "imagined communities,"
   such as nations and ethnic groups, are in any sense less "real"
   than those grounded in face-to-face communication. See Benedict
   Anderson, *Imagined Communities* (New York: Verso, 1983).
6. Anthony Giddens, *The Consequences of Modernity.* Stanford
   University Press, 1990), p. 2. See also, for example, Jean-
   Francois Lyotard, *The Post Modern Condition.* (Minneapolis:
   University of Minnesota, 1985); Sharon Zukin, *Landscapes of
   Power: From Detroit to Disney World* (Berkeley: University of
   California Press, 1991); David Harvey, *The Condition of Post
   Modernity* (New York: Basil Blackwell, 1989); and Frederick
   Jameson, "Postmodernism, or the Cultural Logic of Late Capitalism," *New Left Review*, vol. 146, pp. 53–92.
7. Harvey, *op. cit.*, p. 355.
8. See Anthony Giddens, *op. cit.*, Marshall Berman, *All that is Solid
   Melts into Air* (New York: Simon and Schuster, 1982).
9. If only because the actual production process has been ex-
   ported to other parts of the world. Indeed it could be argued
   the true successors to Dickens' Londoners are now to be found
   in Lagos, Jakarta and Tiajuana.
10. Sharon Zukin, "Postmodern Urban Landscapes: Mapping Cul-
    ture and Power," in Scott Lash and Jonathan Friedman (eds),
    Modernity and Identity (Cambridge: Basil Blackwell, 1992), p.
    221.
11. See, for a history of US suburbanization, Kenneth Jackson,
    Crabgrass Frontier (New York: Oxford University Press, 1985).
12. Hence these places are sometimes dubbed "edge cities".
13. This is further exacerbated by the political complexity of over-
    lapping administrative units that characterize the politics of many
    large metropolitan areas.
14. See Thomas J. Sugrue, "The Structures of Urban Poverty: The
    Reorganization of Space and Work in Three Periods of American
    History," in Michael Katz (ed.), *The Underclass Debate: Views from
    History* (Princeton University Press, 1993); Williams Julius Wilson,
    The Truly Disadvantaged (University of Chicago Press, 1987).
15. See Katz, *op. cit.*
16. See Saksia Saasen, *The Global City: New York, London Tokyo*
    (Princeton University Press, 1991); John Hull Mollonkopf and
    Manuel Castells (eds), *Dual City: Restructuring New York* (New
    York: Russell Sage Foundation: 1991); Alejandro Portes and
    Alex Stepick, *City on the Edge: The Transformation of Miami*
    (Berkeley: University of California Press, 1993).

23 Megalopolis Unbound*
Robert Fishman

"The big city," Frank Lloyd Wright announced prophetically in 1923, "is no longer modern." Although his forecast of a new age of urban decentralization was ignored by his contemporaries, we can now see that Wright and a few other thinkers of his day understood the fragility of the great behemoth – the centralized industrial metropolis – which then seemed to embody and define the modernity of the 20th century.

These capital cities of America's industrial revolution, with New York and Chicago at their head, were built to last. Their very form, as captured during the 1920s in the famous diagrams by Robert E. Park and Ernest W. Burgess of the Chicago School of sociology, seemed to possess a logic that was permanent. At the core was the "central business district," with its skyscraper symbols of local wealth, power, and sophistication; surrounding the core was the factory zone, the dense region of reinforced concrete factories and crowded workers' housing; and finally, a small ring of affluent middle-class suburbs occupied the outskirts. These were the triumphant American cities, electric with opportunity and excitement, and as late as the 1920s they were steadily draining the countryside of its population.

But modernism is a process of constant upheaval and self-destruction. Just when the centralized metropolis was at its zenith, powerful social and economic forces were combining to create an irresistible movement toward decentralization, tearing asunder the logic that had sustained the big city and distributing its prized functions over whole regions. The urban history of the last half-century is a record of this process.

Superficially, the process might be called "the rise of the suburb." The term "suburb," however, inevitably suggests

---
* Reprinted from *The Wilson Quarterly* (Winter 1990).

the affluent and restricted "bedroom communities" that first took shape around the turn of the century in New York's Scarsdale, the North Shore of Chicago, and other locales on the edge of the 19th-century metropolis. These genteel retreats from urban life established the model of the single-family house on its own landscaped grounds as the ideal middle-class residence, just as they established the roles of commuter and housewife as social models for upper-middle-class men and women. But Scarsdale and its kind were limited zones of privilege that strictly banned almost all industry and commerce and excluded not only the working class but even the majority of the less-affluent middle class. The traditional suburb therefore remained an elite enclave, completely dependent on the central city for jobs and essential services.

Since 1945, however, the relationship between the urban core and the suburban periphery has undergone a startling transformation – especially during the past two decades. Where suburbia was once an exclusive refuge for a small elite, U.S. Census figures show that 45 percent of the American population is now suburban, up from only 23 percent in 1950. Allowing for anomalies in the Census Bureau's methods, it is almost certain that a majority of Americans live in the suburbs. About one third remain in the central cities. Even more dramatic has been the exodus of commerce and industry from the cities. By 1980, 38 percent of the nation's workers commuted to their jobs from suburb-to-suburb, while only half as many made the stereotypical suburb-to-city trek.

Manufacturing has led the charge from the cities; the industrial park, as it is so bucolically dubbed, has displaced the old urban factory district as the headquarters of American manufacturing. Commerce has also joined the exodus. Where suburbanites once had little choice but to travel to down-town stores for most of their clothing and household goods, suburban shopping malls and stores now ring up the majority of the nation's retail sales.

During the last two decades, the urban peripheries have even outpaced the cores in that last bastion of downtown economic clout, office employment. More than 57 percent of the nation's office space is now located outside the cen-

tral cities. And the landscaped office parks and research
centers that dot the outlying highways and interstates have
become the home of the most advanced high-technology
laboratories and factories, the national centers of business
creativity and growth. *Inc.* magazine, which tracks the
nation's emerging industries, reported in a survey earlier
this year that "growth is in the 'edge cities.'" Topping its
list of "hot spots" were such unlikely locales as Manchester-
Nashua, New Hampshire; West Palm Beach, Florida; and
Raleigh-Durham, North Carolina.

The complex economy of the former suburbs has now
reached a critical mass, as specialized service enterprises
of every kind, from hospitals equipped with the latest CAT
scanners to gourmet restaurants to corporate law firms, have
established themselves on the fringes. In all of these ways,
the peripheries have replaced the urban cores as the
heartlands of our civilization. These multi-functional late-
20th-century "suburbs" can no longer be comprehended in
the terms of the old bedroom communities. They have become a new kind of city.

The "new city of the 20th century" is not some fantastic
city of towers out of Fritz Lang's celluloid *Metropolis* (1926)
or the visionary architect Paoli Soleri's honeycombed
Arcology. (Soleri's plan for a new city in the Arizona desert
captivated futurists during the 1960s; the stunted model
city that resulted is now a bizarre tourist attraction.) It is,
rather, the familiar decentralized world of highways and
tract houses, shopping malls, and office parks that Americans have built for themselves since 1945. As exemplified
by such areas as the Silicon Valley in northern California,
Route 128 outside Boston, the Route One corridor between
Princeton and New Brunswick, New Jersey, Du Page County
west of Chicago, the Route 285 area north of Atlanta, the
northern Virginia district that surrounds Tysons Corner,
or the immense region that stretches along the southern
California coast from Los Angeles to San Diego, the new
city includes the most dynamic elements in our national
economy. It flourishes in the rocky soil of New Hampshire, the broad prairies beyond Minneapolis, the rainy
shores of Puget Sound and the desert outside Tucson.
From coast to coast, the symbol of this new city is not

the jagged skyscraper skyline of the 1920s metropolis but the network of superhighways as seen from the air, crowded in all directions, uniting a whole region into a vast super-city.

Familiar as we all are with the features of the new city, most of us do not recognize how radically it departs from the cities of old. The most obvious difference is scale. The basic unit of the new city is not the street measured in blocks but the "growth corridor" stretching 50 to 100 miles. Where the leading metropolises of the early 20th century – New York, London, or Berlin – covered perhaps 100 square miles, the new city routinely encompasses two to three *thousand* square miles. Within such "urban regions," each element is correpondingly enlarged. "Planned unit developments" of cluster-housing are as large as townships; office parks are set amid hundreds of acres of landscaped grounds; and malls dwarf some of the downtowns they have replaced.

These massive units, moreover, are arrayed along the beltways and "growth corridors" in seemingly random order, without the strict distinctions between residential, commercial, and industrial zones that shaped the old city. A subdivision of $300 000 single-family houses outside Denver may sit next to a telecommunications research-and-production complex, and a new mall filled with boutiques once found only on the great shopping streets of Europe may – and indeed *does* – rise amid Midwestern corn fields.

The new city, furthermore, lacks what gave shape and meaning to every urban form of the past: a dominant single core and definable boundaries. At most, it contains a multitude of partial centers, or "edge cities," more-or-less unified clusters of malls, office developments, and entertainment complexes that rise where major highways cross or converge. As *Washington Post* writer Joel Garreau has observed, Tysons Corner, perhaps the largest American edge city, boasts more office space than downtown Miami, yet it remains only one of 13 edge cities – including Rockville–Gaithersburg, Maryland, and Rosslyn–Balston, Virginia – in the Washington D.C. region.

Even some old downtowns have been reduced to "first among equals" among the edge cities of their regions. Atlanta has one of the most rapidly growing downtowns in the country. Yet between 1978 and 1983 – the years of its accelerated growth – the downtown's share of regional office space shrank from 34 percent to 26 percent. Midtown Manhattan is the greatest of all American downtowns, but northern New Jersey now has more office space.

If no one can find the center of the new city, its borders are even more elusive.

Low-density development tends to gain an inevitable momentum, as each extension of a region's housing and economy into previously rural areas becomes the base for further expansion. When one successful area begins to fill up, land values and taxes rise explosively, pushing the less affluent even farther out. During the past two decades, as Manhattan's "back offices" moved 30 miles west into northern New Jersey along interstates 78 and 80, new subdivisions and town-house communities began sprouting 40 miles farther west along these growth corridors in the Pocono Mountains of eastern Pennsylvania. "By the time we left [New Jersey]," one new resident of eastern Pennsylvania told the *New York Times*, "there were handyman specials for $150 000 you wouldn't put your dog in." Now such formerly depressed and relatively inexpensive areas as Pennsylvania's Lehigh Valley are gaining population, attracting high-tech industries and office employment, and thus stimulating further dispersion.

Baltimore and Washington, D.C., once separated by mile after mile of farms and forests, are now joined by an agglomeration of office parks, shopping strips, and housing. Census Bureau officials have given up attempting to draw a statistical boundary between the two metropolitan areas and have proposed combining them into a single consolidated region for statistical purposes. Indeed, as the automobile gives rise to a complex pattern of multidirectional travel that largely by-passes the old central cities, the very concept of "center" and "periphery" becomes obsolete.

Although a few prophets like Wright foresaw the downfall of the old city, no one imagined the form of the new. Instead, it was built up piecemeal, as a result of millions of uncoordinated decisions made by housing developers, shopping-mall operators, corporate executives, highway engineers and, not least, the millions of Americans who saved and sacrificed to buy single-family homes in the expanding suburbs. The new city's construction has been so rapid and so unforeseen that we lack even a commonly-accepted name for what we have created. Or, rather, we have too many names: exurb, spread city, urban village, megalopolis, outtown, sprawl, slurb, the burbs, nonplace urban field, polynucleated city, and (my own coinage) technoburb.

Not urban, not rural, not suburban, but possessing elements of all three, the new city eludes all the conventional terminology of the urban planner and the historian. Yet it is too important to be left in conceptual limbo. The success or failure of the new city will affect the quality of life of the majority of Americans well into the 21st century. In a few scattered locales today, one can discern the promise of a decentralized city that fulfills its residents' basic hopes for comfortable homes in sylvan settings with easy access to good schools, good jobs, and recreational facilities of many kinds. More ambitiously, one might hope for a decentralized civilization that finally overcomes the old antithesis of city and countryside, that fulfills in daily life the profound cultural need for an environment that combines the machine and nature in a new unity.

But the dangers of the new city are perhaps more obvious than the promise. The immense speed and scale of development across the nation threaten to annihilate the natural environment of entire regions, leaving the tranquility and natural beauty that Americans seek in the new city perpetually retreating another 10 exits down the interstate. The movement of urban functions to an environment never designed for them has produced the anomaly of urban-style crowding and congestion in a decentralized setting. Through greed and ignorance we could destroy the very things that inspired the new city and build instead a degenerate urban form that is too congested to be efficient, too chaotic to be beautiful, and too dispersed to possess the diversity and vitality of a great city.

The new city is still under construction. Like all new urban types, its early form is necessarily raw and chaotic. The real test of the new city as a carrier of civilization will come when the first flush of hectic building slows down and efforts to redesign and reconstruct begin, as they have in the old downtowns today. But before we can improve the new urban world we are building we need to understand it.

Perhaps the best way to grasp the innovations of the new city is to contrast it with the older metropolis. Lewis Mumford (b. 1895), 20th-century America's greatest urbanist and one of our most clear-sighted prophets of decentralization, expressed this contrast succinctly in his classic work of 1938, *The Culture of Cities*. There he defined "the metropolis of old" as "a single center" that becomes "the focal point of all regional advantages." In the new decentralized city, however, "the whole region becomes open for settlement."

The centralized industrial metropolis that flourished during the 19th and early 20th centuries was the last in a series of urban forms that go back ultimately to Ur and Babylon in the ancient Middle East. At its heart, the traditional city was an attempt to solve the problem of slow and expensive transportation by concentrating people and resources at a single point. Occasionally, this meant locating the city where trade routes crossed or local markets could be established. More often it favored riverside and seaside locations that lent themselves to the construction of a port.

The coming of the railroads during the 19th century amplified the natural advantages of cities like New York and Chicago and transformed them into national centers. Toward the end of the century, as major trunk rail lines were supplemented by similarly converging networks of streetcar and subway lines, the characteristic pattern of the great metropolis emerged: a city formed by its transportation system into a centralized pattern of a hub and spokes. As Mumford argued, such a pattern necessarily concentrated "regional advantages" at the hub and placed all other locations in the region at a disadvantage. A familiar urban ecology emerged, composed of concentric rings with the central business district at the core, the factory zone, and then the suburban ring.

Moralists regarded these crowded "monster metropolises" with horror, but concentration worked. The clustering of office buildings in a central business district multiplied the opportunities for face-to-face communication and the exchange of vital information, opportunities which gave the big-city businessman a significant advantage over his small-town counterparts. Similarly, the subways and trolleys that delivered people from around the region to a single downtown created the dense mass of patrons that made possible such urban institutions as department stores, vaudeville houses, movie palaces and concert halls, museums, sports stadiums, and big-city newspapers.

The complex tangles of branch rail lines that served the factory zone gave enterprises located there a significant advantage over those anywhere else in the region. The factory zone was also the home of a large skilled and unskilled workforce which only those enterprises within the zone could tap. By the 1890s it thus became the natural environment for all manufacturing firms attempting to become national enterprises.

Perhaps the group best served by metropolitan concentration was the middle-class suburban elite, for they enjoyed all the economic benefits of the great city while living in a quiet, leafy-green, smoke-free environment at its edge.

By the 1920s the centralized industrial city had reached its zenith; at the time, only a few lonely prophets noticed that a series of separate and uncoordinated technological innovations were converging to undermine the special advantages of the central city. As Mumford suggested, these innovations all had in common the replacement of networks of communication that focused advantages on the core with networks that distributed them equally over a region.

The great model of such a network was the road system. Although early highway engineers attempted to design major roads on the hub-and-spokes model of the railroads, automobile owners soon discovered that the radical innovation of the roads was to open up to settlement areas remote from rail lines. In a rail-dominated metropolis, most people in cities or suburbs lived no farther than a 15-minute walk from a train or trolley stop; with an automobile, people found that they could fill in the empty spaces between the spokes of the regional rail system without condemning themselves to a kind of exile.

The effect of trucking on industrial location was nearly as dramatic. First used extensively during the 1920s, trucks made it possible for factory owners to leave the crowded streets of the industrial zone for cheaper land on the periphery without sacrificing timely pickups and deliveries from other firms that remained in the city.

Not surprisingly, it was in Los Angeles that these possibilities were first recognized. As late as 1925 Los Angeles was a relatively centralized city organized around a lively and prosperous downtown served by a highly-efficient system of public transportation. The big red streetcars of the Pacific Electric system traveled over more than 1000 miles of track connecting the downtown to even the most remote parts of what was then a vast region of farms and citrus groves. But when downtown traffic reached intolerable levels during the mid-1920s the city was presented with two opposing visions of its future: expand public transportation, or, as the Automobile Club of Southern California proposed, create a massive new grid of roads.

In the debate among the city's civic and business leaders, the issue was put with surprising clarity. Improving public transportation would save the downtown, but it would limit residential development to the narrow rail corridors of the Pacific Electric System. Los Angeles would thus come to resemble eastern cities of the time, with most people living in multi-family dwellings close to public transportation. A new road system, by contrast, might doom the downtown but it would put virtually every acre of land in the 900 square miles of the Los Angeles region within a few blocks of a major road. That would open the whole region to low-density settlement.

Since many of the Los Angeles elite were heavily involved in real-estate speculation, it was never much of a contest. Without hesitation, they chose to sacrifice the downtown and persuaded the citizenry to go along. "Business is pointing the way out of the intolerable congestion situation in our downtown areas," the influential Los Angeles City Club declared in a 1926 report. "Branch banks are going out to the people, factories are seeking outside locations . . . and some of our retail merchants are building, or have established branch stores in outlying sections." In a referendum that year, voters overwhelmingly approved a massive bond issue for new road construction and rejected a modest proposal to improve the streetcar system.

By the mid-1930s, both the Los Angeles downtown and the public transportation system that sustained it were already deteriorating, as the city established what was then a unique pattern of settlement. The downtown was supplanted by many smaller automobile-based centers such as the "Miracle Mile" along Wilshire Boulevard (built, like most of the city's other major streets, with funds from the 1926 bond issue), while the movie studios, the new aircraft factories, and other industry scattered throughout the region. Los Angeles thus established an alternate, decentralized form for the American city based on the automobile and the single-family house.

As Los Angeles demonstrated, transportation was the crucial innovation. But roads and autos could not have achieve their full revolutionary impact without the creation of several other important new networks of decentralization: electricity, telecommunications, mass-market retailing, and new modes of corporate management.

Consider electricity. Until the coming of "giant power" (i.e. regional electricity networks) during the 1920s, utility service rarely extended beyond the metropolis. Thereafter, far-flung homeowners and industry enjoyed the same access to reliable electrical power as those at the core.

The telephone network was the harbinger of the great series of inventions – radio, television, computers, fax machines – that increasingly substituted electronic for face-to-face communication, thus reducing the need for meetings and informal contacts downtown.

The 1920s also saw the fruition of new techniques of mass production, which flooded the nation with consumer goods. This new plenty created the possibility of multiplying the number of retail outlets, thus breaking the monopoly of the great downtown stores. No longer would suburbanites have to go "downtown" to enjoy a wide selection of goods.

Meanwhile, corporate managers had developed techniques (and bureaucracies) that allowed them to supervise a variety of plants at one time, all of them from a great distance. Factories were freed to locate far from the cities, where land and labor were cheaper.

These new networks undermined the functional underpinnings of metropolitan centralization. But the new city

might have emerged slowly and partially if it had not found
an unexpected ally: the American government.

In Europe, governments fearful of losing precious farm
land to the encroaching cities have severely restricted
decentralization wherever they could. As early as 1938
the British government prohibited London and the other
large British cities from expanding beyond their existing boundaries. A decade later it created permanent "green-
belts" of farm and park land around the cities, including
an impressive five-mile-wide Metropolitan Greenbelt which
still rings London. (Paris, on the other hand, is ringed by
a Red Belt, so called because its working-class residents
consistently vote Communist. This reflects another unique
quality of European development: The affluent middle class
generally prefers urban to suburban living.) In the United
States, however, Washington, as well as state and local governments, indefatigably promoted expansion. Government "planning" was largely unconscious and unintended, but that did
not lessen its effects. Between 1930 and 1960, state intervention in four different arenas profoundly affected the shape
of the nation's cities:

First, *Housing.* Although the American preference for
single-family suburban houses was well-established by
the 1920s, it took the New Deal's Federal Housing Administration (1934) to reform the nation's rickety system of
mortgage finance and, ultimately, put the American dream
house within reach of millions of citizens. As historian
Kenneth Jackson has shown, FHA regulations also funneled
mortgage money to newly built suburbs, considered good
credit risks, while virtually starving the cities of residential
construction loans.

Second, *Defense Industries.* During World War II, the new
factories built to manufacture synthetics, alloys, aircraft,
and other products under the auspices of the Defense Plants
Corporation were rarely located in the central cities. For
example, Nassau County, Long Island, future site of the
archetypal postwar suburb of Levittown, became the East
Coast's center for aircraft production during the war, as
Grumman, Republic, and other manufacturers opened plants
there. Unlike the old urban factories, they were built on a
single level on great tracts of land, in accordance with new

ideas of industrial efficiency. Almost overnight these new factories gave the metropolitan peripheries and decentralized sunbelt cities a substantial industrial base on which they could build during the postwar period.

Third, *Highway Construction*. From the beginning, highways were regarded as a public responsibility, entitled to subsidies with tax dollars, while the rail system was not. Rail freight (and often mass transit as well) remained under the control of private corporations. After 1920, the owners were increasingly unable or unwilling to improve their services to attract customers. Highway engineers presided over one of the most massive construction efforts in history, culminating after 1958 in the 44 000 miles of the federal interstate highway system built at a cost of $108 billion. While these Main Streets of the emerging new cities flourished, the rail lines that served the downtowns stagnated or declined.

Fourth, *Local Government*. After the turn of the century, city after city failed to annex its suburbs because of suburban resistance. As a result, cities lost the tax base of the most prosperous and rapidly expanding areas of the region. And since zoning in the American system is essentially a matter of local control, the power to regulate new development passed to the hundreds of suburban governments, which had little interest in restraining growth to create a balanced metropolitan region. Developers learned they could play one small local planning board off another, escaping all control. As the developer Sam Lefrak observed, "There is no zoning: only deals."

Relieved of the task of delivering the full range of services required by a great city, suburbs could tailor public spending to the specific needs of their constituents. With surprising speed, suburban public school systems developed into formidable enterprises, soon rivaling and then surpassing the once-dominant big-city schools.

Without anybody intending for it to happen, all of these seemingly unrelated forces converged to generate enormous momentum behind the great tide of decentralization that washed over the American metropolis after 1945. The tide has continued relentlessly, through booms and recessions, under Democratic and Republican administrations, until the old industrial city became, if not an extinct species, at least a highly endangered one.

The first significant sign was a drop in population. Between 1950 and 1960, all of the large, established cities lost people. Boston, the worst case, shrank by 13 percent, while its suburbs gained 17 percent. New York and Chicago lost less than two percent each, but their suburbs gained over 70 percent. To these blows were added shrinkage of the industrial base. Between 1947 and 1967, the 16 largest and oldest central cities lost an average of 34 000 manufacturing jobs each, while their suburbs gained an average of 87 000. This trend continued through the 1970s, as the cities suffered the elimination of from 25 percent (Minneapolis) to 40 percent (Philadelphia) of the manufacturing jobs that remained.

Building on their growing base of population and jobs, suburban entrepreneurs during the 1950s and 1960s began transforming the new city into a self-sufficient world. "We don't go downtown anymore," became the new city's motto. Shopping centers displaced downtown department stores; small merchants and repairmen deserted Main Street for stores "along the highway" or folded up shop under the competitive pressure of the growing national chain stores. Even cardiologists and corporate lawyers moved their offices closer to their customers.

By the 1970s and 1980s, the new city found itself at the top of a whole range of national and even international trends. The movement from snowbelt to sunbelt meant a shift toward urban areas that had been "born decentralized" and organized on new-city principles. The new city, moreover, moved quickly to dominance in the most rapidly expanding sections of the industrial economy – electronics, chemicals, pharmaceuticals, and aircraft – leaving the old city with such sunset industries as textiles, iron and steel, and automobiles.

Finally, during the 1970s, the new city successfully challenged the old downtowns in the last area of their supremacy, office employment. The "office park" became the locale of choice for many businesses, new and old. Jaded New Yorkers looked on in stunned disbelief as one major corporation after another pulled up stakes and departed for former commuter towns like Stamford, Connecticut, or more distant sunbelt locations. By the 1980s, even social scientists could not ignore the fact that the whole terminology of "suburb" and "central city," deriving from the era of the industrial metropolis, had become obsolete. As Mumford had predicted, the single center had lost its dominance.

But are the sprawling regions *cities*? Judged by the standards of the centralized metropolis, the answer is no. As I have suggested, this "city" lacks any definable borders, a center or a periphery, or a clear distinction between residential, industrial, and commercial zones. Instead, shopping malls, research and production facilities, and corporate headquarters all seem scattered amid a chaos of subdivisions, apartment complexes, and condominiums. It is easy to understand why urban planners and social scientists trained in the clear functional logic of the centralized metropolis can see only disorder in these "nonplace urban fields," or why ordinary people use the word "sprawl" to describe their own neighborhoods.

Nevertheless, I believe that the new city has a characteristic structure – one that departs radically not only from the old metropolis but from all cities of the past.

To grasp this structure we must return to the prophetic insights of Frank Lloyd Wright. From the 1920s until his death in 1959, Wright was preoccupied with his plan for an ideal decentralized American city which he called Broadacres. Although many elements of the plan were openly utopian – he wished, for example, to ensure that every American would have access to at least an acre of land so that all could reap the economic and psychological benefits that he associated with part-time farming – Wright also had a remarkable insight into the highway-based world that was developing around him. Above all he understood the consequences of a city based on a grid of highways rather than the hub-and-spokes of the older city. Instead of a single privileged center, there would be a multitude of crossings, no one of which could assume priority. And the grid would be boundless by its very nature, capable of unlimited extension in all directions.

Such a grid, as it indeed developed, did not allow for the emergence of an "imperial" metropolis to monopolize the life of a region. For Wright, this meant that the family home would be freed from its fealty to the city and allowed to emerge as the real center of American life. As he put it, "The true center, (the only centralization allowable) in Usonian democracy, is the individual Usonian house." (Usonia was Wright's name for the United States).

In the plans for Broadacres – a city he said would be "everywhere or nowhere" – Wright foresaw what I believe to be the essential element in the structure of the new city: a megalopolis based on *time* rather than space.

Even the largest of the old "big cities" had a firm identity in space. The big city had a center as its basic point of orientation – the Loop, Times Square – and also a boundary. Starting from the center, sooner or later one reached the edge of the city.

In the new city, however, there is no single center. Instead, as Wright suggested, each family home has become the central point for its members. Families create their own "cities" out of the destinations they can reach (usually traveling by car) in a reasonable length of time. Indeed, distance in the new cities is generally measured in terms of time rather than blocks or miles. The supermarket is 10 minutes away. The nearest shopping mall is 30 minutes in another direction, and one's job 40 minutes away by yet another route. *The pattern formed by these destinations represents "the city" for that particular family or individual.* The more varied one's destinations, the richer and more diverse is one's personal "city." The new city is a city *à la carte*.

It can be seen as composed of three overlapping networks, representing the three basic categories of destinations that define each person's city. These are the household network; the network of consumption; and the network of production.

The household network is composed of places that are part of family and personal life. For a typical household of two parents and two children, this network is necessarily oriented around childrearing – and it keeps parents scurrying frantically in station wagons and minivans from one place to another. Its set of destinations include the homes of the children's playmates (which may be down the street or scattered around a country), the daycare center, the schools, a church or synagogue, community centers, and the homes of the parents' friends. Although this network is generally more localized than the other two, it is almost always wider than the traditional urban neighborhood.

The two-parent family with children is the archetypical new-city household, but, especially since 1970, the new city has made a place for others. For single or divorced people, single parents, young childless couples or older "empty nest" couples, widows and widowers, the new city offers a measure of familiarity and security that many find lacking in the central city. Its housing is increasingly diverse. No longer confined to single-family homes, it now includes apartment towers, town homes and condominiums, and various kinds of retirement housing, from golf-oriented communities to nursing homes. There are more places to socialize. The same mall that caters essentially to families on weekends and evenings may also serve as an informal community center for older people in the morning, while its bars and restaurants play host to a lively singles scene after the stores close.

The network of consumption – Mallopolis, in economist James Millar's phrase – comprises essentially the shopping centers and malls which, as Wright predicted, have located themselves at the strategic crossroads of the highway system. It also includes movie theaters, restaurants, health clubs, playing fields and other recreational facilities, and perhaps a second home 30 to 100 miles away.

Although this network serves much the same function as the old downtown, it is scattered, and each consumer is free to work out his particular set of preferences from the vast menu of offerings presented by Mallopolis.

Finally, there is the network of production. It includes the place of employment of one or both spouses. It also includes the suppliers – from computer-chip manufacturers to janitorial services – which these enterprises rely upon. Information comes instantaneously from around the world while raw materials, spare parts, and other necessities are trucked in from the firms that cluster along nearby highways.

This network minimizes the traditional distinction between the white-collar world of administration and the blue-collar world of production. Both functions co-exist in virtually every "executive office park." Its most successful enterprises are those where research and development and specialized techniques of production are intimately intertwined: pharmaceuticals, for example, or electronics. Conversely, its most routinized labor can be found in the so-called "back-offices," data-processing centers that perform tasks once done at a downtown corporate headquarters.

Each of these networks has its own spatial logic. For example, primary schools are distributed around the region in response to the school-age population; shopping malls reflect population density, wealth, and the road system; large firms locate where their workers and their suppliers can easily reach them. But because the networks overlap, the pattern on the ground is one of juxtaposition and interpenetration. Instead of the logical division of functions of the old metropolis, one finds a post-modern, post-urban collage.

In some places, a particularly active locale, like Tysons Corner, in Fairfax County, Virginia, may draw together elements from different networks – shopping malls and offices – to form an approximation of an old downtown. But the logic of the new city generally confounds that kind of concentration. Such areas immediately become points of especially bad traffic congestion, denying the ready access that is a hallmark of the new city. (It may be poetic justice that the leaders of the American Automobile Association, patron saint of the suburban motorist, have become so frustrated by the bumper-to-bumper traffic in the area around Tysons Corner that they have decided to move the AAA headquarters to the relatively open roads of Orlando, Florida.) Tysons Corner is an exception. In general, the new city allows and requires each citizen to make connections among the three networks – to make a city – on his own. The new city has no center or boundary because it does not need them.

Women have been a not-so-hidden force behind the new city's economic success. Since 1957, the proportion of married women aged 27 to 54 with jobs has grown from 33 percent to 68 percent. More than half of all women with children aged three years or younger are now employed outside the home. Much of the economic life of the new city, especially with its concentration on retail trade and back-office data processing, would be impossible without these new workers. Indeed, the presence of employment opportunities so close to home – convenient, with decent pay and flexible schedules – is surely responsible for part of the remarkable influx of married women into the work force (although the plentiful supply of workers could just as easily be said to have attracted employers). The outcome is more than a little ironic, considering the fact that the bedroom suburb had originally been designed to separate women from the corruptions of the world of work.

The new city thus decisively breaks with the older suburban pattern that restricted married middle-class women with children to a life of neighborhood-oriented domesticity. Women still work closer to home than men do, and they still bear most of the responsibility for childcare and housekeeping, but, in contrast to the old metropolis, the economic and spatial structure of the new city tends to equalize gender roles.

Indeed, one can argue that the new city has largely been built on the earnings of two-income families and thus reflects their needs more closely than did either the urban core or the traditional bedroom suburb. One large housing developer, Scarborough Corporation of Marlton, New Jersey, found that 72 percent of its customers during the mid-1980s were two-income couples, compared with less than 30 percent a decade earlier. Accordingly, the firm redesigned some of its houses, substituting a "study-office" for the "sewing room," scaling down the formal living room and enlarging the family room, providing more pantry space to cut down on trips to the supermarket, and selecting building materials to minimize maintenance.

In other ways, both trivial and important, the new city has responded to the changing character of families with more flexibility than critics of "the suburbs" are willing to admit. Encouraged by women's groups and planning boards, some developers have set aside space for day-care centers in new office complexes. There are extended school days for "latch-key" children and, during the summer, recreation programs. And only in the new city can one find the extensive array of Pizza Huts, Sizzler's, Denny's, and other inexpensive "family-style" restaurants which, though they may not delight Julia Child, are many a parent's salvation at the end of a hard day of the office.

When Frank Lloyd Wright envisioned Broadacre City, he failed to consider the role of the old centralized industrial cities in the new world of the future. He simply assumed that the old cities would disappear once the conditions that had created them were gone. The reality has not been so simple. Just as the industrial metropolis grew up around the older mercantile city, so the new city of our time has surrounded the old metropolis. What was once the sole center is now one point of concentration among many.

In general, the skyscraper cores of the central cities have adapted to this change and prospered. Even a decentralized region needs a "headquarters," a place of high status and high rents where the movers-and-shakers can rub shoulders and meet for power lunches. By contrast, the old factory zones have not found a function in the new environment. As a result, the central city has reverted to what it was before industrialization: a site for high-level administration and luxury consumption, where some of the wealthiest members of society live in close proximity to many of the poorest.

The recent boom in downtown office construction should not conceal the fact that downtown prosperity rests on a much narrower base than it did in its heyday during the 1920s. Most of the retail trade has fled to the malls; the grand old movie palaces and many of the nightspots are gone. Only the expansion of corporate headquarters, law firms, banks and investment houses, advertising agencies, and other corporate and governmental services has kept the downtown towers filled, and even in these fields there have been major leakages of back-office employment to the new city. Nevertheless, this employment base has enabled most core areas to retain an array of specialized shops, restaurants, and cultural activities unequalled in their region. This in turn encourages both the gentrification of surrounding residential neighborhoods and the "renaissance" of the core as a tourist and convention center.

Yet only blocks away from a thriving core like Baltimore's Inner Harbor one can usually find extensive poverty, decay, de-industrialization, and abandonment that stretches out to encompass the old factory zone. The factory zones have found no new role. Their working-class populations have largely followed the factories to the new city, leaving a supply of cheap, old housing which has attracted poor black, Hispanic, and other minority migrants with no other place to go. If the industrial city in its prime brought people together with jobs, cheap housing in the inner city now lures the jobless to those areas where employment prospects are dimmest. The old factory zone is thus doubly disadvantaged: the jobless have moved in, the jobs out.

Public transportation retains its traditional focus on the core, but the inner-city population generally lacks the education to compete for the high-level jobs that are available there. By contrast, the new city usually has an abundance of entry-level jobs, many of them already going begging as the supply of women and students seeking jobs diminishes. Unfortunately, residents of the new city have generally resisted attempts to build low-income housing in middle-class areas and have discouraged public transportation links. They want to keep the new city's expanding tax base for themselves and to avoid any direct fiscal responsibility for the urban poor. The new city has thus walled itself off from the problems of the inner city in a way that the Social Darwinists of the 19th century could only envy.

If the majority of Americans have voted with their feet (or rather, with their cars) for the new city, we need not conclude that this new environment has been successful, whether judged by the standards of previous cities or even on its own terms.

Comparing the new city with the old metropolis, we can see that the new city has yet to evolve anything comparable to the balance of community and diversity that the metropolis achieved. The urban neighborhood at its best gave a sense of rooted identity that the dispersed "household network" of the new city lacks. The downtowns provided a counterpoint of diversity, a neon-lit world where high and low culture met, all just a streetcar ride away. By comparison, even the most elaborate small pales.

Of course, many residents of the new city were attracted there precisely because they were uncomfortable with both the community and diversity of the old. They wanted to escape from the neighborhood to a "community of limited liability," and they found the cultural and social mix of downtown more threatening than exciting. The new city represents the sum of these choices, but we should beware of accepting the architecture critic Ada Louise Huxtable's snooty judgment of the new city as "slurb" embodying "cliché conformity as far as the eye can see." The new city is rapidly becoming more diverse than the stereotypical suburb of old.

Beyond the inevitable distinctions between more and less affluent residential districts, the new city has begun to generate "communities of shared concerns" formed around areas of special historic, architectural, or environmental value. A neglected town bypassed by the malls and highways attracts homebuyers who want to restore the old houses and merchants who seek to revive its Main Street. An isolated area near a state park attracts those who are willing to sacrifice convenience for access to an unspoiled landscape.

Inevitably, the central city will continue to shelter the dominant institutions of high culture – museums, concert halls, and theaters – but in our electronic age these institutions no longer monopolize that culture. As the French novelist and cultural critic André Malraux wrote in his *Voices of Silence* (1950), there exists a "museum without walls" – a world of high-quality prints, photographs, art books, and other images which are available outside the museums or the galleries. In the age of the compact disc and the VCR, we have concert halls, opera houses, theaters, and movie palaces without walls. The new city is still a cultural satellite of the old, but the electronic decentralization of high culture and the growing vitality of the new city could soon give it an independent cultural base to rival past civilizations.

The most fervent self-criticism coming from the new city has not, however, focused on the lack of art galleries or symphony orchestras. It comes from those who fear that the very success of the new city is destroying the freedom of movement and access to nature that were its original attraction. As new malls and subdivisions eat up acre after acre of land, and as highways clog with traffic, the danger arises that the three networks of communication that comprise the city may break down. Too often the new city seems to be an environment as out of control as the old metropolis.

The machine of growth is yet again gaining the upper hand over any human purpose. The early residents of the new city worried little about regulating growth because there was still a seemingly endless supply of open land. Now that it is disappearing, the residents of the new city must finally face the consequences of get-and-grab development.

Once again we must turn for wisdom to the great prophets of decentralization, especially Frank Lloyd Wright. Wright believed that the guiding principle of the new city must be the harmonization of development with a respect for the land in the interest of creating a beautiful and civilized landscape. "Architecture and acreage will be seen together as landscape – as was the best antique architecture – and will become more essential to each other," he wrote. As his Broadacre City plans and drawings show, he largely ruled out large buildings or even high-rise strucures. His plans show the same juxtapositions of housing, shopping, and industry that exist in the new city today. But they depict a world in which these are integrated into open space through the preservation of farmland, the creation of parks, and the extensive use of landscaping around buildings.

For Wright, an "organic" landscape meant more than creating beautiful vistas. It was the social effort to integrate the potentially disruptive effects of the machine in the service of a higher purpose. Wright, however, gave little practical thought to how this might be achieved. In one of his books he vaguely suggested that each county in Broadacres would have a "County Architect" with dictatorial powers to regulate the environment.

Lacking such a figure in reality, the new city must now undertake the difficult task of moving democratically from its virtually unplanned pell-mell growth to planning with a concern for balanced growth. In New Jersey, a public opinion poll taken in connection with the proposed "State Development and Redevelopment Plan" shows that by a margin of five to one, the residents of the highly-developed Garden State prefer less growth even at the cost of less economic development. Half agreed that controls on development should be "extremely strict," and 25 percent more said regulation should be "very strict."

The ever-present threat of a veto by the state legislature as the plan develops into final form (scheduled for late 1990) shows that these sentiments are still far from determining policy. The New Jersey Plan, however, includes certain proposals that will have to figure in any effective land-use control program in the new city. Limited areas of the state are designated as growth corridors, while development is discouraged in still-rural areas. Scenic or historic sites that give identity to a region are strictly earmarked for preservation. Wherever possible, building is to be channeled back into Newark, Paterson, and other depressed cities. In a creative adaptation of the urban concept of saving historic buildings by selling the air rights to build above them, New Jersey's farmers are allowed to sell the "development rights" to their farms to entrepreneurs who can apply them as credits toward denser development in other areas where new construction is permitted. The farmers are thus allowed to tap the equity in their land without abandoning it to the bulldozer.

Preserving and enhancing the common landscape might become the issue on which the people of the new cities finally come together as communities. Not even Wright's County Architect could accomplish such a task unaided. It will be a slow effort of drafting regulations and making them stick; of patient upgrading of older construction to newer standards, and drawing together the privatized beauties of individual sites into a unified framework. Fifty years ago Lewis Mumford defined his ideal decentralized community as the "biotechnic city," the place where nature and the machine exist in harmony. He saw the coming age of decentralization as a great opportunity to embody the civilizing virtues of the great cities of the past in a new and democratic form. The last half century has not been kind to utopian expectations, but the promise of a new civilization in a new city need not be lost.

24 The Ghetto, the State, and the New Capitalist Economy*

Loïc J. D. Wacquant

People in ghettos don't create [the ghettos]. Those who have and don't give create them. Most people are prejudiced. Those on the outside just play games with poor people's lives. They try to keep a cage around poor people. They lie and say people don't want to work. First they push you on welfare, then they cut the programs. They don't realize they are cutting their own necks too.

> Brick, young resident of Chicago's South Side.[1]

In the two decades since the urban riots of the mid-sixties, the black ghettos of large American cities have undergone a sharp deterioration.[2] The woes of the inner city are the result of profound changes in three interrelated sets of factors: the economic forces that impinge upon the urban core; the internal structure and societal position of the black population; and the public policies that mediate between them and help shape both. The relatively cohesive black community of the 1950s – itself the product of a unified historical experience stamped by the strict and often violent enforcement of a rigid color line – has given way to a deepening division between the relatively secure middle and working classes and an increasingly vulnerable and isolated segment of the minority poor.[3] To be sure, this is only part of a broader shift toward a hardening of class and racial cleavages in the late 1970s and 1980s, as the American economy replaced its crumbling industrial base by a plethora of low-wage and part-time jobs. Both of these trends were in turn abetted and aggravated by state retrenchment: by reneging on the promise of equality of access to housing

---

* Reprinted from *Dissent* (Fall 1989).

and education, by limiting eligibility, and by rolling back sorely needed welfare programs, federal and local governments have contributed to the deepening and concentration of ghetto poverty.[4] All of these developments have hit the urban black poor with special brutality.

Conditions in Chicago's ghetto neighborhoods are emblematic of the dramatic changes that have swept through inner cities and undermined the "Black Metropolises" of yesteryear. I will first sketch the plight of this city's ghetto, then turn to examine the causes that are driving its fateful evolution, including epochal changes in the economy, failed public policies, and the retreat of the American "semi-welfare state" following the "new class war" waged by conservative forces over the past decade,[5] and the subsequent crumbling of public institutions such as low-income housing and schools. In the third section I argue that this new configuration of forces – economic, social, and political – has effected an institutional transformation of the ghetto that effectively dooms ever-larger numbers of inner-city residents to prolonged social marginality and economic redundancy. I outline several dimensions of this process of "hyperghettoization" that has ravaged the inner city before suggesting policy directions.

LIFE IN CHICAGO'S GHETTO TODAY

Author Studs Terkel has nicknamed Chicago's South Side and West Side the city's "Soweto." The sharp segregation and social dislocations visited upon these racial enclaves give him ample motive to do so. In the past three decades, they have harbored growing numbers of poor blacks despite rapid depopulation; their residents have suffered a reduction of real income, sharp increases in joblessness, and record rates of welfare receipt (even though the real dollar value of AFDC in the state was halved between 1970 and 1987). As of 1986–7, conditions in Chicago's ghetto continued to worsen in spite of the national economic recovery and reached unprecedented levels of hardship and deprivation (see Table 24.1).[6]

In the communities that make up the historic core of Chicago's Black Belt, most adults do not hold a job and only

Table 24.1   Economic exclusion and deprivation in Chicago's ghetto (1986–7)

Percentage	All respondents	Females
Class position:		
Not employed	61	69
Working class	33	21
Middle class	6	10
Did not finish high school	51	50
Public aid:		
On aid when a child	41	44
Currently on aid	58	69
Receives food stamps	60	70
Assets:		
Household income , $7,500	51	59
Finances not improved or worse	79	80
Has checking account	12	10
Has savings account	18	14
Household owns home	121	8
Household owns a car	34	26

Source: Urban Poverty and Family Life Survey, 1987.

a tiny fraction of them (6 percent) enjoy employment in a white-collar, credentialed position. Half have not completed their high school education and six in ten are currently on the welfare rolls. Only 22 percent of the residents have never received their own public aid grant and 71 percent of them need at least one of six possible forms of food assistance to feed themselves and their family. Of those receiving welfare, fully one in five expect to remain on aid for a minimum of five years. Such depressing expectations flow from a realistic assessment of the paucity of economic and financial resources available to ghetto blacks in Chicago. Just ever half of them live in a household that declared less than $7500 of yearly income, and an overwhelming majority of 79 percent have experienced either a degradation or no improvement in their financial status in the previous three years, that is, during the supposedly sturdy economic growth of the mid-eighties. A mere 14 percent of them belong to a household with incomes above $25 000 per annum (compared with a national median annual income of $31 000 for white families and $18 000 for blacks). Barely one ghetto resident in ten has a current checking account and fewer than two in ten can afford to maintain a savings account. Threefourths cannot claim to possess even a single one of the following financial assets: a personal checking or savings account, an individual retirement account or pension plan, stocks and bonds, or a prepaid burial. Owning a home and an automobile, two staples of the "American dream," also remain out of the reach of an overwhelming majority of ghetto blacks. And on most counts, black females are notably more disadvantaged than their male counterparts.

The degradation of the housing stock, of the transportation infrastructure, and of municipal services in the inner city, combined with rising levels of crime and street violence, have created conditions of living that are more evocative of a muffled civil war than of life in the richest land on the face of earth. A former Chicagoan explains:

> You couldn't give me a place in Chicago. . . . See, I was there when you could sleep in the park all night and nobody wouldn't bother your pocketbook. I was there when you could sleep with your door open and nobody would bother you. Now my sister's house is barred up like a jail. You go through about three iron doors before you can get inside the house. And they still come in. She put fifteen-hundred dollars' worth of bars around her room – these are wrought iron bars – and she's still afraid to stay at home.[7]

Jobs are so scarce that illegal activities have become the major source of employment and income in many ghetto neighborhoods. Asked what is the best way to get ahead in Chicago today, a young black dishwasher, who lives with his mother and four siblings in a cramped apartment in Grand Boulevard and struggles to survive on $4.85 an hour at a suburban job that offers no health coverage and no security (he has now been working three years running without a single day of vacation for fear of being dismissed), answers bitterly: "I hate to say it, but it, it look to me dealin' drugs, 'cause these guys [gestures to the outside where a band of youths gathered on a porch can be seen] make money out there. This is wrong, but! you know, uh. . . . They make a lot of money, fast. It be a fast way." It is a common occurrence for residents of this neighborhood, one of the poorest in the city, to find themselves out of cash. The consequence is that muggings and theft are routine in this section of Grand Boulevard: "Oh, man, some of them steal, some of them kill, uh. . . . It's hard to say, man: they probably do anything they can to get a dollar in their pocket. Robbin', prostitution, drug sale, anythin'. Oh, boy!"[8]

Public education in the ghetto has slumped to such lows that it merely serves to solidify the social and economic marginalization of most inner-city blacks. First, the system has become the near exclusive preserve of the most under-privileged categories of the urban population: the current enrollment of Chicago's public schools is over 82 percent black and Hispanic and 70 percent of all pupils come from families who live below the official poverty line. Second, educational failure is peaking at record levels: Barely 8 percent of the minority students who enrolled in ninth grade in non-selective segregated public high schools in Chicago in 1980 (and who represented two-thirds of the original class of 1984) graduated with nationally-average reading skills or better.[9] Shut out by the schools and unable to obtain legitimate employment, inner-city black males drop out of the labor market in droves and turn to hustling, crime, and to the underground economy: "The drugs are the only place our folk get jobs or earn money. The other is to steal, knock open heads. Which is the lesser of the two evils, the drugs which is burning their brains out [or] knocking little old laides in the head with their handbags?".[10]

CAPITAL MOBILITY, THE DECONCENTRATION OF METROPOLITAN ECONOMIES AND THE CASUALIZATION OF LABOR

The plight of the ghetto is the outcome of a complex interaction of economic, social, and political factors and no monocausal theory will ever satisfactorily account for it. This being said, there is no denying that the accelerating decline of the inner city finds its deepest roots in the ongoing structural transformation of American capitalism. In the past four decades, the American economy has not only grown erratically, experiencing seven recession years and posting a secular increase in unemployment and stagnation in real wages; it has also undergone major sectoral, occupational, and spatial changes. Whether this marks the "end of organized capitalism," the exhaustion of the mass production paradigm, the transition to a "postindustrial" form of capitalism,[11] or one component of an inevitable cycle of economic "long waves" à la Kondratieff, there has occurred a recentering of the political economy of large American cities around services and credential-intensive industries, dispersed production sites, and high-velocity capital.

This *recomposition of the urban capitalist economy* has translated into massive job destruction in the very sectors that have traditionally supplied the brunt of the employment accessible to the minority poor, and upon which they continue to depend heavily owing to the failure of public schools to prepare them for higher-qualification jobs. In Chicago, deindustrialization reached such magnitude that it has meant nothing short of an uninterrupted "Great Depression" for ghetto blacks. In 1954, over 10,200 manufacturing establishments were located within the city limits, providing nearly half a million blue-collar jobs (production workers up to and including foremen) and over 600,000 in total employment. By 1982, the number of mills and factories had been halved, their overall payroll had gone down 55 percent, and blue-collar jobs had decreased to 172,000, a staggering cut of 63 percent (see Table 24.2). Not only did some 5000 factories close down or leave Chicago in this period; those that stayed on or developed there had a different occupational mix and a notably greater capital intensity, so that the number of employees per establishment dropped by 11 percent while the number of blue-collar jobs per firm declined sharply from 46 to 33 production workers on average (a 28 percent cut).[12] In the meantime, the industrial fabric of the suburbs and exurbs of Chicago was flourishing: from 1963 to 1982, the number of manufacturing establishments doubled to 8700, one and a half-times the city figure.

This mass bleeding of industrial jobs in the central city was further amplified by a loss of trade employment (a 33

Table 24.2   Deindustrialization in Chicago, 1954–82

	1954	*1967*	*1977*	*1982*
Manufacturing establishments	10 288.0	8455.0	6378.0	5203.0
Total manufacturing employment (x 10^3)	616.0	546.0	366.0	277.0
Production workers in manufacturing (x 10^3)	469.0	382.0	241.0	172.0
Employees per establishment	59.9	64.6	57.4	53.2
Production workers per establishment	45.6	45.2	37.8	33.0

Source: US Bureau of the Census, *County and City Data Book* (Washington, DC: GPO, various years).

percent cut, from 332 000 down to 221 000 jobs) that the mild growth in selected services (an additional 55 000 jobs or + 46 percent, excluding health financial, and social services in which few uneducated blacks find employment) could not offset. Urban blacks have been especially hard hit by this spatial and sectoral restructuring of the American economy because they have been disproportionately represented in those industries that have stagnated or declined, and in the central cities that have lost economic muscle. In 1950, fully one-third of all black workers in Chicago were operatives. In the core of the city's South Side, blue-collar workers (operatives, laborers, craftsmen and foremen combined) numbered over 42 000 and over half of all adults were employed; thirty years later, a mere 6200 blue-collar workers remained and 73 percent of the residents were out of a job.

This displacement of manufacturing by service industries and the geographical relocation of firms is part of the globalization of production processes, the internationalization of competition, and the attenuation of regional economies. It has been immensely facilitated by the existence of large pools of cheap, docile labor in the international and national peripheries; by the fragmentation of the labor process that has made possible new forms of sourcing; and by technological innovation in the workplace and the reduction of the cost of transportation and electronic communication. It is important to recognize, however, that the accelerating spatial deconcentration and internal restructuring of the urban economy are by no means the result of a "biotic process" driven solely by the neutral mechanisms of the property and labor markets, as some of the proponents of the "mismatch" hypothesis would have us believe.[13] They result, rather, from the changing balance of power between classes and racial groups in the struggle over space, jobs, and political resources.

And in this struggle, the industrial and financial strategies pursued by corporations have had a heavy hand. Starting in the late sixties, U.S. corporations found their profit margins squeezed out by the pincer of increased foreign competition and rising domestic costs due to employee gains won through union bargaining and the new social legislation. Abetted by government policies of both Democratic and Republican administrations, they sought to recapture the rates of profit of the earlier era of U.S. economic hegemony by launching a systematic attack on wages, unions, and conditions of employment. "The way to cut labor costs, and flexibility to the production process, and reduce tax liability, was simple: move (or merely threaten to move)." This was done by shifting capital from one corporate division to another, by disinvesting in one industry to reinvest in another, and by relocating in those southern states with "right-to-work" legislation, to rural regions, or to cheap, foreign production sites.[14] The proliferation of enterprise zones and subcontracting, the resurgence of sweatshops and domestic labor from the mid-seventies on, evidence these efforts to escape standard labor legislation and lower the wage bill.

The frantic mobility of capital that has come with the new "hegemonic-despotic" phase of American capitalist development,[15] in which organized labor is compelled to consent to the demands of firms under the threat of investment withdrawal, has brought about the peripheralization and recomposition of the core.[16] Corporations have used capital mobility as an instrument to force one group of workers to compete with another and even entire urban communities to scramble for competitive advantage. By thus exacting widespread wage concessions from weakened unions and freezes or cutbacks in salaries and effective tax rates, the corporate sector has set in a drastic and cumulative process of *casualization of employment*, whereby full-time jobs are reorganized into "contingent labor," typified by part-time, seasonal schedules, dwindling benefit packages and growing precariousness. This downward mobility of large fractions of the work force has increased competition to the detriment of the most vulnerable workers and would-be workers, namely, inner-city residents with little education and work experience. It has "hurt most those seeking their first jobs – young adults, particularly those who are black and facing greatly magnified competition by the rapid black concentration of this age segment in the central cities."[17]

Today, not only do labor markets remain strongly segmented racially, blocking the inter-sectoral movement and occupational reconversion of employed blacks and the penetration of new minority workers in certain service sectors.[18] We also observe a resurgence of racism at the bottom of the job ladder, which hampers the efforts of inner-city blacks (and young black males in particular) to enter the labor force. In their report on the collapse of the steel industry in South Chicago, for instance, Bensman and Lynch note that "the impact on black steelworkers was even greater because the mills had been an even larger source of jobs for them. A study of former South Works employees found that far fewer blacks found jobs after being laid off from the mills than had their white counterparts."[19] In a series of interviews conducted by the Urban Poverty Project with a representative sample of Chicagoland employers, it was found that many directors of personnel express considerable reticence at the prospect of hiring young black men and openly acknowledge that they, or their colleagues, do not consider them fit for employment because of insufficient work ethic, education, or proper work experience.[20]

Racial exclusion also operates more visibly at the level of firm location, as part of the larger corporate strategy of union breakup and casualization of labor. Many expanding companies transfer their establishments out of central cities or locate new plants and offices in areas where few blacks live so that they can avail themselves of a predominantly white work force that will be more pliable and less likely to unionize (historically, blacks have often proved more prone to unionize and engage in collective action to defend their economic rights).[21] Many of these new forms of racial closure indirectly affect the inner city by shutting it out from economic development and are difficult to discern as they cloak themselves in the more acceptable and seemingly meritocratic language of class prejudice and lack of proper cultural credentials. Yet another indirect source of black stagnation in the ghetto has been the economic retrenchment of the state. Because the consolidation of the black middle class and stable working class has been largely assisted by the growth of public employment,[22] the rolling back of state and federal payrolls (for example in the post office) has also reduced access to legitimate channels of upward mobility out of the ghetto.

PUBLIC POLICIES AND THE CLASS/RACIAL CLOSURE OF THE INNER CITY

But just as the trends that have metamorphosed the American economy are not wholly the product of a "natural," socially neutral necessity, the plight of today's inner city is not solely the result of blind, impersonal processes ordained by technology, ecology, or the autonomous workings of the market. While it would be preposterous to maintain that some authority has deliberately plotted to manufacture the current ghetto havoc, it would be equally naïve to overlook the considerable degree of *historical and political agency* involved in its creation. Places or neighborhoods, understood as social entities, are *produced institutionally*, within ecological and technical constraints, by social and political struggles over competing uses of space, resources, and people. And no contemporary urban form demonstrates this more incontrovertibly than the black ghettos of America. Today's inner city is in good part the accumulated and contradictory product of the effects, intended and unintended, of the urban, educational, and social policies followed by federal, state, and local governments in the postwar era. And these policies have systematically weakened the position of the ghetto in the urban system.[23]

International comparison reveals that the United States is quite unique in the way it organizes land, granting far more independence and autonomy to local authorities and private developers than most other advanced nations. Yet urban planning does exist in this country, if in a somewhat more chaotic form than in Western European societies, and what exists has "been at the service of the growth machine."[24] Whether it be through regulatory programs (zoning, growth control, environmental impact reports, and so on) or federal incentives (public housing and urban renewal programs, urban development action grants, block grants and revenue sharing, tax increment redevelopment and industrial bonds), local and federal governments have pushed urban policies that have overwhelmingly benefited entrepreneurs, land rentiers, and other local and regional elites at the expense of poor residents. The combination of suburbanization and city incorporation patterns emphasizing home rule, for instance, has sufficed to create fiscal disparities that aggravate and entrench the geography of privilege and set off a vicious cycle that keeps fueling racial and class segregation in the metropolis.

Public policies in transportation and housing have been directly or indirectly instrumental in (re)creating and concentrating persistent poverty in the ghetto. As historian Kenneth Jackson has noted in his *Crabgrass Frontier*,[25] the de-urbanization of America was considerably aided by the Highway Act of 1956, which intensified the dispersal of urban residence and employment and accelerated the downward spiral of public transportation. Freeways in every major city cut through the middle of black settlements in order to connect the central business district to the outlying white suburbs or were deliberately planted as buffers to protect white neighborhoods from the "contamination" of the expanding ghetto (as did, and still does, the Dan Ryan expressway that shelters Mayor Daley's lily-white neighborhood of Bridgeport from the threat of Grand Boulevard). John Mollenkopf has highlighted federal responsibility in suburbanization through the subsidizing of suburban factories and home building. He has established that the National Housing Act of 1949, which was to have afforded "a decent home and a suitable living environment to every American," was in fact harnessed to serve the property investments of the urban establishment. The Federal Housing

Authority channeled loans to whites to build housing in the suburbs while officially denying them to anyone who would unsettle the racial and class makeup of a locale. The ensuing 1954 Housing Act "oriented the urban renewal program toward central-city business interests and the needs of other dominant institutions like hospitals and universities."[26] This is particularly conspicuous in Chicago, where the primary beneficiaries of the "slum clearance" campaign included, *inter alia*, the large Loop business concerns, the Michael Reese Hospital, the New York Life Insurance Company, and the University of Chicago, all of which contributed to the destruction of surrounding black neighborhoods of the South Side. In this particular case, government urban redevelopment and renewal policies, as well as a massive public housing program,

reshaped, enlarged, and transformed the South Side Black Belt. Decaying neighborhoods were torn down, their inhabitants were shunted off to other quarters, and the land upon which they stood was used for middle-class housing and institutional expansion. High-rise housing projects, created, in large part, to rehouse fugitives from "renewed" areas, literally lined up State Street for miles as a new, vertical ghetto supplemented the old. . . . The ghetto was to be reinforced with taxpayers' dollars and shored up with the power of the state.[27]

The devastating impact of urban renewal on poor urban minorities is beyond question and we continue to pay its price today, for it has entrenched ghettos, solidified segregation, and concentrated poverty. In Chicago, public housing became the cornerstone of private redevelopment and was deliberately funneled to maintain the existing color line. The Chicago Housing Authority acted as the bulwark of racial and class segregation: 99 percent of the 10 300 housing units it built after 1955 (which represented a net addition of only 467 housing units to the city's housing supply because of the simultaneous mass destruction of buildings) were located in all-black, slum areas.[28]

Similar observations could be made about the role of school policies: sustained public action toward educational integration of ghetto blacks never materialized either at the

federal or at the local level. Today, schools are routinely
and sometimes purposefully producing dropouts rather than
giving inner-city children a chance to escape the destitution and desperation of poverty.[29] Instead of instituting comprehensive schooling and job training measures, the state
has responded to the rise in social disorientation and crime
that has come along with the increased marginalization of
ghetto youth with a *de facto* penal policy, i.e., by stepping
up incarceration. Troy Duster reports that there are now
more black males in America's jails and penitentiaries than
in classrooms on four-year college campuses; in one year
alone (1979), 15% of all black youth aged 16 to 19 were
arrested at least once; presently, blacks are jailed at a rate
eight times that of whites[30] and inner-city blacks are massively overrepresented among inmates.

Other, private, institutions are party to the transformation of the inner city. Banks, for instance, have pumped
and continue to pump money out of black neighborhoods
by taking in far more deposits than they give out in the
form of home mortgages and they have, over the years,
financed a disproportionately small amount of home pur-
chasing in the inner city. As the recent "racial transition"
of Austin, an area located on the edge of Chicago's West
Side, demonstrates, racial and class isolation in the ghetto
is also helped by, and expands, as an outgrowth of the routine
practices of panic peddling and racial steering of the real
estate industry, of the redlining of banks and insurance
companies, and of laws that encourage unscrupulous "slum
lords" to milk their property for tax benefits while the federal
government sits idle in the face of blatant and repeated
violations of fair-housing laws.[31] In conclusion, "Chicago's
[post-war] ghetto is a dynamic institution, not a dead inherit-
ance from the past," and one that is highly distinctive for
the "deep involvement of government."[32]

THE TRANSFORMED SOCIAL-INSTITUTIONAL STRUCTURE OF THE GHETTO

According to the model of urban sociologists Logan and
Molotch, "[N]eighborhood futures are determined by the

ways in which entrepreneurial pressures from outside intersect with internal material stakes and sentimental attachments."[33] We have seen how, in the last half-century, economic and political pressures have downgraded the commodity status of the inner city in the urban system (especially in the rent-generation process) and undermined its traditional material underpinnings. Here, we want to emphasize how its internal constitution has also been altered. Indeed, the staggering increases in joblessness, infrastructural dilapidation, and educational exclusion in the urban core reveal not merely a quantitative concentration of poverty but a transformation of the social and institutional structure of the inner city, which places its inhabitants in a radically more constraining situation that their counterparts of earlier times or the poor of other neighborhoods.

In the first place, the ghetto has lost much of its already limited economic and social resources as a consequence of the outmigration of working- and middle-class black families. As argued by William Julius Wilson, the exodus of stably employed residents has removed an important *social and economic buffer* and made the ghetto poor considerably more vulnerable to the prolonged and rising joblessness that has plagued inner-city communities since the early 1970s, thanks to the periodic recessions and uneven growth of the American economy.[34] The dwindling presence of regularly employed households and individuals makes it more difficult for those who remain mired behind to sustain resident institutions. "The sixties gave us people in higher places," reflects a former inhabitant of Chicago's ghetto, "but the rank and file is worse off than they was then. They're on a destruction course. We have more killings, more murder. We have dropouts. Our schools is gone. Our churches is gone. And our business is gone."[35] Institutions that depend on local patronage to flourish have indeed either disappeared entirely (as in the case of most banks and scores of stores and professional practices) or have sharply reduced their activities and programs, as with churches, block clubs, community groups, and recreational facilities. Means of formal and informal social control have declined along with these organizations; this has contributed in turn to the rising incidence of street crime and to spreading a sense of insecurity that helps further speed up the deterioration of the neighborhood.

A second major impact of the concentration of inner-city poverty is on the school. The lowering of the class composition of the student body and of the volume of "cultural capital" that children bring into the classroom from the outside has substantially diminished objective chances of academic success.[36] The high density of low-achieving students undermines teachers' morale and discipline. The prevalence of joblessness weakens the perception of a meaningful connection between education and work and decreases academic aspirations accordingly, making it exceedingly difficult for the school to compete with other available sources of income and status, including illegal ones. An important mediation of educational and job success (especially in an economy increasingly oriented toward personal services that require frequent face-to-face interaction and extensive social skills of self-management and communication) is language. One of the most worrisome implications of the increasing isolation of the ghetto is that the black English vernacular spoken in inner cities is growing more different from standard English. For sociolinguist William Labov, the fact that "the majority of inner-city blacks are diverging from and not converging with the dominant linguistic pattern" is evidence of their decreasing contacts with the dominant culture; he views it as the linguistic correlate of "the formation of what has been called 'a permanent underclass.'" This *deepening of black–white linguistic opposition* is furthermore becoming less transparent and functions more often than not below the level of social awareness. "When a child enters school and faces the problem of learning to read and write the standard language, unknown and unrecognized differences in the structural base can interfere with the cognitive process of learning to read and deepen the problem of establishing sound social and emotional relations to the school system. . . . When we look at the divergence of black and white vernaculars in the inner city, we see conflict without contact, and therefore conflict without structure."[37]

The single most significant consequence of the increased class segregation of the inner city, however, has to do with its disruption of the networks of occupational contacts that are so crucial in moving individuals into and up job chains. Not only have employment openings been drastically reduced in the ghetto due to the demise of hundreds of local businesses, service establishments and stores; the prevalence of joblessness and the associated changes in the local social structure have also caused a *transformation of both the structure and content of the job networks* that sharply reduces the individual and collective employment chances of most residents. "Members of any group suffering from an unusual degree of unemployment or underemployment have the problem that friends will be disproportionately un- or underemployed, and thus in a poor position to offer job information"[38] or to recommend them for a position. Social isolations means that ghetto residents lack parents, friends, and acquaintances who are stably employed and can therefore function as diversified ties to firms, critical at a time when labor recruiting practices are becoming more and more formal, by telling them about a possible opening and assisting them in applying and retaining a job. Furthermore, the job tenures of the privileged minority who are employed are frequently too short for them to accumulate useful job contacts. Unlike earlier generations of inner-city minorities or contemporary poor whites who live in predominantly working-class neighborhoods that are sheltered from acute poverty, ghetto blacks cannot build the "reservoirs of personal contacts" that Granovetter has shown to channel job entry and mediate occupational mobility. Poverty concentration and social isolation thus exert a cumulative negative effect on work opportunities and mobility that goes well beyond the mere shortcomings of aggregate job supply.

Instead, networks based on cooperation in illegal activities such as drug dealing, petty theft, or fencing stolen goods provide a readily available alternative for many teenagers from these communities to obtain the income they need. As a result, numerous inner-city adolescents routinely become involved with gangs and crime rather than work at an early age.[39] All of these objective transformations are in turn further reinforced by changes in the subjective experiences and aspirations of ghetto residents. Living in a neighborhood plagued by material decay and continued exclusion from the economy makes it arduous to maintain a commitment to the labor force and a belief in the rosy promises of "mainstream" society. Long and repeated spells of forced unemployment, a succession of low-paying jobs, and the persistent economic insecurity that come with them are experiences that go a long way toward explaining the reluctance of many inner-city blacks to keep making efforts to find stable employment. There is no way to quantify the *demoralization effect* of persistent economic and sociocultural exclusion but everything indicates that it is one of the heaviest human costs of the marginalization of the ghetto.[40]

Through a rough, practical "spontaneous statistic," ghetto residents come progressively to evaluate their objective chances of escaping poverty and to adjust their social and economic conduct to the closed opportunity structure they face. Thus a circular process sets in that feeds back onto itself, whereby subjective expectations and hopes act to reinforce the objective mechanisms that limit their already meager chances of mobility. Far from being born of the alleged disincentives of (at any rate dwindling) welfare handouts, a self-reproducing "culture of poverty" or the moral defects of poor individuals mystified by the spell of an all-powerful (and mythical) "welfare mentality," the disposition towards the future and towards the economy of inner-city residents, and the discouragement and hopelessness that their conduct often manifests, are nothing other than a realistic expression of their objective future.[41]

TOWARD A NEW POLICY DEBATE

Public discussion of poverty and welfare has been severely hampered by the recent barrage of conservative rhetoric and by the rapid erosion of the influence of the poor and working class upon government, attendant upon the reorganization of the linkages between corporations, the ruling class and political parties.[42] The current debate on the so-called "black underclass" has been paradigmatic of this myopia. Recently, liberals and conservatives have reached an agreement that the problem of the ghetto should be tackled primarily by means of welfare reform, that public assistance should be based on "reciprocal responsibilities" between society (represented by the state) and public aid recipients, and that able-bodied adult recipients should be coerced to work or to prepare themselves for employment if necessary. This agreement is predicated on two patently false assumptions: First, that welfare can provide a way out of the predicament of the ghetto; second, that it is not the economic and political structure of society that has produced the latter but, somehow, deficiencies in the moral or cultural makeup of individual poor persons. Both of these premises do not withstand for one second the test of careful empirical investigation, historical analysis and cross-national comparison.

Instead of addressing the structural factors that are producing inner-city dislocations, including the tenacious and rising economic insecurity of meager pay and joblessness policy advocates have fastened on the personal characteristics of ghetto residents.[43] As a result, policy initiatives have mistakenly focused on devising renewed incentives or means of administrative coercion to reform the assumed habits of the apathetic, deviant, and destructive individuals that supposedly make up the "underclass." Such *disciplining*, in Foucault's sense of the term, will do little to alleviate the plight of inner-city minorities, for "it is not deviance – culture of poverty – that is keeping most poor blacks down, but the persistence of unemployment and the spread of low-wage, unsteady employment."[44]

Insofar as the range of policy solutions envisaged is largely predetermined by how one defines the problem, the first item on the political agenda is to recognize that the false consensus that currently obtains between conservatives and liberals is hiding the real issues. It rests on a *depoliticization and a dehistoricization* of the problem that denies its collective nature and origins. Since ghetto poverty is the product of economic and political forces and struggles, not the result of the aggregation of free individual choices or moral failures, remedies to it must likewise be economic and political.

Any realistic attempt at progressive reform here needs to take into account the peculiar legacy of American state formation and social policy experience. Historical analysis demonstrates conclusively that the pattern of social and economic intervention launched during the New Deal,

anchored by the sharp bifurcation between "social security" (aimed mainly at the stable working class and middle
class and blessed with strong administrative capacities and
a broad base of public support) and the disjointed patch-
work of programs known under the rubric of "welfare" (serving mainly minorities and the poor, and thus devoid of strong
popular and institutional backing), continues to stamp state
programs and thinking in dealing with poverty and that,
as long as this bifurcation persists, there is little hope for
meaningful change. Consequently, *programs aimed at improving
the lives of society's most disadvantaged members must be inclusive* in order to diminish, not aggravate, the political isolation of the poor, and particularly the black poor, from the
working and middle classes in the American policy-making
process. "The persistence of poverty, particularly among
black Americans, can be addressed only by new universal
policies – and correspondingly broad political coalitions –
that transcend the limits of the New Deal system."[45] Thus
the peculiar paradox of the politics of American social
provision: it is necessary to provide for the majority in order to help the most disadvantaged minority.

What would such a comprehensive, social-democratic
agenda include? Its centerpiece would have to be "a qualitatively defined full employment,"[46] including provision of
public employment when necessary, and, short of this, a
national guaranteed minimum income of the kind instituted
by numerous Western European countries to weather the
transition to the new world and domestic economic order.
For this, a full employment federal tax and expenditure
strategy must be combined with greater regulation of labor
markets (including stricter legislation on plant closures and
an increase in the minimum wage, which has yet to be raised
since 1981 after being increased four times between 1978
and 1981), flexible industrial reconversion, relocation, and
retraining programs, and the amelioration of the social wage
by means of universal family allowances. There is no reason,
other than political ones, for goods and services necessary
to satisfy basic human and social needs not to be available
to all. Child and health care must be universally provided,
along with low-cost housing, and expanded educational
chances. Today, less than one percent of the federal budget

is expended on either training and job programs or education.

The gravity of the situation of the ghetto calls for bold experimentation, of the mind and in reality, not for fine tuning and modest expansion of existing interventions. Rather than revive once more the perennial conservative discourse of moral obligations and individual initiative, we must muster the imagination and political will to try out new ideas and to pass innovative legislation by learning, not turning away, from the successes of other capitalist democracies.[47] Most important, we must no longer be fainthearted in our defense of democratic social policies by the state and we must never again let the free-market dogmas and delusions of conservatives set the tone and terms of the debate. For while the programs that are urgently needed to expand social and economic opportunity and turn the tide of inequality – in the inner city and beyond – will no doubt be costly to the public coffers, they do not begin to compare to the economic, social, and human costs of the current do-nothing policy.

POSTSCRIPT, OCTOBER 1992: MORNING IN AMERICA, DUSK IN THE DARK GHETTO

A mere six months after the single most deadly and destructive urban upheaval in a century, the riots of South-Central Los Angeles seem to have vanished in thin air.[48] How could an event of such magnitude slip out of the national consciousness to the point where it was mentioned not once in the presidential debates? How, on the morrow of a social eruption of this intensity and scale, could the issues of segregation, poverty, and rising class inequalities in the metropolis be so completely censored from the national public debate?

The answer is that the Los Angeles uprising was, for most Americans and for politicians and the media alike, little more than another "reality show," if a particularly vivid and shocking one. It might as well have happened in a foreign land. And in many ways it has. For the ghetto has become of sort of *domestic Bantustan*, a separate and inferior territory lodged at the heart of American society but cut off from it by a wall of racial fear, public indifference, and government neglect.

In 1965, Kenneth Clark portrayed the "dark ghetto" as "a philanthropic, economic, business and industrial colony" of the wider society.[49] Twenty five years later, the white metropole has discarded its former colony and pushed it outside of its sphere of responsibility – though, as in every neo-colonial regime, not from that of its deadly influence. Indeed, the two main roots of the tragic degradation of the ghetto since the "long hot summers" of the mid-60s do not reside within it but are found in the growing economic and political dualization of American society.

The first root, as cogently argued by William Julius Wilson in *The Truly Disadvantaged*, is the restructuring of the American economy.[50] Deindustrialization, the transfer of millions of jobs from central cities to the suburbs and exurbs as well as to "right-to-work" states in the Sunbelt or overseas, the polarization of labor demand, and the persisting racial segmentation of the low-wage labor market have eviscerated the economic base of the ghetto. By eliminating its traditional function of reservoir of cheap, unskilled labor, these changes have condemned working-class blacks trapped in the inner city by segregation to sheer economic redundancy. But a second and deeper root of the demise of the "Black Metropolis" is distinctively political: it is the *collapse of public institutions in the urban core* resulting from the policy of abandonment and punitive containment of the minority poor pursued at all levels of government since the mid-1970s.

The shift from the aborted War on Poverty of the 1960s to the escalating War on the poor of the 1980s has proceeded on many fronts simultaneously. There is first the rolling back of welfare through a combination of benefit cuts and new restrictions on eligibility. In most big cities, the real dollar value of the standard public assistance package has decreased by one half and more since 1977 and only 55 percent of the population eligible for AFDC nationwide presently receive the meager payments they are entitled to. The coverage of unemployment insurance has likewise shrunk from one in two jobless workers to less than 30 percent, hurting poor minorities the hardest since they are the most likely to have insecure job tenures. Today government cash transfers no longer play the compensating role they fulfilled in the 60s and early 70s, when poverty in the ghetto was slowly receding.[51]

Second, federal resources directed at cities have declined abruptly in the 1980s in order to satisfy the needless military expenditures and the fiscal redistribution of income to the upper class that made up Reagan's agenda of "warfare and wealthfare." The termination of the CETA job training program, of general revenue sharing and of urban development grants, the replacement of public housing funds by federal sharing grants controled by local elites who diverted them to the benefit of the real estate industry and property owners, all amounted to a dismantling of the web of programs, originally set up under the Great Society umbrella,[52] that had helped keep the fragile institutions of the inner city afloat.

As big-city machines and local parties lost their pull in national politics with the rise of PAC financing and the demographic predominance of the suburbs, cities were forced to compete in a cutthroat race to provide corporate services and urban amenities for upper- and middle-class families at the expense of social programs for their poorest residents and at the cost of further fragmenting the revenue base upon which the financing of public institutions rests. The New Federalism of Bush and Reagan translated locally into a policy of "planned shrinkage" which has meant additional curtailment of infrastructural outlays and city services in the ghetto.

No organization is more revealing of the institutional debilitation suffered by the inner city as a result of government retrenchment than public education. Because they cater to a population that public officials consider politically expendable, big-city public schools have been allowed to deteriorate into a *quasi-custodial academic reservation* which serves more to ensnare the black and Latino (sub)proletariat than to open an escape hatch out into the wider society. Segregated by both color and class, inner-city public schools are plagued by aging and overcrowded facilities, undertrained and underpaid teachers, and outdated and grossly insufficient supplies. Under duress of chronic budgetary crisis and bureaucratic stasis, they deliver substandard education and deficient vocational training, offer little counseling and no programs to ease the transition from school to work. The students who manage, against formidable odds, to attain some level of literacy are stigmatized for having graduated from an inner-city public school and cannot find employment. Those who enter the equally segregated system of city colleges soon discover that it leads nowhere. Under such conditions, it is not hard to agree with a Chicago alderman who famously exclaimed: "Nobody in their right mind would send their kids to public school."[53]

Because of grievous shortages of funds and manpower, public authorities in the urban core likewise can guarantee neither minimal physical security, nor effective legal protection, nor the routine municipal services that are taken for granted by residents of other city and suburban neighborhoods. The public health system, for instance, is falling apart. With the closure of countless community hospitals due to insufficient (or inexistent) insurance coverage and tardy Medicaid reimbursement, ghetto residents are denied access to the most basic care, such as immunizations for children, blood pressure tests, and cholesterol screening. Precious few private hospitals dispense prenatal care for the poor and the "perinatal dumping" of uninsured women with "risky" pregnancies is common in many cities. The result is that, counter to worldwide trends, rates of infant mortality in the ghettos of America have been going *up* and now exceed in many areas those of many Third World nations.

The breakdown of the public sector has also accelerated the degradation of the social fabric of the ghetto by decimating its indigenous institutional base. The local businesses, churches, lodges, recreational facilities, and neighborhood associations that used to give structure to life in the inner city and a sense of collectivity to its residents have disappeared by the thousands, leaving behind an *organizational desert* filled largely by gangs, currency exchanges, liquor stores, and virulent relations with police and the courts, to institutions whose role is reduced to creating a protective buffer between the ghetto and the larger society. Those who ask in bewilderment why the youths of South-Central Los Angeles "destroyed their own neighborhoods" naïvely forget that those neighborhoods had *already* been hollowed out by the twofold, mutually reinforcing, economic and political abandonment of the ghetto.

The vacuum created by the concurrent withering away of the wage-labor market and the crumbling of public institutions has supplied the room and impetus for the blossoming of an underground economy dominated by the only expanding employment sector to which poor minority youths miseducated by public schools can readily accede: the retail trade of drugs. Much of the crime that has engulfed the ghetto, creating a veritable climate of terror on the streets and spawning mortality rates rivaling those of frontline troops at the height of the Vietnam war, results from the growth of a form of "booty capitalism" in which each becomes an individual entrepreneur in violent predation. Where there are no jobs, no social programs, and no hope to get out through education, people strive to generate an economy with the only asset left at their disposal, namely physical force. Sadly, the best means of "getting paid," as the ghetto idiom puts it, in the irregular street economy of the inner city only contributes to the latter's continued dilapidation and decline.[54] All that the so-called "War on Drugs" – a misnomer for a guerrilla warfare on poor drug users and dealers of color designed more to placate white suburban fears than to address the real causes of substance abuse – has done in this respect is to give added momentum to a policy of *criminalization of the consequences of poverty* whose only tangible outcome is the doubling of the incarcerated population in the short span of a decade. But when a sojourn at the "Graybar Hotel" is no worse than a daily life of misery and humiliation in the ghetto, jail ceases even to be a deterrent.

In short, instead of forming a protective buffer and a panoply of mechanisms to prop up the most vulnerable members of society and to tie them into the national collectivity, public institutions, from schools and health care to housing and welfare, serve only to further isolate, stigmatize, and exclude them. Not, as in the imaginary world of neoconservative ideologues, because they obstruct the magical workings of the market, but, on the contrary, because they have been so weakened that they can no longer protect one from it and accomplish the integrative mission which is theirs in every other democratic society. It is not the expansion but the dramatic *erosion of the public sphere* that has damaged the ghetto poor – and, beyond them, the working and middle classes, black and white. For, when government pursues a policy of systematic debasement of the public organizations it is entrusted to steward and nurture, it not only undermines the sole institutional support upon which the urban poor can rely when the market casts them out; it also deepens the racial and class divisions that fragment society and undermines the collective good.

Aptly, the *de facto forcible secession* of poor urban minorities from American society has found its fullest expression in the current political campaign. It is perceptible not only in the conspicuous absence of a serious urban agenda in the platforms of both major parties and in their dogged avoidance of the issues of racial separation, city blight, and poverty, but also, and more strikingly, in the very terms used by Presidential contenders of all stripes. Their appeals are invariably addressed to the "decent," "responsible," "hard-working," "tax-paying" families that make up the mythically all-encompassing "middle class," whose mild ailments have monopolized all attention. This rhetoric suggests that those who do not work (though not for lack of wanting to), do not "play by the rules" (whose rules, anyway?), and do not gain sufficient income to contribute their "fair share" to the financing of those very public institutions which enforce their exclusion, are not *bona fide* members of the citizenry. Thus are most residents of the ghetto – and other dispossessed families throughout America – symbolically cast out of the civic community after been having been driven out of the economy and written off the polity.

The Kerner Commission warned in 1968 of a "time-bomb ticking in the heart of the nation."[55] One big bomb exploded in Los Angeles last Spring and countless smaller explosions go off everyday in the "quiet riots" of deprivation, destitution, and despair that have turned the decaying racial enclaves of the city into so many urban hellholes. How many more deaths, how much more suffering, how much more human wastage will it take before Americans realize the cost of separatism and muster the political will to tear down the walls of the new apartheid they and their government are busy erecting?

Notes

1. Quoted in Arne Duncan, "Profiles in Poverty: An Ethnographic Report on Inner-City Black Youth" (paper presented at the Urban Poverty Workshop, The University of Chicago, October 1987), p. 14.
2. See Fred Harris and Roger W. Wilkins, eds., *Quiet Riots: Race and Poverty in the United States* (New York: Pantheon, 1988) for a synopsis. Robert Blauner's remarkable collection of interviews with blacks over a twenty-year period, *Black Lives, White Lives: Three Decades of Race Relations in America* (Berkeley: University of California Press, 1989), brings out time and again the notion that "this is a worse kind of ghetto."
3. See William Julius Wilson, *The Truly Disadvantaged: The Inner City, the Underclass and Public Policy* (Chicago: The University of Chicago Press, 1987), and Martin Kilson, "Social Classes and Intergenerational Poverty," *The Public Interest* 64 (Summer 1981), pp. 58–78.
4. June Axinn and Mark J. Stern, *Dependency and Poverty: Old Problems in a New World* (Lexington, Mass.: Lexington Books, 1988).
5. Frances Fox Piven and Richard A. Cloward, *The New Class War* (New York: Pantheon Books, 1982).
6. These data are based on a survey of a multistage random sample of black residents of Chicago's poverty areas, ages 18 to 45 conducted by the Urban Poverty and Family Structure Project at the University of Chicago (under the direction of William Julius Wilson). The preliminary results summarized in this table concern only the 364 black respondents who lived in tracts with more than 40 percent poor persons in them, 82 percent of which were located on Chicago's South and West Sides. See Loïc J. D. Wacquant and William Julius Wilson, "The Cost of Racial and Class Exclusion in the Inner City," *Annals of the American Academy of Political and Social Science*, 501, January 1989, pp. 8–25, for further precisions on this survey and a more detailed sociography of Chicago's ghetto that contrasts it with other working- and lower-middle class black neighborhoods. On the persistence of near-total racial segregation in Chicago, see for instance Joe T. Darden, "Socioeconomic Status and Racial Residential Segregation: Blacks and Hispanics in Chicago," *International Journal of Comparative Sociology*, 1(2), 1987, pp. 1–13.
7. Cited in Bob Blauner, *Black Lives, White Lives*, p. 174.
8. Interview by Loïc J. D. Wacquant for the Urban Poverty and Family Structure Project, summer 1987. Such descriptions could be repeated over and over in inner cities throughout the country. Thus in the San Francisco Bay Area, a black community worker reports:

"See those guys standing over there in the street right now? Those are young men – they don't have any jobs. Young people should be able to get jobs, young people need to be given an opportunity not to become animals. With all the CETA programs and everything, we have not raised the level of ninety percent of the young blacks out there. Blacks now are beginning to go into banks and rob. And that's not all drug money – that's desperation for food money. And the sad part about it is that they are breaking into blacks' homes. We had less of that kind of thing than we have now" (quoted in Blauner, *op. cit.*, p. 192).

9. Designs for Change, *The Bottom Line: Chicago's Failing Schools and How to Save Them*, Chicago, Chicago School Watch, Research Report #1, 1985.

10. Quoted in Robert Blauner, *Black Lives, White Lives*, p. 185. See also Douglas G. Glasgow, *The Black Underclass: Poverty, Unemployment, and Entrapment of Ghetto Youth* (New York: Vintage, 1981), and the vivid personal testimonies collected in Leslie Dunbar, *The Common Interest* (New York: Pantheon, 1988), chapter 3, "A Just Entitlement: That There Be Work."

11. See Scott Lash and John Urry, *The End of Organized Capitalism* (Madison: University of Wisconsin Press, 1988); Michael J. Piore and Charles F. Sabel, *The Second Industrial Divide: Possibilities for Prosperity* (New York: Basic Books, 1984); and Fred Block, *Revising State Theory: Essays on Politics and Postindustrialism* (Philadelphia: Temple University Press, 1987), for three insightful discussions of these theses.

12. This is in no way unique to Chicago but characterizes all major Rustbelt megalopolises with large black ghettos, as was shown elsewhere (Loïc J. D. Wacquant and William Julius Wilson, "Poverty, Joblessness and the Social Transformation of the Inner City," in Phoebe H. Cottingham and David Ellwood, eds, *Welfare Policy for the 1990s* (Cambridge: Harvard University Press, 1989), pp. 70–102). For example, from 1958 to 1982, the number of production workers in New York City dropped from 670 000 to 311 000 (–54 percent); in Philadelphia from 208 000 to 81 000 (–61 percent); in Detroit from 145 000 to a mere 59 000 (59 percent).

13. The key deficiency of the literature on the so-called "mismatch hypothesis" is that it mistakes the *description* of the outcomes of political-economic processes and of ongoing class-racial struggles over their social allocation for their *explanation*, in effect "naturalizing" them. Cf. John Kasarda, "Urban Change and Minority Opportunities" (in Paul Peterson, ed., *The New Urban Reality*, Washington, D.C.: Brookings Institution, 1985, pp. 33–67), for a particularly lucid and sophisticated restatement of this ecological model, and David T. Ellwood, "The Spatial Mismatch Hypothesis: Are there Teenage Jobs Missing in the Ghetto?" (in Richard B. Freeman and Harry J. Holzer, eds., *The Black Youth Employment Crisis* (Chicago: The University of Chicago Press, 1987), pp. 147–197) for a typical approach by an economist which "explores the so-

called mismatch hypothesis as an *explanation* for the poor labor market experiences of young blacks" (p. 147, my emphasis).

14. Barry Bluestone, "Deindustrialization and Unemployment in America," *The Review of Black Political Economy*, 17 (2), Fall 1988, pp. 29–44, quote p. 38. This section also draws upon Barry Bluestone and Bennett Harrison, *The Great U-Turn* (New York: Basic Books, 1988), as well as on a lecture by Bennett Harrison, "How the Lower Half Lives," delivered at the Urban Poverty Workshop, the University of Chicago, March 1988.

15. Defined as the "rational" tyranny of capital mobility over the collective worker." For an analysis of this new "factory regime" in advanced capitalism, see Michael Burawoy, *The Politics of Production* (London: Verso, 1985), chapter 3. One could list here tens of examples of cities or states blackmailed by large employers into providing more collective investment for private profit. The panic created among city and state politicians and officials by Sears's threat to move out of Chicago is emblematic of this strategy. Shortly after Sears announced it was considering relocating its 6,600 jobs elsewhere, possibly to Raleigh, Charlotte or Dallas, Mayor Daley and Republican Governor Thompson joined hands in packaging an assistance plan (some might call it a hand-out) worth an estimated $300 million, including 80 acres of prime property near O'Hare Airport virtually for nothing, free site and infrastructural improvements, new highway access, a property tax abatement, job training subsidies and enterprise zone incentives (*Chicago Tribune*, June 15, 1989, Business section, pp. 1–2). An even more striking instance is that of Detroit's Poletown as recounted by Barry Bluestone in his article "Deindustrialization and Unemployment in America."

16. See Alejandro Portes and John Walton, *Labor, Class, and the International System* (New York, Wiley, 1981), and Sassia Sassen-Koob, "Recomposition and Peripheralization at the Core," *Contemporary Marxism*, 5, 1982, pp. 88–100.

17. Daniel T. Lichter, "Racial Differences in Underemployment in American Cities," *American Journal of Sociology*, 93(4), January 1988, pp. 771–792, quote p. 789.

18. Thomas D. Boston provides evidence of this in his *Race, Class, and Conservatism* (Boston: Unwin and Hyman, 1988). Also Norman Fainstein, "The Underclass/Mismatch Hypothesis as an Explanation of Black Economic Deprivation," *Politics and Society*, 15(4), 1986–87, pp. 403–452.

19. David Bensman and Roberta Lynch, *Rusted Dreams: Hard Times in a Steel Community* (Berkeley: University of California Press, 1987), pp. 102–103.

20. Not surprisingly, many of those who are wary of inner-city black males are more favorably disposed toward black females, whom they see as more reliable and willing to take on low-paying jobs because of the weight of their family responsibilities. The apparently neutral and well-founded requirement of work experience is in fact a circular argument that sets up a catch-22 situation for

inner-city youth: they cannot find work because they do not have sufficient job experience, which they do not get because employers do not hire them.

21. The ferocity of the employer drive to eliminate and prevent unions is documented by Rick Fantasia in his remarkable *Cultures of Solidarity: Consciousness, Action and Contemporary American Workers* (Berkeley: University of California Press, 1988), chapter 2. Michael Golfield, *The Decline of Organized Labor in the United States* (Chicago: the University of Chicago Press, 1987) has shown that de-unionization is the result, not of sectoral or occupational changes driven by technology, but of concerted anti-union attacks of the part of corporations.

22. According to Bart Landry, *The New Black Middle Class* (Berkeley: University of California Press, 1987). It is possible that the recent decline of black college attendance, which has puzzled many observers, constitutes partly a response to this decreased commitment of the state to provide paths of occupational ascent for blacks.

23. Ted Robert Gurr and Desmond S. King argue in *The State and the City* (Chicago: the University of Chicago Press, 1987) that, even in the United States, national and local states play significant material and regulatory roles that have as great an impact on cities as private economic activities.

24. This paragraph builds on John R. Logan and Harvey L. Molotch, *Urban Fortunes: The Political Economy of Place* (Berkeley: University of California Press, 1987), passim and especially p. 153 and pp. 196–199.

25. Kenneth Jackson, *Crabgrass Frontier: The Suburbanization of the United States* (New York: Oxford University Press, 1985), p. 233.

26. John Mollenkopf, *The Contested City* (Princeton: Princeton University Press, 1983), p. 121.

27. Arnold Hirsch, *Making the Second Ghetto: Race and Housing in Chicago, 1940–1960* (Cambridge: Cambridge University Press, 1983), p. 10.

28. Hirsch, *Making the Second Ghetto*, p. 243. Roger Friedland (*Power and Crisis in the City*, London, Macmillan, 1982, and "The Politics of Profit and the Geography of Growth," *Urban Affairs Quarterly*, 19, 1983, pp. 41–54) has found that urban renewal destroyed far more housing than it created at a time of great shortage of low-income housing, especially among ghetto blacks.

29. On the failure of federal school policies, see Gary Orfield, "Race and the Liberal Agenda: The Loss of the Integrationist Dream, 1965–1974," in Margaret Weir, Ann Shola Orloff, and Theda Skocpol, eds, *The Politics of Social Provision in the United States* (Princeton: Princeton University Press, 1988); on the institutional debilitation of ghetto schools and how they can deliberately push students out, see the remarkable research of Michelle Fine, including "Why Urban Adolescents Drop Into and Out of High School," *Teachers College Record*, 7, 1986; "Silencing in Public Schools," *Language Arts*, 64(2), February 1987; pp. 157–174, and "Bein' Wrapped Too Tight: When

Low-Income Women Drop Out of High School," in Lois Weis, ed., *Dropouts in Schools: Issues, Dilemmas, Solutions* (Albany: State University of New York Press, 1988).

30. Troy Duster, "Social Implications of the 'New' Black Urban Underclass," *The Black Scholar*, 19(3), May–June 1988, pp. 2–9. There is more than a touch of irony in the fact that the term "underclass," which has recently been consecrated as the new label to designate an allegedly new, if ill-defined, "group" of inner-city poor, is also used in criminology to refer to the regular jail population – unbeknownst to most specialists of the "underclass." See, e.g., John Irwin, *The Jail: Managing The Underclass in American Society* (Berkeley: University of California Press, 1985). For an effective critique of the uses of this term, which owes its success more to its ideological malleability than to its analytical usefulness, read William Kornblum, "Lumping the Poor: What Is the Underclass?," *Dissent*, Summer 1984, pp. 275–302.

31. Cf. Tom Brune and Eduardo Camacho, *A Special Report: Race and Poverty in Chicago* (Chicago: The Chicago Reporter and the Center for Community Research and Assistance, 1983), pp. 16–17. See my discussion of the fate of the adjacent neighborhood of North Lawndale in "Poverty, Joblessness, and the Social Transformation of the Inner City." For comparable evidence on another city, see Harriett Taggart and Kevin Smith, "Redlining: An Assessment of the Evidence in Metropolitan Boston," *Urban Affairs Quarterly*, 17(1), 1981, pp. 91–107.

32. Hirsch, *Making the Second Ghetto*, p. 254.

33. Logan and Molotch, *Urban Fortunes: The Political Economy of Place*, p. 123.

34. William Julius Wilson, *The Truly Disadvantaged*, especially pp. 46–62.

35. Cited in Bob Blauner, *Black Lives, White Lives*, p. 175.

36. Pierre Bourdieu ("Les trois états du capital culturel," *Actes de la recherche en sciences sociales*, 30, 1979, pp. 3–6; also Pierre Bourdieu and Jean-Claude Passeron, *Reproduction in Education, Society and Culture*, London: Sage, 1977) discusses the three forms of cultural capital – embodied, objectified, and institutionalized – involved in the transmission of cultural inequality.

37. William Labov, "Language Structure and Social Structure," in Siegwart Lindenberg, James S. Coleman, and Stephan Nowak, eds., *Approaches to Social Theory* (New York: Russell Sage, 1986), pp. 265–284, quotes pp. 277–78 and pp. 281–282 respectively.

38. Mark Granovetter, *Getting A Job: A Study in Contacts and Careers* (Cambridge: Harvard University Press, 1974), p. 136.

39. John Agedorn (*People and Folks; Gangs, Crime, and the Underclass in a Rustbelt City*, Chicago: Lakeview Press, 1988) has turned up a fairly direct link between deindustrialization, social isolation, and gang activities in Milwaukee's inner city. It should be stressed that gangs and crime are not, public perceptions to the contrary, coterminous with one another.

40. It is perhaps particularly acute (or more visible) among black

men, for whom masculinity remains defined essentially in terms of steady employment and the ability to provide for their family. For moving accounts of how joblessness erodes the ability to be a father, a husband, and to maintain a sense of self-worth as "a man" in the black community, see the interviews in Blauner, *Black Lives, White Lives*, Mercer Sullivan ("Absent Fathers in the Inner City," *Annals of the American Academy of Political and Social Science*, 501, January 1989, pp. 48–58) also discusses the impact of male joblessness upon family life.

41. See Lawrence Mead, *Beyond Entitlement: The Social Obligations of Citizenship* (New York: The Free Press, 1985), for a statement of the conservative myth of the "welfare mentality," and Jay McLeod, *Ain't No Makin' It* (Boulder: Westview Press, 1987), on the complex (and sometimes counterintuitive) dialectic of objective chances and subjective aspirations among black and white youth in a Northeastern urban housing project.

42. This aspect of the transformation of American politics is discussed by Thomas Byrne Edsall in *The New Politics of Inequality* (New York: W. W. Norton, 1984).

43. David Ward has unearthed the "long ancestry" of such views, "going back to the second quarter of the nineteenth century, when the first wave of mass immigration from Europe exacerbated anxieties about the social order," in his remarkable book, *Poverty, Ethnicity, and the American City, 1840–1925* (Cambridge: Cambridge University Press, 1989). The historical roots of this vision, which turns a *societal* problem into a question of *individual* attributes and incentives, is explored provocatively by Frances Fox Piven and Richard A. Cloward in "Sources of the Contemporary Relief Debate," in Fred Block *et al.*, *The Mean Season: The Attack on the Welfare State* (New York: Pantheon, 1988). See also Michael B. Katz, *In the Shadow of the Poorhouse* (New York: Basic Books, 1986).

44. Axinn and Stern, *Dependency and Poverty*, p. 118.

45. Margaret Weir, Ann Shola Orloff, and Theda Skocpol, "The Future of Social Policy in the United States: Political Constraints and Possibilities," in their edited volume, *The Politics of Social Provision in the United States, op. cit.*

46. Michael Harrington, "The First Steps and a Few Beyond," *Dissent*, Winter 1988, pp. 44–56, quote p. 50.

47. Paul Osterman's *Employment Futures* (New York: Oxford University Press, 1988) offers a stimulating reflection on job training policy alternatives by contrasting the German and Swedish models of comprehensive vocational education and flexible labor markets to the haphazard and disjointed U.S. system. Sheila B. Kamerman and Alfred J. Kahn ("What Europe Does for Single-Parent Families," *Transatlantic Perspectives*, 19, Spring 1989, pp. 9–11) do the same on family policies and their impact on poverty in single-parent households.

48. For an account of the events and their underlying factors, see *Inside the LA Riots: What Really Happened and Why it Will Happen Again* (New York: Institute for Alternative Journalism, 1992).

49. Kenneth B. Clark, *Dark Ghetto: Dilemmas of Social Power* (New York: Harper, 1965).
50. William Julius Wilson, *The Truly Disadvantaged: The Inner City, the Underclass and Public Policy* (University of Chicago Press, 1987).
51. Herbert H. Gans, *People, Plans and Policies: Essays on Poverty, Racism, and Other National Urban Problems* (New York: Columbia University Press, 1991).
52. Gary Orfield and Carole Askinaze, *Closing the Door: Conservative Policy and Black Opportunity* (University of Chicago Press, 1991).
53. Jonathan Kozol, *Savage Inequalities: Children in America's Schools* (New York: Crown Publishers, 1991).
54. Mercer Sullivan, *"Getting Paid": Youth, Crime, and Work in the Inner City* (Ithaca: Cornell University Press, 1989).
55. *The Kerner Report. The 1968 Report of the National Advisory Commission on Civil Disorders* (New York: Pantheon, 1989, 1st pub. 1968).

25 Civil Society as a Polyarchic Form: The City*

Franco Ferrarotti

The development of Rome proceeds in fits and starts. It is not, and indeed never has been, a rational development, provided with its own plan and able to answer for itself in a general sense, in the context of an explicit public interest perceived as such by the people of Rome as a whole. It is an intermittent, whimsical expression, set under way by the erratic accumulation of the happenstance of a long history. It is also driven by ravenous appetites, made urgent by hunger, and with anxious deadlines tied to contingencies. Rome's structure is now very complex, and no longer to be synthesized in a simple, or indeed dichotomous, image. To talk of city and anti-city, as was acceptable in the 1960s, now borders on schematism.[1]

Yet the main way we have considered Rome's shanties and the shanty-towns has been seen through the lens of simple schemes and solutions, as the result of a now-superseded under-development, though the solution would lie in setting out targets for planning the area, organizing city services, guaranteeing the collective use of space and resources previously purloined, in short working with the conviction that it is possible to restore the city to all citizens through a simple effort of rationalization.

While these plans may be necessary, they are not sufficient. Passed over in silence is the strength and mastery, still potent, of the 'construction bloc'. The political and social group which has been master of Rome for over a century is still living: this is an alliance of economic power – those who own and build on land and speculate for de-

* Reprinted from the *International Journal of Politics, Culture and Society*, vol. 10, no. 6 (1992).

velopment – and political decision-makers. At times, for a certain period, the players in the capital have fallen out, but the tables upon which power games are played are many. It is not demographic pressures which today act as sparkplugs for the expansion of the city. It is the process of tertiarization of the city which guarantees other means of opening up new spaces upon which the 'construction bloc' can press its claims and make its mortgages felt.

In this sense, and for these reasons, the categories of critical urban sociology must be redefined. They are no longer able to grasp reality and make it understood. Even if it be admitted that the modern city is still a class phenomenon, the concept of class itself has changed profoundly. The Marxian 'class in itself' has changed appearance, has fragmented into a series of roles and functions, and no longer has the monolithic compactness it once had.[2] Is it therefore still possible to infer from the class character of the city the idea of the city as 'social factory'?

The class-in-itself has dissolved. That does not mean that social class as an important category for understanding industrial societies and what are called 'post-industrial' ones no longer exists, nor that it has no further importance. At all events, the 'class for itself', a system of affiliations, however diverse and on different levels in the productive and distributive cycle, remains for the subaltern world of labor. However, the crude equation which not so long ago seemed plausible, between the 'factory struggles' and 'urban struggles' is thereby made impossible and explodes. It is no longer possible to equate employer and landlord, on the one hand, and working class and ghetto or marginal population on the other. One must go ahead cautiously in this field, and refer to empirical checks on propositions which run the risk of spilling over into the realm of pure ideology.

The marginal, the sub-proletariat – without adopting Marx's harsh condemnation of them as only 'the putrid layer of society', – cannot be systematically exploited for the simple reason that they are not incorporated into a regular, controlled or controllable, labor force.[3]

To understand today's conditions, in which marginals and lumpenproletariat are subject to new forms of exploitation, we must look beyond the local level. One must put oneself on the level of the overall system and grasp its logic. One must point out the dialectical relationship which, instead of being generic and unidimensional, appears as coordinated and multi-dimensional. The overall system is capable of compensating dominant groups for the immediate loss of income or profit connected with urban ghettoes with the political advantages that derive from maintaining a considerable and growing part of the population in a position of relative social segregation, and political impotence.

In a certain analogous but quite exact sense, "political commerce" is restricted too, with the accumulation of parasitic income, and the definition and organization of monopolies reducing 'democratic representation' to a fiction. That is, democracy becomes a ritualistic facade, removing from the subordinate, segregated population any real possibility of politically effective reprisal.[4] The current phenomenon of localistic 'Leagues', movements for local autonomy which are violently anti-centralist – together with that of growing electoral abstention – are evident symptoms of a crisis which it would be an illusion to hope to correct with devices of pure 'social engineering.'"[5]

The city is not just a conglomeration of buildings, a 'built-up area'. It cannot be reduced to the material interests which nonetheless ground it and uphold it like an invisible, powerful web. The city is also a collection of messages, a world of meanings, a grid of communications.[6]

The modern urban phenomenon remains basically a theatre for the struggle among counterposed material interests.[7] Clearly, these material interests, as the expression of strongly differentiated groups, strata, layers, and classes, do not tell us all about it. This, however, is the essential datum which defines and, at least in part, explains it. First of all, it explains it as a multiplicity that is not mechanistic but dialectical, that is, as a real (historical), structural movement. At the same time, it is a contradiction experienced, a daily exaltation and suffering, a tension surrounding conflict; it is political but also interpersonally competitive. It exists in a nonfunctionalist logical context; one, that is, which does not make all the structural elements equally indispensable to the functioning of the system, and thus unchangeable. Rather it is historically open, kept in motion by the great historical subjects, as well as by the more limited tensions of the groups and subcultures to which these elements give rise.

In this way the city occupies a strategic position in the modern world. It is the chosen seat of capital and its workings. We may legitimately ask what will happen when capital changes its abode, as it were, and changes from being productive capital invested in real goods into a highly mobile finance capital? This capital, without a fixed address, speculative and manipulative rather than productive, and no longer connected to a specific commodity sector or a personal or public company with a precise social purpose, becomes the resource of 'treasure' of the conglomerates, the multinationals, which, immense and ineffable, are, like God, everywhere and where.

After the fall of so-called 'real' socialism, capitalism is consolidating its undoubted 'victory'. It has penetrated and permeated all aspects of life with its logic, and the city has fragmented, as a finished aesthetic form, and is forced to transform itself into the amorphous, outspreading metropolitan region. The former bipolarity between city and countryside has become the urban continuum, which finally ends in the simple extinction of the terms of the problem, and their subsumption in the schema 'production–consumption–profit'. One may manage a large firm with three phone calls from offshore Florida. The billionaire Howard J. Hughes controlled his industrial empire from his secret residence in the Bahamas.

The city is no longer a built-up area, as the Chicago School proposed. Nor is it a 'neocropolis', as Lewis Mumford foretold. It is merely a series of messages supported by a solid structure of powerful interests which I have defined as 'without fixed abode': nomadic capital. Every specific responsibility towards the local community has collapsed or at most remained a sentimental residue. Every personal tie between worker and his counterpart has been severed. The structure of these interests is at once omnipotent and anonymous. It can exist equally in the center of the city destined to be a museum, or at all events alive only from nine a.m. to five p.m. – already dead, in other words. Or it may live in the grey sadness of suburbia. The cultural richness of 'demographic density' and the intellectual and moral stimuli which, according to Durkheim, ought to result from this, are already a memory or a happy, fragile exception.

Humanity may be entering a post-urban phase. After the 'idiocy of rural life' (Marx), and the massification of urban concentrations, man may find a new, historically unheard-of, form of coexistence, mark the end of pre-history, and put an end to unnecessary suffering.[8] However, the contradictions of modern cities do not seem resolvable just by way of the cumulative effect of little repair jobs, case by case. The hope for planning needs much stronger legs. The crisis and exhaustion of the city as a place of industrial production and market may become the precondition for the construction of the city as human community. However, this will not be a gift by chance, nor by historical progress conceived of as chronological determinacy. There is nothing painless nor automatic. As I have remarked elsewhere, the city may reasonably be viewed as a multiplicity of systems: (a) an economico-ecological or productive system in the first instance; (b) a political system; (c) a cultural system; (d) a family system, reproductive and relatively educational; (e) a symbolic system, determined by religious faiths, sacred and profane, revealed or immanent.

CITY SYSTEMS

This multiplicity does not develop in historical reality on a horizontal plane or synchronically, on one of pure abstraction, on the basis of stages rationally predictable by means of theoretical calculations. This is perhaps what philosophers and armchair urban sociologists would like. The different systems, evolving at varying speeds, and not on the basis of some mysterious Leibnizian postulate of 'pre-established harmony,' come into contact with one another, but also into collision. It is precisely this impact, the fractions and potential clash which underpin and act as motive powers for urban development. In other words, development of the city is a function of the conflict of which the city is at once protagonist and theater. The scars are both the essential precondition and the price to be paid. This holds good because in this development there is nothing impersonal, or automatic. Nor can it be hypothesized as the painless childbirth or inevitable outcome of the blind, cumulative series of impersonal evolutionary impulses. Rather, it is a political fact in the full sense. It is the result of the conflict between specific social forces, not abstract ones but historically determinate and identifiable ones.

There is no doubt that at the base and in the origins of the modern city there is a technological imperative, but there also exists, and this should be remembered, peasant centers, such as Madras, or the integrated *polis* of classical antiquity, or the feudal and noble cities. The modern city is both, from the need to concentrate physically a labor force that is sufficiently various as regards its attitudes, and close to the place of production, so as to make less negative the results of the 'friction of space'.[9] Moreover, the primary source of energy, steam, requires a fairly high level of concentration, given its nebulousness. This is all true, but a purely technical explanation cannot clarify the more important aspects of the phenomenon. It cannot explain the political context, nor the social results of the relations of production as social relations. It is, for example, instructive to note that even when new energy sources, such as electricity, would permit an efficient decentralization, this does not occur. On top of the original, technically induced, concentration (though also bearing in mind the influence of the impoverishment of the rural population under specific statues such as the English enclosure acts), a parasitic status income has already accumulated. This, becoming an hereditary class privilege, halts the logic of purely technical development. It perverts it and makes it a valuable means of mystification to justify the indefinite protraction of a deeply asymmetrical social situation of exploitation and expropriation.[10]

Then, the fabric of the city is torn apart. The city takes the form of a divided social reality. It becomes the permanent scene of a slow, institutionally masked violence. This only explodes in swift bursts of open conflict from time to time. From this point of view, it seems clear that the future of the metropolises (if they have one) cannot be left to chance. It requires an urban planning policy in the real sense, rooted in a general plan, not just in outline, but worked out in every aspect. It must be coordinated overall, or risk the reduction of the metropolis to a structure for dissipation, for pure consumption, turning in on itself and ultimately becoming unlivable.

Unfortunately we must observe that, in Italy as perhaps elsewhere, there is no real urban planning. There is a plurality of schools and town planning and architectonic trends. However, even in the larger cities, there is no urban planning policy which does not restrict itself more or less fortuitously to patching up what exists. Moreover, the Communes of Italy are short of efficiently equipped offices for carrying out an urban planning policy. At the most, they restrict themselves to ruling on the 'practicability' of projects worked out by others: financial groups, firms, banks and so on. The national and council bureaucracy is still stationary at the conception and practice of legalist-guaranteeing policy. This does not go to meet the problem, proposing rational solutions, but rather acts as an organ of pure *ex-post facto* legal control.[11] In conditions like these, urban planning remains quite logically a prologue in heaven, when it does not just turn into a convenient alibi for real urban chaos.

It is too easy to 'shoot the politicians'; in other words, restrict oneself to criticizing, however harshly, the mayors, controllers and councillors. One can guess at their drama in Italy today. Power administered according to clientelistic criteria 'pays.' The efforts at planning and planning rationally, applying the laws, lose votes and reduce consensus. An American political scientist, Joseph Lapalombara, has even theorized the Italian client system as a kind of model, clearly not a normative one, of democracy as petty corruption, and more flexible and innovatory than those democratic practices which respect the legal norms.[12]

This glorification of clientelism as a form of democracy is disturbing. In Italy, unfortunately, it is confirmed every day, and not only in the three regions 'at risk': the traditionally mafia ones of Sicily, Calabria and Campania. Here, even the President of the Republic has recognized the impotence of the legal state and the dangerous, arrogant emergence of organized crime, with its three facts – mafia, 'ndrangheta, camorra – as an unprecedented, anomalous, but real, power of government which controls territory and persons efficiently.[13] The efficiency of clientelistic power is real and empirically verifiable elsewhere too. A single, and not the most dramatic example, suffices: the ex-mayor of Rome, Amerigo Petrucci was re-elected whilst he was being held on a charge of administrative irregularities.

A policy of urban planning based on rational criteria is simply impossible in these conditions, not only because there are no detailed plans, and technically equipped and functionally adequate offices are lacking, but because a culture of urban planning, diffused in a capillary manner and on average at a good level, is non-existent. This lack obviously goes beyond the council administrators and local political personnel in general. It directly involves the quality of Italian culture, its ability to form consciences, awareness, and the civic education of its citizens.

Awareness of this crisis has penetrated deeply among the scholars of urban planning and architecture. The split between the idea of the city and the specific historical reality of urban centers is growing to the point of becoming a contradiction and estrangement. Architects and urban planners now explicitly denounce the conceptual and executive deficiencies of their disciplines. They ask, with a degree of anxiety which, if not genuine, at least goes beyond the usual aesthetic self-congratulation, "who makes the cities"? In a clearly provocative vein, it has been said, "I propose dealing with the architectural mode or presence as a classic 'black box', recognized by what it produces but unknown as regards it contents. It should not be confused with 'good design', since architecture is obviously present – for example in the work of Lutyens – in buildings which from other points of view are rather opaque designs. To separate architecture from good design in this way may disturb those who do not call in question the mythologies on which architecture has functioned for centuries, but does not necessarily imply that the two things are incompatible, simply that one may have one without the other. The situation has been made confused by the tendency of the modern movement from the time of William Morris to group together all modestly decent buildings under the name of 'architecture'. This was a warmhearted, friendly and egalitarian gesture, but it should not be considered historically crude and dangerously acritical, like Nikolaus

Pevsner's assertion that Lincoln Cathedral is architecture and that the bicycle shed is not. The distinction rests on the fact that Lincoln Cathedral has aesthetic pretensions whereas the bicycle shed does not."[14]

The question is not fully dealt with in scholastic disputees. Alberto Samona, to cite the name of a foremost exponent of Italian town planning, has often observed that the city and open sites today express a level of demands whose quality finds at best a partial response in the current conceptual and practical instruments of town planning. For Samona, the latter tries to find firm ground upon which to base the essence of its 'transformatory expressions', so as to be able to direct the best layout of the city and the land. However, thereby is created a deep split between the concrete reality of the environment and presumption regarding the reality as forecast in the plan's proposals. Samona, correctly, believes this gap has widened disproportionately in Italy during the past twenty years; that is, since there was rigidly superimposed on the generalized scheme of zoning – until that time directed for good or ill by a 'design' – the system of 'standards' declared by ministerial decree in April 1968. This gradually but inexorably replaced any form of 'design with quality' by pre-established quantities, zone by zone. Thus all differences regarding the true reality were eliminated. These, however, were differences which should lie at the bottom of any study, plan or design of city and site. This ministerial regulation also reduced, quite drastically, the sphere of architecture schools which for almost forty years have been widening their own areas of involvement, spilling over from their original boundaries. (Today, the critically prepared architect has also to be an historian, sociologist, economist and planner.) This multi-disciplinary standpoint of the activity and preparation of the urban planner and architect is basic. However, it finds fearful obstacles in the `tendency to standardize' by central political and financial agents and, simultaneously, in the trend toward fragmentation and hyperspecialization which characterizes the modern world.

Francesco Tentori's recent remarks are clear and acceptable.[15] The tendency to subdivide reality in a resumé of components now seems to be asserted to its fullest extent.

"The world is subdivided into a summation of news already ripe for the pages of the newspapers: the city into an aggregate of heterogeneous buildings; society, into an aggregate of neurotic and hostile individuals." Rarely do urban planners, architects and planners in general manage to consider the individual building in its context. They seem to have no sensitivity, no ear for surroundings, those which encircle and give meaning to the building, and in some way frame it. And yet Tentori, with a critical, enlightened sociological sense, notes that cities need those formal syntheses constituted by the main thoroughfares, the squares, the open spaces, the parks. The traditional way of establishing a kind of hierarchy by means of buildings with towers, domes and belfries has definitely undergone a crisis. Seen from the Arc de Triomphe, in the Etoile, the cube set up in la Defense, 114 metres high, is merely an 'insignificant speck'.

The contribution of the famous Chicago School of urban sociology (Robert Park, R. D. Mckenzie, Ernest W. Burgess, Louis Wirth) was an idea of the city as a collective representation, a complex – not necessarily harmonious or easily harmonized – of symbols, politico-cultural agencies of socialization, institutions for mediating between interests. That is, there was the idea of a city as a grid of systems and subsystems, whose analysis necessarily involved not confusing the analytical plane with that of specific historical context, at the risk of losing the research in the irrelevance of generic abstraction.[16]

In the 1960s, urban 'Roman studies' proposed an alternative subjecting the most accredited and up-to-date readings of the urban phenomenon to criticism:

1. The ecologico-mechanistic reading, in which the city was a natural eco-system with a post-community *Gesellschaft*, was an intellectual product of social Darwinism. It reduced, if it did not eliminate, the role of consciously directed human action.
2. The materialist reading posed the city as a pure reflection of class interests.
3. The economistic one had the city as center of commercial transactions (cf. as in Max Weber, the 'market', which lays out the city).

4. The spiritualistic reading presumed communitarian survival, at times tracing its expressions in solidaristic subareas.

Research on the Roman areas of urban decay and social marginality (in particular in the Borgata Alessandrina, Valle Aurelia or Valle dell'Inferno, at Magliana, Acquedotto Felice, the parish of San Policarpo, and the Borghetto Latino and Borghetto Prenestino, as well as the shanty-town of Villa Gordiani) allows us to challenge the implicit apologetics of current urban sociology, so potent in its authoritative teachers and ancestors.[17] At the same time, this research helped to destroy any leftover illusion about possible linear readings of the phenomenon, and that any easy transposing of categories of urban planning into the fabric of sociological analysis was possible. The nature of urban planning was made clear. It appeared as a genuine politico-social science, entrusted with the identification and scientific testing of the choices which govern land-use, and upon which the future and the form (or its absence) of cities depend.

Against the myth that the community finds natural expression in the city as social seat of progress, and the related one of natural harmony, perhaps predetermined by the secret design of a history endowed with automatic organizational powers, the changing and contradictory character of the urban phenomenon became clear. So too did the close systemic functionality between areas of marginality and situations of privilege typical of the 'rich suburbs.' The high and growing share constituted by the tertiary population, along with a steady real decrease of the working population, gives Rome a special characteristic as laboratory-city. The phenomenon of urbanization without industrialization, typical of the metropolises of the Third and Fourth Worlds, produced peculiar effects not explicable by any traditional category of analysis. The existence of a double bureaucracy (legalistic, conservative, nestling in the parasitic sectors of government, as against dynamic sectors linked to the interests and initiatives of capitalistic modernization) was reflected on the one hand in difficult administrative equilibria and the system of representation. On the other hand, it was interlinked with the traditional conflict between urban income and entrepreneurial profit. The analysis of the mechanisms of social exclusion reinforced the image of a city developing erratically, in fits and starts, and blindly expansionist. This type of development produced a peripheral layer, purulent and constructed illegally, capable of compromising, and perhaps suffocating, the city.

Overall, the classic readings in urban sociology appeared quite inadequate. The need for a more flexible, systematic but not ahistorical, interpretation was forced upon us. This would make the economic and ecological sphere (land, resources, social wealth) interact with the political and cultural sphere (education, mass media, reproduction), and that of the symbolic apparatuses and the sub-system of the family. However, a systematic approach was needed that would not hesitate to grasp the conflictual, historically rooted and deeply political aspect of this interaction. Provocatively they hypothesized the city as 'social factory', echoing the political culture of the 60s.

The urban 'evil' was thus identified with a mesh of social situations and structural, symbolic and political connections which gave lie to every evolutionary reading. At the same time, it compelled us to adopt a reading directed towards historical data. This identified in Rome an urban model that could not be reduced to the model of other great European capitals, in that it was not industrial, at least initially, and was marked by an ambivalent love–hate relation with the national community. Nor could it be likened to the degraded agglomerations of the Third and Fourth Worlds, if only because of its important historical presence from time immemorial. Generally, however, phenomena of a decay in the urban socio-environmental fabric accompanied:

1. the privatization of the public – 'public' not in the purely party-political or juridico-state sense, but as synonymous with the 'social' (absence and/or complicity of public power);
2. the existence of areas of social emargination which are mobile but not easily reabsorbed into the overall context;
3. a lack of politico-cultural hegemony.

There further was a challenge to the canonic approach based on the identification of structural, self-explanatory variables of the Chicago School.[18] These variables include the resident population, the density, the heterogeneity of the inhabitants although Louis Wirth himself attempted to consider the variable of history as a phase in the formation of identity (cf. especially *The Ghetto*), and relative processual indeterminacy.[19] The analysis based on the interrelationship of three possible levels of incidence seems more convincing. These are: the physico-ecological; that of the system of social organization; and that of the mechanisms of integration and control. The inconsistency of the classical dichotomies – urban versus rural, traditional versus modern, rational versus customary – seemed confirmed.

Recent estimates by the Brundtland Commission show for the end of the century a situation wherein half the population of the world will live in urban environments. From 1950 to today, the proportion of urban dwellers has tripled, with a variegated and concentrated tendency for the metropolitan areas in under-developed countries. Even today, we are bordering on a situation where one person in ten lives in a metropolis with over a million inhabitants. These data are marked by sharp imbalances which, however, should be compared with the base figures. In 1920, the phenomenon was at a tenth of these levels. The insights of urban sociology at its beginnings were thus, analytically speaking, very exact.

It is clear that one must avoid approximate and romantically catastrophical reading of the statistics, which must, however, be taken into account. Some points, expressed in synthesis, are in any event worth considering by today's analysts:

1. Even in the degraded metropolises of the Third and Fourth Worlds, there are signs of the slowing of growth as a result of two simultaneous and partially connected causes. These are government policies to slow urbanization (clearly a very delicate question), and the crisis in financial and food resources.

2. In the technically developed countries, the phenomenon shows signs of a clear inversion of the trend – de-urbanization and a flight from the metropolis. This is caused above all by socio-demographic dynamics, and by cultural ones – fall in births, growth of new suburban residential areas, the mobility of the middle strata.

3. Intervention aimed at environmental conditions, at traffic and movement, and at housing, has produced actual improvements in the quality of life, though with two phenomena encountered in all comparable metropolitan contexts: an abnormal and barely controlled expansion of tertiarization and massive decentralization of polluting industrial activity, plus a crisis in the peripheral eco-systems.

4. It is precisely the intensive urbanization of recent centuries which has shown the progressive loss of power of the "cement culture," seen as a dividing line, cultural and physical, with the rural world from which recent immigrants originate. We are moving towards an urban–rural continuum (the US East Coast, 'Padania,' Tokyo–Osaka). Here, the city is deprived of its natural center of attraction, its core. This is replaced by a capillary, widespread system of long-range communications, which runs from the 'invisible' power source, electricity, to the electronics revolution, informatics and telematics.

When we examine the trends emerging today, it appears useful to free social-science analysis not just from the constraints of old theories but from the politico-cultural influence derived from popular interpretations of the urban phenomenon. These have the city as:

1. epiphenomenon of the *myth of its foundation*, with considerable psychological, ideological and symbolic weight. The rational designs, total planning, seen from Romulus to the utopian reformers and urban planners, reaching the claims for totalizing rational management of physical and human space; and as

2. a typical example of the *unintentional effect* (cf. Karl Popper, [Ludwig] von Mises and Ludwig Wittgenstein, with analogies in the linguistic system). This leads one to reflect on the city as a purely accidental construct, never really projected or plannable. And yet this does not see or does not mention the actual, partial or sectoral 'planning' determined and carried out by the interests of the various economic and financial potentates, in more or less organic alliance with political power.

Research and analysis of the case of Rome seem to show

the usefulness of an attempt to assist the transition from a *culture of expansion to one of transformation,* a transition often merely verbal at present. This means giving the right weight to the growing complexity and incontestable pressure towards atomization acutely present in metropolitan areas. It means also attributing due significance to the accompanying processes of concentration of financial and decision-making powers and resources. At the same time, one should cultivate a *salutary distrust of standard models,* both in urban planning and social intervention. It is fair to ask if we have reflected adequately and critically on the social effects of a dogmatic policy of "directional centers" of the 1960s, which often led irreversibly and determinedly to the destruction of traditional agencies of urban socialization, from politico-union headquarters to taverns. What idea of the city can be drawn concretely from intervention restricted to building standards in area plans or specialized subsystems such as parks?

One should probably support recovery of the role of local powers to contrast the galloping crisis of the municipalities – even if this does not have the power to lead back to 'autocephalous cities'. Max Weber described these as the social core and vital force of modern Europe, entering in crisis with industrialism and urbanism. This is perhaps the first step in reactivating the political sense, in a non-centralistic, non-authoritarian way. For this reason too one should rethink the *center–periphery relation,* bearing in mind the new and sometimes heterogeneous characteristics of the metropolitan periphery. The flight towards the suburban areas, now manifest also in Italy, reproduces cultural models and deeply disparate social situations from a sociological standpoint.

On the one hand, there is a re-emergence of the privileged classes' anti-urbanism – the race to the status symbol; the need for privacy as separateness; the search for life-rhythms and environmental surrounds 'of a human size'. However, on the other hand one sees the phenomenon of the marginal population driven out by the high rents, the effects of massive tertiarization, and syndromes of collective insecurity.

Starting from this observation, one can devise structural interventions and even hypotheses for new divisions of administrative powers. These should not merely prefigure an awareness of spontaneous social dynamics devoid of political and planning governability. One should explore more deeply and at the same time, the cultural trend that emerges from *residential polivalence* – the recent shape of uses of free time and holidays linked to high mobility. (It is enough to remember the boom in campers, caravans and generally in tourist–residential nomadism.)

The experience of research in urban surroundings suggests that plans and projects are often necessary to rehumanize the city. However, they are almost never in themselves adequate to change the quality of metropolitan life. Spaces for social *voluntary activity* must be made available, spaces for experimentation with informal activity. To give a few examples, these would involve self-management of services, initiatives for the environment as common heritage and resource, 'urban agriculture,' and the culture of reuse and recycling as a structural dimension of metropolitan society. It also means counterposing a *culture of aggregation and solidarity* to the tendencies toward 'segregation' caused by the very specialization of urban functions. This must take place in full consciousness of the problematic tangle represented by the contemporary city, of which the poet Volponi reminds us most effectively:

> If the city is uncontainable
> regression too is insatiable
> and is climbing up a utopia takable
> like an old branch, unbreakable,
> stretched out towards a high colour believable
> above the dust; a point, stable
> growing and open, reachable
> and, for sure, safe and maneuverable;
> to take as far as possible
> forwards and back: to immeasurable
> site, space, body – able –
> lines of everything and all thinkable
> residue, pain, scene; hostile
> fact and obstacle, even inescapable
> duty, task, lack, even civil
> law, as implacable
> impulse of spirit, or attack of bile.[20]

Notes

1. Cf. F. Ferrarotti et al., *Vite di periferia*, (Milan: Mondadori, 1981), esp. pp. 9–20.
2. cf. The preface to the new edition of my *Roma da capitale a periferia* (Rome-Bari: Laterza, 1979), pp. xii–xiii (in the series 'Tempi nuovi', after the fourth in 'Libri del tempo'): "As regards those employed in the production of goods in manufacturing industries, their incidence is greater in the slum areas: 22% of the active population, plus another 14–18% employed in construction. So, in these areas, between 31% and 36% of the working population produces goods. In the central areas, the percentage falls to 17.7%–20%, or half."
3. To extract from this situation and theorize a 'revolutionary vocation' for the sub-proletariat or 'wretched of the earth' is essentially a more literary than scientific operation. The formula of the 'wretched' is Franz Fanon's, but also derives from the marginalia of a stubborn neo-Hegelian like Herbert Marcuse (in all his works, but especially that bedside book of youth contestation in 68, *One-dimensional man*), and in the wake of economists, such as Baran and Sweezy (*Monopoly Capital*). Or again, it may express very respectable principles of personal preference, but not intersubjectively binding propositions.
4. Cf. for a pre-critical view on the problem, linked to a moralizing inspiration, G. Simoncini, *Il futuro e la citta*, (Bologna: Il Mulino, 1970), p. 33.
5. At this point, urban social movements, including the narrowest ones that have demonstrators at the Capitol demanding a publicly-owned apartment, take on a pedagogical function of inter-individual solidarity. At the same time, they present themselves as opportunities and instruments of scientific field work. Marx said, "If I scratch the man, I find the German." Scratching the man today, I find the construction worker, the auto worker, the employee, the boss – the essence of the social forces. They are more diversified today than in the past, but they act in flesh and blood behind the formal facade, the legal fictions and conceptual abstractions. Urban social movements bring home to us directly that the contemporary urban phenomenon escapes and refutes the traditional categories. It is a reality in motion which we may continue to call 'dialectical' for want of a better word. This tells us that its various, divergent aspects affect each other reciprocally through a network of mediations, and also of contradictions. This network is basically driven by the conflict of economic interests, but not only by this. There is the space, the symbols, the mobile, evocative images of the city: there are monuments, the collective memory turned to stone in the buildings, the arches, the walls and the tombs of the famous. There are fashions, collective behaviour, the totality of the so-called superstructural phenomena, the ideological state of the experience of human groups and classes, their more or less false consciousness – which it would be ingenuous and illicit to consider only as a mask, a veil of illusion, a trick and a rationalization. Cf. F. Ferrarotti

(ed.), *La protesta silenziosa. Evoluzione e significato dell'astensionismo elettorale* (Rome: SIARES, 1989).

6. For a theorization of the city as a collection of signs and flow of information, from the formal layout to the functional, practical consequences in an organizational sense, cf. *Verso una societa dell'informazione Il caso giapponese*, Introduction by R. Olivetti, (Milan: Ed. di Comunita, 1974). For the social and strictly political dimension of the problem, lacking in the former, cf. my 'Social information as a fundamental requisite for human development', *Social Praxis*, 1, 4, 1974, pp. 300–410. Later, with special concern for urban reality as crime-breeding framework cf. my *Alle radici della violenza* (Milan: *Rizzoli, 1978*); L'ipnosi della violenza, (Milan: Rizzoli, 1979); *La citta come fenomeno di classe* (Milan: F. Angeli, 1985). A whole literature has blossomed around these urban features, which tends to remain silent concerning their directly productive, structural and material aspects in favor of what is often called 'post-industrial society'. By 'post-industrial' is meant a society of services, seemingly no longer producing 'products' but, rather, 'messages' to the point of dissolving the working class itself into a generic, amorphous, subdivided and strongly individualized tertiary population. This is seen paradoxically as both privatized and equally devoid of specific identity.

7. Cf. for an analytical overview of urban struggles, especially in Italy, G. Della Pergola, *Diritto alla citta e lotte urbane*, (Milan: Feltrinelli, 1974). In a broad theoretical perspective, see also the works of Manuel Castells which, however, especially in the first phase of the 1960s, is redolent of the narrowness typical of the scholastic, dogmatic Marxism of the time.

8. For an exploration of some themes in urban sociology from a strictly Marxist position, cf. W. K. Tabb and L. Sawyers (eds), *Marxism and the Metropolis* (New York: Oxford University press, 1978).

9. Even though Adam Smith used this formula, the phenomenon is ancient. It has been remarked that "Cato, the famous Roman statesman and writer on scientific agriculture, bought an olive press in Pompei for 384 sestertii. To transport it from the city to his farm, a distance of about 70 miles, cost him about 280 sestertii! It is not surprising in these circumstances that industry often migrated towards the market instead of sending its products there." V. G. Childe, *Il progresso nel mondo antico*, (Turin: Einaudi, 1949), p. 256.

10. It is hardly necessary to recall that the contrast between the real 'captains of industry' and 'captains of business' had its supreme theorist in Thorstein Veblen.

11. For an interesting examination of the difficulties met in some Italian cities, including the most advanced both civilly and economically, with special reference to the question of jurisdictions and responsibilities which end up paralyzing each other through their convoluted complexity, cf. B. Dente, L. Bobbio, P. Fareri and M. Morisi, *Metropoli per progetti. Attori e processi di trasformazione urbana a Firenze*, (Milano; Torino; Bologna: Il Mulino, 1990).

12. Cf. J. Lapalombara, *Democracy, Italian Style* (New Haven: Yale University Press, 1987). The author is one of the most acute and persistent commentators on the Italian scene, with noteworthy studies on the role of kinship and clientelism in Italian political structure and behavior.

13. For the consequences of the essential de-legitimization affecting the state, unable to protect its citizens from the fear (*metus*) of violent death as Thomas Hobbes put it, cf. my recent *L'Italia in bilico: elettronica e borbonica* (Rome-Bari: Laterza, 1990).

14. Cf. "A black box – the secret profession of architecture," *New Statesman and Society*, 12 (October 1990), p. 23.

15. The positions of Francesco Tentori and Alberto Samona are taken from the proceedings of the international conference of *La sfida architettonica*, Rome 25–27 October 1990. On the 'planning policy' of the Paris region, the scene of a series of ideological, juridical and financial measures, rather than of an 'abstractly rational will,' where the struggle between the socially subordinate classes and the interests of the ruling groups is reflected, cf. J. Lojkine, *La politique urbaine dans la region parisienne* (1945–1927) (Paris, The Hague: Moutnon, 1972).

16. Aside from the works mentioned, see too the 'notebooks' published by the Centro di documentazione su Roma moderna Ernesto Nathan, director Giancarlo Dosi, which issued three numbers between 1977 and 1978. Of special interest is the work edited by Marcello Lelli, *La "Critic sociologica" di F. Ferrarotti*, (Rome: Savelli, 1976), wherein the author of *Dialettica del baraccato*, still at the start of his scientific career, showed exceptional analytical perception and proof of overall understanding of the phenomenon, gifts that certainly cannot be obscured by the not always coherent choices he exhibited before his premature death.

17. Cases in point are Emile Durkheim – the city produces freedom and richer, more intense human relations. Georg Simmel – the city is the site of liberty and loneliness, competition between men as counterposed to the common struggle for subsistence. Even Marx and Engels in the Manifesto have no hesitation in letting themselves go, in a kind of cosmopolitanism typical of *clerici vagantes*, wandering scholars, against the 'idiocy of rural life'.

18. Cf. especially Appendix 1 of *Roma da capitale a periferia*, op. cit., "Osservazioni sulla sociologia urbana," esp. pp. 227–33.

19. This crucial point was grasped by G. Bettin, *I sociologi della citta* (Bologna: Il Mulino, 1979), p. 164: "Wirth avoids considering ecology as a branch of sociology and prefers to speak of it as 'a perspective, method'." See too D. Pacelli, "Rileggendo i'opera di Louis Wirth," *La critica sociologica*, no. 93, Spring 1990.

20. P. Volponi, *Nel silenzio campale* (Lecce: Ed. Manni, 1990).

Acknowledgements

The following essays are reprinted with the permission of their original publishers.

Chapter 2, "The Culture of Cities" by Lewis Mumford (excerpts), reprinted with the permission of Harcourt Brace and Company from Lewis Mumford, *The Culture of Cities*. Copyright © 1938, renewed in 1966 by Lewis Mumford.

Chapter 3, "The Metropolis and Mental Life" by Georg Simmel (Edward Shills, Translator), reprinted with the permission of The University of Chicago Press from Georg Simmel, *On Individuality and Social Forms* (Donald Levine, Editor). Copyright © 1971.

Chapter 4, "Paris: Capital of the Nineteenth Century" by Walter Benjamin (excerpts), reprinted with the permission of Harcourt Brace and Company from Walter Benjamin, *Reflections, Essays, Aphorisms*, Autobiographical Writing. English translation copyright © 1978.

Chapter 5, "Urbanism as a Way of Life" by Louis Wirth, *American Journal of Sociology*, vol. 44, no. 1 (1938). Copyright © 1938 The University of Chicago Press.

Chapter 7, "New York is not a Completed City" by Le Corbusier (excerpt) (Francis E. Hyslap, Translator), reprinted with the permission of Harcourt Brace and Company from Le Corbusier, *When the Cathedrals Were White*. Copyright © 1947, renewed in 1975 by Francis E. Hyslap, Jr.

Chapter 8, "The Uses of Sidewalks" by Jane Jacobs (excerpt), reprinted with the permission of Random House Inc. from Jane Jacobs, *The Death and Life of the Great American Cities*. Copyright © 1961 Jane Jacobs.

Chapter 9, "In the Forest of Symbols: Some Notes on Modernism in New York" by Marshall Berman (excerpt), reprinted with the permission of Georges Borchardt, Inc. from Marshall Berman, *All that is Solid Melts into Air*. Copyright © 1982 Marshall Berman.

Chapter 11, "Urbanism and Suburbanism as Ways of Life: A Reevaluation of Definitions" by Herbert J. Gans, reprinted with the permission of The Columbia University Press and Russell Sage Foundation from Herbert J. Gans, *People, Plans and Policies*. Copyright © 1991.

Chapter 12, "Race, Ethnicity and New Forms of Urban Community" by Joseph Bensman and Arthur J. Vidich, reprinted with the permission of Franklin Watts from Joseph Bensman and Arthur J. Vidich (eds), *Metropolitan Communities: New Forms of Urban Sub-Communities.* Copyright © 1994 Arthur J. Vidich.

Chapter 13, "Private, Parochial and Public Social Orders: The Problem of Crime and Incivility in Urban Communities" by Albert Hunter, reprinted with the permission of Ablex Publishers from G. Suttles and M. Zald (eds), *The Challenge of Social Control.* Copyright © 1985.

Chapter 14, "Community Becomes Uncivilized" by Richard Sennett (excerpts), reprinted with the permission of Alfred A. Knopf, Inc. from Richard Sennett, *The Fall of Public Man.* Copyright © 1974, 1976 Richard Sennett.

Chapter 15, "City Life and Difference" by Iris Marion Young (excerpt), reprinted with the permission of Princeton University Press from Iris Marion Young, *Justice and the Politics of Difference.* Copyright © 1990.

Chapter 18, "The Pleasures and Costs of Urbanity" by Michael Walzer, *Dissent* (Fall 1986). Copyright © 1986 *Dissent.*

Chapter 19, "Street Etiquette and Street Wisdom" by Elijah Anderson (excerpt), reprinted with the permission of The University of Chicago Press from Elijah Anderson, *Streetwise.* Copyright © 1990.

Chapter 20, "Fortress Los Angeles: The Militarization of Urban Space" by Mike Davis (excerpt), reprinted with the permission of Hill and Wand, a division of Farrar, Strauss and Giroux, Inc. from *Variations on a Theme Park.* Michael Sorkin (ed.), Copyright © 1990 Mike Davis.

Chapter 21, "Reclaiming Our Public Spaces" by Fred Siegel, *The City Journal,* vol. 2, no. 2 (Spring 1992). Copyright © 1992 *The City Journal.*

Chapter 23, "Megalopolis Unbound" by Robert Fishman, *The Wilson Quarterly* (Winter 1990). Copyright © 1990 *The Wilson Quarterly.*

Chapter 24, "The Ghetto, the State and the New Capitalist Economy" by Loïc J.D. Wacquant, *Dissent* (Fall 1989). Copyright © 1989 *Dissent.*

Chapter 25, "Civil Society as a Polyarchic Form: The City" by Franco Ferrarotti, *International Journal of Politics, Culture and Society,* vol. 10, no. 6 (1992). Copyright © 1992 *International Journal of Politics, Culture and Society.*

Notes on the Contributors

SERIES EDITORS

Robert Jackall is Willmott Family Professor of Sociology and Social Thought at Williams College. His most recent book is *Moral Mazes: The World of Corporate Managers.*

Arthur J. Vidich is Senior Lecturer and Professor Emeritus of Sociology and Anthropology at the Graduate Faculty, New School for Social Research. He is the co-author of *Small Town in Mass Society* and *American Society: The Welfare State and Beyond.*

AUTHORS

Elijah Anderson, is Professor of Sociology at the University of Pennsylvania. His works include *A Place on the Corner* and *Streetwise: Race Class and Change in an Urban Community,* which received the 1990 Robert Park Award of the American Sociological Association. He writes frequently on various aspects of ghetto life in the United States.

Walter Benjamin (1892–1940) was a leading German-Jewish literary critic and essayist during the years between the two world wars and an early associate of the "Frankfurt School" of social theorists. While his writing covers a wide variety of subjects he is perhaps best remembered for his portraits of cities. He fled Germany for France when the Nazis came to power in 1933 and began work on a never completed study of Paris in the nineteenth century, an excerpt of which is presented in this volume. Several collections of his essays are available in English, among them *Reflections* (edited by Gary Smith) and *Illuminations* (edited by Hannah Arendt). He committed suicide after the fall of Paris in 1940.

Joseph Bensmen (1922–1986) was professor of Sociology and the City University of New York. His books include *Dollars and Sense, Ideology, Ethics and the Meaning of Work in Profit and Non-Profit Organizations, Craft and Consciousness: Occupational Technique and the Development of World Images* and he was the coeditor (with Arthur J. Vidich) of *Metropolitan Communities: New Forms of Urban Sub-Communities.*

Marshall Berman is the author of *The Politics of Authenticity,* and *All That is Solid Melts into Air.* A graduate of Columbia University, he holds advanced degrees from Columbia and Harvard Universities and teaches political theory and urbanism at City College and the Graduate Center of the City University of New York. He is now at work on *Living for the City,* a book on life in New York today.

Mike Davis teaches urban planning and political economy at the Southern California Institute of Architecture and the University of the California at Los Angeles. He is the author of *City of Quartz*, nominated for the National Books Critics Circle Award, and *Prisoners of the American Dream*.

Franco Ferrarotti is Professor of Sociological Theory at the University of Rome "La Sapienzo" and was founder and first editor the *Quaderini du Sociologia*. He was an independent member of the Italian parliament during the third legislature (1958–63) and in 1960 was awarded the first full-time chair established in sociology in the Italian university system. Among his books are *Max Weber and the Destiny of Reason, An Alternative Sociology, Time, Memory and Society*, and *The Paradox of the Sacred*.

Robert Fishman teaches urban history at Rutgers University in Camden, New Jersey. He is the author of *Urban Utopias in the Twentieth Century*, and *Bourgeois Utopias: The Rise and Fall of Suburbia*.

Herbert J. Gans, Robert S. Lynd Professor of Sociology at Columbia University, is the author many books on cities, urban planning, mass media, culture and politics. Among them are *The Urban Villagers. The Levittowners, More Equality, Deciding What is News, Middle American Individualism*, and *People, Plans and Policies*. A former President of the American Sociological Association, he has been a consultant to many planning and antipoverty agencies.

Albert Hunter is Professor of Sociology at Northwestern University. He is the author of *Symbolic Communities: Persistence and Change of Chicago's Local Communities*, and has published numerous articles on neighborhoods, local community organizations, and urban politics. He is a former editor of *Urban Affairs Quarterly* and chair of the Urban and Community section of the American Sociological Association.

Jane Jacobs, a critic, journalist, and independent scholar, originally from Scranton Pennsylvania, became well known as both a writer and neighborhood activist in New York City before moving to Toronto Canada, where she now lives. Among her books are *The Death and Life of the Great American Cities, The Economy of Cities, Cities and the Wealth of Nations, The Question of Separatism*, and *Systems of Survival*. From 1952 to 1962 she was an associate editor of *Architectural Forum*.

Philip Kasinitz teaches sociology at Hunter College and the Graduate Center of the City University of New York, and formerly taught at Williams College. He is the author of *Caribbean New York: Black Immigrants and the Politics of Race*, and is currently writing a book on deindustrialization and poverty on the Brooklyn waterfront.

Le Corbusier (1887–1965), born Charles-Edouard Jeanneret, was an influential urban planning theorist as well as a central figure in the history of modern architecture. Born in Switzerland, he lived in Paris for most of his adult life and first came to prominence as author of the "Plan Voisin," a 1925 proposal for the massive rebuilding of that city that was loudly rejected by the paris City Council. Among his dozens of books are *The City of Tomorrow and its Planning, The Radiant City, When the Cathedrals were White,* and *Concerning Town Planning.*

Lewis Mumford (1895–1990) was a journalist, sociologist, architecture critic, and historian as well as an early and important advocate of urban and regional planning in the United States. He was the author of over thirty books, among them *Techniques and Civilizations, The Culture of Cities, The Human Prospect, The City in History,* and *Architecture as a Home for Man.* During most of his lifetime Mumford was probably best known for his regular contributions on architecture and urban planning in *The New Yorker* magazine.

Richard Sennett is University Professor of the Humanities, and Professor of History and Sociology at New York University. His writings include *Families Against the City, The Uses of Disorder, The Hidden Injuries of Class* (with Jonathan Cobb), *The Fall of Public Man, Authority, The Conscience of the Eye,* and *Flesh and Stone: The Body and the City in Western Civilization.* He is currently the representative to the United Nations of the International Social Science Council. His works also include three novels.

Fred Siegel is Professor of History at the Cooper Union. He is a former fellow of the Institute for Advanced Study in Princeton, and a former editor of *The City Journal.* He has taught at the City University of New York, The State University of New York, Columbia University, and the Sorbonne and has written for the *Atlantic, The New Republic, Commonweal, Dissent,* and *The American Spectator.*

Georg Simmel (1858–1918) is today remembered as one of the founding fathers of sociology. In his own time, however, he had a somewhat marginal career in the academy. Starting in 1885 he held a series of low-ranking positions at the University of Berlin but was not appointed to a regular professorship until 1914, when he was appointed to the University of Strasbourg. Nevertheless he was famous as a lecturer and his writing was widely influential, particularly in the United States. Among his best-known works available in English are, *The Sociology of Georg Simmel* (edited by Kurt Wolff), *Conflict and the Wed of Group Affiliations,* and *The Philosophy of Money.*

Arthur J. Vidich is Senior Lecturer and Professor Emeritus of Sociology and Anthropology of the Graduate Faculty of the New School for Social Research. He is the author of *The Political Impact of Colonial Administration,* coauthor (with Joseph Bensmen) of *Small Town in Mass Society,*

Notes on the Contributors

and coauthor (with Stanford Lyman) of *American Sociology: Worldly Rejections of Religion and Their Directions.*

Loïc J. D. Wacquant learned sociology in Montpellier, Paris, Chapel Hill, New Caledonia, and the South Side of Chicago. His writings span the areas of race and class, comparative urban inequality, social theory and the anthropology of the body. A former member of the society of Fellows at Harvard University, he now teaches at the University of California at Berkeley.

Michael Walzer is Professor of Politics at the Institute for Advanced Study in Princeton New Jersey and coeditor of *Dissent* magazine. Among his books are *The Revolution of the Saints, Just and Unjust Wars, Spheres of Justice: A Defense of Pluralism and Equality,* and *Exodus and Revolution.*

Jeff Weintraub is a social and political theorist who has taught at Harvard, The University of California at San Diego, and Williams College. His recent work includes *Freedom and Community: The Republican Virtue Tradition and the Sociology of Liberty,* and *Public and Private in Thought and Practice* (coedited with Krishan Kumar).

Louis Wirth (1897–1952), a central member of the "Chicago School" of urban sociology, received his doctorate from the University of Chicago in 1926 and, except for a one-year appointment at Tulane University, was affiliated with that university for the rest of his life. In addition to his scholarly work, he was a consultant to numerous housing, antipoverty and planning agencies and served as president of the American Sociological Association, the International Sociological Association, and the American Council on Race Relations. Among his books are *The Ghetto, Urban and Rural Living* (with Ray Lussenhop), and *On Cities and Social Life* (edited by Albert J. Reiss Jr.)

Iris Marion Young teaches ethics and political philosophy at the Graduate School of Public and International Affairs of the University of Pittsburgh. She is the author of *Throwing Like a Girl and Other Essays in Feminist Philosophy and Social Theory,* and *Justice and the Politics of Difference.*

Index

structure of, 408–17; overlapping
networks in, 409–11; recent
construction in, 413; housing
programs in, 428–29; hypostatized
as social factory, 451, 461; as a
struggle of interests, 452–53; as a
multiplicity of systems, 454–65;
bureaucracy in, 460; components of
decay in, 461. *See also* Chicago
School, Community, Public spaces,
Sidewalks, Strangers, Streets,
"Urban" and "Suburban" listings,
and specific authors

City life: and sociability, 299–301

City systems: as a theoretical view,
454–65; and technology, 455; and
urban planning, 455–59; need for
historical data, 461

Civil society: and social order, 215–16;
and strangers, 222

Civilization: and the city, 25, 28, 58–60;
and urban safety, 113; and public/
private dichotomy, 297–98; suburb
as heart of, 397. *See also* Strangers

Civil Society: in social theory, 293, 294,
306–07; as public, 296

Clark, Kenneth: on the ghetto, 438

Class war: by intellectuals, 189

Collective: versus individual, 285

Communitarianism: meaning of, 253–54;
and mutuality, 255–57; and
copresence of subjects, 256–60;
versus liberalism, 292–93

Community: loss of, 163–64; of limited
liability, 164–65, 212, 214;
solidarity of, 165–66; Gans' studies
of, 166–67; and politics, 167, 198,
204–07, 235–44; and sociological
analysis, 185; and spatial patterns,
196–97; as voluntary construct,
197–200; and values, 198–99;
conflict in, 202–03; and ethnicity,
204–05, 241–44; and formal
organizations, 207; and
countercommunities, 207–08; power
relations in, 214; and crime control,
219, 220–21; and urban planning,
226; and withdrawal, 228, 234–35,
247–48; as a social issue, 231;
liberal ideal of, 250; normative ideal
of, 251; opposed to individualism,
252–54; as mutuality, 255–57, 262;
as copresence of subjects, 256–60;
myth of, 258, 261, 460; in common

speech, 260–61; and antiurban
appeals, 263; and citizenship,
292–93; and violence, 331–34,
339–41, 349–54; shared concerns
in, 332, 338, 340–41, 353–54;
invisible networks in, 337;
preventive behavior in, 344; and
industrial production, 390, 394n.9;
in the new city, 414–15. *See also*
City, Ideal types, Neighborhoods

Computers: and virtual reality, 392

Consumption: as an urban network, 410

Cosmopolites: as an urban type, 173,
175, 187

Crime: in the city, 113, 201, 216–20,
460–61; urban statistics of, 114;
and street safety, 331–35, 339–41,
344–45, 349–54; and racial coding,
333–34, 339–40, 345; and drug
use, 372, 380; in Chicago, 422, 431,
443–44n.8; and poverty, 441. *See
also* Fear, Strangers

Critical theory: of community relations,
250–64; purpose of, 250; of the
city, 251; critique of liberalism,
252–55; ideal of community,
254–58; criticism of, 258–64; of
city life, 264–69; and urban
sociology, 451. *See also* Social
theory, Urban theory

Crowds: and alienation, 227; imagery of,
231–34; and violence, 233–34

Cuomo, Mario M.: diary of, 168, 235–44

Cynicism: and the past, 7–8; about the
city, 373

Darwin, Charles: on differentiation, 70

Davis, Gordon: parks policies of, 374–75

Davis, Mike: study of Los Angeles, 277;
on urban war, 371

*The Death and Life of Great American
Cities. See* Jane Jacobs

Decentralization: as a modern trend,
391–93, 395–417; statistics on,
396; key examples of, 397–98; key
elements of, 405–07; projections
on, 462–63

Delinquency: in urban settings, 113,
201

Democracy: fictionalization of, 452.

de Tocqueville, Alexis: on political
suppression, 294–95, 313n.25

Dickens, Charles: on the city, 7; in
London, 9

CPSIA information can be obtained at www.ICGtesting.com
Printed in the USA
LVOW062158140812

294312LV00006B/121/P